The Paradox of Self-Consciousness

Representation and Mind

Hilary Putnam and Ned Block, editors

Representation and Reality
Hilary Putnam

Explaining Behavior: Reasons in a World of Causes
Fred Dretske

The Metaphysics of Meaning
Jerrold J. Katz

A Theory of Content and Other Essays
Jerry A. Fodor

The Realistic Spirit: Wittgenstein, Philosophy, and the Mind
Cora Diamond

The Unity of the Self
Stephen L. White

The Imagery Debate
Michael Tye

A Study of Concepts
Christopher Peacocke

The Rediscovery of the Mind
John R. Searle

Past, Space, and Self
John Campbell

Mental Reality
Galen Strawson

Ten Problems of Consciousness: A Representational Theory of the Phenomenal Mind
Michael Tye

Representations, Targets, and Attitudes
Robert Cummins

Starmaking: Realism, Anti-Realism, and Irrealism
Edited by Peter J. McCormick

A Logical Journey: From Gödel to Philosophy
Hao Wang

Brainchildren: Essays on Designing Minds
Daniel C. Dennett

Realistic Rationalism
Jerrold J. Katz

The Paradox of Self-Consciousness
José Luis Bermúdez

The Paradox of Self-Consciousness

José Luis Bermúdez

A Bradford Book
The MIT Press
Cambridge, Massachusetts
London, England

© 1998 Massachusetts Institute of Technology

This book was set in Sabon on the Miles 33 typesetting system by Graphic Composition, Inc., Athens, Georgia, and was printed and bound in the United States of America.

First printing, 1998.

Library of Congress Cataloging-in-Publication Data

Bermúdez, José Luis.
  The paradox of self-consciousness / José Luis Bermúdez.
      p.   cm. — (Representation and mind)
  "A Bradford book."
  Includes bibliographical references and index.
  ISBN 0-262-02441-1 (alk. paper)
  1. Self (Philosophy) 2. Self-consciousness. 3. Thought and thinking.
  4. Psycholinguistics. I. Title. II. Series.
  BD450.B436   1998
  126—dc21   97-40757
                                                                CIP

Contents

Preface   xi

Acknowledgments   xiii

A Note to the Reader   xv

1   **The Paradox of Self-Consciousness**   **1**

1.1   'I'-Thoughts   2

1.2   Two Types of First-Person Content   5

1.3   The First-Person Pronoun and a Deflationary Account
of Self-Consciousness   9

1.4   Explanatory Circularity and Capacity Circularity   14

1.5   Capacity Circularity: An Innatist Solution?   21

1.6   The Paradox of Self-Consciousness   24

2   **The Form of a Solution**   **27**

2.1   The Functionalist Account of Self-Reference   28

2.2   Rejecting the Classical View of Content   39

2.3   The Outline of a Solution   43

3   **Content, Concepts, and Language**   **49**

3.1   Conceptual and Nonconceptual Content: The Richness of
Perceptual Experience   50

3.2   Extending the Notion of Nonconceptual Content: The
Autonomy Principle   58

3.3   Defending the Autonomy Principle: Evidence from
Developmental Psychology   62

3.4   The Autonomy Principle: Further Evidence and
Applications   76

4   **The Theory of Nonconceptual Content   83**
     4.1 Attributing States with Autonomous Nonconceptual
           Content   83
     4.2 The Form of Autonomous Nonconceptual Content   94

5   **The Self of Ecological Optics   103**
     5.1 Self-Specifying Information in the Field of Vision   103
     5.2 The Content of Ecological Perception   115
     5.3 The Ecological Self in Infancy   123
     5.4 Moving beyond Perception   128

6   **Somatic Proprioception and the Bodily Self   131**
     6.1 The Modes of Somatic Proprioception   132
     6.2 Somatic Proprioception and the Simple Argument   134
     6.3 Somatic Proprioception as a Form of Perception   135
     6.4 Somatic Proprioception as a Form of Self-Consciousness   145
     6.5 The Content of Somatic Proprioception   151

7   **Points of View   163**
     7.1 Conceptual Points of View and Nonconceptual Points
           of View   163
     7.2 Self-Specifying Information and the Notion of a Nonconceptual
           Point of View   168
     7.3 Three Intersecting Distinctions and the Acquisition
           Constraint   188

8   **Navigation and Spatial Reasoning   193**
     8.1 From Place Recognition to a Nonconceptual Point of View:
           Navigation and Spatial Awareness   193
     8.2 Spatial Awareness and Self-Consciousness   198
     8.3 Cognitive Maps and Integrated Representations of the
           Environment   203
     8.4 Navigation Deploying an Integrated Representation of the
           Environment over Time   207
     8.5 The Notion of a Nonconceptual Point of View and Primitive
           Self-Consciousness   220

9   **Psychological Self-Awareness: Self and Others   229**
     9.1 The Symmetry Thesis: An Unsuccessful Defence   230

9.2 The

9.3

9

Note.

Referenc

Index   3.

Preface

The phenomenon of self-consciousness provides one of the enduring themes of philosophy. Many philosophers from the great to the insignificant have thought that a philosophical account of self-consciousness would be an Archimedean point upon which the whole of philosophy might stand. This book has no such pretensions. My concern is solely with understanding the internal articulation of the phenomenon of self-consciousness. In fact, my concern is primarily with those forms of self-consciousness that are more primitive, both logically and ontogenetically, than the conceptual and linguistic forms of self-consciousness to which philosophers have traditionally devoted their attention.

My concern with these primitive forms of self-consciousness stems from a paradox that strikes hard at traditional understandings of the relation between linguistic self-reference and self-conscious thought. I develop what I term the *paradox of self-consciousness* in chapter 1. The core of the paradox is the apparent strict interdependence between self-conscious thought and linguistic self-reference. This paradox is insoluble, I argue in chapter 2, if it is assumed that the conceptual and linguistic forms of self-consciousness are the only forms. In chapters 3 and 4, I set out a framework for thinking about the intentional explanation of behavior that allows truly ascribing content-bearing representational states to creatures who lack both conceptual abilities and linguistic abilities. Chapters 5 through 9 are devoted to showing that among those content-bearing representational states, there are several types that properly count as forms of primitive self-consciousness. Finally, in chapter 10, I show how a recognition of the existence and nature of these forms of primitive self-consciousness can be used to solve the paradox of self-consciousness.

The perspective from which this book is written is *philosophical naturalism*. I take it, for example, that philosophical accounts of concepts must accord not just with what is involved in the fully-fledged mastery of a concept but also with how it is possible for a thinker to acquire that concept in the normal course of cognitive development. The distinction between logical issues about concepts and psychological issues about concepts is, of course, a real one, but to my mind it does not provide a clear demarcation between the areas of competence of two separate disciplines, or of two distinct levels of explanation. Throughout this book I make free use of empirical work from various areas in scientific psychology in making philosophical points. I hope that the book as a whole may serve as an indirect argument for the utility of this approach.

Acknowledgments

This book was conceived and written during my tenure (1993–1996) of a British Academy Postdoctoral Research Fellowship, hosted initially by the University of Cambridge and subsequently by the University of Stirling. I am extremely grateful to the academy for making it possible for me to spend three years unencumbered by teaching and administrative commitments. I also owe a very great debt to my colleagues at the University of Stirling for encouraging my research, most particularly by allowing me seven months leave to complete this book before taking up my teaching duties. Peter Sullivan read a complete draft of the text with great care and is responsible for numerous improvements. While at Stirling I have benefited enormously from daily discussions on the philosophy of mind with Alan Millar.

I first began thinking about some of the issues in this book during the academic year 1992/1993, when I was a member of the Spatial Representation Project at King's College, Cambridge. Discussions during the project with Bill Brewer, Naomi Eilan, and Anthony Marcel were very helpful. As will be apparent from the text, I have been greatly inspired by the writings of John Campbell and Christopher Peacocke, who were also associated with the project. An intermittent correspondence with Susan Hurley over the last few years has helped me to sharpen many thoughts, and I am extremely grateful for the care and rigour with which she read a penultimate draft of the manuscript as well as for the opportunity to learn from her own unpublished writings.

A version of chapter 1 was delivered to the Sapientia Colloquium at Dartmouth College, where I was a visiting scholar in the summer of 1996. Chapters 3 and 4 draw heavily on my paper "Nonconceptual Content:

From Perceptual Experience to Subpersonal Computational States" (1995e). Chapter 7 is based on "Ecological Perception and the Notion of a Nonconceptual Point of View," my contribution to *The Body and the Self* (MIT Press, 1995), which I edited with Anthony Marcel and Naomi Eilan. Section 6.1 is drawn from the coauthored Introduction to that work.

It has been a pleasure to work once again with the MIT Press. Amy Brand has seen the project through with tact and forbearance. I am particularly grateful to her for securing the services of an excellent but sadly anonymous reviewer who made more useful suggestions than any author deserves. The final text has been greatly improved by the copyediting skills of Alan Thwaits.

A Note to the Reader

This book has been written in an interdisciplinary spirit, and I very much hope that it has things to say that will be of interest to workers in disciplines cognate to philosophy, particularly empirical psychology and cognitive science. Some readers may well find that they can more easily grasp the main line of my argument if they bypass some of the more narrowly philosophical discussion involved in identifying the paradox of self-consciousness and in setting up a possible framework for its resolution. On an initial reading, therefore, they could omit the first four sections of chapter 1, moving directly to sections 1.5 and 1.6. This should provide an outline of the central issues posed by the paradox of self-consciousness, which can subsequently be filled in by referring back to the earlier sections of the chapter. Sections 2.1 and 2.2 might also be omitted on a first pass. Section 2.3 should be sufficient to give a sense of the general strategy which I propose to adopt. In chapter 3, section 3.1 is likely to be of interest primarily to a philosophical audience. After that, I would hope to be able to hold my audience.

The Paradox of Self-Consciousness

1

The Paradox of Self-Consciousness

It is very natural to think of self-consciousness as a cognitive state or, more accurately, as a set of cognitive states. Self-knowledge is an example of such a cognitive state. There are plenty of things I know about myself. I know the sort of thing I am: a human being, a warm-blooded rational animal with two legs. I know many of my properties and much of what is happening to me, at both physical and mental levels. I also know things about my past: things I have done and places I have been, as well as people I have met. But I have many self-conscious cognitive states that are not instances of knowledge. For example, I have the capacity to make plans for the future—to weigh up possible courses of action in the light of goals, desires, and ambitions. I am also capable of a certain type of moral reflection, tied to moral self-understanding and moral self-evaluation. I can pursue questions like, What sort of person am I? Am I the sort of person that I want to be? Am I the sort of person that I ought to be?

When I say that I am a self-conscious creature, I am saying that I can do all of these things. But what do they have in common? Are some more important than others? Are they all necessary? Could I lack some and still be self-conscious? These are central questions that take us to the heart of many issues in metaphysics, the philosophy of mind, and the philosophy of psychology. In reflecting on them, however, we have to start from a paradox that besets philosophical reflection on self-consciousness. This paradox emerges when we consider what might seem to be the obvious thread that ties the various manifestations of self-consciousness together. I call it the paradox of self-consciousness. It is a paradox that raises the question of how self-consciousness is even possible. Some preparatory work is required before it can be appreciated, however.

1.1 'I'-Thoughts

Confronted with the range of putatively self-conscious cognitive states listed above, one might naturally assume that there is a single ability that they all presuppose. This is my ability to think about myself. I can only have knowledge about myself if I have beliefs about myself, and I can only have beliefs about myself if I can entertain thoughts about myself. The same can be said for autobiographical memories and moral self-understanding. These are all ways of thinking about myself.

Of course, much of what I think when I think about myself in these self-conscious ways is also available to me to employ in my thoughts about other people and other objects. My knowledge that I am a human being deploys certain conceptual abilities that I can also deploy in thinking that you are a human being. The same holds when I congratulate myself for satisfying the exacting moral standards of autonomous moral agency. This involves concepts and descriptions that can apply equally to myself and to others. On the other hand, when I think about myself, I am also putting to work an ability that I cannot put to work in thinking about other people and other objects. This is precisely the ability to apply those concepts and descriptions to myself. It has become common to refer to this ability as the ability to entertain 'I'-thoughts. I shall follow this convention.

What is an 'I'-thought? Obviously, an 'I'-thought is a thought that involves self-reference. I can think an 'I'-thought only by thinking about myself. Equally obviously, though, this cannot be all that there is to say on the subject. I can think thoughts that involve self-reference but are not 'I'-thoughts. Suppose I think that the next person to get a parking ticket in central Cambridge deserves everything he gets. Unbeknownst to me, the very next recipient of a parking ticket will be me. This makes my thought self-referring, but it does not make it an 'I'-thought. Why not? The answer is simply that I do not know that I will be the next person to get a parking ticket in central Cambridge. If A is that unfortunate person, then there is a true identity statement of the form $I = A$, but I do not know that this identity holds. Because I do not know that this identity holds, I cannot be ascribed the thought that I will deserve everything I get. And so I am not thinking a genuine 'I'-thought, because one cannot think a genuine 'I'-thought if one is ignorant that one is thinking about oneself. So it is natural to conclude that 'I'-thoughts involve a distinctive type of self-reference. This is the sort of self-reference whose natural linguistic expression is the first-person pronoun 'I', because one cannot use the first-person pronoun without knowing that one is thinking about oneself.

We can tighten this up a bit. When we say that a given thought has a natural linguistic expression, we are also saying something about how it is appropriate to characterize the content of that thought. We are saying something about what is being thought. This I term (without prejudice) a propositional content. A propositional content is given by the sentence that follows the 'that' clause in reporting a thought, a belief, or any propositional attitude. The proposal, then, is that 'I'-thoughts are all and only the thoughts whose propositional contents constitutively involve the first-person pronoun.

This is still not quite right, however, because thought contents can be specified in two ways. They can be specified directly or indirectly. An example of a direct specification of content is (1):

(1) J. L. B. believes the proposition that he would naturally express by saying, 'I will be the next person to receive a parking ticket in central Cambridge'.

A direct specification of content involves specifying what I would say in *oratio recta,* if I were explicitly to express what I believe. In contrast, an indirect specification of content proceeds in *oratio obliqua.* The model here is reported speech. So the same content indirectly specified would be (2):

(2) J. L. B. believes that he will be the next person to receive a parking ticket in central Cambridge.

Proposition (2), however, can also be used as a report of the belief that would be directly specified as follows:

(3) J. L. B. believes the proposition that he would naturally express by saying, 'J. L. B. will be the next person to receive a parking ticket in central Cambridge'.

Nonetheless, (1) and (3) are not equivalent. This is easily seen. J. L. B. could be suffering from an attack of amnesia and struggling to remember his own name. So even though a kindly soul has just put it to him that

J. L. B. will be the next person to get a parking ticket in central Cambridge and he believes that kindly soul, he fails to realize that he is J. L. B. Because of this, (1) is not a correct report of his belief, although (3) is. Nonetheless, as it stands, (2) is a correct indirect report of both (1) and (3). This creates a problem, because only (1) is a genuine 'I'-thought, according to the suggested criterion of having a content that constitutively involves the first-person pronoun, and yet there appears to be no way of capturing the distinction between (1) and (3) at the level of an indirect specification of content.

This problem can be solved with a device due to Hector-Neri Castañeda (1966, 1969). Castañeda distinguishes between two different roles that the pronoun 'he' can play in *oratio obliqua* clauses. On the one hand, 'he' can be employed in a proposition that the antecedent of the pronoun (i.e. the person named just before the clause in *oratio obliqua*) would have expressed using the first-person pronoun. In such a situation, Castañeda holds that 'he' is functioning as a *quasi-indicator*. He suggests that when 'he' is functioning as a quasi-indicator, it be written as 'he*'. Others have described this as the *indirect reflexive* pronoun (Anscombe 1975). When 'he' is functioning as an ordinary indicator, it picks out an individual in such a way that the person named just before the clause in *oratio obliqua* need not realize the identity of himself with that person. Clearly, then, we can disambiguate between (2) employed as an indirect version of (1) and (2) employed as an indirect version of (3) by distinguishing between (2.1) and (2).

(2.1)   J. L. B. believes that he* will be the next person to receive a parking ticket in central Cambridge.

Proposition (2.1) is an example of the indirect reflexive, while (2) is not. So, we can tie up the definition of an 'I'-thought as follows.

Definition   An *'I'-thought* is a thought whose content can only be specified directly by means of the first person pronoun 'I' or indirectly by means of the indirect reflexive pronoun 'he*'.

It was suggested earlier that all the cognitive states under consideration presuppose the ability to think about oneself. This is not only what they all have in common. It is also what underlies them all. We can now see in more detail what this suggestion amounts to. The claim is that what makes all those cognitive states modes of self-consciousness is the fact that they all have contents that can only be specified directly by means of the first person pronoun 'I' or indirectly by means of the indirect reflexive pronoun 'he*'. I will term such contents *first-person contents*.

1.2   Two Types of First-Person Content

The class of first-person contents is not a homogenous class. There is an important distinction to be drawn between two different types of first-person contents, corresponding to two different modes in which the first person can be employed. The existence of this distinction was first noted by Wittgenstein in an important passage from *The Blue Book*.[1] He gives the following examples of the two different modes:

> There are two different cases in the use of the word "I" (or "my") which I might call "the use as object" and "the use as subject." Examples of the first kind of use are these: "My arm is broken," "I have grown six inches," "I have a bump on my forehead," "The wind blows my hair about." Examples of the second kind are: "*I* see so-and-so," "*I* try to lift my arm," "*I* think it will rain," "*I* have a toothache." (Wittgenstein 1958, 66–67)

The explanation he gives of the distinction hinges on whether or not they are judgements that involve identification. The passage continues thus:

> One can point to the difference between these two categories by saying: The cases of the first category involve the recognition of a particular person, and there is in these cases the possibility of an error, or as I should rather put it: The possibility of an error has been provided for. . . . It is possible that, say in an accident, I should feel a pain in my arm, see a broken arm at my side, and think it is mine when really it is my neighbour's. And I could, looking into a mirror, mistake a bump on his forehead for one on mine. On the other hand, there is no question of recognizing a person when I say I have toothache. To ask "are you sure that it's *you* who have pains?" would be nonsensical. (Wittgenstein 1958, 67)

Wittgenstein is drawing a distinction between two types of first-person contents. The first type, which he describes as invoking the use of 'I' as object, can be analyzed in terms of more basic propositions. Suppose that the thought 'I am ϕ' involves such a use of 'I'. Then we can understand it as a conjunction of the following two thoughts: '*a* is ϕ' and 'I am *a*'. We can term the former a predication component and the latter an identification component (Evans 1982, 185). The reason for breaking the original thought down into these two components is precisely the possibility of error that Wittgenstein stresses in the second of the quoted passages. One can be quite correct in predicating that someone is ϕ, even though mistaken in identifying oneself as that person.

One way of putting this distinction, derived ultimately from Sydney Shoemaker, is in terms of immunity to a certain sort of error. First-person contents in which the 'I' is used as subject are immune to error through misidentification relative to the first-person pronoun. Shoemaker explains this as follows:

> To say that a statement "a is ϕ" is subject to error through misidentification relative to the term 'a' means that the following is possible: the speaker knows some particular thing to be ϕ, but makes the mistake of asserting "a is ϕ" because, and only because, he mistakenly thinks that the thing he knows to be ϕ is what 'a' refers to. (Shoemaker 1968, 7–8)

The point, then, is that one cannot be mistaken about who is being thought about. In one sense, Shoemaker's criterion of immunity to error through misidentification relative to the first-person pronoun (henceforth simply "immunity to error through misidentification") is too restrictive. Beliefs with first-person contents that are immune to error through misidentification tend to be acquired on grounds that usually do result in knowledge, but they do not have to be. The definition of immunity to error through misidentification needs to be adjusted to accommodate this by formulating it in terms of justification rather than knowledge.

The connection to be captured is between the sources or grounds from which a belief is derived and the justification there is for that belief. Beliefs and judgements are immune to error through misidentification in virtue of the grounds on which they are based. This is very important. The category of first-person contents being picked out is not defined by its subject matter or by any points of grammar. What demarcates the class of judgements and beliefs that are immune to error through misidentification is the evidence base from which they are derived, or the information on which they are based (Evans 1982, chap. 7). So, to take one of Wittgenstein's examples, my thought that I have a toothache is immune to error through misidentification because it is based on my feeling a pain in my teeth. Similarly, the fact that I am consciously perceiving you makes my belief that I am seeing you immune to error through misidentification. This suggests that we can modify Shoemaker's definition as follows:

Definition To say that a statement "*a* is ϕ" is *subject to error through misidentification relative to the term 'a'* means that the following is possible: the speaker is warranted in believing that some particular thing is ϕ, because his belief is based on an appropriate evidence base, but he makes the mistake of asserting '*a* is ϕ' because, and only because, he mistakenly thinks that the thing he justifiedly believes to be ϕ is what '*a*' refers to.[2]

First-person contents that are immune to error through misidentification can be mistaken, but they do have a prima facie warrant in virtue of the evidence on which they are based, because the fact that they are derived from such an evidence base is closely linked to the fact that they are immune to error through misidentification. Of course, there is room for considerable debate about what types of evidence base are correlated with this class of first-person contents, and this will be discussed further below.

It seems, then, that the distinction between different types of first-person content originally illustrated by Wittgenstein can be characterized in two different ways. We can distinguish between those first-person contents that are immune to error through misidentification and those that are subject to such error. Alternatively, we can discriminate between first-person contents with an identification component and those without such a component. For the purposes of this book I shall take it that these different formulations each pick out the same classes of first-person contents, although in interestingly different ways.

It will be obvious that these two classes of first-person contents are asymmetrically related. All first-person contents subject to error through misidentification contain an identification component of the form 'I am *a*'. Now, consider the employment of the first-person pronoun in that identification component. Does it or does it not have an identification component? If it does, then a further identification component will be implicated, of which the same question can be asked. Clearly, then, on pain of an infinite regress, at some stage we will have to arrive at an employment of the first-person pronoun that does not presuppose an identification component. The conclusion to draw, then, is that any first-person content subject to error through misidentification will ultimately be anchored in a first-person content that is immune to error through misidentification.[3]

This leaves us with a class of self-ascriptions that are identification-free. How are we to explain what is going on in this class of self-ascriptions? Shoemaker's suggestion is that to see how such identification-free self-reference is possible, we need to investigate the class of predicates that can be employed in such self-ascriptions. He writes, "There is an important and central class of psychological predicates, let us call them P^* predicates, each of which can be known to be instantiated in such a way that knowing it to be instantiated in that way is equivalent to knowing it to be instantiated in oneself" (Shoemaker 1968, 16). It is a matter of some controversy just what predicates fall into this class, and indeed, whether they are all psychological, as Shoemaker claims. This will be discussed below. For present purposes, we can just take being in pain to be a canonical example of a P^* predicate. Shoemaker's claim is that no self-identification is required to move from the judgement 'There is pain' to the judgement 'I am in pain', provided that the judgement is based on actually experiencing the pain. But how are we to flesh this out? One way of doing so is to employ the idea of a primitively compelling inference, an inference that a subject both can and should make without any further reasoning or justification (Peacocke 1992). The thought is that when the predicate 'pain' is applied on the basis of feeling the pain, the inference from the existential statement 'There is pain' to the self-ascription 'I am in pain' is primitively compelling in virtue of the status of pain as a P^* predicate. Another way (and one that might be closer to Shoemaker's view) would be to deny that any such inference is required at all. Knowing that there is pain just is knowing that one is in pain, which in turn can be understood as a disposition to think 'I am in pain'. On this view, thinking 'There is pain' is just another way of thinking 'I am in pain' (provided, of course, that the thought is grounded on experiencing the pain).

Neither of these suggestions, though, can *explain* what it is to possess the capacity to make self-ascriptions that are immune to error through misidentification. Both make essential reference to the capacity to think thoughts like 'I am in pain', and these thoughts fall squarely into the category of identification-free self-ascriptions, which we are trying to explain. Clearly, we need to take an alternative tack to make progress here.

1.3   The First-Person Pronoun and a Deflationary Account of Self-Consciousness

Since we cannot explain what immunity to error through misidentification consists in through the class of predicates that feature in identification-free judgements, the obvious alternative is to look at the other component of identification-free judgements, namely the first-person element, naturally expressed with the first-person pronoun. And in fact there is at least one good reason to think that the semantics of the first-person pronoun might hold the key to immunity to error through misidentification. This emerges when one reflects that the first-person pronoun has guaranteed reference. It is commonly and correctly held that the practices and rules governing the use of the first-person pronoun determine what its reference will be whenever it is employed, according to the simple rule that whenever the first-person pronoun is used correctly, it will refer to the person using it (Barwise and Perry 1981, Strawson 1994). It follows from this rule that the correct use of 'I' is enough to guarantee both that it has a referent and that the referent is the user. So it is impossible for the first-person pronoun (correctly and genuinely employed) to fail to refer or for it to refer to someone other than the person using it.

Guaranteed reference and immunity to error through misidentification are clearly very closely related. It is natural to suggest that immunity to error through misidentification (relative to the first-person pronoun) is simply a function of the meaning rule for the first-person pronoun.[4] The claim here is not, of course, that the set of judgements with guaranteed reference maps onto the set of judgements immune to error through misidentification. There are clear instances of judgements expressible with the first-person pronoun that ipso facto have guaranteed reference but that fail to be immune to error relative to the first-person pronoun. Suppose, for example, that a baritone singing in a choir hears a tuneful voice that he mistakenly judges to be his own when it is in fact the voice of his neighbour (also a baritone). He then judges, 'I am singing in tune'. This is a clear instance of misidentification relative to the first-person pronoun, because the baritone makes the mistake of assuming that the baritone whom he justifiably believes to be singing in tune is the baritone to whom

'I' refers. Nonetheless, this is not a counterexample to the suggested view, because the evidence base upon which the baritone judges is not one of the categories of evidence bases that generates judgements immune to error relative to the first-person pronoun. Reformulating the issue will make it more perspicuous. The evidence base is such that the ensuing judgement has to be analyzed conjunctively in terms of an identification component and a predication component ('That baritone is singing in tune' and 'I am that baritone').

It seems natural to combine this close connection with our earlier conclusions by proposing an account of self-consciousness in terms of the capacity to think 'I'-thoughts that are immune to error through misidentification, where immunity to error through misidentification is a function of the semantics of the first-person pronoun. This would be a *deflationary* account of self-consciousness. If we can straightforwardly explain what makes those first-person contents immune to error through misidentification with reference to the semantics of the first-person pronoun, then it seems fair to say that the problem of self-consciousness has been dissolved, at least as much as solved. The proposed account would be on a par with other noted examples of deflationism, such as the redundancy theory of truth.

Let me break this deflationary theory down into a set of distinct claims. The first claim is that what is distinctive about the various forms of self-consciousness is that they involve thinking 'I'-thoughts. As a thesis about explanation, this comes out as the following claim:

Claim 1   Once we have an account of what it is to be capable of thinking 'I'-thoughts, we will have explained everything distinctive about self-consciousness.

The second claim is a claim about the form that such an account will have to take. It stems from the thought that what is distinctive about 'I'-thoughts is that they are either themselves immune to error through misidentification or they rest on further 'I'-thoughts that are immune in that way. This yields the following claim:

Claim 2   Once we have an account of what it is to be capable of thinking thoughts that are immune to error through misidentification, we will have explained everything distinctive about the capacity to think 'I'-thoughts.

The final claim derives from the thought that immunity to error through misidentification is a function of the semantics of the first-person pronoun:

Claim 3 Once we have an account of the semantics of the first-person pronoun, we will have explained everything distinctive about the capacity to think thoughts that are immune to error through misidentification.

The suggestion is that the semantics of the first-person pronoun will explain what is distinctive about the capacity to think thoughts immune to error through misidentification. Of course, this needs to be fleshed out a little. Semantics alone cannot be expected to explain the capacity for thinking such thoughts. The point must be that all that there is to the capacity to think thoughts that are immune to error through misidentification is the capacity to think the sort of thoughts whose natural linguistic expression involves the first-person pronoun, where this capacity is given by mastery of the semantics of the first-person pronoun. This yields the following reformulation:

Claim 3a Once we have explained what it is to master the semantics of the first-person pronoun, we will have explained everything distinctive about the capacity to think thoughts immune to error through misidentification.

So on this view, mastery of the semantics of the first-person pronoun is the single most important explanandum in a theory of self-consciousness.[5]

One immediate question that might be put to a defender of the deflationary theory is how mastery of the semantics of the first-person pronoun can make sense of the distinction between first-person contents that are immune to error through misidentification and first-person contents that lack such immunity. Both types of first-person content are naturally expressed by means of the first-person pronoun. So how can mastery of the semantics of the first-person pronoun capture what is distinctive about those first-person contents that are immune to error through misidentification? One can see, however, that this is only an apparent difficulty when one remembers that those first person contents that are immune to error through misidentification (those employing 'I' as object) have to be broken down into their two constituent elements: the identification component and the predication component. It is the identification component of such judgements that mastery of the semantics of the first-person pronoun is being called upon to explain, and the identification component is, of course, immune to error through misidentification.

There are grave problems with the deflationary account, as will emerge in the next section, but at this stage it is important to stress how well it meshes with one persuasive strand of thought about self-consciousness. Many philosophers have thought that what is distinctive about beings who are self-conscious is that they are capable of ascribing predicates to themselves. Those predicates are sometimes taken to be psychological (by those of a Cartesian bent) and sometimes both psychological and physical. If it is assumed that the predicates in question have a constant sense, whether they are applied to oneself or to others, then everything distinctive about the self-conscious grasp of those predicates that apply to one seems to fall on the act of self-ascription, and in particular, on the first-person pronoun by which that self-ascription is effected. A move toward the deflationary view is therefore a natural next step.

It is also important to stress how the deflationary theory of self-consciousness, and indeed any theory of self-consciousness that accords a serious role in self-consciousness to mastery of the semantics of the first-person pronoun, is motivated by an important principle that has governed much of the development of analytical philosophy. This is the principle that the philosophical analysis of thought can only proceed through the philosophical analysis of language. The principle has been defended most vigorously by Michael Dummett. Here is a particularly trenchant statement:

Thoughts differ from all else that is said to be among the contents of the mind in being wholly communicable: it is of the essence of thought that I can convey to you the very thought that I have, as opposed to being able to tell you merely something about what my thought is like. It is of the essence of thought not merely to be communicable, but to be communicable, without residue, by means of language. In order to understand thought, it is necessary, therefore, to understand the means by which thought is expressed. (Dummett 1978, 442)

Dummett goes on to draw the clear methodological implications of this view of the nature of thought:

We communicate thoughts by means of language because we have an implicit understanding of the workings of language, that is, of the principles governing the use of language; it is these principles, which relate to what is open to view in the employment of language, unaided by any supposed contact between mind and mind other than via the medium of language, which endow our sentences with the senses that they carry. In order to analyse thought, therefore, it is necessary to make explicit those principles, regulating our use of language, which we already implicitly grasp. (Dummett 1978, 442)

Many philosophers would want to dissent from the strong claim that the philosophical analysis of thought through the philosophical analysis of language is the fundamental task of philosophy. But there is a weaker principle that is very widely held:

The Thought-Language Principle   The only way to analyze the capacity to think a particular range of thoughts is by analyzing the capacity for the canonical linguistic expression of those thoughts.

The Thought-Language Principle dictates an obvious methodology for the analysis of thought. To understand what it is to be capable of thinking a particular range of thoughts, one must first find the canonical linguistic expression for the thoughts in question and then explain the linguistic skills that must be mastered for the use of that linguistic expression.

When the methodology associated with the Thought-Language Principle is combined with the point just made about predicates having a constant sense irrespective of whether they are being used for first-, second-, or third-person ascriptions, the deflationary theory falls out very naturally. The weaker thesis tells us that the only way to understand self-conscious thoughts is through understanding the linguistic expression of those self-conscious thoughts. The fact that the paradigm cases of self-conscious thoughts (like instances of self-knowledge) involve ascribing certain properties to oneself means that attention must be directed to the distinctive features of the linguistic means whereby a subject is able to apply certain predicates to himself in the appropriate way. Since the constancy-of-sense thesis means that the distinctive features cannot lie in the relevant predicates, we soon arrive at the deflationary theory.

Despite these two powerful motivations for it, the deflationary theory runs into two very serious problems that together constitute what I term the paradox of self-consciousness. In the following section I will bring these problems out.[6]

1.4   Explanatory Circularity and Capacity Circularity

According to claim 3a, once we have explained what it is to master the semantics of the first-person pronoun, we have explained everything distinctive about the capacity to think thoughts that are immune to error through misidentification, and hence everything distinctive about self-consciousness. We can start evaluating this by being a little more precise about what the semantics are that have to be grasped. I suggested earlier that the rule governing the use of the first-person pronoun is that it refers to the person using it. More precisely, we can state the following token-reflexive rule:

Token-reflexive rule, version 1   When a person employs a token of 'I', in so doing he refers to himself.[7]

This token-reflexive rule is the key to the semantics of the first-person pronoun. So, according to the deflationary account, mastery of this rule is the explanatory key to the capacity to think thoughts immune to error through misidentification.

An obvious problem with this suggestion emerges from the points made earlier about the third-person pronoun 'he'. It can be employed as the ordinary reflexive 'he' or as the indirect reflexive, which, following Castañeda, can be written 'he*'. Clearly in the context of the token-reflexive rule it is the indirect reflexive that is required. Reporting self-reference by means of the ordinary reflexive 'he' leaves open the possibility that the person who is referring to himself might be referring to himself without realizing that he is so doing, and this is clearly not possible with the first-person pronoun. So the token-reflexive rule needs to be reformulated:

Token-reflexive rule, version 2   When a person employs a token of 'I', in so doing, he refers to himself*.

This creates obvious problems of circularity, however, because we can only understand how a person can refer to himself* by understanding how a person can refer to himself by employing the first-person pronoun. The indirect reflexive in indirect speech needs to be explained through the first-person of direct speech, which is, of course, 'I'.[8] This circularity appears damaging to the deflationary account of self-consciousness. Recall that I characterized a first-person content as one that can be specified directly only by means of the first-person pronoun 'I' or indirectly only by means of the indirect reflexive 'he*'. If, as the deflationary account suggests, we take the capacity to think thoughts with first-person contents to be what we are trying to explain, then it is viciously circular to suggest that this capacity can be explained by mastery of a rule that contains a first-person content.

Perhaps, though, the token-reflexive rule can be formulated in a way that avoids this difficulty. Consider the following suggestion:

Token-reflexive rule, version 3   Any token of 'I' refers to whoever produced it.[9]

This seems on the face of it to avoid the problem, in the sense that it does not employ the third-person pronoun and therefore does not force us to choose between direct and indirect reflexive construals of that pronoun in *oratio obliqua*. But how are we to construe it? In one sense version 3 of the rule can be read as just a notational variant of version 1 and hence subject to precisely the same ambiguity between ordinary and indirect reflexive pronouns. But there is a way of construing it that is more promising:

Token-reflexive rule, version 4   If a person employs a token of 'I', then he refers to himself in virtue of being the producer of that token.

In version 4 it is plausible to suggest that 'himself' can be read as an ordinary reflexive pronoun. The possibility that a person might refer to himself without realizing that he is doing so is what forced us toward the indirect reflexive in version 1. But in version 4 it seems that this possibility is ruled out by the fact that the person is referring to himself as the producer of the token of 'I'.

Again, though, there is a difficulty.[10] What is it for someone to refer to himself in virtue of being the producer of a given token? It seems clear that such a person will not succeed in referring to himself unless he knows that he produced the token in question. But this brings us straight back to the circularity problem. Employing a token of the first-person pronoun in a way that reflects mastery of its semantics (as construed by the token-reflexive rule, version 4) requires knowing that one is the producer of the relevant token and that is a piece of knowledge with a first-person content.[11] This is the first strand of what I term the *paradox of self-consciousness*. Any theory that tries to elucidate the capacity to think first-person thoughts through linguistic mastery of the first-person pronoun will be circular, because the explanandum is part of the explanans, either directly, as in version 2, or indirectly, as in version 4. Let me call this *explanatory circularity*.

It is important to keep the problem of explanatory circularity distinct from a closely related problem. Elizabeth Anscombe has controversially argued that 'I' is not a referring expression. As part of her argument for that bizarre conclusion, she maintains that no version of the token-reflexive rule can provide a noncircular account of the meaning of the first-person pronoun. She supports this with considerations much like those I have adduced. The version of the token-reflexive rule she considers is this:

Token-reflexive rule, version 5   'I' is a word that each speaker [of English] uses only to refer to himself.

She points out, very much as I have done, that although version 5 truly fixes the reference of the first-person pronoun, it does not capture what is distinctive about 'I', because it fails to distinguish between genuine self-reference and accidental self-reference. But if, she continues, version 5 is adjusted to accommodate the distinction by replacing the direct reflexive pronoun with the indirect reflexive pronoun, then she identifies problems of circularity: "The explanation of the word 'I' as 'the word which each of us uses to speak of himself' is hardly an explanation!—At least, it is no explanation if that reflexive has in turn to be explained in terms of 'I'; and if it is the ordinary reflexive then we are back at square one" (Anscombe 1975, 48). This dilemma comes about, she thinks, only because the first-person pronoun is being treated as a referring proper name. The only solution she sees is to deny that 'I' is a referring expression at all.

I must stress that the notion of explanatory circularity I have outlined in no way commits me to Anscombe's position, although both Anscombe and I are stressing the same features of token-reflexive accounts of the semantics of the first-person pronoun. The conclusion I draw from those features is that the deflationary theory of self-consciousness (and by extension, any account of self-consciousness that tries to explain what is distinctive about self-conscious thoughts in terms of mastery of the first-person pronoun) will end up being viciously circular because mastery of the semantics of the first-person pronoun involves the capacity to think first-person thoughts. This has no implications for the question Anscombe addresses of whether the token-reflexive rule yields an adequate account of the semantics of the first-person pronoun. And in fact it seems to me that, on this question, Anscombe is surely wrong. The token-reflexive rule is an adequate account of the semantics of the first-person pronoun precisely because it fixes the reference of any token utterance of 'I', and that is all that a meaning rule for 'I' needs to do. The token-reflexive rule *as it stands* is not circular. It becomes circular only if it is adjusted to rule out the possibility of accidental self-reference either by replacing the direct reflexive pronoun with the indirect reflexive pronoun or by requiring that the utterer of a token of 'I' should know that he produced the relevant token. But neither of these modifications is required for an account of the meaning of 'I'. To hold that there is any such requirement is to confuse the semantics of the first-person pronoun with the pragmatics of the first-person pronoun. The problem of explanatory circularity arises because it is not sufficient for the deflationary account, or any comparable account of self-consciousness, simply to provide an account of the semantics of the first-person pronoun. As stressed in the previous section, the deflationary account needs to provide an account of mastery of the first-person pronoun, and this will have to include both the semantics and the pragmatics. Hence the modifications have to be made, with the ensuing circularity.

The second problem with the deflationary account is closely related. What creates the difficulty with version 4 of the token-reflexive rule is that the reflexive self-reference achieved with the first-person pronoun requires that the person referring to himself know that he is the producer of the token in question (although, to repeat, I am offering this merely as a necessary condition rather than as a sufficient condition). This knowledge, of course, is knowledge with a first-person content. So the deflationary account of self-consciousness needs to advert to precisely the first-person thoughts it is attempting to explain if it is to provide an understanding of the mastery of the semantics of the first-person pronoun able to anchor the explanation of self-consciousness. This makes the deflationary theory viciously circular, because the explanandum is required to explain the explanans. This is *explanatory circularity*. It is important to note, however, that this is not the only type of circularity created by the mutual interdependence of first-person thought and mastery of the semantics of the first-person pronoun. Another form of circularity arises because the attempt is being made to explain one capacity (the capacity to think thoughts with first-person contents) in terms of another capacity (mastery of the semantics of the first-person pronoun). What is at stake is the relation between the relevant capacities that underlie the explanans and the explanandum respectively. The point here is that the capacity for reflexive self-reference by means of the first-person pronoun presupposes the capacity to think thoughts with first-person contents, and hence cannot be deployed to explain that capacity. In other words, a degree of self-consciousness is required to master the use of the first-person pronoun. It is natural to describe this as an instance of *capacity circularity*.

But what is wrong with capacity circularity? Why should we take capacity circularity to be as vicious as explanatory circularity? It would be in keeping with the general spirit of the deflationary account to hold that the existence of capacity circularity just shows that we have reached the limits of explanation. Pointing out the interconnections and interdependencies between various forms of self-consciousness is, on this view, as far as we can go. The thought is that we are dealing with a set of abilities that can be explained from within but not from without. No explanation of the constituents of that set of abilities in terms of abilities that are more fundamental can be expected, and, it might be suggested, capacity circularity merely reflects this. On this view, capacity circularity is merely a reflection of the fact that certain cognitive abilities form what Christopher Peacocke (1979) has called a *local holism*.

That there are such local holisms is indisputable. And in many cases the existence of such local holisms presents no difficulties of circularity.[12] There is nothing troubling per se about an interdependence of explanation. In the case of self-consciousness, however, problems of circularity are not so easily dismissed, because they go far beyond a putative interdependence of explanation. Capacity circularity has implications for the *ontogenesis* of self-consciousness. In brief, if we hold that the various abilities at the root of self-conscious thought form a local holism and consequently can only be explained in terms of each other, then we are ruling out the possibility of explaining how any or all of those abilities can be acquired in the normal course of cognitive development. But this needs to be made more explicit.

Let me begin with the following constraint, which seems to me to be operative in all discussions of cognition.

The Acquisition Constraint   If a given cognitive capacity is psychologically real, then there must be an explanation of how it is possible for an individual in the normal course of human development to acquire that cognitive capacity.

There is a potential ambiguity in the concept of explanation. On the one hand, 'explanation' might be taken to refer to the actual account that is offered to explain a particular phenomenon. On the other, 'explanation' might be thought to refer to the metaphysical basis of such an account, that is to say, to the facts that are characterized by such an account if it is true. I intend the Acquisition Constraint in the second of these two senses (which might be termed the metaphysical sense as opposed to the epistemological sense). In this metaphysical sense the Acquisition Constraint is truistic. It does not demand that philosophers or anybody else should be able to provide an account of how the capacity in question is, or could be, acquired. What it does provide, however, is a contrapositive test for the psychological reality of any putative cognitive ability. For any proposed cognitive ability, if it is impossible for an individual to acquire that ability, then it cannot be psychologically real.

Of course, the usefulness of the Acquisition Constraint depends on how we understand its being satisfied. Let me briefly outline one such way, which seems to me to be paradigmatic. Every individual has an innate set of cognitive capacities that it possesses at birth. Let me call that S_0. At any given time t after birth an individual will have a particular set of cognitive capacities. Let me call that S_t. Now consider a given cognitive capacity c that is putatively in S_t. Suppose that for any time $t - n$ the following two conditions are satisfied. First, it is conceivable how c could have emerged from capacities present in S_{t-n}. Second, it is conceivable how the capacities present in S_{t-n} could have emerged from the capacities present in S_0. By its being conceivable that one capacity could emerge from a given set of capacities, I mean that it is intelligible that (in the right environment) the individual in question could deploy the cognitive capacities it already has to acquire the new capacity. If those conditions are satisfied, then we have a paradigm case of learning.

It is precisely here that capacity circularity bites, for the following reason. If mastery of the first-person pronoun is to meet the Acquisition Constraint, then clearly there must be some time t when S_t includes the capacity for linguistic mastery of the first-person pronoun, and a corresponding time $t - n$ when S_{t-n} does not include that capacity but includes other capacities on the basis of which it is intelligible that an individual could acquire the capacity for linguistic mastery of the first-person pronoun. The implication of capacity circularity, however, is that any such S_{t-n} will have to include the capacity to think thoughts with first-person contents, and hence that any such S_{t-n} will have to include the capacity for linguistic mastery of the first-person pronoun. Clearly, then, there can be no such S_{t-n} in terms of which the Acquisition Constraint could be satisfied.

There will be philosophers unprepared to accept that the Acquisition Constraint, or anything like it, can have a role to play in philosophical accounts of concepts and conceptual abilities. The most obvious basis for such a view would be a Fregean distrust of "psychologism" that leads to a rigid division of labor between philosophy and psychology. The operative thought is that the task of a philosophical theory of concepts is to explain what a given concept is or what a given conceptual ability consists in. This, it is frequently maintained, is something that can be done in complete independence of explaining how such a concept or ability might be acquired. The underlying distinction is one between philosophical questions centering around concept possession and psychological questions centering around concept acquisition. This distinction is, to my mind, suspect.[13] For my present purposes, though, all that I need to point out is that, however strictly one does adhere to the distinction, it provides no support for a rejection of the Acquisition Constraint. The neo-Fregean distinction is directed against the view that facts about how concepts are acquired have a role to play in explaining and individuating concepts. But this view does not have to be disputed by a supporter of the Acquisition Constraint. All that the supporter of the Acquisition Constraint is committed to is the principle that no satisfactory account of what a concept is should make it impossible to provide an explanation of how that concept can be acquired. The Acquisition Constraint has nothing to say about the further question of whether the psychological explanation in question has a role to play in a constitutive explanation of the concept in question, and hence is not in conflict with the neo-Fregean distinction.

1.5 Capacity Circularity: An Innatist Solution?

Although the notion of capacity circularity just defined has emerged from what might initially appear to be narrow philosophical concerns, the problems it generates are far wider in their application.

The capacity circularity of the first-person pronoun 'I' arises because mastery of the first-person pronoun requires the capacity to think certain self-conscious thoughts that can only be expressed with the first-person pronoun 'I'. For genuine employment of the first-person pronoun it is not enough that a speaker should utter 'I' in full knowledge of the token-reflexive rule that a token of 'I' refers to the utterer of that token. The speaker also needs to grasp that he himself is the utterer of that token, which is a thought that can only be expressed in terms of the first-person pronoun for reasons that I have tried to bring out. This has implications for thinking about how the first-person pronoun can be learned. It is not simply a matter of learning that there is an expression governed by the token-reflexive rule that it refers to whoever utters it. Rather, it is a matter of learning that there is an expression governed by the rule that it refers to its utterer when that utter intends to refer to himself*. To put it in the first person, I can only learn to employ the first-person pronoun by learning that there is an expression governed by the rule that it refers to me when I intend to refer to myself.

The problem that this creates is a simple one. It seems to make it impossible to understand how mastery of the first-person pronoun could ever be genuinely learned. The thought that I need to grasp if I am to learn how to employ the first-person pronoun is not a thought that I can entertain before I have mastered the first-person pronoun—not, at least, according to any theory that accepts the widely held view that a thought cannot be entertained by a creature who lacks the ability for the canonical linguistic expression of that thought. So, to master the first-person pronoun, I must already have mastered the first-person pronoun.

It might be thought that capacity circularity as thus described both confirms, and can be resolved by, an innatist account of the relevant abilities, because it is only threatening on a crude empiricist account of learning and concept acquisition. Much of contemporary cognitive science and linguistics postulates the existence of innate modules as a way of explaining how cognitive abilities can be acquired.[14] This is offered as an explicit contrast to learning-based developmental theories (Gazzaniga 1992). In an innatist account the learning environment serves merely as a source of triggers determining the selection of one of a range of circuits or parameters. There are two areas in which such theories have become prominent. The first and most celebrated is the nativist theory of language acquisition pioneered by Chomsky. According to the nativist view, languages can be learned only if the language user is already innately aware of their essential *syntactic* structure.[15] The second is the modular version of the nativist theory of mind in humans and (more controversially) in some higher primates.[16] Combining these two theories offers the prospect of an innatist response to the capacity circularity of the first-person pronoun, by showing how the relevant cognitive abilities are present in what I earlier termed the individual's *innate endowment.*

There are several reasons, however, why this initial reaction should be resisted. The first is quite straightforward. Despite the complexity and sophistication of the dominant government-binding (GB) paradigm in transformational grammar (Chomsky 1981, Haegman 1993), the theory has nothing to say about the first-person pronoun that will help with the problem of capacity circularity. When the first-person pronoun is employed nominatively as the subject of a sentence, it counts simply as an R expression (referring expression) and as such is governed solely by the third constraint of binding theory, namely, that R expressions occurring in noun phrases are always free. When the third-person pronoun is used anaphorically in indirect-speech reports, it is subject to the first constraint of binding theory, namely, that anaphoric pronouns are bound in the governing category, but this is, of course, impervious to the distinction between the direct reflexive 'he' and indirect reflexive 'he himself' (or 'he*', as Castañeda writes it). But none of this is surprising, since the peculiarities and complexities of the first-person pronoun arise at the semantic level and GB theory is a theory about syntax.

The second point follows from this. The existence of an innate universal grammar, no matter what its degree of complexity and no matter how its parameters are set, does not mean that language is not learned. The postulation of an innate universal grammar is not in itself a theory of language acquisition. Although motivated by the thought that without such an innate grammar the acquisition of language would be impossible (the famous "poverty of the stimulus" argument), it leaves open the crucial question of how the innately given parameters are set. What governs the transition from the initial state of the language faculty to the steady state of adult linguistic competence? There are, broadly speaking, three candidate theories here. According to the "no growth" theory, language ①️ acquisition does not involve a process of learning, and the parameters are set purely by exposure to linguistic data. The partial and extended nature of the process of language acquisition is explained in terms of the development of nonlinguistic cognitive capacities, such as memory or attention, that expand the range of linguistic data to which children can be exposed. According to the "maturation" theory, on the other hand, dif- ②️ ferent components of universal grammar mature at different times, and this explains the appearance of linguistic learning.

Neither of these theories will help with capacity circularity, however, for familiar reasons. Both the no-growth and maturation theories deal solely with the acquisition of syntax, and the problems of capacity circularity arise at the level of semantics. This leads into the third theory of language acquisition. Stephen Pinker's recognition of the need for what he terms the "semantic bootstrapping hypothesis" (according to which ③️ the child uses rough-and-ready semantic generalizations to map innate syntactic structures onto natural language) is a clear recognition that the postulation of innate syntactic structures cannot *suffice* to show how language acquisition meets the Acquisition Constraint, and he attempts to develop an alternative (Pinker 1987). The motivations that lead to his alternative clearly indicate that advocates of innate syntactic structures still have to answer general questions like these: How are innate syntactic principles to be applied to the natural language that the child encounters? How is the transition made from innate (tacit) knowledge of general syntactic principles to the ability to manipulate and combine words that have both syntactic and semantic properties? It should be clear that an answer to these questions will involve an answer to the question of how it is possible for the child to learn to manipulate a pronoun with the semantic properties of the first-person pronoun, and at this point the problems of capacity circularity become salient once again.

1.6   The Paradox of Self-Consciousness

A paradox is an unacceptable conclusion or set of conclusions reachable by apparently valid argument from apparently true premises. The clearest way to appreciate a paradox is to list the incompatible propositions that form the premises and conclusions. In the case of the paradox of self-consciousness, they are as follows:

1. The only way to analyze what is distinctive about self-consciousness is by analyzing the capacity to think 'I'-thoughts.
2. The only way to analyze the capacity to think a particular range of thoughts is by analyzing the capacity for the canonical linguistic expression of those thoughts (the Thought-Language Principle).
3. 'I'-thoughts are canonically expressed by means of the first-person pronoun.
4. Mastery of the first-person pronoun requires the capacity to think 'I'-thoughts.
5. A noncircular account of self-consciousness is possible.
6. Mastery of the semantics of the first-person pronoun meets the Acquisition Constraint (in the paradigmatic way defined earlier).

What I have argued in this chapter is that propositions (1) through (6) cannot be maintained together. More specifically, neither proposition (5) nor proposition (6) can be maintained in conjunction with propositions (1) through (4).

Clearly, if the arguments I have offered are valid, then one or more of these propositions must be abandoned, and possible solutions to the paradox of self-consciousness can be classified according to which proposition(s) they reject in order to restore consistency. The problem, of course, is that each proposition is both intuitively and philosophically appealing, which is why the term 'paradox' seems appropriate. Proposition (1) seems to be entailed by the thesis that self-ascribable psychological and physical predicates have a constant sense across first- and third-

Right

person uses. There are powerful epistemological reasons for not wanting to reject that thesis. Proposition (2) has been described as, and widely accepted to be, a fundamental principle of analytical philosophy. Propositions (3) and (4) are indisputable. Both propositions (5) and (6) are highly desirable. If (5) is not true, then it follows that the capacity to think 'I'-thoughts is unanalyzable, which is a highly undesirable result, while the alternative to (6) is to deny that linguistic mastery of the first-person pronoun is psychologically real in anything like the way we understand it.

Nonetheless, these six propositions cannot all be true. In the first two sections of chapter 2, I identify the proposition that I think needs to be rejected if the paradox is to be solved. That proposition is proposition (2), the Thought-Language Principle. Of course, any solution to the paradox will be ad hoc, and hence unacceptable, unless the rejection of the proposition in question can be independently motivated. In section 2.3 of chapter 2 and in chapters 3 and 4, I outline in more detail what needs to be shown if the Thought-Language Principle is to be plausibly rejected in a way that will solve the paradox of self-consciousness. The remainder of the book is devoted to the twofold task of, first, motivating the rejection of the Thought-Language Principle and, second, showing how the paradox of self-consciousness can be solved once the Thought-Language Principle is abandoned.

2

The Form of a Solution

One possible reaction to the paradox of self-consciousness as outlined in the previous chapter is that it arises only because unrealistic and ultimately unwarranted requirements are being placed on what are to count as genuinely self-referring first-person thoughts. Support for such an objection will be found in those theories that attempt to explain first-person thoughts in a way that does not presuppose any form of internal representation of the self or indeed any form of self-knowledge. The paradox of self-consciousness arises because mastery of the semantics of the first-person pronoun is available only to creatures capable of thinking first-person thoughts whose contents involve reflexive self-reference and thus seem to presuppose mastery of the first-person pronoun. If, though, it can be established that the capacity to think genuinely first-person thoughts does not depend on any linguistic and conceptual abilities, then arguably the problems of circularity will no longer have purchase.

There is an account of self-reference and genuinely first-person thought that can be read in a way that poses just such a direct challenge to the account of self-reference underpinning the paradox of self-consciousness. This is the functionalist account. On the functionalist view, reflexive self-reference is a completely unmysterious phenomenon susceptible to a functional analysis. Reflexive self-reference is not dependent upon any antecedent conceptual or linguistic skills. Nonetheless, the functional account of reflexive self-reference is deemed to be sufficiently rich to provide the foundation for an account of the semantics of the first-person pronoun. If this is right, then the circularity at the heart of the paradox of self-consciousness can be avoided.

In the first section of this chapter I examine the functionalist account of self-reference as a possible strategy. I will argue that, although it is not ultimately successful, attention to the functionalist account reveals the correct approach for solving the paradox of self-consciousness. The second section shows how a successful response to the paradox of self-consciousness must reject what I call the classical view of content. In the final section I set the agenda for the rest of the book.

2.1   The Functionalist Account of Self-Reference

The circularity problems at the root of the paradox of self-consciousness arise because mastery of the semantics of the first-person pronoun requires the capacity to think first-person thoughts whose natural expression is by means of the first-person pronoun. It seems clear that the circle will be broken if there are forms of first-person thought that are more primitive than those hitherto discussed, in the sense that they do not require linguistic mastery of the first-person pronoun. What creates the problem of capacity circularity is the thought that we need to appeal to first-person contents in explaining mastery of the first-person pronoun, combined with the thought that any creature capable of entertaining first-person contents will have mastered the first-person pronoun. So if we want to retain the thought that mastery of the first-person pronoun can only be explained in terms of first-person contents, capacity circularity can only be avoided if there are first-person contents that do not presuppose mastery of the first-person pronoun.

On the other hand, however, it seems to follow from everything I said earlier about 'I'-thoughts that self-conscious thought in the absence of linguistic mastery of the first-person pronoun is a contradiction in terms. First-person thoughts have first-person contents, where first-person contents can only be specified in terms of either the first-person pronoun or the indirect reflexive pronoun. So how could such thoughts be entertained by a thinker incapable of reflexive self-reference? How can a thinker who is not capable of reflexively referring to himself as English speakers do with the first-person pronoun be plausibly ascribed thoughts with first-person contents? The thought that, despite all this, there are indeed first-person contents that do not presuppose mastery of the first-person pronoun is at the core of the functionalist theory of self-reference and first-person belief, which I will examine in this section.

The best developed functionalist theory of self-reference has been provided by Hugh Mellor (1988–1989). The basic phenomenon he is interested in explaining is what it is for a creature to have what he terms a subjective belief, that is to say, a belief whose content is naturally expressed by a sentence in the first-person singular and the present tense. The explanation of subjective beliefs that he offers makes such beliefs independent of both linguistic abilities and conscious beliefs. From this basic account he constructs an account of conscious subjective beliefs and then of the reference of the first-person pronoun 'I'. These putatively more sophisticated cognitive states are causally derivable from basic subjective beliefs.

Mellor starts from the functionalist premise that beliefs are causal functions from desires to actions. It is, of course, the emphasis on causal links between belief and action that make it plausible to think that belief might be independent of language and conscious belief, since "agency entails neither linguistic ability nor conscious belief" (Mellor 1988–1989, 21). The idea that beliefs are causal functions from desires to actions can be deployed to explain the content of a given belief via the equation of truth conditions and utility conditions, where utility conditions are those in which the actions caused by the conjunction of that belief with a single desire result in the satisfaction of that desire. We can see how this works by considering Mellor's own example (1988–1989, 24–25). Consider a creature x who is hungry and has a desire for food at time t. That creature has a token belief $b(p)$ that conjoins with its desire for food to cause it to eat what is in front of it at that time. The utility condition of that belief is that there be food in front of x at that time. Moreover, for $b(p)$ to cause x to eat what is in front of it at t, $b(p)$ must be a belief that x has at t. For Mellor, therefore, the utility/truth conditions of $b(p)$ is that whatever creature has this belief faces food when it is actually facing food. And a belief with this content is, of course, the subjective belief whose natural linguistic expression would be 'I am facing food now'. On the other hand, however, a belief that would naturally be expressed with these words can be ascribed to a nonlinguistic creature, because what makes it the belief that it is depends not on whether it can be linguistically expressed but on how it affects behavior.

What secures self-reference in belief $b(p)$ is the contiguity of cause and effect. The essence of a subjective belief is the effects that it has on actions. It can only have those effects conjointly with a desire or set of desires, and the relevant sort of conjunction is possible only if it is the same agent at the same time who has the desire and the belief:

For in order to believe *p*, I need only be disposed (*inter alia*) to eat what I face if I feel hungry: a disposition which causal contiguity ensures that only *my* simultaneous hunger can provoke, and only into making *me* eat, and only *then*. That's what makes my belief refer to me and to when I have it. And that's why I need have no idea who I am or what the time is, no concept of the self or of the present, no implicit or explicit grasp of any 'sense' of 'I' or 'now', to fix the referents of my subjective beliefs: causal contiguity fixes them for me. (Mellor 1988–1989, 24–25)

Causal contiguity, according to Mellor, explains why no internal representation of the self is required, even at what other philosophers have called the subpersonal level. Mellor believes that reference to distal objects can take place only when an internal state serves as a causal surrogate for the distal object, and hence as an internal representation of that object. No such causal surrogate, and hence no such internal representation, is required in the case of subjective beliefs. The relevant causal components of subjective beliefs are the believer and the time.

The necessary contiguity of cause and effect is also the key to the functionalist account of self-reference in conscious subjective belief. Mellor adopts a relational theory of consciousness, equating conscious beliefs with second-order beliefs to the effect that one is having a particular first-order subjective belief. It is, on Mellor's view, simply a fact about our cognitive constitution that these second-order beliefs are reliably, though of course fallibly, generated so that we tend to believe that we believe things that we do in fact believe. Certain first-order beliefs cause the relevant second-order beliefs. These second-order beliefs are subjective beliefs, whether or not the relevant first-order beliefs are subjective, because they are beliefs with the content that one is oneself having a particular belief at a particular time. And they refer indirectly to the referents of the relevant first-order beliefs. When those first-order beliefs are subjective beliefs, then the first-order reference is to the person having them, and by causal contiguity, so is the reference of the second-order beliefs that they cause in that person. Neither the first-order belief nor the second-order belief that it causes requires any internal representation of the self.

The last link in the chain is extending this account to the linguistic capacity to master the first-person pronoun. Here, according to Mellor, the key is the linguistic habit, which need not, of course, be conscious, that my desire to express a belief linguistically should cause me to use the first-person pronoun 'I' when the belief I want to express is first-personal. What governs the choice of 'I' is not any beliefs about myself but simply the belief that 'I' is the right word to express the belief I want to express. And what makes this belief true is that everyone else shares my habit of using 'I' to refer to themselves when they want to express a first-person belief. Mellor concludes, "A knowingly shared habit is therefore all it takes for me to use 'I' and 'now' successfully at any time *t*. I still don't need a concept of the self or of the present; nor need I believe that my 'now' refers to a present now, or to *t*, or that my 'I' refers to my I, or to Hugh Mellor" (Mellor 1988–1989, 29).

What are the implications of the functionalist account of self-reference for the paradox of self-consciousness? The paradox of self-reference arises because of a postulated two-way interdependence between the capacity to think thoughts with the first-person contents characteristic of self-consciousness and the capacity to understand and use the first-person pronoun. The first dependence claim is that the first-person contents characteristic of self-consciousness can be understood only in terms of their canonical linguistic expression with the first-person pronoun and hence that they presuppose mastery of the first-person pronoun. The second dependence claim is that mastery of the first-person pronoun presupposes the first-person contents characteristic of self-consciousness. The first dependence relation opens up the possibility of what I termed the deflationary theory of self-consciousness, while the second dependence relation threatens to make any such theory circular. The functionalist theory of self-reference takes issue with the first dependence claim. It argues that there are first-person contents (the so-called subjective beliefs) that do not presuppose mastery of the first-person pronoun. These first-person contents can be put to work to explain what it is to master the semantics of the first-person pronoun. Such mastery requires only the presence of certain subjective beliefs, some of which are conscious, a shared linguistic habit of using the first-person pronoun in particular situations, and a belief that this linguistic habit is indeed shared.

If we adopt the functionalist theory, the paradox of self-consciousness seems to disappear. We can accept, as the deflationary theory does, that there are forms of first-person content (those implicated in the capacity for moral self-evaluation, for example, or the capacity to entertain autobiographical memories) that presuppose mastery of the first-person pronoun and are to be elucidated through explaining what such mastery consists in. When it comes to explaining what mastery of the first-person pronoun consists in, however, the functionalist theory can avoid both capacity and explanatory circularity by appealing to subjective beliefs that do not presuppose those higher forms of first-person content. The real question, therefore, is whether the functionalist theory is correct and adequate. This question has two sides. The first is whether the functionalist theory provides everything that a theory of self-reference needs to provide. Second, though, we also need to ask whether the functionalist theory is based on a satisfactory and plausible account of belief and, more particularly, of what it is for a given belief to have a given content.

I begin with the first side of the question: can the functionalist theory of self-reference accommodate the crucial distinctions that any satisfactory theory of self-consciousness has to accommodate? One such distinction is the distinction between what I termed genuine first-person contents (namely, those which can only be specified directly by means of the first-person pronoun 'I' or indirectly by means of the indirect reflexive pronoun 'he*') and those contents that are self-referring but are not genuinely first-personal. A belief content is self-referring but not genuinely first-personal when it refers to the believer though the believer is not aware that it does. Can the functionalist theory capture this distinction? I introduced the distinction through the following example:

(1)   J. L. B. believes that he* will be the next person to receive a parking ticket in central Cambridge.

(2)   J. L. B. believes that he will be the next person to receive a parking ticket in central Cambridge.

To appreciate the difference between (1) and (2), consider the anomalous situation in which J. L. B. believes that J. L. B. will be the next person to receive a parking ticket in central Cambridge but does not realize that he is J. L. B. This situation can be properly described with (2) but not with (1).

How might the functionalist theory of self-reference deal with this? The difference between (1) and (2) in the actual contents of the beliefs (when directly specified in *oratio recta*) is this:

(C.1)   I will be the next person to receive a parking ticket in central Cambridge.

(C.2)   J. L. B. will be the next person to receive a parking ticket in central Cambridge.

This difference certainly seems to be one that the functionalist theory can accommodate. According to Mellor, (C.1) is a semantic function $s(i, t, x)$ from whoever, x, produces a token $s(i, t)$ to an impersonal truth condition: x will be the first person after t to receive a parking ticket in central Cambridge. In contrast, (C.2) is a constant function $s(jlb, t)$ to the effect that J. L. B. will be the first person after t to receive a parking ticket in central Cambridge. These are two distinguishable contents with clearly distinguishable functional roles. As this makes clear, then, the functionalist theory of self-reference can make perfectly good sense of the thought that (C.1) and (C.2) are different contents, and that is how it undertakes to accommodate the distinction between (1) and (2) and, more generally, between genuine first-person contents and contents that are self-referring but not genuinely first-personal. According to Mellor, when J. L. B. believes that he* will be the next person to receive a parking ticket in central Cambridge, what he believes is that whoever is thinking that thought will be the next person to receive a parking ticket in central Cambridge. And this is clearly a different thought from the thought that J. L. B. will be that person, even though he is J. L. B.

The capacity to mark this sort of distinction is clearly an important criterion of adequacy for theories of self-reference, and the fact that the functionalist theory can do so without apparently falling afoul of the paradox of self-consciousness is important presumptive evidence in its favor. But it cannot be conclusive until we have looked more closely at the bases on which the relevant belief contents are ascribed, because the functionalist theory needs to provide not just an explanation of the distinction in the abstract but also a guarantee that the different belief contents will be ascribed in the relevant contexts. This brings us, however, to the general issue of whether the functionalist account is based on a satisfactory account of belief ascription, and it is here that problems arise.

Let me start by mentioning one possible line of objection to the general concept of belief underlying Mellor's position. For many philosophers, it is axiomatic that beliefs are propositional attitudes to contents composed of concepts. To such a philosopher, the functionalist account of self-reference is in danger of committing the (putative) solecism of attributing belief contents where it does not seem appropriate to attribute concepts. Although in the following chapters I will defend a version of this theory, I do not want to press it against Mellor at this point.[1] One reason for setting this line of objection aside is that it might justifiably be thought to beg the question against Mellor. If it is indeed the case that Mellor's account of self-reference is embedded within a theory of belief that separates belief ascription from concept ascription, then in the absence of any independent reasons for rejecting the functionalist account of belief, this might well be taken by an unbiased observer as evidence against the view that beliefs are constitutively composed of concepts. A second reason for not pursuing this line of thought is that it is far from clear that Mellor's account cannot be supplemented by a theory of what would warrant attributing to a creature the concepts invoked in the relevant content. There is no reason in principle why the functionalist account of belief cannot be matched with a functionalist account of concepts so as to allow it to conform to the postulated requirement that beliefs be composed of concepts. What this brings home, of course, is that this is not a line of argument that can be pressed without a clearer understanding of what concepts are (as well as an argument supporting the presupposed dependence of beliefs on concept possession).

Let us go back to Mellor's original example of the hungry creature facing food. The creature has a token belief that conjoins with its desire for food to cause it to eat what is in front of it. Mellor's analysis of truth conditions in terms of utility conditions leads him to identify that token belief with the subjective belief whose linguistic expression would be 'I am facing food now'. This belief clearly has what I have been terming a genuine first-person content. Now, as Mellor stresses, there is a very close connection between beliefs with genuine first-person contents and dispositions to actions, and this connection is one way of marking the distinction between the two classes of self-referring beliefs I have been discussing. A genuine first-person content, when conjoined with the appropriate desire(s) in the appropriate circumstances and provided there are no countervailing factors, will lead to action. In contrast to this, belief contents that are self-referring but not genuinely first-personal will only issue in action when conjoined with beliefs that are genuinely first-personal—as when my attack of amnesia lifts and it suddenly dawns upon me that I am that J. L. B. who will shortly receive a parking ticket, and I start running back to my car.[2]

It is beyond dispute, then, that all beliefs with genuinely first-person contents have direct and immediate implications for action. To the extent that Mellor's theory is based on this idea, it cannot be faulted. The problem with the theory, however, is that it seems to be based on the unargued-for assumption that something like the converse of this principle also holds and is all that we need to guide us in the ascription of beliefs. Let me explain. Mellor's position seems to rest on two fundamental thoughts. The first of these is the thought that all cases of action to be explained in terms of belief-desire psychology have to be explained through the attribution of first-person beliefs. This is what underwrites his treatment of the example. The utility conditions, and hence truth conditions, of whatever belief motivates the creature facing food are, according to Mellor, that 'there is food in front of me' or 'I am facing food'. Let me call this the *first-person-motivation thesis*. It will be noticed, of course, that my statement of the first-person-motivation thesis contains an important qualification: it is claimed to hold only for those actions for which explanation in terms of beliefs and desires is required. It turns out, though, that (at least for Mellor) there is little need for such a qualification, because he also seems to subscribe to a thesis that I shall label the *universality-of-belief thesis*, according to which all apparently purposeful behavior is to be explained in terms of the conjunction of beliefs and desires. My reason for holding that Mellor subscribes to the universality-of-belief thesis is his insistence that the functionalist account of self-reference explains how nonlinguistic animals can have first-person beliefs. His assumption seems to be that (to stick with the example he uses) whenever a hungry animal eats the food in front of it, it will have been caused to do so by the conjunction of its hunger with a first-person belief of the type he discusses.

The problem with Mellor's theory is that neither the first-person-motivation thesis nor the universality-of-belief thesis are true. Let me consider them in reverse order. The universality-of-belief thesis that every instance of apparently purposeful behavior should be explained in terms of beliefs and desires is at odds with a very basic principle at the heart of the psychological study of animal behavior, namely, the principle that intentional explanations in terms of beliefs and desires are to be deployed in explaining animal behavior only when simpler and more parsimonious explanations are demonstrably inadequate. Apparently purposive actions that can be explained without recourse to beliefs and desires include those explicable through classical or Pavlovian conditioning, for example. Here the classically conditioned associative links between stimulus and response are what explains the fact that a creature behaves in certain ways in certain situations. There are also various types of explanation appealing to innate, hard-wired determinants of behavior, such as the concept of innate releasing mechanisms (preprogrammed responses to events with a common structure). Explanation in terms of instrumental (operant) conditioning is more complex. Instrumental conditioning is the name given to processes of learning that make the receipt of a reward conditional upon an animal's performance of the behaviour being learned, and some psychologists have argued that this type of learning is possible in certain circumstances only if the animal in question has beliefs about the contingent relation between response and reward (Russell 1980 and Dickinson 1988). But even if instrumental conditioning is set to one side, a range of psychological explanations are available that are genuine alternatives to intentional explanations in terms of belief-desire psychology. A methodological assumption almost universal in psychology and animal ethology is that there is a place for intentional explanation only when those other modes of explanation are demonstrably inapplicable.

It is, I think, a definite shortcoming in Mellor's theory as it stands that it is too prodigal with the ascription of beliefs. Nonetheless, it might be thought that some modification of the theory could accommodate this point—most obviously, specifying the circumstances in which belief-desire explanations are to be deployed. But matters are not as simple as this. On the functionalist theory, beliefs are causal functions from desires to actions. This creates a problem, however, because all of the different modes of psychological explanation mentioned also appeal to states that fulfill a similar causal function from desire to action. Of course, it is open to a defender of the functionalist approach to say that it is only beliefs, and not, for example, innate releasing mechanisms, that interact causally with desires in a way that generates actions. But this sort of response is of limited effectiveness unless some sort of principled reason is given for distinguishing between a state of hunger and a desire for food. It is no use, of course, simply to describe desires as functions from belief to actions.

The moral to draw from this, I think, is that the functionalist theory of belief needs to be expanded so as to explain how and why beliefs are different from innate releasing mechanisms, conditioned responses, and other such states featured in nonintentional psychological explanation (henceforth, 'nonintentional psychological states'). The theory as stated does not have the resources to deal with this problem, because all these states, including beliefs, can plausibly be described as causal functions from desires to actions. Of course, to say that the functionalist theory of belief needs to be expanded is not to say that it needs to be expanded along nonfunctionalist lines. Nothing that has been said rules out the possibility that a correct and adequate account of what distinguishes beliefs from nonintentional psychological states can be given purely in terms of their respective functional roles.[3] The point is just that until we have such an account, it will be hard properly to evaluate the functionalist theory of self-reference. The core of the functionalist theory of self-reference is the thought that agents can have subjective beliefs that do not involve any internal representation of the self, linguistic or nonlinguistic. It is in virtue of this that the functionalist theory claims to be able to dissolve the paradox of self-consciousness. The problem that has emerged, however, is that it remains unclear whether those putative subjective beliefs really are beliefs.

Let us assume for the moment that this problem has been solved, and that belief states can be adequately distinguished from nonintentional psychological states. The functionalist theory is still not out of the woods. There remains its reliance on what I termed the first-person-motivation thesis, according to which all cases of action to be explained in terms of belief-desire psychology have to be explained through the attribution of first-person beliefs. The first-person-motivation thesis is clearly at work in Mellor's assumption that the utility conditions, and hence truth conditions, of the belief that causes the hungry creature facing food to eat what is in front of him are first-personal—thus determining the content of the belief to be 'There is food in front of me' or 'I am facing food'. The problem, however, is that it is not clear that this is warranted. There are a range of other possible contents, none of them first-personal, that such a belief could have. One possibility would be the demonstrative content 'That's food'. Another would be the indexical content 'There's food here'. Either of these would satisfy the requirements posed by Mellor's equation of truth conditions with utility conditions. Each of them would explain why the animal would eat what is in front of it. Nonetheless, on the face of it these are significantly different thoughts, only one of which is a genuine first-person thought.

Although there is a sense in which these three beliefs are all functionally equivalent, because they all serve a similar causal function from desires to action, the distinction between them is not trivial. Only one of them, for example, can plausibly be taken as expressive of any type of self-consciousness. Of course, putting the point like this may well seem like begging the question to a defender of the functionalist theory of self-reference. And such a defender might press the question of whether there really is a genuine difference between these three possible thoughts. After all, it is arguable that no one could assent to one of them without simultaneously assenting to the others. It would seem to be only in very contrived situations that someone might assert 'I am facing food now' while denying 'There is food here now' or 'That's food'.

But there is one very fundamental difference that the functionalist theory seems unable to capture. To bring it out, we need to consider the general distinction between structured and unstructured thought. A structured thought is one composed of separable and recombinable elements. What makes a given thought a structured thought is that its distinct parts can be separated out and put to work in other thoughts.[4] So in attributing to a creature a structured thought, one is ipso facto attributing to it the distinct cognitive abilities associated with the elements composing that thought. An unstructured thought, on the other hand, is not composed of such distinguishable components. It is more like a primitive response to the presence of a given feature, perhaps best understood on the model of an exclamation. Now, the content of the belief that Mellor's functionalist theory demands that we ascribe to an animal facing food is 'I am facing food now' or 'There is food in front of me now'. These are, it seems clear, structured thoughts. So too, for that matter, is the indexical thought

'There is food here now'. The crucial point, however, is that the causal function from desires to actions, which, according to Mellor, is all that a subjective belief is, would be equally well served by the unstructured thought 'Food!'

This inability to mark the distinction between a structured and an unstructured thought is a significant problem for the functionalist account of self-reference, because the subjective beliefs that the theory is trying to capture are, of course, structured beliefs and yet the theory is not sufficiently fine-grained to pick out only structured beliefs. Again, however, I do not put this forward as a principled argument against the possibility of providing a satisfactory functional account of self-reference. As before, the point is simply that the functional account under consideration will need to be supplemented, and it remains perfectly possible that the extension will be along functional lines.

For present purposes, however, the conclusion must be that the functionalist theory of self-reference is not of immediate use in dissolving the paradox of self-consciousness. Although it is true that the capacity circularity at the heart of the paradox of self-consciousness does not arise on the functionalist theory, the price paid for this is an inadequate theory of self-reference. What it does do, however, is to point us very clearly in the right direction, as will emerge in the next two sections.

2.2   Rejecting the Classical View of Content

One central idea that emerges from the functionalist account of self-reference discussed in the previous section is that content-bearing states can be independent of language mastery. Mellor emphasizes that his theory is intended to explain how nonlinguistic creatures can be in belieflike content-bearing states, and even though he characterizes the content of a belief in terms of the sentence that would be its natural linguistic expression, it is very clear that the creature to which the belief is ascribed need not be capable of uttering that sentence or indeed any sentence at all.

In this respect the functionalist theory is very much at odds with what might be described as the conventional understanding of the nature of content and how it should be ascribed. This conventional understanding is clearly expressed in the Thought-Language Principle, which, it will be remembered, was one of the inconsistent set of propositions that together constitute the paradox of self-consciousness:

The Thought-Language Principle   The only way to analyze the capacity to think a particular range of thoughts is by analyzing the capacity for the canonical linguistic expression of those thoughts.

The functionalist theory of self-consciousness entails the rejection of the Thought-Language Principle for the following reason. The functionalist account tackles the problem of first-person thoughts not by considering their canonical linguistic expression but instead by considering their functional role, particularly their role in the explanation of action. On the functionalist view, the best way to understand first-person thoughts is through understanding first-person beliefs, and first-person beliefs are themselves best understood as a particular sort of function from desires to action. An understanding of the canonical linguistic expression of first-person beliefs comes after, not before, an understanding of those beliefs themselves.

It seems to me that, although the functionalist account of first-person thought, as it stands, is not adequate to solve the paradox of self-consciousness, it provides a clear indication of both a general strategy and a specific strategy that any adequate solution to the paradox will have to adopt. The general strategy is a rejection of the Thought-Language Principle. The specific strategy concerns what is to replace the Thought-Language Principle, namely, an analysis of first-person thoughts based on the role of first-person thoughts in the explanation of behavior. I will develop both of these ideas in the remainder of this chapter. First, though, we need to take a step back to consider further some of the views about the relation between the content of thought and the content of language that underlie the Thought-Language Principle.

There is an obvious but central question that arises in considering the relation between the content of thought and the content of language, namely, whether there can be thought without language as theories like the functionalist theory suggest. The conception of thought and language that underlies the Thought-Language Principle is clearly opposed to the proposal that there might be thought without language, but it is important to realize that neither the principle as outlined nor the considerations adverted to by Dummett directly yield the conclusion that there cannot be thought in the absence of language. According to the principle, the capacity for thinking particular thoughts can only be *analyzed* through the capacity for the linguistic expression of those thoughts. On the face of it, however, this does not yield the claim that the capacity for thinking particular thoughts cannot *exist* without the capacity for their linguistic expression. And let me quote again the passage from Dummett cited in the previous chapter:

Thoughts differ from all else that is said to be among the contents of the mind in being wholly communicable: it is of the essence of thought that I can convey to you the very thought that I have, as opposed to being able to tell you merely something about what my thought is like. It is of the essence of thought not merely to be communicable, but to be communicable, without residue, by means of language. In order to understand thought, it is necessary, therefore, to understand the means by which thought is expressed. (Dummett 1978, 442)

This point about thoughts being wholly communicable does not entail that thoughts *must always be* communicated, which would be an absurd conclusion. Nor does it appear to entail that there must always be a possibility of communicating thoughts in any sense in which this would be incompatible with the ascription of thoughts to a nonlinguistic creature. There is, after all, a prima facie distinction between thoughts being wholly communicable and it being actually possible to communicate any given thought. But without that conclusion there seems no way of getting from a thesis about the necessary communicability of thought to a thesis about the impossibility of thought without language.

So at least one vital question about the relation between thought and language is left undetermined by the Thought-Language Principle. The missing link is provided, I think, by two fundamental principles at the heart of what I shall term the classical view of content. The first is the principle that the type of thoughts which can be ascribed to a creature are directly circumscribed by the concepts that the creature possesses:

The Conceptual Requirement Principle   The range of contents that one may attribute to a creature is directly determined by the concepts that the creature possesses.

The second principle is a requirement on concepts that a creature can possess. It holds that the range of concepts that a creature can possess is a direct function of its degree of language mastery. There is, of course, a spectrum of different ways of understanding the assumed connection between mastery of concepts and mastery of a language. On the strongest and simplest view of the matter, mastery of a concept is exhausted by the capacity properly to manipulate certain terms of a language. An example of a weaker view would be that certain linguistic abilities are essential criteria of conceptual mastery. The following thesis does, however, seem to be common to all the views on this spectrum:

The Priority Principle   Conceptual abilities are constitutively linked with linguistic abilities in such a way that conceptual abilities cannot be possessed by nonlinguistic creatures.

When the Priority Principle is conjoined with the Conceptual Requirement Principle, it follows that nonlinguistic creatures cannot be in states with content.

   With all this in mind, let me return to the functionalist theory. Mellor's account is clearly opposed to the classical view of content encapsulated in these two principles. Mellor's contents do not involve concepts, and they are available to nonlinguistic creatures. However, his theory suffers from the lack of discriminative power noted in the preceding section. There seems to be a range of different and incompatible contents that can fulfil the causal roles with which he identifies beliefs. One response to this would be to reject the functionalist approach and to return to the classical view of content. I do not think that this would be the correct reaction, however, because there are good reasons for thinking that the classical view of content is wrong. As even defenders of the classical view of content frequently accept, there are difficult borderline cases involving animals and young children that do seem to require the ascription of representational states with content to creatures with no linguistic abilities and hence, given the Priority Principle, with no conceptual abilities. One standard strategy for dealing with these has been to retain the Priority Principle while allowing that there are protoconcepts available to nonlinguistic creatures (Dummett 1993, chap. 12, is a good example). But this is an obviously unstable position. If protothoughts really are representational, then it follows on the classical view that they cannot be available to nonlinguistic creatures.

In the following two chapters I will explain why I think that the classical view of content is wrong. My objections to it, however, are quite compatible with retaining the Priority Principle, because I shall be arguing principally against the first component of the classical view of content, that is, the thesis that content is constrained by concept possession. There are, it seems to me, very good reasons for thinking that there are ways of representing the world that are *nonconceptual,* in the sense that they are available to creatures who do not possess the concepts required to specify how the world is being represented. This can be accepted (and the Conceptual Requirement Principle rejected), however, without any need to revise the idea that there is a constitutive connection between language mastery and conceptual mastery. Quite the contrary. Hanging on to the Priority Principle allows us to make a very clear distinction between conceptual and nonconceptual modes of content-bearing representation, because the connection between language and concepts gives us a clear criterion for identifying the presence of conceptual representation, as opposed to nonconceptual representation. On the other hand, though, one consequence of holding onto the Priority Principle while rejecting the Conceptual Requirement Principle would be that we have to recognize the restricted application of the Thought-Language Principle. The methodological principle that the only way in which to analyze particular thoughts is through analyzing the canonical linguistic expression of those thoughts does not seem plausible when applied to thoughts whose content is not connected in any way with linguistic abilities.

2.3   The Outline of a Solution

This distinction between conceptual and nonconceptual modes of content-bearing representation is highly relevant to the paradox of self-consciousness, for precisely the reasons that emerged during my discussion of the functionalist theory. The circularity at the heart of the paradox arises from the assumption that the capacity to think thoughts with the first-person contents characteristic of self-consciousness is available only to creatures who have mastered the semantics of the first-person pronoun. This in turn rests on the thought that first-person contents are conceptual in the sense under discussion. That is, the restriction of first-person contents to creatures who have mastered the semantics of the first-person pronoun is an obvious consequence of the thought that content ascription is constrained by concept possession, combined with the Priority Principle, affirming a constitutive connection between language mastery and conceptual mastery. The desirability of retaining the Priority Principle has already been indicated. Suppose, however, that the conceptual constraint on content ascription is lifted by allowing the possibility that a creature might be in representational states despite not possessing the concepts required to specify the relevant content. This would open up the possibility that there might be nonconceptual first-person contents that would not require mastery of the concept 'I' and hence, by the Priority Principle, of the semantics of the first-person pronoun. These would be first-person contents that do not involve linguistic mastery of the first-person pronoun. If such contents do exist and if they can be put to work to explain mastery of the semantics of the first-person pronoun, then the paradox of self-consciousness will be solved.

Let me be more precise about how this works. Recall the following six incompatible propositions at the root of the paradox of self-consciousness:

1. The key to analyzing self-consciousness is to analyze the capacity to think 'I'-thoughts.

2. The only way to analyze the capacity to think a particular range of thoughts is by analyzing the capacity for the canonical linguistic expression of those thoughts (the Thought-Language Principle).

3. 'I'-thoughts are canonically expressed by means of the first-person pronoun.

4. Mastery of the first-person pronoun requires the capacity to think 'I'-thoughts.

5. A noncircular account of self-consciousness is possible.

6. The capacity to think 'I'-thoughts meets the Acquisition Constraint (in the paradigmatic way defined earlier).

My proposal is that proposition (2) be rejected, in other words, that it be denied that the only way to analyze the capacity to think a particular range of thoughts is by analyzing the capacity for their canonical linguistic expression. More precisely, I shall be arguing that there is an important class of thoughts for which the Thought-Language Principle fails to hold because the Conceptual Requirement Principle fails to hold.

If proposition (2) is rejected, then consistency will indeed be restored. Clearly, however, to reject proposition (2), we have to find a satisfactory way of analyzing first-person thoughts that does not proceed via their canonical linguistic expression and yet that is compatible with the truth of the other propositions, most particularly (5) and (6). In fact, it is hard to see how a proposed solution to the paradox of self-consciousness could establish its credentials without providing a clear indication both of how a noncircular account of the capacity to think 'I'-thoughts might be derived and of how that capacity might meet the Acquisition Constraint. Without these three things, we will in fact not know *whether* the Conceptual Requirement Principle can be rejected in discussions of self-consciousness.

It is in meeting these conditions that the theoretical notion of nonconceptual content has a crucial role to play. I shall ultimately be arguing that proposition (4), to the effect that mastery of the first-person pronoun involves the thinking of thoughts with first-person contents, can be reconciled both with the existence of a noncircular account of mastery of the first-person pronoun and with the Acquisition Constraint if at least some of the relevant thoughts can be taken to have nonconceptual contents in the way discussed. The central idea will be that both in explaining what mastery of the first-person pronoun actually is and in explaining how such a capacity can be acquired in the normal course of human development, we can appeal to nonconceptual first-person thoughts. These are thoughts that, although first-personal in the sense that their content is to be specified directly by means of the first-person pronoun and indirectly by means of the indirect reflexive pronoun 'he*', can nonetheless be correctly ascribed to creatures who have not mastered the first-person concept (as evinced in mastery of the first-person pronoun).

Of course, this blueprint for solving the paradox of self-consciousness is highly dependent on two things. The first is the legitimacy of the general notion of nonconceptual content, and hence of the falsity of that part of the classical view of content captured by the Conceptual Requirement Principle. Showing the legitimacy of the general notion of nonconceptual content, however, is not sufficient on its own. What also needs to be shown is that the general notion can be applied within the area we are concerned with and that there are indeed nonconceptual first-person thoughts.

I undertake the first of these tasks in chapters 3 and 4. There I outline in more detail the conception of nonconceptual content with which I wish to work and begin the task of legitimating it by showing that we need such a notion of nonconceptual content for a proper characterization of the content of perceptual experience. This is only the first step, however. Some philosophers who accept that the content of perceptual experience has a nonconceptual component maintain this in conjunction with the view that correct ascriptions of states with nonconceptual content can only be made to creatures who possess at least a minimal conceptual repertoire. Against this I defend the Autonomy Principle, to the effect that there are no dependence relations between concept possession and states with nonconceptual content. Of course, any satisfactory theory of nonconceptual content must be able to provide an account of the conditions under which it is appropriate and warranted to ascribe states with nonconceptual content, particularly since the Autonomy Principle deprives us of the potential evidence that might otherwise have been provided by language use. The account that I develop follows the functionalist theory discussed earlier in stressing the importance of content-bearing states in the explanation of behavior. Unlike the functionalist account, however, it places constraints upon the types of behavior that require content-bearing explanation, as well as upon the nature of those content-bearing states. The account I offer is intended as a corrective to what I earlier termed the universality-of-belief thesis.

In chapters 5 through 9, I move on to the second task of showing that the notion of nonconceptual content can profitably be applied to first-person thought. I argue that nonconceptual first-person contents are to be found in somatic proprioception, in certain navigational abilities, and in certain nonlinguistic social contexts. The foundations for this account of first-person nonconceptual contents are laid in chapter 5, where I show how a Gibsonian perspective on perception reveals the presence of nonconceptual first-person contents in the very structure of perceptual experience. At various points in arguing for the existence of these different types of nonconceptual first-person thought, I adopt a form of the principle of inference to the best explanation. In such cases my modus operandi is to identify certain types of behavior that, it seems to me, can best be explained by assuming the causal efficacy of states with nonconceptual first-person contents. I take it that this will lay to rest the worries about indiscriminate attributions of first-person contents that arose in the context of the functionalist theory of self-reference. In chapter 10, I draw the various strands of the argument together and show how the nonconceptual first-person contents identified can be put to work to defuse both the explanatory circularity and the capacity circularity at the heart of the paradox of self-consciousness.

Let me close this programmatic chapter with a methodological comment. This book contains much closer attention to empirical work in various areas of psychology than it is usual to find in works on the philosophy of mind. This is in no way accidental. As has emerged in this chapter, and as I continue to stress throughout the book, the ascription conditions of content-bearing states, particularly first-person content-bearing states, are closely bound up with the potential that such states have for the explanation of different types of behavior. One central reason why philosophers have generally been unprepared to countenance or even contemplate the existence of nonconceptual content-bearing states is that they have had relatively little exposure to those forms of behavior that might seem to demand explanation in terms of such states. Animal behavior and the behavior of prelinguistic infants paradigmatically raise the problems for which, so I believe, theoretical appeal to states with nonconceptual content is the only solution (or at least the best so far available). But the behavior of animals and prelinguistic infants needs to be approached experimentally if we are to have a clear sense of what the data are that need to be explained. This is partly because it is only in certain experimental contexts that particular problematic forms of behavior can be isolated and identified, a good example being the infant-dishabituation experiments to be discussed in chapter 3. But it is also partly because experimental work is required to establish the parameters of particular explanations and to test their adequacy. Any explanation that one offers of why an animal behaves thus and so in a particular situation has implications for how it might be expected to behave in certain other situations. Experimentally producing those situations allows given explanations to be confirmed or disconfirmed.

It should not be assumed, however, that finding a solution to the paradox of self-consciousness is a purely empirical matter. The empirical work that I adduce is more than purely illustrative, since many of the theoretical points that it is brought in to illuminate could not be independently formulated without it. Nonetheless, that empirical work cannot bring us any closer to a solution to the paradox of self-consciousness without being integrated into a theoretical account that is ultimately driven by concerns that are more traditionally philosophical—concerns about the nature of an adequate explanation, about the nature of representation, about the structure of perception, and most important, about what it is to be self-conscious.

3

Content, Concepts, and Language

What gives bite to the paradox of self-consciousness as developed in chapter 1 is the assumption that it is incoherent to ascribe thoughts with first-person content to an individual who is not capable of employing the first-person pronoun to achieve reflexive self-reference. This yields the paradoxical conclusion that any explanation of mastery of the semantics of the first-person pronoun will presuppose mastery of the semantics of the first-person pronoun. One of the important points that emerged from the discussion of the functionalist theory of self-reference in the previous chapter, however, was that this assumption can be challenged. This chapter further questions the view of content on which this assumption rests, what I termed the classical view of content. It argues that there are good reasons for thinking that the classical view of content is mistaken in ways that will, when properly understood, reveal how the paradox of self-consciousness can be resolved.

I shall be outlining a theory of content on which there can exist states with *nonconceptual first-person contents*. A nonconceptual content is one that can be ascribed to a thinker even though that thinker does not possess the concepts required to specify that content. Nonconceptual first-person contents are those that fall into this category and that can only be specified by means of the first-person or indirect reflexive pronouns (as discussed in chapter 1). These nonconceptual first-person contents offer a way of breaking both forms of circularity identified in chapter 1. Developing and defending a theory of nonconceptual content as a way of defusing the paradox of self-consciousness is a complicated task, particularly in view of the power and popularity of the classical theory of content. Any defence of nonconceptual content will, ipso facto, be an attack on the classical theory. In the remainder of this chapter I will lay out some of the reasons why a notion of nonconceptual content seems preferable to the classical theory of content. I begin in the next section by explaining the importance of nonconceptual content in providing a satisfactory account of the richness of perceptual experience. This will provide an initial legitimation of the notion of nonconceptual content, which will then be extended in the following section.

3.1   Conceptual and Nonconceptual Content: The Richness of Perceptual Experience

A dominant view among philosophers is that the ways in which a creature can represent the world are determined by its conceptual capacities. This is associated with a widespread rejection of the traditional empiricist distinction between sensation and belief. Recently, though, the existence of mental states with nonconceptual representational content has been discussed among philosophers of mind (Evans 1982, Peacocke 1992).[1] The general thought is that it is theoretically legitimate to refer to mental states that represent the world but do not require the bearer of those mental states to possess the concepts required to specify how they present the world as being. These are states with nonconceptual content. A nonconceptual content can be attributed to a creature without thereby attributing to that creature mastery of the concepts required to specify that content.

The central impetus for legitimating a notion of nonconceptual content has come from the study of perceptual experience. Like traditional theorists who see sensations as ineliminable components of perceptual experience, theorists have been attracted to nonconceptual content by the thought that the richness and grain of perceptual experience is not constrained by the concepts that a perceiver might or might not possess. What distinguishes the theory of nonconceptual content from theories of the sensational component of perceptual experience is that nonconceptual content is representational. If a given perceptual experience has a nonconceptual content that ϕ, this means that the experience represents ϕ as holding in the world. Conceptual and nonconceptual contents are distinguished not by whether they are representational but according to how they represent. They are distinguished according to whether, in specifying how they represent the environment as being, we need to restrict ourselves to concepts possessed by the perceiver. This is in stark contrast to the traditional distinction between sensation and belief, according to which the sensational component has no role to play in explaining how the experience represents the world as being.

The first stage in imposing a principled distinction between conceptual and nonconceptual content is that perceptual experiences can represent the world in ways fundamentally different from those in which perceptual beliefs can represent the world. Although perceptual experiences are representational, rather than sensational, they cannot always be assimilated to perceptual beliefs. Perceptual experience can have a richness, texture, and fineness of grain that beliefs do not and cannot have. A useful illustration of this has been provided by Christopher Peacocke (1986, 1992), who stresses that perceptual experiences have contents that are analogue in character: "To say that the type of content in question has an analogue character is to make the following point. There are many dimensions— hue, shape, size, direction—such that any value on that dimension may enter the fine-grained content of an experience. In particular, an experience is not restricted in its range of possible contents to those points or ranges picked out by concepts—*red, square, straight ahead*—possessed by the perceiver" (1992, 68). As Peacocke notes, it is prima facie plausible to suppose that the analogue nature of perceptual experience can only be explained by assuming that the content of perceptual experience is not constrained by the concepts that the perceiver possesses. Observational concepts pick out salient features of experience; there are many other discriminably different ways that experience could have represented the world, even though those ways can only be specified through those very same observational concepts. This fact about perceptual experience cannot be accommodated if the content of perceptual experience is deemed to be conceptual.

Suppose we combine the two ideas, first, that perceptual experience has a nondoxastic component that is nonetheless representational, and second, that the nondoxastic component of perception is analogue and finer-grained in a way that the doxastic component is often unable to capture. A natural next step would be to map the distinction between doxastic and nondoxastic onto the distinction between conceptual and nonconceptual. On such a view, the contents of perceptual belief are necessarily limited by the conceptual resources of the perceiver, while this restriction does not apply to the content of perceptual experience.[2] This proposal seems to me to be the right way to proceed. Before it can be defended, however, it needs to be sharpened up.

Peacocke has proposed defining a conceptual content simply as a content composed of concepts. A nonconceptual content, therefore, is a content not composed of concepts. One source of worry with this proposal is that it unnecessarily forecloses on the possibility of contents being conceptual without being composed of concepts. Contents understood in Russellian terms are not composed of concepts, for example, but this does not automatically make them nonconceptual. It could still be the case that a Russellian content cannot be ascribed to an individual unless that individual possesses the concepts associated with the individuals and properties that make up that content. Nonetheless, Peacocke's suggestion that conceptual and nonconceptual contents be distinguished in terms of their constituents is very helpful. I take it that the constituents of a given content are identifiable in terms of the concepts used to specify that content. Those constituents do not have to be concepts themselves, but they can be (on some theories). On this construal, then, a content is nonconceptual if and only if none of its constituents are conceptual, where a conceptual constituent is one that can feature in a content only if the thinker possesses the concept required to specify that constituent. A content is conceptual, in contrast, if and only if any of its constituents are conceptual.

The key question, therefore, is whether there are any good reasons to hold that the contents of perceptual beliefs, and indeed of propositional attitudes in general, are necessarily conceptual, that is, whether such contents can properly be attributed to a thinker only if that thinker possesses the concepts required to specify them. It seems to me that there is a persuasive argument here trading on certain crucial parallels between the normative dimensions of believing a particular content and the normative dimensions of possessing a particular concept.[3] Belief contents are individuated in part according to the rational connections they have with other propositional-attitude contents, including, but not confined to, other belief contents. A belief has a particular content in virtue of the inferences that it licenses to other propositional-attitude contents, where an inference is licensed by a belief content if and only if having a belief with that content makes it rational for the believer to draw those inferences. By the same token, concepts are also individuated in normative reason-giving terms. This emerges particularly clearly when we reflect on the "normative liaisons" built into the conditions of possessing a particular concept (Peacocke 1992, chapter 5). Not only will any acceptable account of what it is to possess a concept have to specify the circumstances in which it is appropriate for a thinker to apply that concept, but also part of what it is to possess a given concept is that one should be able to recognize circumstances that give one good reasons to take particular attitudes to contents containing that concept. Moreover, concept mastery is also evidenced in dispositions to make, and accept as legitimate, certain inferential transitions between judgements.

Of course, it follows trivially from these points that the normative dimensions of concept possession depend on the normative dimensions of the belief and other attitudinal contents in which they might feature. But this does not yet warrant the conclusion that belief contents, and attitude contents in general, must be conceptual. To derive that further conclusion, we need two further lemmas. The first is the very familiar point that the content of a belief is determined by its constituents. If a belief has a conceptual content, then that content will be determined by the nature of its conceptual constituents, and if it has a nonconceptual content, then its content will be determined by the nature of its nonconceptual constituents. The second lemma is that if a content constituent is individuated in normative and reason-giving terms, then it is a concept. This follows from the definition of a concept, because concepts just are those content constituents that are individuated in normative and reason-giving terms. I should stress, however, that this is not meant to imply that contents with nonconceptual constituents cannot stand in reason-giving relations to other contents. That would be patently false. The claim is rather that those reason-giving relations do not serve to individuate those nonconceptual content constituents.

The conclusion that belief contents must be conceptual can be derived as follows. Since the content of a belief is determined by its constituents, the normative dimensions of a belief content must be determined by the normative dimensions of its constituents. Since belief contents are individuated in terms of the normative dimensions of their inferential role, it follows that they must play their respective inferential roles essentially. Putting these two thoughts together yields the conclusion that belief contents must be determined by constituents that themselves essentially possess a normative dimension. These constituents, by the second lemma, must be conceptual. So, to return to the general question of how the distinctive features of perceptual experiences can best be accommodated, we now seem to be in a position to make a clear distinction between the (nonconceptual) contents of perceptual experiences and the (conceptual) contents of perceptual beliefs (and propositional attitudes in general). The possible contents of propositional attitudes are constrained by the conceptual repertoire of the thinker in a way that the possible contents of perceptual experiences are not.

Some philosophers would resist this suggestion that perceptual experience has nonconceptual content. There are, broadly, two strategies for such resistance. First, it might be argued that the content of perception is exhausted by dispositions to acquire beliefs (see Armstrong 1968 for a classic statement of this epistemic theory of perception). Clearly, if perception has no nondoxastic elements, then, given the above argument that the contents of belief are fully conceptual, issues of nonconceptual content do not arise. I will say no more about this possible line of argument, however, as I suspect that it ultimately collapses into a version of the nonconceptual theory. The idea that there is no more to perceptual content than can be given by perceptual beliefs or dispositions to acquire such beliefs is only plausible if the notions of belief and of content possession are weakened so far that they effectively come into the domain of nonconceptual content.

The second strategy for denying the need for nonconceptual content is more promising. Its general thrust is that the fine grain and richness of perceptual experience can be accommodated within a fully conceptual account of perception. John McDowell is a sophisticated proponent of such a strategy (McDowell 1994, particularly lecture 3). Unlike proponents of the first strategy, he does accept that perceptual experience has a richness that cannot *directly* be captured by concepts. He agrees that a given perceiver can, and often does, have perceptual experience that is more fine-grained than his conceptual repertoire, but he takes this point to hold in only a limited sense that does not warrant talk of nonconceptual content. This can best be explained through the example that he himself discusses, color experience. It is clear that normal perceivers can discriminate a far wider range of colors than they have concepts for. This is the uncontroversial starting-point from which it is tempting to conclude (as above) that perceptual experience has a nonconceptual content. McDowell, though, thinks that the uncontroversial starting-point can be accommodated without any such theoretical move:

It is possible to acquire the concept of a shade of a colour, and most of us have done so. Why not say that one is thereby equipped to embrace shades of colour within one's conceptual thinking with the very same determinateness with which they are presented in one's visual experience, so that one's concepts can capture colours no less sharply than one's experience presents them? In the throes of an experience of the kind that putatively transcends one's conceptual powers—an experience that *ex hypothesi* affords a suitable example—one can give linguistic expression to a concept that is exactly as fine-grained as the experience, by uttering a phrase like "that shade," in which the demonstrative exploits the presence of the sample. (McDowell 1994, 56–57)

An obvious question to ask is why this should count as a conceptual capacity, on a par with mastering the concept of red, for example. Such demonstrative thoughts can exist only in the presence of the particular shade of color that they pick out, and this is hardly comparable to the capacity to identify and reidentify appropriately colored objects over time, which is integral to the mastery of color concepts. But McDowell has a response to this:

In the presence of the original sample, "that shade" can give expression to a concept of a shade; what ensures that it is a concept—that thoughts that exploit it have the necessary distance from what would determine them to be true—is that the associated capacity can persist into the future, if only for a short time, and that, having persisted, it can be used also in thoughts about what is by then the past, if only the recent past. What is in play here is a recognitional capacity, possibly quite short lived, that sets in with the experience. (McDowell 1994, 57)

The suggestion is that a minimal apparatus, containing solely the concept of a shade of color and ability to employ the demonstrative pronoun, can capture all the richness and fine grain of color experience. What makes it a proper conceptual capacity for identifying colors is that it can serve as the foundation for recognizing particular shades of color and for thinking about them in their absence.

This general strategy is not, of course, confined to colors. Theorists of nonconceptual content often appeal to spatial features of the perceived environment that they hold to be more finely individuated than would be possible if individuation proceeded according to the perceiver's repertoire of spatial concepts. It seems plausible to hold that perceivers can perceive the differences between a circle, an ellipse, and a sphere without possessing all three relevant concepts. McDowell's position would accommodate this by appeal to the conceptual capacities minimally required to think demonstratively about shapes (*that shape,* for example).

McDowell's position is unattractive, however, because it has to concede precisely the point that it is trying to rule out: that color experience often has a richer and finer content than can be captured in terms of concepts possessed by the perceiver. Although he offers a sense in which one can think demonstratively about shades of color that one can discriminate but nonetheless cannot directly conceptualize, he nonetheless has to describe the exercise of basic color-recognition abilities as involving "thoughts that are not necessarily capable of receiving an overt expression that fully determines their content" (McDowell 1994, 58). It is worth reminding ourselves that the import of placing a conceptual constraint on perceptual content is to capture the idea that the type of perceptual experiences a perceiver can have is determined by the concepts he possesses.[4] The thought often canvassed in support of this is that one cannot see, for example, a post box without possessing the concept *post box,* because perceiving a post box requires the ability to classify it as a post box and that just is a conceptual ability (or so the argument runs). It follows from this that if we know what concepts a perceiver possesses, we will be able to define what might be termed a *perceptual space* limiting the colors, shapes, objects, etc., that he can properly be described as perceiving. It seems clear, however, that McDowell's minimal recognitional capacities do not permit this. If the relevant conceptual capacities are not those associated with the concepts of particular shapes or particular colors but rather those associated with the demonstrative pronoun and the general concepts *shade* and *color,* then no such definition of a perceptual space will be possible. The range of perceivable colors and perceivable shapes will be unlimited, in which case it is far from clear that the notion of conceptual content is doing much work here.

The significance of this emerges when one asks what the truth conditions are for such demonstrative thought in cases where the color sample is no longer present (in cases where we really do have what McDowell is proposing as a recognitional capacity). A particular application of the recognitional capacity will be true if and only if the particular shade currently being perceived really is the same shade as the shade originally perceived. But what about cases when the currently perceived shade is not the same as the previously perceived shade, as when a perceiver mistakenly confuses the lilac that he is now looking at with the maroon that he saw previously? Suppose that a perceiver does something that we can explain only by attributing to him just such a confusion of shade (such as, for example, making a mistake in sorting objects). The natural way of describing what is going on would be that he is perceiving lilac and confusing it with maroon, whether or not he possesses the relevant concepts. McDowell's demonstrative account is committed to denying this. McDowell would presumably say that the recognitional capacity for recognizing *that* shade that persists in thought (namely, maroon) is being misapplied. This, however, does not allow us to describe what is going on in sufficient detail to allow us to distinguish this case from one in which a perceiver makes a similar mistake, but this time between maroon and mauve. This confusion would also be described as a misapplication of the persisting recognitional capacity for recognising *that* shade. Nonetheless, McDowell is committed to a picture of perceptual experience on which there really is a salient phenomenological difference between these two cases. And if there is a salient phenomenological difference, then the obvious way to capture it is by identifying the colors that are actually perceived, even if the perceiver is not (conceptually) capable of identifying them as such. The reason that McDowell-type demonstrative thought is possible about perceptually encountered shades of color is that those shades of color are encountered in experience, and this is something that should be reflected in an adequate account of what is actually perceived. But this brings us back to the idea that perceptual experience has nonconceptual content.

Bearing in mind, then, that the only alternative to a McDowell-type strategy is a version of the epistemic theory, the balance of the evidence appears to be in favor of an account of perceptual experience that allows it to have a component that is nondoxastic but nonetheless representational. We seem driven to the idea of nonconceptual content by the need for an adequate characterization of color experience. But, to return to the matter in hand, we are still a long way away from a conception of nonconceptual content that is of obvious theoretical use in explaining primitive forms of self-consciousness. That would require a notion of nonconceptual content with application beyond the realm of colour experience. It is to this that I turn in the following section.

3.2   Extending the Notion of Nonconceptual Content: The Autonomy Principle

In this section I make a start on explaining how the notion of the non-conceptual content of perception can be put to use to solve the paradox of self-consciousness. I distinguish two different explanatory projects within which the notion of nonconceptual content can be deployed. These two projects can be correlated with the different strategies required to dissolve the two types of circularity at the heart of the paradox of self-consciousness.

One way of putting the notion of nonconceptual content to work is in explaining what it is to possess certain concepts. In the case of a large and probably foundational class of concepts, an adequate explanation of what it is for a subject to possess a given concept will have to contain a clause stipulating how that subject responds when enjoying experiences with an appropriate content. There is an obvious danger of circularity, however, if the content in question is conceptual. This danger of circularity makes the notion of nonconceptual content appealing, because one promising way of overcoming it is to specify the conditions for concept possession so as to require responding in appropriate ways (say, by applying the concept in question) when enjoying experiences with the appropriate nonconceptual content.

We can see how this might work with the example of color concepts. Any adequate account of what it is to have mastery of a particular color concept will obviously have to require a certain sensitivity to the presence of samples of the color in question, and it is natural to think that this sensitivity will involve responding appropriately when experiencing objects of the color in question. So an account of what it is to master a particular colour concept will mention perceptual experience of that color. But then we seem driven to the thought that such perceptual experience has a nonconceptual content, because of the obvious circularity that there would be in the account of conceptual mastery if the content of the perceptual experience demands mastery of the concept we are trying to explain. The suggestion, then, is that a specification of the conditions that must be satisfied by any individual who can properly be ascribed mastery of a particular color concept will involve a clause stipulating that he be sensitive to experiences with a nonconceptual content featuring the color in question.

This use of the notion of nonconceptual content in specifying what it is to possess given concepts has been pressed by Christopher Peacocke (1992, 1994). Peacocke offers a specification of the *possession conditions* for certain concepts that takes two parts. The first part of the specification for a particular concept hinges on the constraint that the subject be in a state with an appropriate nonconceptual content and that he be willing to apply the concept when in that state. The second part is a version of the Generality Constraint first proposed by Gareth Evans, namely that the subject be capable of generalized concept application (Evans 1982, sec. 4.3). Broadly speaking, the idea is that if a subject is to be properly credited with mastery of the concepts in the thought *a is F*, then that subject must be capable of thinking *a is G* for any property G of which he has a conception, and similarly of thinking *b is F* for any object *b* of which he has a conception. When these two conditions are satisfied, then, Peacocke holds, the subject has mastered the concept in question. That the subject has experiences with nonconceptual content is central to this account, and this centrality derives from the noncircularity mentioned earlier. The specified concept will feature in the specification of the first condition, but it will not do so in a way that presupposes that the subject possesses the concept in question. The subject's possession of the concept in question is neither mentioned in, nor required by, a specification of the content of the appropriate perceptual experience.

A *possession-conditions explanation* of concepts canvassed by Peacocke needs to be sharply distinguished from another potential way in which the machinery of nonconceptual content might be employed to elucidate conceptual content and concept mastery in general. This second form of explanation, which one might term a *developmental explanation of conceptual content*, explains the acquisition of conceptual abilities from states with nonconceptual content in terms of a developmental progression over time. On this view, nonconceptual content comes first, as a basis from which conceptual content can emerge. Cussins (1990) gives an account of conceptual content along these lines, suggesting that the gradual development of a conception of objectivity should be understood in terms of a progressive construction of concepts from a basis of structured nonconceptual content. He describes this as "the transition from a preobjective stage where no concepts are possessed to an objective concept-exercising stage" (Cussins 1990, 409). The possibility of this sort of developmental explanation of conceptual content is of considerable interest to developmental psychologists studying the ontogeny of concept development (as will be discussed at greater length in the following section), as well as to evolutionary biologists studying the phylogeny of conceptual abilities.

This broad distinction between a possession-conditions explanation and a developmental explanation is directly relevant to the different explanatory projects posed by the two strands of the paradox of self-consciousness. The distinction there, it will be remembered, is between the unwelcome implications that stem from explanatory circularity and those that derive from capacity circularity. Explanatory circularity poses problems for the project of providing a noncircular account of self-consciousness (because of the need for first-person thoughts in an account of mastery of the first-person pronoun). Insofar as a solution to this strand of the paradox of self-consciousness involves deploying nonconceptual first-person contents to give a noncircular account of mastery of the first-person pronoun, it seems clearly to fall within the broad category of a possession-conditions explanation. The solution to problems arising from capacity circularity, on the other hand, will not be an instance of a possession-conditions explanation. What is at stake is the possibility of showing how mastery of the first-person pronoun can emerge in the normal course of human development, which clearly counts as an instance of developmental explanation.

One reason why this is significant is that a possession-conditions explanation and a developmental explanation involve differing degrees of commitment to what we can, following Peacocke (1992, 90), term the Autonomy Principle:

The Autonomy Principle   It is possible for a creature to be in states with nonconceptual content, even though that creature possesses no concepts at all.

Given what, in chapter 2, I identified as the Priority Principle (namely that conceptual abilities are constitutively so linked with linguistic abilities that conceptual abilities cannot be possessed by nonlinguistic creatures), it follows that the Autonomy Principle, if true, leaves open the possibility of a nonlinguistic creature being in states with nonconceptual content.

A philosopher who holds that the notion of nonconceptual content can provide a developmental explanation of conceptual content is likely to be sympathetic to the Autonomy Principle, to the extent that his project is one of explaining how a creature possessing only states with nonconceptual content can develop into a full-fledged concept user.[5] A philosopher committed only to a possession-conditions explanation, however, does not have to accept the Autonomy Principle (although there is no requirement to deny it). He can, for example, maintain that the nonconceptual content of experience will yield a noncircular account of possession conditions for certain primitive concepts, even if the Autonomy Principle is denied.[6] What makes this possible is, of course, that nonconceptual content is defined as content that does not require mastery of any of the concepts required to specify it; it is not defined as content that requires mastery of no concepts whatsoever. Indeed, one can be in a state with nonconceptual content despite possessing the relevant concepts. The point is that being in such a state does not depend on possession of the concepts required to specify it.

On the other hand, however, if the Autonomy Principle is rejected, then it will ipso facto be impossible to give at least one type of developmental explanation of conceptual content in terms of nonconceptual content, namely the type of developmental explanation that involves explaining how a creature in states with only nonconceptual content, such as, for example, a newborn human infant, can develop into a full-fledged concept user. By the same token, it will also rule out any account of the phylogenetic development of conceptual content on which it appears at a far later stage of evolution than nonconceptual content.[7] Moreover, it is plausible that a primitive form of intentional explanation is required to account for the behavior of creatures that one might not want to describe as concept-using, and obviously, any form of intentional explanation requires attributing to the creature representations of its environment. One area in which this emerges is animal-learning theory (see, for example, Dickinson 1988, where it is argued that certain cases of instrumental conditioning in rats support an intentional interpretation, as well as Premack and Woodruff 1978), but it also seems highly relevant to the study of infant cognition. The suggestion that there are experiential states that represent the world but do not implicate mastery of the concepts required to specify them is potentially important here. Clearly, however, it can only be of theoretical use if the Autonomy Principle is accepted.

For present purposes, the important point to bring out is that a solution to the strand of the paradox of self-consciousness created by capacity circularity seems prima facie to involve a commitment to the Autonomy Principle, because such a solution requires showing how mastery of the first-person pronoun (and hence the first-person concept) can meet the Acquisition Constraint and it is natural to think that this will involve showing how mastery of the first-person pronoun can be constructed on the basis of states with nonconceptual content that can exist in the absence of any form of concept mastery. Accordingly, in the next section I shall offer a defence of the Autonomy Principle.

3.3   Defending the Autonomy Principle: Evidence from Developmental Psychology

Developmental psychology has long been concerned with the question, At what stage, in early childhood or infancy, is it appropriate to ascribe a grasp that objects exist even when not being perceived? On the traditional view, derived ultimately from Piaget, object permanence does not appear until relatively late in development, toward the end of the sensorimotor period. Prior to the end of the sensorimotor period the infant

Habituation

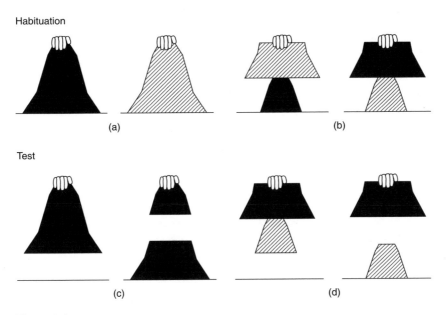

(a)   (b)

Test

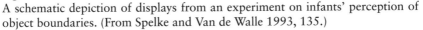

(c)   (d)

Figure 3.1
A schematic depiction of displays from an experiment on infants' perception of
object boundaries. (From Spelke and Van de Walle 1993, 135.)

universe is almost completely undifferentiated. Much recent work in developmental psychology, however, has attacked this view (see Spelke 1990
and Spelke and Van de Walle 1993 for overviews). There is strong experimental evidence that infants have the capacity from a very young age to
parse the array of visual stimulation into spatially extended and bounded
individuals that behave according to certain basic principles of physical
reasoning.

Elizabeth Spelke, whose laboratory has produced much of the interesting work in this area, has identified four such principles governing the
unity of individuals in the perceived array. It will be helpful briefly to
outline the results. The first principle she terms the *principle of cohesion*,
according to which surfaces lie on a single individual if and only if they
are in contact. It is evidence for the principle of cohesion, for example,
that infants do not appear to perceive the boundary between two objects
that are stationary and adjacent, even when the objects differ in color,
shape, and texture (figure 3.1 gives an example). Three-month-old infants

are habituated to two objects, one more or less naturally shaped and homogenously colored, and the other a gerrymandered object that looks rather like a lampshade. When the experimenter picks up the objects, they either come apart or rise up cleanly. Infants show more surprise when the object comes apart, even if (as in the case of the lampshade) the object does not have the Gestalt properties of homogenous color and figural simplicity. The conclusion drawn by Spelke and other researchers is that the infants perceive even the gerrymandered object as a single individual because its surfaces are in contact.

The principle of cohesion clearly suggests that infants will perceive objects that have an occluded center as two distinct individuals, since they cannot see any connection between the two parts. And this indeed is what they do perceive, at least when dealing with objects that are stationary. Thus it seems that infants do not perceive an occluded figure as a single individual *if the display is static.* After habituation to the occluded figure, they showed no preference for either of the test displays.

On the other hand, however, infants do seem to perceive a center-occluded object as a single individual if the object is in motion, irrespective, by the way, of whether the motion is lateral, vertical, or in depth (see figure 3.2). According to Spelke, this is because there is another principle at work, which she terms the *principle of contact.* According to the principle of contact, only surfaces that are in contact can move together. When the principle of cohesion and the principle of contact are taken together, they suggest that since the two parts of the occluded object move together, they must be in contact and hence in fact be parts of one individual.

Spelke also identifies two further constraints governing how infants parse the visual array. These emerge from experiments involving hidden objects and their motions. A distinctive and identifying feature of physical objects is that every object moves on a single trajectory through space and time, and it is impossible for these paths to intersect in a way that would allow more than one object to be in one place at a time. One might test whether infants are perceptually sensitive to these features by investigating whether they are surprised by breaches of what Spelke calls the *continuity* and *solidity* constraints. Renée Baillargeon's well-known drawbridge experiments are often taken as evidence that infants are perceptu-

Habituation

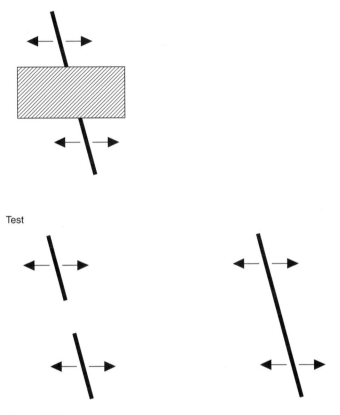

Test

Figure 3.2
A schematic depiction of displays from an experiment on infants' perception of partly occluded objects. Arrows indicate the direction and relative extent of the rod's motion. (From Spelke and Van de Walle 1993, 140.)

ally sensitive to the solidity constraint. In one version (Baillargeon 1987), Baillargeon habituated 4½-month-old infants to a screen rotating vertically 180° on a table, rather like a drawbridge. She then placed a stationary object behind the screen so that it was completely occluded by the time the screen had been raised 60°. She was interested in whether infants would distinguish between trials in which the screen stopped when it reached the place occupied by the object and trials in which the screen

Continuity violation

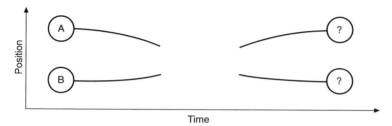

Figure 3.3
A schematic depiction of events violating the continuity constraint. The solid lines
indicate each object's path of motion. (From Spelke and Van de Walle 1993, 148.)

continued rotating (apparently passing through the object). In fact, the
infants looked longer at the second type of trial, which thus indicates that
they found this novel and surprising. Spelke takes this as evidence of the
infants' sensitivity to the impossibility of there being more than one object
in a single place at one time.

Figure 3.3 gives a schematic representation of an experiment to test
whether infants parse their visual array in accordance with the continuity
constraint. Two objects disappear and reemerge without having appeared
in the space between. This contravenes the continuity constraint because
an object can only move on a single path through space-time if that path
is continuous.

I won't go into any more details about the experimental work on infant
perception. The point to extract is that if we accept the general methodology of habituation followed by tests for preferential looking, we have to
conclude that the perceptual world of young infants is not at all the undifferentiated chaos of noises, smells, patches of color, and flashes of light
that it was believed to be by both Piaget and the early sense-data theorists.

Suppose, then, that we accept that Spelke is right to deny Piaget's conception of the universe of early infancy as almost completely undifferentiated. This raises two fundamentally important questions. The first is
whether the capacities to which she draws attention should be reflected
in accounts of the content of the perceptual experience of young infants?
An affirmative answer is compelling here. The crux of the experimental
evidence is that what young infants perceive is not a "blooming, buzzing

confusion" of sensations but rather a world composed of determinate and bounded individuals behaving in reasonably fixed and determinate manners. And if that is how they perceive the world, then it is clear that such a world must feature in an account of their perceptual experiences.

This brings us to a second, considerably more controversial question: must we conclude from an affirmative answer to the first question that the infants in question are to be ascribed mastery of the concept of an object, or can we say what we want to say about their perceptual experience at the level of nonconceptual content? Denying the Autonomy Principle would certainly force us in the direction of a conceptual interpretation. Moreover, anyone who does not accept the Autonomy Principle is committed to holding that the infants in question will have to possess the basic conceptual abilities required to support a rudimentary conception of an objective world, because no creature that lacks these basic conceptual abilities could count as a concept user.[8] Whatever detailed account is favored of what it is to conceive the world as objective, it will clearly have to include the following: mastery of the concept of a place, mastery of some form of the first-person concept, mastery of the connectedness of space, and mastery of the concept of an object. These conceptual abilities are at the core of any account of what it is to apprehend the objectivity of the world, in however rudimentary a way.

Any detailed theory of concept possession that is accepted will have to reflect the close connection between possessing a concept and carrying out certain forms of inference. Mastery of a concept is tied up with grasp of its inferential role, where a concept's inferential role can be understood in terms of its contribution to the inferential powers of propositions in which it features. It is interesting, then, that there does seem to be an analogue for this in infant behavior. It is clear that the notion of solidity or impenetrability is essential to the concept of an object, so that if something is an object, it follows that it will be solid and hence that nothing can pass through it. So we may take the following inference as a basic example of the type of inference licensed by possession of the concept of an object:

x is an object.

Nothing will pass through x.

Let us return, then, to Baillargeon's drawbridge experiments (Baillargeon 1987). At one level, it seems possible to describe what is going on in the drawbridge and similar experiments in terms of a primitive application of the inference pattern connecting objects with solidity and impenetrability. This seems a natural way of understanding the idea that the infants are engaged in a form of physical reasoning. On this view, they show surprise because they have seen that something is an object, inferred that it must therefore be solid and impenetrable, and yet seen a drawbridge apparently pass through it.

It seems plausible on this view to ascribe mastery of the concept of an object to infants who demonstrated the appropriate dishabituation behavior in a range of contexts sufficiently wide to indicate that they had grasped several such inference patterns. This is Spelke's own interpretation of the dishabituation results:

I suggest that the infant's mechanism for apprehending objects is a mechanism of thought: an initial *theory* of the physical world whose four principles jointly define an initial *object concept*. This suggestion is motivated not only by evidence of the centrality of the mechanism for apprehending objects, but also by a consideration of the principles governing its operation. The principles of cohesion, boundedness, substance, and spatio-temporal continuity appear to stand at the centre of adults' intuitive conceptions of the physical world and its behaviour: our deepest conceptions of objects appear to be the notions that they are internally connected and distinct from one another, that they occupy space and that they exist and move continuously. (1988, 181)

On such a view, the basic elements of the concept are in place very early on in life. What happens subsequently in development is their refinement and incorporation into a body of knowledge about the physical, mechanical, and dynamic properties of objects.[9]

There is, of course, a simple answer to this proposal. It follows from the Priority Principle, which I adopted in chapter 2, that conceptual abilities are constitutively linked with language mastery in a way that rules out the ascription of conceptual abilities to nonlinguistic or prelinguistic creatures. Since Baillargeon's infants are clearly prelinguistic, this would immediately rule out the conceptualist interpretation. This simple answer should be treated with prima facie suspicion, however, because the Priority Principle has not yet been defended. I propose to proceed instead by offering a general argument against the conceptualist interpretation of the empirical evidence, showing how these general considerations can be employed in support of the Priority Principle. What follows will, I hope, fulfill the promissory note for a defence of the Priority Principle issued in chapter 2.

The conceptualist interpretation blurs some very important distinctions. According to the interpretation, the experimental infants are applying a primitive inference pattern connecting the concept *object* with the concept *impenetrability*. But the fact that young infants are surprised when certain expectations they have are thwarted does not mean that they have drawn inferences from the fact that something seems to be an example of an object. This is so for (at least) two reasons.

Identifying something as an object is something that one does for *reasons*. An individual identifies something as an object if he knows what the criteria for objecthood are and can recognize that they are by and large satisfied. The subject is making a judgement that can be justified or unjustified, rational or irrational. It does not seem, however, that anything like this is going on in the infant behavior under consideration. The fact that infants are capable of parsing their visual array into bounded segments that (more or less) correspond to objects does not warrant the thought that there are reasons for this that can be evaluated according to the standards appropriate for ascriptions of justified belief. Of course, there are reasons why such parsing abilities are in place, but they are of a different type and are to be judged by different standards. It might, for example, be explicable purely at the level of early visual processing. This point can be appreciated by considering what the appropriate response would be to an infant who shows surprise when an object passes through something that, although bounded, is not an object (say a shadow). It would be totally inappropriate to describe such an infant as making an unjustified judgement. It is not the infant's standards of rational assessment that are at fault (he hasn't got any). The problem is that his visual processing is not sufficiently discriminating within the general category of bounded segments.

The second problem follows from this. If a subject justifiably thinks that something exemplifies the concept of an object, then this licenses him in drawing certain inferences, a good example of which is the inference from something's being an object to its being impenetrable. But whatever drawing an inference means, it must mean more than having certain expectations that manifest themselves only in the presence or absence of surprise. Drawing inferences requires grasping general rules of inference and recognizing that their application is appropriate in a given situation. The paradigm cases of inference are conscious reflective acts, and although many of the inferences that mature concept users make are unconscious and unreflective, they are exercises of capacities that could be made conscious and reflective. There seem to be no reasons for thinking that there is anything like this, or even approaching it, going on in dishabituation behavior.[10]

The contrast between genuine inference and what might best be termed sensitivity to the truth of inferential transitions can easily be illustrated.[11] Piaget's well-known discussions of searching behavior (1954) provide good examples of a case where inference is obviously absent. Consider the *A*, not-*B* error (the stage 4 error). An object that an 8-month-old infant has successfully found at place *A* is moved in full view of the infant and hidden at place *B*. Instead of searching at *B*, the infant searches again at *A*. It would clearly be inappropriate to describe this behavior in terms of the infant making any inferences about the object still being where it was first found. Consider, on the other hand, the classic experiments by Susan Carey (1982) on 4-year-olds. Carey told the children that people had a greenish internal organ called a 'spleen'. She then showed them a toy mechanical monkey and a live earthworm and asked them which was more likely to have a spleen. Although a toy mechanical monkey obviously looks much more like a human being than an earthworm does, the children decided that the worm was more likely to have a spleen. How did they come to this conclusion? It seems natural to say that they made use of inference patterns linking the concepts *human being, living animal,* and *internal organs*. To explain what is going on in these experiments, in stark contrast to the drawbridge experiments, we really do need to talk about concepts and inferences.

It is not coincidental that the example of genuine inference comes from the domain of linguistic competence. A clear understanding of the grounds for drawing a sharp contrast between genuine inference and sensitivity to the truth of inferential transitions supports the idea that there is a constitutive link between language mastery and concept mastery. The sort of inferences that can plausibly be taken as good evidence of concept mastery are carried out for reasons, as is the classification of objects under the relevant concepts. Indeed, there are obvious rational connections between classifying objects in certain ways and being prepared to accept certain inferences on the basis of those classifications. The plausibility of the Priority Principle emerges when one starts to reflect on the constraints on being able to appreciate rational grounds for certain inferences. Certainly, it is possible to be justified (or warranted) in making a certain inferential transition without being able to provide a justification (or warrant) for that inferential transition. It is a familiar epistemological point, after all, that there is a difference between being justified in holding a belief and justifying that belief. What does not seem to be true is that one can be justified in making an inferential transition even if one is not capable of providing any justifications at all for any inferential transitions. But providing justifications is a paradigmatically linguistic activity. Providing justifications is a matter of identifying and articulating the reasons for a given classification, inference, or judgement. It is because prelinguistic creatures are in principle incapable of providing such justifications that the priority thesis is true. Mere sensitivity to the truth of inferential transitions involving a given concept is not enough for possession of that concept. Rational sensitivity is required, and rational sensitivity comes only with language mastery.

For all these reasons, then, the phenomena that developmental psychologists interpret in terms of object permanence are not a sign of mastery of the concept of an object. Maintaining the Autonomy Principle is the only way in which we can reconcile this with the earlier thought that young infants' capacities to register object permanence should feature in an account of the content of their perceptual experience. Denying the Autonomy Principle leaves one with the choice between either ascribing to the infants mastery of certain basic objective concepts or denying that the infants have experience with representational content and that this content has a role to play in explaining their behavior. Neither of these possibilities is plausible. The first has already been discussed, while the second seems to be vitiated by the truth of counterfactuals like the following: 'If the infants had perceived an array of unstructured visual sense data rather than bounded segments, they would not have shown surprise when an apparently continuous surface comes apart'. The infants in dis-habituation experiments show surprise because they see things a certain way, and it is natural to describe how they see things by saying that they parse the visual array into bounded segments, even though they have no conceptual grasp of what those bounded segments are.

Nonetheless, some caution is needed here. Even if it is granted that the infants' perceptions need to be explained at the nonconceptual level, there is still the important question as to how the nonconceptual content of those perceptions is to be elucidated. The question can be focused by asking whether it follows from the preceding discussion that the infants perceive the world as divided up into objects. The reason I have formu-lated the discussion so far in terms of bounded segments and individuals has been precisely to leave this question open. It is a substantive question whether the bounded segments into which the infant universe is divided up map at all cleanly onto the objects into which the actual universe is divided up. If those bounded segments do map onto objects, then it will be right to describe the experimental infants as nonconceptually perceiv-ing objects. That is to say, specifications of the content of the infants' visual perceptions will have to be made in terms that include the concepts pertaining to objects. If, on the other hand, the bounded segments into which infants parse the visual array turn out not to be equivalent to ob-jects, then some other concepts will have to be employed in specifying how the infants perceive the world.

How might we settle this question? What conditions would have to be satisfied for the contents of infant perceptions to be properly described in terms of objects? The necessary conditions, it seems to me, are ultimately derivable from a specification of the properties that can plausibly be seen as essential to objects. Let me call these *object properties*. Object proper-ties are properties constitutive of objects, so that any individual of which a suitable set of object properties can be truly ascribed will ipso facto count as an object. Examples of object properties are these:

• The property of following a single continuous trajectory through space-time
• The property of continuing to exist when unperceived
• The property of having a determinate shape
• The property of being impenetrable

- The property of being subject to gravity
- The property of being internally causally connected
- The property of having a certain mass
- The property of posing resistance to touch
- The property of having its state of motion or rest explicable in terms of the mechanical forces acting upon it
- The property of having its state of motion or rest exert forces on other objects

There are no doubt other object properties, and some of the properties on this list may well be reducible to others. Correctly determining the set of object properties is obviously a significant philosophical task. For present purposes, however, all that is required is that there actually be such a set and that we can uncontroversially identify at least some of its core members.

Given that object properties define objecthood, it is natural to hold that a perceiver perceives objects to the extent that he is perceptually sensitive to object properties.[12] This is, of course, an application of a general principle governing all attributions of perceptual content, namely, that a perceiver cannot properly be described as perceiving a given thing unless he can perceptually discriminate that thing. To return to the original question, the following seems a plausible answer. Infants, and indeed any other perceivers at the nonconceptual level, can properly be described as perceiving objects to the extent that they are perceptually sensitive to object properties. Of course, there is an important distinction between those object properties that are, and those that are not, perceptually manifest at a time. The object property of having a determinate shape is an obvious example of one that is perceptually manifest at a time. By definition, though, the object property of existing unperceived is not perceptually manifest at a time. The evaluation of perceptual sensitivity to object properties that are not perceptually manifest at a time will need to take into account behavioral dispositions and expectations. A good example (and one rather familiar to developmental psychologists) of the sort of behavior that would be prima facie evidence of perceptual sensitivity to unperceived existence would be searching for an object that is hidden. Here, as always when dealing with nonconceptual content, considerations of parsimony must be paramount.

There seems to me to be no doubt that an important element in infant cognitive development is increasing sensitivity to an increasing range of object properties. Although this is a purely empirical matter (and a profitable avenue for research in developmental psychology[13]), it seems natural to conjecture that the most basic and primitive ability is the ability to parse the visual array into bounded segments that are, as cognitive development proceeds, perceptually endowed with progressively richer properties, among which will feature an increasing range of object properties. When sensitivity to object properties is sufficiently developed the bounded segments which are perceived will map closely onto the objects which really exist in the environment. However, at some stages in infant cognitive development there will not be perceptual sensitivity to a sufficient number of object properties for it to be appropriate to describe infants at that stage of development as perceiving objects, even at the nonconceptual level. Clearly, therefore, a different conceptual framework is required to specify the nonconceptual content of perception for infants at that stage, and this is an issue to which I shall return at the end of the next chapter.

Enough has been said, however, for it to be clear not only why the notion of autonomous nonconceptual content is legitimate but also how it can have a crucial role to play in a *developmental explanation* of concept acquisition. As the passage quoted earlier from Spelke and Van de Walle stresses, the operation of the cohesion, contact, and other similar principles will eventually help infants towards a position in which they can pick out objects as objects. Young infants who have acquired sufficient perceptual sensitivity to object properties will be able to represent the world in a way that divides it up into objects. Accounting for this in terms of autonomous nonconceptual content gives us the basic raw material from which the process of concept acquisition develops. It seems plausible that a (theoretical) understanding of the reasons for thinking that something exemplifies the concept of an object, together with an understanding of what inferences it is legitimate to draw from that fact, emerges from certain basic representational abilities that permit the subject to pick out the extension of the concept and that support certain expectations about how the things that fall under that extension will behave.

An adequate account of how the concept of an object meets the Acquisition Constraint will involve tracing this process of making representational abilities explicit. How does the infant move from the primitive recognitional abilities tapped in dishabituation experiments to explicit and articulated mastery of the concept of an object? As suggested above, this process is partly a process of increasing sensitivity to a wider range of object properties. But that can only be half of the story. The infant must also move from an implicit understanding to an explicit understanding, from a cognitive level at which understanding is manifested in thwarted expectations and reactive behavior to a cognitive level at which the reasons and grounds of those expectations and reactive behavior are themselves appreciated.

Let me end this section by offering a hypothesis about a vital stage in this process of moving from an implicit to an explicit understanding. As already noted, an important reason for the shift in developmental psychology away from the Piagetian perspective has been the increasing use of dishabituation experiments. This is because dishabituation experiments do not tap the motor abilities required for success on Piaget's favored tests for understanding of object permanence. The picture that emerges from comparing performance on Piaget's search tasks with performance on dishabituation paradigms strongly suggests that the first stage in the move from implicit to explicit understanding involves developing the ability for behavioral, rather than purely reactive, manifestation of the relevant representational abilities (Russell 1996). There seem to be two significant developments in motor competence that ground successful performance on Piagetian tasks like the *A*, not-*B* search task (Diamond 1991). Infants need to be able to inhibit their prepotent action responses if they are to engage in appropriately sophisticated manipulatory behavior, and they also need to be able to develop sequences of actions and to link information over a separation in space and/or time. The acquisition of these abilities is known from lesion studies to be correlated with maturational changes in the frontal cortex, particularly in the supplementary motor areas (including callosal connections between the supplementary motor areas in the left and right hemispheres) and in the dorsolateral prefrontal cortex (Diamond 1991).

Accordingly, it seems plausible to suggest that a crucial bridge between, on the one hand, the implicit nonconceptual understanding of object properties implicated in infant performance in dishabituation experiments and, on the other, the rational explicit understanding implicated in full mastery of the object concept is an increasing ability to put that nonconceptual understanding to work in the manipulation and exploration of the environment.[14] This initial stage in the process is relatively well understood at both developmental and neurophysiological levels. Subsequent stages in the process are less well understood, although I hope to shed some light on them in later chapters of this book. In the final section of this chapter, I turn to reviewing further evidence for the explanatory utility of autonomous nonconceptual content.

3.4   The Autonomy Principle: Further Evidence and Applications

Developmental psychology, particularly infancy research, provides the clearest and most unambiguous examples of the explanatory power of the notion of nonconceptual content. But there are other areas in which the notion of nonconceptual content also seems applicable, including cognitive ethology (which I will discuss in greater detail in the next chapter). I will conclude this chapter more speculatively by pointing to the role that the notion of autonomous nonconceptual content can play in understanding, first, the phylogeny of language and, second, the *visual agnosias* (disorders of visual perception following brain damage). I will conclude by noting how a version of the distinction between conceptual and nonconceptual content seems to be built into the computational theory of vision developed by David Marr.

The phylogeny of language
It is often suggested that ontogeny recapitulates phylogeny (Brown 1988). In this spirit it makes sense to move from developmental psychology to evolutionary theory. The solution that I am proposing to the paradox of self-consciousness is that we need to recognize the existence of primitive, prelinguistic forms of self-consciousness if we are to explain the possibility of mastery of the first-person pronoun emerging naturally in the normal course of development. This in turn might be viewed as an appli-

cation of the general thought that an organism already needs to be think-ing before it can acquire the capacity to employ a language. That general thought, in turn, might be defended in one of (at least) two ways. It might be defended on conceptual grounds, by maintaining that learning a lan-guage is itself a process of thought, and hence that it would be impossible for a language to be learned by a creature not capable of some sort of language-independent thought. Some such argument is often held to be a powerful motivation for a language of thought (Fodor 1975). Alterna-tively, it might be defended empirically. The two obvious avenues for such an empirical defence would be ontogenetic and phylogenetic. A possible ontogenetic defence for the claim would be the familiar developmental view of the language-learning child as a little linguist, for example. Com-parable phylogenetic evidence would emerge if it could be shown that the evolutionary emergence of language was preceded by a stage at which early humans were clearly capable of thinking.

Of course, because of the paucity of evidence, it is hard to imagine anything being *shown* about the phylogeny of language. But the evidence that exists from paleoneurology and comparative primate neuroanatomy is certainly consistent with the hypothesis that significant cognitive abili-ties emerged before the evolution of language. Researchers are largely in agreement that the two brain regions most closely involved in language mastery are Broca's area and the parieto-occipital-temporal cortex (in-cluding the region known as Wernicke's area). The parieto-occipital-temporal cortex serves to integrate visual, auditory, and somatosensory information and then feeds structured and integrated information for-ward to Broca's area. Neither of these areas is present in primate brains. Nor, more interestingly, do they appear to be present in the early homi-nids, that is, the early members of the primate lineage which separated off between 10 and 4 million years ago from the African apes and eventually evolved into *Homo sapiens sapiens*. The first genus of hominid, *Austra-lopithecus,* is, from endocast studies, thought likely to have had an ape-like, rather than a human-like, parietal cortex (Donald 1991, Corballis 1991).[15] There is some dispute about dating the emergence of a human-like neural organization, but recent authors are largely in agreement that the crucial event in the emergence of language was the speciation of ar-chaic *Homo sapiens* approximately 300,000 years ago, following a massive expansion in brain size and, perhaps most significant, the descent of the larynx (Lieberman 1991, Corballis 1991, Donald 1991).[16] Only once the larynx has descended is anything like the full range of human speech sounds available.

Now this view of the evolution of language poses a prima facie problem for the opponent of the Autonomy Principle for the following reason. There is considerable evidence that early hominids, considerably prior to the speciation of archaic *Homo sapiens,* were cognitively highly evolved, certainly far more so than any nonhuman primate. *Homo habilis,* the first species in the genus *Homo* (approximately 2 million years ago), is known to have created and used stone tools (scrapers and choppers) and so is believed to have had precursors of Broca's area and a developed parietal cortex (Tobias 1987). However, a major cognitive breakthrough is believed to have been made in the transition period leading to the speciation of *Homo erectus* approximately 1.5 million years ago. The relative brain size of *Homo erectus* was much larger than previous hominids (approximately 70 percent of the modern human brain), and it continued to increase until the speciation of *Homo sapiens.* The brain of *Homo erectus* is believed to have expanded particularly in the association cortex, the hippocampus, and the cerebellum. This is associated with well-confirmed evidence of significant cognitive evolution. *Homo erectus* is known to have developed sophisticated stone tools, to have employed complex long-distance hunting strategies (some of them tool-based), and to have moved out of Africa to cover much of Eurasia.

Tool-making obviously requires sophisticated instrumental reasoning, as does the social coordination involved in implementing large-scale migrations. If the modern consensus of opinion is right that the emergence of language (in the sense of a communication system marked by generativity and a lexicon containing thousands of items) did not emerge until nearly 2 million years after the start of tool-making and social coordination, then a nonlinguistic framework is required to make sense of these more primitive, and yet undeniably cognitive, abilities.[17] This is a task that the theory of nonconceptual content that I will be developing in this book is suited to perform. Such a framework would still be required even if it were held that language neither did evolve, nor could have evolved, by natural selection (Piatelli-Palmarini 1989). It would still be necessary to explain the cognitive abilities that preceded language even if language was held to have emerged independently of them. But on the plausible assumption that some sort of natural-selection account is indeed correct (Pinker and Bloom 1990), the theory of nonconceptual content also offers scope for a phylogenetically developmental account of the acquisition of conceptual mastery to match the ontogenetically developmental account sketched in the previous section.

Visual agnosias
Neuropsychologists have long been familiar with a range of deficits in visual object recognition that are collectively termed the *visual agnosias*. These deficits (as opposed, for example, to disorders like blindsight) are characterized by the relative preservation of elementary visual functions, such as acuity, brightness discrimination, and color vision. As is often the case with neuropsychological disorders, the first problem that confronts workers in the area is providing a workable taxonomy of the range of deficits. The taxonomy is particularly important because how visual deficits are classified has obvious implications for (and is equally informed by) the analysis of normal visual processing. What I suggest is that the distinction between conceptual and nonconceptual content offers scope for developing and refining what is by now a standard classification of visual agnosias.

Students of visual agnosias have generally drawn a broad distinction between the so-called *apperceptive agnosias* and the so-called *associative agnosias* (Brown 1988, Farah 1990). In very broad terms, the distinction is between deficits in object perception (the apperceptive agnosias) and object recognition (the associative agnosias). Apperceptive agnosias are due to impairments in visual perception that, although at a higher level than, for example, visual-field deficits, nonetheless appear to be perceptual rather than recognitional. Objects are not properly perceived, and hence are not recognized. Classic examples of apperceptive agnosias include *simultagnosia,* in which patients seem to be incapable of recognizing more than one stimulus at a time and unable to make even the simplest forms of shape discrimination.[18] In the associative agnosias, on the other hand, objects do seem to be properly perceived but are nonetheless not recognized. Such deficits appear to be more cognitive than perceptual. Standard examples of associative object agnosias involve impairment in the recognition of (certain categories of) visually presented objects, coupled with normal recognition of those objects in nonvisual modalities and with intact visual perception (as measured, for example, by the ability to draw a fair copy of the stimulus).[19] Impaired visual recognition is manifested both verbally and nonverbally (e.g., in abilities to mime the use of the relevant objects or to sort pictures of visually dissimilar but functionally similar objects). *Prosopagnosia,* the inability to recognize faces, is usually classified among the associative agnosias, as is *alexia,* an inability to read, coupled with a preserved ability to write.

It is standard to take the two contrasts between normal vision and agnosic vision and between the apperceptive and associative agnosias to show that there are several different levels of visual processing (Marr 1982, Farah 1990). The first level is often described as the level of purely sensory processing, where dedicated sensory analyzers and filters, generally thought to be located in anatomically distinct but nonetheless functionally integrated areas of the visual cortex, yield information about features of the environment, such as color, motion, luminance, etc. (Ts'o and Roe 1995). This level is preserved in both the apperceptive and associative agnosias. A second level of visual processing might be identified programmatically as what is lacking in the apperceptive agnosias although nonetheless present in the associative agnosias (and, of course, in normal vision). The third processing level can be equally programmatically specified as what is lacking in the associative agnosias but not in the apperceptive agnosias. The associative and apperceptive agnosias yield a dissociation between two distinct components of the visual-processing system. One standard way of describing the functional architecture revealed by this dissociation is in terms of a distinction between object perception and object recognition or between form perception and meaning perception (Brown 1988). Other more complex classifications have been proposed. Martha Farah has proposed a tripartite analysis of higher vision. Grouping operations on the outputs of purely sensory processing yield a grouped array operated on in parallel by the spatial-attention and object-recognition systems (Farah 1990). The apperceptive agnosias reveal impairments in the initial grouping processes, while the associative agnosias implicate one or another of the spatial-attention and object-recognition systems.

The existing classifications can usefully be supplemented by thinking about the functional differences revealed by the visual agnosias in terms of the distinction between nonconceptual and conceptual content. The grouping operations impaired in the apperceptive agnosias and preserved in the associative agnosias produce representations of the world at the level of nonconceptual content. The grouping operations parse the visual array into spatially extended and bounded individuals that stand in spatial relations to each other, and that, of course, is how the world seems to be represented in the instances of infant perception that were taken as paradigm examples of nonconceptual content. The visual world of the infant and the visual world of the associative agnosic can be understood in terms of each other. Of course, the comparison is of necessity a restricted one, since associative visual agnosias are always messy and often highly localized (*prosopagnosia* is an obvious example). But there seems to be a clear analogy to be drawn between how the infant sees the world and how the world would be seen by an idealized global associative agnosic—a patient whose representations of the world are devoid of semantic features but for whom the elementary grouping and parsing elements of higher vision are fully operational. Conversely, those functionally distinct elements of higher vision that are absent or severely impaired in the associative agnosias are best viewed as generating representations of the world at the conceptual level. Although there is considerable evidence that the associative agnosias are not simply impairments in naming, and hence purely linguistic, it is highly relevant that they are associated with damage to the left hemisphere (the hemisphere specialized for language), particularly to the occipital-temporal junction.

The computational theory of vision
Since one of Marr's motivations came from reflecting on what disorders in visual processing revealed about the functional architecture of vision, it is perhaps not surprising that a subpersonal analogue of the personal-level distinction between conceptual and nonconceptual content seems to be built into Marr's pioneering computational theory of vision (Marr and Nishihara 1978, Marr 1982).[20]

Marr's account of vision describes the stages by which variations in illumination are parsed to yield an image of objects in space, in terms of a series of representations, termed 'sketches', each of which is the product of a limited series of specialized processes dedicated to discriminating distinct features of the available information. In the first stage, the primal sketch, a scene is represented in terms of groupable edges, bars, and blobs with a range of basic properties (orientation, contrast, length, width, and position). In the second stage, cues for depth, such as stereopsis and contour occlusion, are added to the primal sketch. In the third stage, a 3D structural description of the object in object-centered space is computed using a catalog of stored structural descriptions. The fourth stage involves the imposition of a semantic interpretation upon the structured object.

For the theorist of nonconceptual content, the crucial point here is the sharp separation between the third and fourth stages. The third stage yields a parsing of the perceived array into spatially extended and spatially related bounded individuals of the sort characteristic of representations with nonconceptual content. This is a stage carried out in complete independence of the semantic and categorizing steps in the fourth stage. Of course, the 3D sketch is part of the mechanism that subserves vision. It is neither the object nor the content of vision.[21] Nonetheless, Marr's key idea that the structural description of objects is computed independently of the semantic classification and conceptualization of those objects lends support both to the distinction between conceptual and nonconceptual content and to the Autonomy Principle.

4

The Theory of Nonconceptual Content

In chapter 3, I provided an existence proof of autonomous nonconceptual content. If we are to do justice both to the differences and to the similarities between infant and adult cognition then we will have to recognize the existence of states that represent the world in a way that is independent of concept mastery and, moreover, that can be ascribed to creatures who possess no concepts whatsoever. What we now need is a closer understanding of the circumstances in which such states can be attributed, as well as a more detailed specification of the form that such attributions will take.

4.1 Attributing States with Autonomous Nonconceptual Content

On many philosophical construals, content is whatever is specified in a 'that' clause when attributing a propositional attitude. In attributing belief, desire, fear, or any other propositional attitude to an individual, we do three things: identify a particular person; attribute a particular attitude to that person; and specify the proposition to which that attitude is held. Specifying the proposition to which an attitude is held is equivalent to giving the content of that attitude, i.e., what is believed, desired, or feared.

If this familiar conception of propositional content is deemed the only appropriate one, then it seems natural to resist the suggestion that there might be forms of content that are nonconceptual in the sense discussed in section 1.2, because propositional attitudes are paradigmatically conceptual (for reasons that I brought out in chapter 3). To make any progress, then, we need an account of what it is for a state to have content that will not rule out the notion of nonconceptual content as a matter of definition. A promising start is provided by Peacocke's (1992) suggestion that a state has content if and only if it has a correctness condition. On Peacocke's view (the *minimal account of content possession*), a state presents the world as being in a certain way if and only if there is a condition or set of conditions under which it does so correctly, and the content of the state is given in terms of what it would be for it to present the world correctly. This certainly leaves open the possibility of nonconceptual content, but it leaves several important questions unanswered.[1]

Suppose that we distinguish two different tasks that a general account of content possession might be called upon to perform. The first (*constitutive*) task would be to give an account of what the content of a given state is, on the assumption that such a state has content. The second (*criterial*) task would be to explain how one might tell whether a state has content at all. The minimal account certainly fulfils the constitutive task, but it is not clear that it satisfies the criterial task. Correctness conditions are conditions of some state of affairs being represented correctly. So before we can determine whether a state has a correctness condition, we must determine whether it is a representational state.

Consider, for example, how the minimal account would deal with the question of whether carrying information betokens the presence of content. As standardly construed (Dretske 1981), a state of affairs carries information about another state of affairs if and only if there is nomological covariance between the respective types of which they are tokens. Familiar examples are the rings of a tree, which carry information about the age of the tree, and fossils, which carry information about the bone structure of extinct animals.

In both cases it would seem that a correctness condition can be provided. In the first example the correctness conditions would be 'The rings on the tree correctly indicate the age of the tree if and only if the number of rings = the number of years the tree has been in existence'. But would these be *genuine* correctness conditions? Many would think not. They might argue as follows. No state could count as a representational state unless it were possible for it to *misrepresent* the environment. But it is the lawlike connection between, for example, the number of rings and the number of years that makes it plausible to speak of the former as carrying information about the latter, and what makes it a lawlike connection is the fact that the number of rings and the number of years invariably coincide.[2] Such invariable coincidence, however, clearly rules out the possibility of misrepresentation.[3]

In cases like these, then, the minimal account is not sufficient to settle the question of whether we are dealing with genuine content or not. We need to supplement it with an account of representation—of what it is for a creature to be representing the environment. As is required by the argument rejecting the Autonomy Principle (section 3.3), this account will have to identify the conditions that must be satisfied for nonconceptual content to be ascribed to non-concept-using creatures. On the other hand, such an account should also be able to explain what is going on in ascriptions of conceptual content. Conceptual and nonconceptual content are both forms of content because there is a single notion of representation applicable to both of them. What is needed is an account of the general conditions under which it makes theoretical sense to hold that creatures are representing the environment.

What is at stake here is the appropriateness of distinct types of explanation. Theorists have traditionally distinguished between two different categories of explanation of behavior: mechanistic explanations and intentional explanations (Taylor 1964). Intentional explanations have several distinguishing characteristics. First, they are teleological. That is, they explain an organism's behavior in terms of the purposes and desires that the behavior is intended to satisfy. Second, intentional explanations cannot be eliminated in favour of nonintentional explanations. Third, intentional explanations appeal to desires and purposes in conjunction with nonmotivational representational states. Simply specifying a desire that an organism could satisfy by performing a particular action cannot provide a satisfactory explanation. Two different types of representation have to be involved: perceptual representations of the environment and representations of how performing that action can satisfy the desire in question. It is not the case, however, that there have to be two different representations. Quite often a single perceptual representation of the environment will also illustrate how performing a given action will satisfy the desire in question.[4]

Explanations of behavior, particularly when dealing with the cognitive abilities of nonlinguistic creatures, quite rightly operate with a principle of parsimony. Appeals to representational states should be made only where it is theoretically unavoidable, where there is no simpler mechanistic explanation of the behavior (*pace* Fodor [1987, Preface]). This raises the question, of course, of how 'behavior' is being understood here. It is natural to ask whether what is at stake is behavior narrowly construed in terms of independently characterizable bodily movements or behavior broadly construed in terms of bodily movements related in certain ways to the environment. This is a complicated question, and I state my position without argument. It seems to me that the distinction between narrow and broad construals of behavior maps cleanly onto the distinction between mechanistic and intentional explanations of behavior. Mechanistic explanations of behavior are appropriate when, and only when, the behavior to be explained can be specified in terms of nonrelational bodily movements. Intentional explanations, in contrast, go hand in hand with relationally characterized bodily movements. So, to return to the issue of parsimony, this provides a further way of conceptualizing the difference between behavior that needs to be explained through representational states and behavior that does not. The latter, but not the former, can be satisfactorily characterized nonrelationally.

As a first step towards building on this, consider the thesis that representational states are intermediaries between sensory input and behavioral output (theoretically) required to explain how behavioral output emerges on the basis of sensory input. We can identify situations, such as the operation of primitive evolutionarily hard-wired connections, where the connections between sensory input and behavioral output do not demand the attribution of representational states. Consider a creature genetically programmed to respond in a certain way to a certain stimulus, say to move away from the perceived direction of a particular stimulus. One can explain why it made such a movement in any particular situation without saying that it was representing the distal cause of the stimulus. Registering the relevant stimulus causes the appropriate response, and this can be fully understood, explained, and predicted without any appeal to an intermediary between stimulus and response. By the same token, the movement can be satisfactorily described in bodily terms. It does not have to be described relationally as a movement away from whatever the distal cause happens to be.

So for situations in which the connection between sensory input and behavioural output are invariant in this way, we do not need to bring in representational states. This does not just rule out primitive hard-wired forms of reflex behavior. Consider the classic situation of hungry rats for whom the sound of a tone regularly signals the delivery of food to a magazine. Suppose (as is in fact the case) that after exposure to this set-up the rats acquire an approach response—they approach the magazine during the sound of the tone. There seem to be two ways of describing this behavior. The first and perhaps the most intuitively appealing would be to describe the situation in representational terms. This would involve two different representations: a representation of the goal (the food) and a representation of the instrumental contingency between approaching the magazine and attaining the goal. The goal is taken to be intrinsically motivating, and what drives the approach response is a comprehension that the response will lead to the goal. Alternatively, a completely nonrepresentational account might be given in which there is appeal simply to lawlike connections, built up through associative conditioning, between the rat hearing the sound and his approaching the magazine.

How can we decide between these two options? One way of doing so discussed in the psychological literature (Holland 1979, Dickinson 1980) would be to employ an omission schedule. An omission schedule inverts the connection between the approach response and the reward. If the rat approaches the food source during the sound of the tone, no food is delivered. There is no reason to think that this would interfere with the rat's initially learning the association between tone and food, because in the initial trials it would not approach the magazine (there being no reason for it to approach the magazine before it has learned the association). Once it *has* learned the association, however, the rat will approach the magazine in the familiar way. But by the omission schedule, the approach will lead to the food being withheld. What will the rat do now? The operative idea here is that if the rat's response (approaching the magazine) is really determined by a representation of the instrumental contingency between approaching the magazine and gaining food, then the response will not occur when the instrumental contingency ceases to hold, especially when it actually results in nonachievement of the goal. Experiments on rats show that rats do indeed maintain the approach response even in omission schedules (Holland 1979).[5]

There are two comments to be made here. The first is that the persistence of the original behavior militates strongly against the idea that the rat's behavior is driven by a representation of the instrumental contingency between performing the action and attaining the goal, since it continues to perform the action even when the goal is not attained. The second is that the invariance of the behavior is an integral part of its being explicable solely in terms of lawlike connections between stimulus and response built up by associative conditioning.

This is closely connected with the earlier point about the importance of the connection between representation and misrepresentation. The reason that tropistic and classically conditioned behavior can be explained without reference to representational perceptual states is, as already stressed, that the response is invariant if the creature in question registers the relevant stimulus. What this means, of course, is that the behavior can be explained by how things are in the immediate environment. There is, therefore, no need to appeal to how things are taken to be (how they are represented as being). The need to appeal to how things are taken to be comes in only when the law-governed correlation between stimulus and response breaks down. This can come about either when the response occurs in the absence of the stimulus or when the stimulus occurs and is registered without the response following. In the first of these cases one might say that there is a representation of the stimulus and that this is what generates the response, and in the second case one might say that even though the stimulus is there, it is not represented so as to bring about the appropriate response. Both of these are different types of misrepresentation, and the existence or possibility of misrepresentation is a good criterion for the necessity of bringing in representational perceptual states.

It will be helpful, I think, if I situate my position relative to the account of "registration" developed by Jonathan Bennett in the detailed account of teleological explanation of animal behavior that he develops in the justly influential *Linguistic Behaviour* (Bennett 1976). The technical notion of registration that Bennett develops has many features that make it appear that when a creature registers something, it is ipso facto in a perceptual state with representational content. According to Bennett, a creature c registers that p if c is in a sensory state that is sufficiently like some p-operative state, where a p-operative state is one that implies that c's acting on p is noncoincidental (Bennett 1976, 56). This is considerably weaker than the criteria that I favour for the attribution of representational states. The notion of registration is, for example, weak enough to be involved in conditioned behavior.[6] If, as a result of Pavlovian conditioning, an animal salivates whenever it hears a tone, then its actions will certainly be noncoincidental. But, although there is a case to be made for viewing instrumental conditioning as involving representational states, Pavlovian conditioning seems fundamentally different. What is significant is that, although Bennett stresses that there is no entailment between p and 'c registers that p', his notion of registration is perfectly compatible with the existence of laws of the form 'Whenever a c-like creature registers that p, it will ϕ'.[7] In such a case, then, Bennett's account fails to distinguish between cases in which creatures react invariantly to a stimulus and those in which they do not. I take it to be an advantage of my own account that it respects this important distinction.

Jerry Fodor has made some interesting suggestions about how the possibility of misrepresentation might be explained by the lack of a lawlike correlation between stimulus and response (Fodor 1986, 14–16). Explaining why there should be an invariant connection between stimulus and response requires postulating the existence of *transducers* (devices that transfer sensory stimuli into physical output in a suitable form to interact with the motor system). We need transducers to explain how an organism can pick up stimuli at all, and when there is an invariant connection between stimulus and response, we need to postulate the existence of transducers sensitive to specific properties (what are often known as *dedicated* transducers). The existence and operation of these dedicated transducers, hooked up in the appropriate ways to the motor system, is all that we need to explain the invariant behavior in question. Now in the case of intentional behaviour, which does not involve a lawlike connection between stimulus and response, it is clear that we are not dealing with dedicated transducers. Creatures who are behaving intentionally are, of course, sensitive to particular properties of the stimulus, but these are not properties that can be detected by dedicated transducers. So how are they detected? One answer is that their presence is inferred from the presence of properties that can be picked up by transducers. The need for such a process of inference, however, brings with it the possibility of error, because it is inductive, not deductive, inference. Hence the possibility of misrepresentation.

This connects with another strand in the notion of representation. When we appeal to representational states to explain behavior, we rarely, if ever, appeal to single states operating in isolation. The behavior of organisms suitably flexible and plastic in their responses to the environment tends to be the result of complex interactions between internal states. As Robert Van Gulick notes, "Any adequate specification of the role which a given state or structure plays with respect to the system's behaviour will have to be in terms of the partial contributions which that state makes to the determination of behaviour in conjunction with a wide variety of internal state combinations" (1990, 113–114). There are several reasons for this.

First, interaction between internal states is one possible way of explaining why there do not exist lawlike correlations between input and output. It is a familiar point from the philosophy of perception that the same state of affairs can be perceptually represented in different ways determined by the influence of varying beliefs governing what one expects to see or to what one has just seen.

Second, it seems right to draw a broad distinction within the general class of representational states between "pure" representational states on the one hand and motivational states on the other. In many situations in which it is appropriate to appeal to representational states in explaining behavior, a theorist will be compelled to appeal to instances of both types of representational states. And, of course, it is not just the conjunction of representational states and motivational states that is relevant, but their interaction.

Third, representational states have to interact with other representational states. Organisms respond flexibly and plastically to their environments partly in virtue of the fact that their representational states respond flexibly and plastically to each other, most obviously through the influence of stored representations on present representations. The possibility of learning and adapting depends on past representations' contributing to the determination of present responses, and hence interacting with them. Moreover, representing a particular feature of the environment does not have effects on behavior just when a creature is confronted by that very feature. It can also be effective when the creature is confronted by something that is relevantly similar to the represented feature, or when the feature is absent and there is nothing relevantly similar in the environment (as when a creature determines to leave its shelter because it cannot detect either a predator or anything predatorlike in the vicinity).

Two separate constraints follow from this. First, there must be pathways enabling a given representational state to connect up with other states, both representational and motivational. There must be *cognitive integration* of the relevant states. This point is most familiar in the context of propositional attitudes. Part of what it is, for example, to have a belief is that it should be open to modification from newer, incompatible beliefs, or that it should hook up, in appropriate cases, with desires in order to bring about actions, or with fears in order to prevent action.

Second, part of what is involved in the integration of representational states is that a creature representing the environment should be capable of registering when the environment is relevantly similar over time. The simplest example would be when the represented current environment is identical in all respects to the represented previous environment. But the appropriate sort of flexibility requires being able to register in what respects there is a match in the environment as represented and in what respects there is no such match, so that a suitable response can be determined by integrating the relevant match with previous experience and current motivational states.

This means that representational states must be structured so that they can be decomposed into their constituent elements, which can then be recombined with the constituent elements of other representational states. Suppose, for example, that a creature represents its environment as containing food in an exposed place with a predator within striking distance. If its ensuing behavior is not to be driven either by the association food-eat or by the association predator-flee, the creature will need to evaluate whether it can reach the food without the predator noticing, whether the food is worth the risk, whether having gained the food it can then escape to safety, etc. These primitive forms of inference require being able to distinguish the various elements in the original representation and to integrate them with comparable elements in other representational states.

This requirement of compositional structure is at the core of one important recent discussion of the conditions for ascribing conceptual content. Evans (1982) understands thoughts as essentially structured, composed of distinct conceptual abilities that are constitutively recombinable in indefinitely many distinct thoughts. This is the Generality Constraint, which he imposes on genuine concepts. The idea of concepts as the essentially recombinable constituents of thought is familiar enough not to require further discussion, falling naturally, as it does, out of the parallelism widely assumed to hold between conceptual thought and language. What is perhaps less clear is how this requirement of structure is met by the nonconceptual perceptual states discussed in the previous chapter. What can count as the recombinable elements of a perceptual state? It seems to me that the key here is the thought that nonconceptual perceptual experience nonetheless involves parsing the perceived array into distinct elements. In the case of vision, this involves the ability to parse the array of visual stimulation into spatially extended bodies. Placing this parsing ability in the context of perceptual recognitional abilities that allow such spatially extended bodies to be reidentified in subsequent experiences makes the structure of nonconceptual perceptual experiences much clearer.

The requirement of compositional structure is closely related to the generativity usually taken to be the defining feature of language. It is hard to see how generativity could be explained without compositionality. This is not to say, however, that wherever there is compositional structure, there must be generativity. That would be to obscure the distinction between conceptual and nonconceptual content. Linguistic generativity comes with the conjunction of compositional structure and global recombinability. It is not just that grammatical sentences can be decomposed into their constituent elements. The crucial point is that those grammatical elements can be recombined to yield infinitely many grammatically well-formed new sentences. It is this feature of language that Evans's Generality Constraint aims to capture at the level of thought. Theorists have frequently held that structured content must be recombinable content. What leaves space open for the possibility of nonconceptual content, however, is that compositional structure can exist in the absence of global recombinability. And this is exactly how we should understand nonconceptual content.

For the reasons given above, nonconceptual thought must be structured to allow recognition of partial similarities and to allow primitive forms of inference. But the structural components of nonconceptual content cannot be recombined at will. At the nonconceptual level there are only limited behavior-driven and environment-constrained possibilities for generating further nonconceptual contents out of a given set of nonconceptual contents. It is plausible to think that the transition from nonconceptual content to conceptual content is at least in part a matter of moving from partially recombinable content constituents to globally recombinable content constituents. Part of the motivation for the Thought-Language Principle is the thought that only through some form of syntax can the possibility of global recombinability be explained. This may well be true, but it clearly leaves conceptual space open for structured content that has only limited combinatorial properties.

It should not be thought that a requirement of compositionality at the level of content imposes a strong requirement of compositionality in the vehicle of that content. Fodor and Pylyshyn (1988) have famously suggested that when this compositionality requirement is properly understood, it entails that the computational theory of cognition (CTC) is the only viable cognitive architecture. They argue that the main alternative to CTC, the parallel-distributed-processing (PDP) paradigm, is faced with either being a mere implementation of CTC (if it does satisfy the compositionality requirement) or failing to provide an adequate account of cognition (if it does not). The debate that this challenge has raised is enormous, and this is not the place to discuss it in any detail. I have two brief points, however. First, it does not seem to me that Fodor and Pylyshyn's challenge can be defused by the sort of instrumentalist moves made in Clark (1989). At a minimal level, the compositionality requirement entails that representational states have constituents that are causally efficacious, because the only alternative is to make constituent structure epiphenomenal. The vehicle of content does have to be structured. On the other hand, however, and this is the second point, it is far from obvious that this minimal level of structure ipso facto counts as an implementation of CTC. Smolensky (1991) has argued that there is an important class of PDP representations (which he terms *tensor product* representations) that are compositionally structured in a way that approximates rather than implements a CTC architecture (see also Horgan and Tienson 1992). If he is right about this, then this would provide good reasons for thinking that the compositionality requirement that flows from the nature of intentional explanation is neutral with regard to cognitive architecture.[8]

The discussion in this section suggests that the following four criteria need to be satisfied before given states can properly be described as representational states.

· They should serve to explain behavior in situations where the connections between sensory input and behavioral output cannot be plotted in a lawlike manner.
· They should admit of cognitive integration.
· They should be compositionally structured in such a way that their elements can be constituents of other representational states.
· They should permit the possibility of misrepresentation.

As has emerged at various points during the discussion of these four marks of content, they are all satisfied paradigmatically by the conceptual contents that are the objects of folk-psychological propositional attitudes. On the other hand, it does not follow from them that conceptual propositional content is the only genuine form of content. This gives us a way of determining the issue of nonconceptual content. When confronted with states that are candidates for the ascription of nonconceptual content, we can ask whether these states satisfy the four conditions of content and thus qualify as representational states. If the four conditions are satisfied, then this will show that the states in question are contentful in virtue of features shared with the conceptual contents of folk psychology.

4.2   The Form of Autonomous Nonconceptual Content

As I have stressed, the type of autonomous nonconceptual content we are interested in is perceptual. We need an understanding of perceptual content that will capture how the world is perceived by creatures who need not have the conceptual apparatus needed to conceptualize what they perceive. Given the irrelevance of conceptual mastery for the matter in hand, standard accounts of content in terms of senses and other propositional objects are clearly irrelevant. A radically different understanding of perceptual content is needed.

The framework within which such an understanding can be developed has been provided by Christopher Peacocke (1989, 1992). Peacocke develops an account of the content of perceptual experience based on the idea that a given perceptual content should be specified in terms of all the ways in which space could be filled out around the perceiver that are consistent with that content being a correct representation of the environment:

The idea is that specifying the content of a perceptual experience involves saying what ways of filling out a space around the origin with surfaces, solids, textures, light and so forth, are consistent with the correctness or veridicality of the experience. Such contents are not built from propositions, concepts, senses, or continuant material objects. (Peacocke 1989, 8–9)

In specifying such a content, we need to start by organizing the space around the perceiver. This is done by specifying origins and corresponding axes based on the perceiver's body. There will be a range of such origins, and they will vary according to the modality in question. In the case of touch, for example, the possibilities include origins at the center of the palm of each hand, as well as certain other origins that will capture the sensitivity to touch of the remainder of the body surface. Once we have selected a particular origin and defined a set of axes in terms of them, we can identify points (or rather point types) in terms of those axes. This provides a framework within which the account of how space is "filled out" can be completed as follows:

For each point (strictly, I should say point-type), identified by its distance and direction from the origin, we need to specify whether there is a surface there and, if so, what texture, hue, saturation and brightness it has at that point, together with its degree of solidity. The orientation of the surface must be included. So must much more in the visual case: the direction, intensity, and character of light sources; the rate of change of perceptible properties, including location; indeed, it should include second differentials with respect to time where these prove to be perceptible. (Peacocke 1992, 63)

The conceptual resources with which this specification is carried out are not, of course, attributed to the perceiver. This is what makes it an account of nonconceptual content.

The account is completed as follows. Selecting an origin and axis and specifying the relevant values for each of the points in the perceivable space around that origin determines a spatial type, which Peacocke terms a *scenario*. This spatial type determines a class of ways of filling out the space, any of which could be instantiated in the real world. The next step is to assign to the origin and axes real places and directions in the world, and to assign a time. This yields a content that Peacocke terms a *positioned scenario*. This positioned scenario is correct if and only if the volume of perceptually discriminable space around the perceiver at a specified time instantiates the spatial type specified by the scenario.

It is straightforward how this notion of scenario content helps with the problem with which I began this chapter. Some aspects of what I described as the fine-grainedness of perceptual experience can be accommodated without difficulty. This is particularly clear with regard to color perception. Specifying the precise color and shade of particular points on a surface is an integral element in specifying the scenario content for any creature sensitive to color. Once this is done, justice will have been done to the idea that a creature can perceive shades of color that it cannot conceptualize. What is not yet clear, however, is how this notion of scenario content can help us with the far more complicated idea that an account of the contents of infants' perception should reflect their perception of object permanence, which they cannot conceptualize.

To make progress here, we need to consider a further level of nonconceptual representational content that Peacocke introduces. Peacocke notes that it is possible for two experiences to represent the world in different ways at the nonconceptual level, despite having identical scenario contents. He gives the familiar example of perceiving an object that is in fact square as a square, as opposed to perceiving it as a diamond. Whether the object is perceived as a square or as a diamond, the scenario content is the same (because the same values hold at each of the points identified by their distance and direction from the axes). But there remains a significant phenomenological difference. One way of capturing this difference is in terms of what symmetries are perceived. Perceiving something as a square involves perceiving symmetries about the bisectors of its four sides. If the same figure is perceived, but the perceived symmetry is about the bisectors of its four angles, then it will be perceived as a diamond. One way of dealing with this difference would be at the level of conceptual content, by invoking the perceiver's possession of some or other of the relevant concepts, such as the concept of a square, the concept of a diamond, or the concept of something being symmetrical. On the other hand, however, it does seem that the difference between perceiving an object as a square and perceiving it as a diamond is available in the absence of such concept mastery. Moreover, it is desirable to be able to appeal to it in giving a possession-conditions explanation of what such conceptual mastery consists in. Accordingly, Peacocke offers a further level of nonconceptual representational content that he terms *protopropositional content*:

The contents at this second layer cannot be identified with positioned scenarios, but they are also distinct from conceptual contents. These additional contents I call *protopropositions*. These protopropositions are assessable as true or false. A protoproposition contains an individual or individuals, together with a property or relation. When a protoproposition is part of the representational content of an experience, the experience represents the property or relation in the protoproposition as holding of the individual or individuals it also contains. (Peacocke 1992, 77)

Just as scenario content is built up out of real space-time points, protopropositional content is built up out of real individuals and real properties. Again, this qualifies as nonconceptual representational content because the perceiver need not have any conceptual grasp of those individuals and properties.

It is, I shall suggest, at the level of protopropositional content that we can capture the phenomenology of object permanence. Before going into this, however, it is important to stress that this is an employment of Peacocke's theoretical machinery that he himself is not prepared to countenance. Peacocke opposes the Autonomy Principle and does not believe that either scenario or protopropositional content can be ascribed to creatures who lack the conceptual skills necessary to generate a rudimentary conception of an objective world. I shall not take issue with his argument here. He claims that a primitive form of the first-person concept must be possessed by any creature capable of being in states with scenario content. My own position on this is that the work that Peacocke thinks can only be performed by the first-person concept can in fact be done by the first-person nonconceptual contents that I shall be discussing in the following chapters. At the moment I can only issue a promissory note (see section 8.2 below).

One point that does need to be made with regard to Peacocke's own development of the notion of protopropositional content is that it contains a crucial ambiguity that might well play into the hands of the defender of autonomous nonconceptual content. Protopropositional content, as we have seen, contains an individual or set of individuals, together with one or more property or relation. It is natural to ask what these individuals are, since they are obviously not the space-time points picked out in the positioned scenario. According to Peacocke, "These properties and relations can be represented as holding of places, lines, or regions in the positioned scenario, or of objects perceived as located in such places" (Peacocke 1992, 77). This raises a very important issue. If a property is being represented as holding of an object in the positioned scenario, then it is clear that the object itself is being represented. But the account of scenario content so far given does not provide any clues as to what this might amount to. Even though a positioned scenario might contain objects, that fact is not manifest in the scenario content, because scenario content is specified in terms of points. So, whatever basis there might be for thinking that objects are represented as such in the protopropositional content of a given experience (for thinking, for example, that *that* object is being represented as a square rather than as a diamond), it cannot come from the scenario content.

One possible position here (which may be Peacocke's own) would hold that an object is perceived as such in virtue of certain forms of conceptual mastery. It is the conceptual content of the experience in question that permits objects to be represented as objects, thereby making possible the relevant protopropositional content. Thus, to continue with Peacocke's own example, when a subject perceives a particular object as a diamond rather than a square, that is a fact about that subject's experience that needs to be explained at the level of protopropositional content. The explanation takes the following form: the perceiver's experience represents the object in question as instantiating the property of being symmetrical about the bisectors of its four angles (rather than the property of being symmetrical about the bisectors of its four sides). This is an explanation at the level of nonconceptual content because a perceiver's experience can take this form without the perceiver having to possess all or any of the concepts *symmetrical, bisector,* or *angle* (or for that matter, *diamond*).

Nonetheless, the perceiver's experience represents the object in question as instantiating those properties, and on the current view, that is only possible if the perceiver possesses at least the concept of an object in general. So, although to perceive an object as instantiating various properties (like being diamond-shaped) there is no need for the perceiver to have a conceptual grasp of those properties, the perceiver must at least have the concept of an object.

The position just sketched out is perfectly consistent, but it is not compulsory. Indeed, it seems prima facie incompatible with the possibility of autonomous nonconceptual content at the protopropositional level, since it makes the possibility of an important class of protopropositional contents depend on the perceiver's possession of at least one concept. To that extent, therefore, the arguments in the previous chapter defending the notion of autonomous nonconceptual content clearly count against it. The question arises, therefore, of how the defender of autonomous nonconceptual content can accommodate the possibility of protopropositional content. The obvious alternative is simply to deny the general principle that objects can only feature in the content of perception if the perceiver possesses the concept of an object in general. However, considerable caution is required here. The denial of the general principle can be developed in both a narrow and a broad manner. Let me go back briefly to Peacocke's characterization of protopropositional content:

A protoproposition contains an individual or individuals, together with a property or relation. When a protoproposition is part of the representational content of an experience, the experience represents the property or relation in the protoproposition as holding of the individual or individuals it also contains. . . . These properties or relations can be represented as holding of places, lines or regions in the positioned scenario, or of objects perceived as located in such places. (Peacocke 1992, 77)

Suppose we ask, what different types of thing can occupy the subject position in a protoproposition? In the final sentence quoted, Peacocke offers four candidates, namely, places, lines, spatial regions, and perceived objects. Now, after rejecting the general principle that the perception of objects depends on possession of the concept of an object, one way to proceed would be to take Peacocke's four candidates as exhausting the field. On this (*narrow*) construal, there can be no protopropositional individuals that are neither places, lines, spatial regions, or perceived objects.

The discussion of infant cognition in the previous chapter provides clear reasons for thinking that the narrow construal cannot be correct. As I noted there, infants from an early age seem to represent the world as divided into bounded segments. However, the basic perceptual capacity to parse the perceived array into bounded segments is not in itself equivalent to the perception of objects, even at the nonconceptual level. The extent to which infants (and, of course, prelinguistic and nonlinguistic creatures in general) can appropriately be described as perceiving objects is determined by the extent of their perceptual sensitivity to what I earlier termed *object properties,* that is, those properties that constitutively mark out individuals as objects. There are levels of cognitive development at which there is insufficient perceptual sensitivity to object properties for it to be appropriate to describe perceivers as perceiving objects. This can be marked in two ways. First and most straightforward, there are perceptually discriminable features that are clearly object properties but to which infants at relatively early stages of development fail to be perceptually sensitive. For example, it seems to be the case that neonates do not perceive continuously moving center-occluded objects as a single individual with a hidden part (Slater et al. 1990). Second, infants can be perceptually sensitive to properties that are not object properties and that in fact divide up the perceived array in a way that does not map at all cleanly onto how the perceived real-world situation is composed of objects. For example, it is well documented that three-month-old infants parse the perceived array in accordance with the principle that single individuals are spatially connected bodies that retain their connectedness when they move. But this often leads them to take to be a single object what is really a composite.

Since, however, even in such cases the requirements of inference to the best explanation will often require the ascription of states with nonconceptual content to such perceivers and such states will often have protopropositional content, it follows that there must be protopropositional individuals to which properties and relations can be ascribed other than objects (and lines, places, and regions of space). Some technical vocabulary is required to specify these protopropositional individuals. Let me introduce the notion of an object*. An object* is defined as a bounded segment of the perceived array. The notion of an object* is intended to capture minimal differentiation of the perceived array of the sort that is to be found in early infancy. By saying that objects* feature as individuals in the protopropositional content of perceived experience, I mean to distinguish them from protopropositional properties and relations. An object* is a unified and coherent segment of the perceived array that can be perceived as having certain properties and as standing in certain relations to other objects*. Some of those properties will be what I have termed object properties (such as the property of having a determinate shape), and others not (such as the property of having a particular color). Indeed, it is plausible to hold that for a given sense modality, certain object properties have to be perceived if a perceiver is to perceive an object* in that modality. In the visual modality, for example, it seems clear that objects* will have the object property of possessing a determinate shape. In the tactile modality, objects* will have to possess the dynamic object property of resistance to touch.

With this notion of an object*, Peacocke's account of scenario and protopropositional content can be developed so as to accommodate the possibility of autonomous nonconceptual content, and in particular so as to allow us to specify how the infants discussed in the previous chapter are perceiving the world. The first component will be a specification, formulated in terms of scenario content, of how the very general contours of the environment are perceived. This will specify what colors are seen where, for example. The second component is the novel one. It uses the notion of objects* to specify how the perceived array is parsed into spatially extended and bounded segments, and then specifies the properties that those spatially extended and bounded segments are perceived as having, as well as the relations that are perceived as holding between them.

By now the form that a specification of autonomous nonconceptual content should take should be clear. The modification that I have proposed to Peacocke's theory of protopropositional content allows us to do justice to the powerful evidence that the best explanation of the behavior of infants and other nonlinguistic and prelinguistic creatures requires attributing to them states with nonconceptual content, even though they are not properly described as perceiving objects. We now have a theoretical framework in play that should overcome resistance to the idea of autonomous nonconceptual contents. The next stage is to employ this theoretical framework to avoid the paradox of self-consciousness. This project begins in the following chapter.

5

The Self of Ecological Optics

The ground is now clear for a start to be made on defusing the paradox of self-consciousness. I suggested in the last two chapters that the key to defusing the paradox lies in primitive forms of self-consciousness with nonconceptual first-person contents, and most of those chapters was taken up with establishing the legitimacy of the general notion of nonconceptual content. The next stage is to illuminate what these primitive forms of self-consciousness are and to show how the theory of nonconceptual content can be brought to bear on them. In this chapter I discuss some of the distinctive claims of the theory of ecological optics developed by J. J. Gibson, to see how they might serve as the basis for a form of primitive self-consciousness.

5.1 Self-Specifying Information in the Field of Vision

It is open to a sceptic about the possibility of nonconceptual first-person contents to concede everything said in the previous two chapters about the legitimacy of a theory of autonomous nonconceptual content while objecting in principle to the idea that there are forms of primitive self-consciousness that such a theory can help us to understand. The whole raison d'être of using the theory of nonconceptual content to explain infant understanding of object permanence is provided by the considerable experimental evidence that shows that infants are capable of parsing the visual array into bounded segments. But, a sceptic might argue, even if there is such a thing as primitive self-consciousness, it cannot be understood on these lines for the simple reason that the self is not phenomenologically salient in a way that demands to be incorporated into an account of the content of perceptual experience. The theory of nonconceptual content is a theory of what is perceived, whereas the self is not something that can be perceived—so how can there be nonconceptual first-person contents? If the self is not perceived, then how can it feature in the content of perception?

It is important to distinguish the claim at the heart of this objection from Hume's familiar claim that the self is not directly encountered in introspection. As he famously puts it in the *Treatise,*

For my part, when I enter most intimately into what I call *myself,* I always stumble on some particular perception or other, of heat or cold, light or shade, love or hatred, pain or pleasure. I never catch *myself* at any time without a perception, and can never observe anything but the perception. (Hume 1739–1740/1978, 252)

What Hume is worried about is his introspective failure to encounter the putative owner of his sensations. The sceptical worry expressed in the previous paragraph is related but importantly different. It is a worry about the contents of perception. Whereas Hume is noting that he cannot find the self in which his perceptions are supposed to inhere, the worry at stake here is about the contents of those perceptions. The self, it is being suggested, cannot appear in the content of any ordinary, outwardly directed perception (I leave aside the question of whether it can feature as the owner of such outwardly directed perceptions in the content of any inwardly directed introspective perception).

It is not to Hume that we must turn to find the view under discussion, but to Schopenhauer, and after him to Wittgenstein. Here's a passage from Schopenhauer's well-known essay "On Death and Its Relation to the Indestructibility of Our Inner Nature":

But the I or the ego is the dark point in consciousness, just as on the retina the precise point of entry of the optic nerve is blind, and the brain itself is wholly insensible, the body of the sun is dark, and the eye sees everything except itself. Our faculty of knowledge is directed entirely *outwards* in accordance with the fact that it is the product of a brain-function that has arisen for the purpose of mere self-maintenance, and hence for the search for nourishment and the seizing of prey. (Schopenhauer 1844/1966, 2: 491)

A similar theme occurs during the discussion of solipsism in Wittgenstein's *Tractatus Logico-philosophicus,* which many commentators have held to be directly inspired by Schopenhauer:

5.633   Where *in* the world is a metaphysical subject to be found?
   You will say that this is exactly like the case of the eye and the visual field. But really you do *not* see the eye.
   And nothing in the visual field allows you to infer that it is seen by an eye. (Wittgenstein 1921/1961, 57)

According to this view, the self or subject cannot appear in the content of perceptual experience, simply because the self or subject is never perceived. In Wittgenstein's useful phrase, the self does not feature in the visual field, because it is not in the world but limits it. Both Schopenhauer and Wittgenstein deployed this thought about the perceptual invisibility of the subject to rather different and idiosyncratic ends, into which there is no need to digress. For present purposes, we need only note that they provide a very clear statement of the view that the self cannot be perceived. This view is strong prima facie support for the objection that there is no place for the self in the content of perceptual experience. In the following, I will term the conjunction of the view that the self cannot be perceived with the view that there is no place for the self in the content of perceptual experience as the Schopenhauer/Wittgenstein view. Obviously, I appeal to these two writers purely for illustrative purposes. The Schopenhauer/Wittgenstein view is suggested by the passages I have quoted, but it matters little whether either of them actually held it.

   This is where the relevance of Gibson's theory of ecological optics initially emerges. It is relevant in several ways, the first of which is the crudest but also the easiest to grasp. Gibson's concept of a field of view is, I take it, more or less the same as Wittgenstein's notion of the visual field. It is the solid angle of light that the eyes can register. This is not the same as the images that appear on the two retinas, and nor is it to be understood as a melange of visual sensations. It is the panorama that reveals itself to the two eyes working together. Gibson stresses certain peculiarities of the phenomenology of the field of vision. Notable among these is the fact that the field of vision is bounded. Vision reveals only a portion of the panorama to the perceiver at any given time (roughly half in the human case, because of the frontal position of the eyes). The fact that the field of view is bounded is itself phenomenologically salient. The boundedness of the field of vision is part of what is seen, and the field of vision is bounded in a way quite unlike how spaces are bounded within the field of vision:

The edges of the field of view hide the environment behind them, as those of a window do, and when the field moves there is an accretion of optical structure at the leading edge with deletion of structure at the trailing edge, as in the cabin of a steam shovel with a wide front window and controls that enable the operator to turn the cabin to the right or the left. But the edges of the field of view are *unlike* the edges of a window inasmuch as, for the window, a *foreground* hides the background whereas, for the field of view, the *head of the observer* hides the background. (J. J. Gibson 1979, 112)

He continues, evocatively,

Ask yourself what it is that you see hiding the surroundings as you look out upon the world—not darkness surely, not air, not nothing, but the ego! (J. J. Gibson 1979, 112)

From a Gibsonian perspective, then, the Schopenhauer/Wittgenstein view misreads the data. Gibson agrees with Wittgenstein that the self is the limit of the visual field, or field of view, but he thinks that it is precisely in virtue of this that the self features in the content of perception. The self appears in perception as the boundary of the visual field, a moveable boundary that is responsive to the will.

The boundedness of the visual field is not the only way in which the self becomes manifest in visual perception, according to Gibson. The field of vision contains other objects that hide, or *occlude,* the environment. These objects are, of course, various parts of the body. The nose is a particularly obvious example, so distinctively present in just about every visual experience:

The nose is *here.* It projects the largest possible visual solid angle in the optic array. Not only that, it provides the maximum of crossed double imagery or crossed disparity in the dual array, for it is the furthest possible edge to the right in the left eye's field of view and the furthest possible edge to the left in the right eye's field of view. This also says that to look at the nose one must converge the two eyes maximally. Finally, the so-called motion parallax of the nose is an absolute maximum, which is to say that, of all the occluding edges in the world, the edge of the nose sweeps across the surfaces behind it at the greatest rate whenever the observer moves or turns his head. (J. J. Gibson 1979, 117)

The cheekbones and perhaps the eyebrows occupy a slightly less dominant position in the field of vision. And so too, to a still lesser extent, do the bodily extremities: hands, arms, feet, and legs. They protrude into the field of vision from below in a way that occludes the environment and yet differs from the way in which one nonbodily physical object in the field of vision might occlude another. They are, as Gibson points out, quite peculiar objects. All objects, bodily and nonbodily, can present a range of solid angles in the field of vision (where by a solid angle is meant an angle with its apex at the eye and its base at some perceived object), and the size of those angles will, of course, vary according to the distance of the object from the point of observation. The further away the object is, the smaller the angle will be. This gives rise to a clear and phenomenologically very salient difference between bodily and nonbodily physical objects:

The visual solid angle of the hand cannot be reduced below a certain minimum; the visual solid angle of a detached object like a ball can be made very small by throwing it. These ranges of magnification and minification between limits link up the extremes of *here* and *out there,* the body and the world, and constitute another bridge between the subjective and the objective. (J. J. Gibson 1979, 121)

Of course, the further away a particular body part is from the point of observation and the more moveable it is, the greater the range of solid angles will be. This leads Gibson to another provocative conclusion:

Information exists in the normal ambient array, therefore, to specify the nearness of the parts of the self to the point of observation—first the head, then the body, the limbs and the extremities. The experience of a central self in the head and a peripheral self in the body is not therefore a mysterious intuition or a philosophical abstraction but has a basis in optical information. (J. J. Gibson 1979, 114)

Perceived body parts are, according to Gibson, "subjective objects" in the content of visual perception.

At a crude level, then, Gibson's theory of ecological optics offers an account of the phenomenology of visual experience that denies the Schopenhauer/Wittgenstein claim that the self is not, and cannot be, perceived. Of course, no defender of the Schopenhauer/Wittgenstein view will accept the lessons that Gibson draws from the phenomenology, for obvious reasons. All Gibson's points about the boundedness of the field of vision and the peculiarities of bodily surfaces can be accepted without accepting his gloss in terms of the ego being what blocks out the unperceived hemisphere. What is clear, however, is that Gibson's account of the phenomenology of visual experience cannot be ignored. The way in which he describes the situation is accurate and important (and it is remarkable that the points he makes should have had to wait so long to come into the open). But once this is recognized the way is open for a less crude deployment of ecological optics against the Schopenhauer/Wittgenstein position.

The crucial claim in the Schopenhauer/Wittgenstein position is that because the self is not directly perceived, there is no place for the self in accounts of the content of perceptual experience. It is this inference, rather than the initial premise, that the theory of ecological optics provides us with the material to challenge. The crucial thought is that even if it is conceded, *pace* Gibson, that the self is not directly perceived, it is still the case that the self has a place in the content of perceptual experience in virtue of the self-specifying information that is an integral part of that perceptual experience. Before going into more detail here, though, a little more background about ecological optics is required.

Perhaps the most basic notion in ecological optics is the notion of a *perceptual invariant*. One of Gibson's central complaints against traditional theories of perception is that they fail to accommodate the fact that perception is an active process that involves movement and takes place over time. Whereas traditional theories have tried to understand vision by simplifying it, Gibson's starting point is not the laboratory but the real environment. What happens when an animal moves around the world? What does it see? The starting point is obvious. The animal sees a huge number of surfaces illuminated from a range of different directions. Even if there is just a single source of light, the light from that source will illuminate all the surfaces from different directions, depending on the path that the animal takes. Complicated enough at any given moment, the array of these illuminated surfaces obviously changes as the animal moves around. How can the animal make sense of this confusion of surfaces under illumination? How can a constantly changing pattern of stimulation yield constant perceptions?

Traditional empiricist theories of perception resort to constructive and serial accounts in terms of information processing and stored memories, starting from information on the retina and building up to a three-dimensional representation of the world (Marr 1982). Gibson, in contrast, thinks that the relevant information is already there in the field of vision. Gibson's approach to perception shifts the emphasis from the retinal image to the changing patterns in the *optic array* that we experience as we move around the world.[1] He stresses that the illuminated surfaces in the field of vision do not change completely at random. Consider the relatively straightforward example of moving toward a wall and looking ahead of one to the point of impact. As one approaches the wall, the array of illuminated surfaces will obviously change. But there is a certain order to the change. The part of the wall at which one is looking remains stationary, although, of course, the magnification of the solid visual angle will accelerate drastically as the wall is approached (the phenomenon of *looming*). But around the stationary part of the wall there are textured surfaces radiating outward in what Gibson terms patterns of *optic flow*. These textured surfaces expand in a lawlike manner as one approaches them (and, obviously, contract if and when they pass beyond the head). Both the immobility of the part of the wall where one will impact and the patterns of optic flow are perceptual invariants. They are higher-order patterns that remain constant during change in the field of vision brought about by the perceiver's movement, the movement of the environment, or a combination of the two. The immobility of the wall is an example of a *structural invariant*, while the changing patterns in the optic flow are *transformational invariants*. According to Gibson, it is the underlying invariant structure of the field of vision that allows perceptual order to emerge from what should, by all rights, be complete chaos.[2]

This sketchy background should be enough to allow the points relevant to the current discussion to emerge. The first point to make is that all the phenomenological points mentioned earlier can be glossed in a less provocative manner. What was formerly described as the self being directly perceived can be reinterpreted in terms of the existence of *self-specifying structural invariants* in the field of vision.[3] Whether or not it is correct straightforwardly to deny the Schopenhauer/Wittgenstein view on the basis of the ecological analysis of what is perceived, this analysis does show beyond reasonable doubt that there is self-specifying information available in the field of vision. The outline and contours of the body impose a high-order invariant structure on the field of vision, which will vary, of course, across individuals as well as across species. But this is only a fraction of the self-specifying information available in visual perception. There are two more important types of self-specifying information.

The ecological emphasis on explaining the perceptions of creatures as they move about in the world brings out the first type of self-specifying information. The very fact that motion through the environment is perceptually controlled poses a very significant problem for psychologists, as this passage brings out:

Drivers of cars see where they are going, if they pay attention. Viewers of a Cinerama screen see where they are going in the represented environment. A bee that lands on a flower must see where it is going. And all of them at the same time *see the layout of the environment through which they are going.* This is a fact with extremely radical implications for psychology, for it is difficult to understand how a train of signals coming in over the optic nerve could explain it. How could signals have two meanings at once, a subjective meaning and an objective one? How could signals yield an experience of self-movement and an experience of the external world at the same time? How could visual motion sensations get converted into a stationary environment and a moving self? (J. J. Gibson 1979, 183)

The mass of constantly changing visual information generated by the subject's motion poses an immense challenge to the perceptual systems. How can the visual experiences generated by motion be decoded so that subjects perceive that they are moving through the world? Gibson's notion of *visual kinesthesis* is his answer to this traditional problem. Whereas many theorists have assumed that motion perception can only be explained by the hypothesis of mechanisms that parse cues in the neutral sensations into information about movement and information about static objects, the crucial idea behind visual kinesthesis is that the patterns of flow in the optic array and the relations between the variant and invariant features make available information about the movement of the perceiver, as well as about the environment:

Vision is *kinesthetic* in that it registers movements of the body just as much as does the muscle-joint-skin system and the inner ear system. Vision picks up both movements of the whole body relative to the ground and movement of a member of the body relative to the whole. Visual kinesthesis goes along with muscular kinesthesis. The doctrine that vision is exteroceptive, that it obtains "external" information only, is simply false. Vision obtains information about *both* the environment and the self. (J. J. Gibson 1979, 183)

As an example of such a visually kinesthetic invariant, consider the optical flow in any field of vision when the perceiver is moving. The optical flow starts from a center, which is itself stationary. This stationary center specifies the point that is being approached. That is, the aiming point of locomotion is at the vanishing point of optical flow. In combination with the phenomenon of looming mentioned earlier, this is a powerful source of information about the direction of movement.

A good way of appreciating the significance of the claim that the movement of the perceiver is directly perceived is by distinguishing it from the common explanation of the phenomena in question in terms of feedback mechanisms. In cases of voluntary movement, the operation of *efference copy* ensures that information about the motor command to move the relevant limbs, sent to the motor center from the higher centers of the brain, is processed by the perceptual centers in the brain, and then well-known proprioceptive mechanisms provide feedback on the motor action actually being performed.[4] When further information reaches those perceptual centers indicating movement in the field of vision, the calibration of that information with the efference copy and proprioception allows those changes in (reafferent) input that are due to the perceiver's own movement to be separated out from those changes in input due to the movement of the environment. On this view, the information that the perceiver is moving is not actually present in the field of vision. Visual input just specifies movement, and the movement due to the perceiver's own movement is separated out and compensated for on the basis of nonvisual information.

The most obvious difficulty with this as a complete account of the discrimination of self-motion is that it cannot explain the perception of passive movement (when the perceiver moves but is not responsible for this movement). Striking experiments have brought out the significance of passive movement. In the so-called "moving room" experiments, subjects are placed on the solid floors of rooms whose walls and ceilings can be made to glide over a solid and immoveable floor (Lishman and Lee 1973). If experimental subjects are prevented from seeing their feet and the floor is hidden, then moving the walls backwards and forwards on the sagittal plane creates in the subjects the illusion that they are moving back and forth. This provides strong support for the thesis that the movement of the perceiver can be detected purely visually, since visual specification of movement seems to be all that is available. An even more striking illustration emerges when young children are placed in the moving room, because they actually sway and lose their balance (Lee and Aronson 1974).

Adults will not normally lose their balance in the moving-room experiments. But they do lose their balance if they are in unfamiliar postures, like standing on a beam for example. The optical flow yields the information that they (the subjects) are moving, and when they compensate for this apparent movement they fall over.

The significance of visual kinesthesis is that information specifying the movement of the perceiver is present in visual perception. This is, of course, self-specifying information, and as such it means that the self has a place in the content of visual experience. Of course, much remains to be said about how the self can feature in visual contents. Before going into this, however, I should mention that there is a further important form of self-specifying information available in the field of vision, according to the theory of ecological optics. This is due to the direct perception of a class of higher-order invariants that Gibson terms *affordances*. It is in the theory of affordances that we find the most sustained development of the ecological view that the fundamentals of perceptual experience are dictated by the organism's need to navigate and act in its environment, that the organism and the environment are complementary. The uncontroversial premise from which the theory of affordances starts is that objects and surfaces in the environment have properties that are relevant to the abilities of particular animals, that allow different animals to act and react in different ways:

If a terrestrial surface is nearly horizontal (instead of slanted), nearly flat (instead of convex or concave), and sufficiently extended (relative to the size of the animal) and if its substance is rigid (relative to the weight of the animal), then the surface *affords support*. It is a surface of support, and we call it a substratum, ground or floor. It is stand-on-able, permitting an upright position for quadrupeds and bipeds. It is therefore walk-on-able and run-over-able. It is not sink-into-able like a surface of water or a swamp, that is, not for heavy terrestrial animals. Support for water bugs is different. (J. J. Gibson 1979, 127)

This much is indisputable. The bold and interesting claim that Gibson then goes on to develop is that affordances like these can be directly perceived. Information specifying affordances is available in the structure of light to be picked up by the creature as it moves around in the world. The possibilities that the environment affords are not learned through experience, nor are they inferred. They are directly perceived as higher-order invariants. And, of course, the perception of affordances is a form of self-perception, or at least a way in which self-specifying information is perceived. The whole notion of an affordance is that of environmental information about one's own possibilities for action and reaction.

An important point to bear in mind is that affordances are properties that objects and surfaces have relative to the organisms that perceive them, or at least could perceive them; they are not properties of the perceiving organisms.[5] They are to be sharply distinguished from what psychologists often refer to as *valences,* the subjective properties of pleasure and pain that can come to be associated with supposedly neutral perceptions of objects and surfaces. According to the ecological theory, there are no such neutral perceptions. The meanings and values that objects and surfaces have for perceivers are directly perceived, not learned by association. This emerges particularly clearly in the striking visual-cliff experiments carried out by Eleanor Gibson with a range of collaborators (E. J. Gibson 1969).

The visual-cliff experiments were done with a glass floor strong enough to support the weight of the animals and young infants placed on it. One half of the glass floor was backed with an opaque surface, so that it could not be seen through. A similar opaque surface was placed some distance below the other half of the glass floor. Thus a clifflike effect was created, with a sharp divide between a "shallow" half and a "deep" half. A range of animals were placed on the glass floor (including infant rats and snow-leopard cubs). They all showed a preference for the shallow side over the deep side. Infants and young children were also placed in the experimental situation. When young children capable of walking or crawling were placed on the glass floor, they crawled and walked normally when on the shallow side, but froze and showed distress on the deep side. When very young infants of 6 weeks or so were placed on the floor, their cardiac responses showed that they too were distressed.

The crucial point about the visual-cliff experiments is that visual information conflicts with haptic information (from the sense of touch). The animals and infants are in contact with a surface of support, whether they are on the shallow side or the deep side of the visual cliff. Wherever they are on the glass floor, the haptic information tells them that they are on a surface that will bear their weight. As far as vision is concerned, however, this information exists only when they are on the shallow side. On the deep side the visual information is that the supporting surface is far below them (just as if one were on a glass-bottomed balcony on the side of a precipice). The distress behavior manifested in the experimental situation shows that the visual information dominates over the haptic information. The conclusion that Eleanor Gibson and her coworkers drew from this is that the capacity to perceive depth is innate. They reasoned that what causes the distress is the visual perception of depth together with a fear of heights.[6] James Gibson, in contrast, has an explanation in terms of affordances:

But the sight of a cliff is *not* a case of perceiving the third dimension. One perceives the affordance of its edge. A cliff is a feature of the terrain, a highly significant, special kind of dihedral angle in ecological geometry, a falling-off place. The edge at the top of the cliff is dangerous. It is an occluding edge. But it has the special character of being an edge of the surface of support, unlike the edge of a wall. One can safely walk around the edge of a wall but not off the edge of a cliff. To perceive a cliff is to detect a layout but, more than that, it is to detect an *affordance,* a negative affordance for locomotion, a place where the surface of support ends. (J. J. Gibson 1979, 157)

It is not that the infants and animals perceive depth and then are driven to distress behavior by their fear of heights. Rather, they show distress because they directly perceive that they are in an environment that affords falling.

On the basis of Gibson's theory of ecological optics, then, we can identify the following three different types of self-specifying information in visual experience:

• Information about bodily invariants that bound the field of vision
• Information from visual kinesthesis about the movement of the perceiver
• Information about the possibilities for action and reaction that the environment affords the perceiver

Putting these three types of self-specifying information together provides a powerful counterbalance to the view that perceptual experience provides information only about the external world. Instead, we find that information about the ambient environment is inextricably combined with self-specifying information, without which the former would be of little use. This duality of exteroceptive and proprioceptive information in perceptual experience is at the core of the theory of nonconceptual first-person contents.

5.2   The Content of Ecological Perception

It would be natural at this stage in the argument to suggest that the insights of ecological optics into the phenomenology of perception show
that perceptual experience is itself a source of nonconceptual first-person
contents. Subject to certain qualifications, I think that this is correct. This
section explains why and explores some of the qualifications.

The self-specifying information that ecological optics discerns in perceptual experience is clearly available to a wide range of creatures, as well
as to humans from the earliest days of infancy.[7] There is no question that
concepts are required to pick up this self-specifying information. Here we
are clearly in the realm of autonomous nonconceptual content, if we are
in a realm of content at all. In chapters 3 and 4, I noted that there are
considerable difficulties in attributing states with autonomous nonconceptual content to non-language-using creatures, and I pointed out certain general constraints on such attributions. It is from these constraints
that we must start.

States with representational content are intermediaries between sensory input and behavioral output that are (theoretically) required to explain how behavioral output emerges on the basis of sensory input. The
theoretical requirement to deploy states with content emerges only when
the connections between sensory input and behavioural output are not
invariant. As was discussed above, states with autonomous nonconceptual content play a role in intentional explanation, and intentional explanations are teleological. This means that they explain behavior in terms
of a conjunction of representational states and motivational states. Now
there is no reason to think that all creatures whose perceptual systems can
be correctly described as picking up self-specifying information behave in
ways that can only be explained intentionally in this way. Quite the contrary. The relevant self-specifying information can be deployed in the sort
of conditioned behavior that is entirely explicable by stimulus-response
psychology. By the same token, there is no absurdity in describing tropistic behavior, like that of the Sphex wasp, as guided by self-specifying invariants and visual kinesthesis in the wasp's limited field of vision. Only
a small subset of creatures sensitive to self-specifying information in the
field of vision behave intentionally. Picking out the members of that small

subset is an experimental task, to be achieved by determining whether their behavior can be explained nonintentionally. If it can be explained nonintentionally, then obviously the parsimonious nonintentional explanation should be adopted. But if nonintentional explanation is impossible, then inference to the best explanation drives us to an intentional explanation. It is only here that the issue of nonconceptual first-person contents arises. This is the first constraint. Perceptual experience cannot be a source of nonconceptual first-person contents if the behavior of the creature in question can be explained in a nonintentional manner. But how does the coperception of self and environment in perceptual experience contribute to intentional explanations of behavior in instances where such explanation is required?

The need for intentional explanation arises in the absence of lawlike correlations between environmental stimulus and behavioural response—when, for example, the response occurs in the absence of the stimulus. This, in turn, is connected with the possibility of misperception: of perceiving things as being where they are not, or of perceiving something that is there as having properties that it does not have. Instances of misperception like these are what make it impossible to formulate lawlike correlations between environmental stimulus and behavioral response, because misperception generates behavioral responses that cannot be predicted from the layout of the environment. Part of the significance of the ecological analysis of perception is that it makes comprehensible both how such misperception can occur and how it can directly feed into action. A possible example is provided by the moving-room experiments discussed in the previous section. The movement of the room creates deceptive visual-kinesthetic information. Subjects misperceive the movement of the room relative to them as their own movement relative to the room, and they behave accordingly (most spectacularly in the case of the young children who fall over). The visual cliff is another potential case in point. The misperception of an affordance generates distress behavior that is not a function of the presence of any real danger. As Gibson puts the point, "If information is picked up perception results; if misinformation is picked up misperception results" (1979, 142).[8]

There is a broader point to be extracted here. The direct perception of visual kinesthesis and affordances has immediate salience for the launching and control of action. The optical information for visual kinesthesis specifies the perceiver's movement relative to the environment. It specifies the imminence of collisions and the consequences of maintaining a particular trajectory. This obviously has immediate implications for how the perceiver behaves—whether he modifies or maintains his trajectory, for example. The situation is even clearer with the perception of affordances. Perceiving an affordance just is perceiving the possible actions and reactions that the environment affords. This immediate salience of perception for action is at the core of ecological optics. And this leads us to the idea that when we are dealing with behavior that supports an intentional explanation, perception is a source of nonconceptual first-person contents. An analogy with indexical beliefs will illustrate the point. It is widely held that indexical beliefs are required to explain why an individual behaves as he does.[9] Among those indexical beliefs, beliefs with first-person contents are particularly important. The thought is that we will not be able to explain why an individual behaves as he does unless we understand the beliefs that support and drive his behavior, and that we can explain why those beliefs support and drive his behavior only if they are beliefs about himself and his possible courses of action. The first person is, in Perry's famous phrase, an essential indexical. It is essential, he argues, in order to capture the immediate salience of an agent's beliefs to what he actually does.

Of course, indexical beliefs in Perry's sense occur at the level of conceptual content. They are available only to thinkers who have attained a sophisticated mastery of concepts, including mastery of the concept of the first-person. But Perry's central point can be carried over to the level of nonconceptual content. The salience of an agent's beliefs to what he actually does, which, according to Perry, requires the thinking of first-person thoughts, is directly parallel to the salience of perception to action that is highlighted in the ecological theory of perception. A vital part of what it is to describe a belief as a first-person belief is that the belief makes a given action immediately comprehensible (as my fleeing becomes immediately comprehensible in light of my belief that a bear is about to attack me, to continue with Perry's familiar example). This is directly applicable to the perceptual case. Perception is directly salient to action in virtue of the self-specifying information that is coperceived with information about the environment, and this is what makes it appropriate to describe the content of perception as a first-person content. Perceptual contents are first-person contents in virtue of their immediate connections with behavior. The conclusion to draw, then, is that in cases where the behavior of non-language-using creatures demands an intentional explanation, such explanations can draw on first-person perceptual contents just as explanations of the behavior of more conceptually sophisticated creatures can draw on first-person beliefs.

It might well be asked how perceptual contents can play a part in intentional explanation at the nonconceptual level, since intentional explanation is generally understood to proceed in terms of beliefs and desires, which are, of course, propositional attitudes with paradigmatically conceptual content. Let me first introduce terms for the analogues of beliefs and desires at the level of nonconceptual content.[10] I will call these *proto-beliefs* and *protodesires,* to avoid the conceptual implications of the notions of belief and desire. I take it that the possibility of nonconceptual protodesires is relatively uncontroversial. I have not encountered any defenders of the view that all motivational states must be conceptual. The possibility of protobeliefs is more controversial, however.

Let me start by recalling that protobeliefs fall into two broad classes: perceptual protobeliefs and instrumental protobeliefs. A perceptual protobelief is a representation of the layout of the immediate environment. An instrumental protobelief has to do with how a particular protodesire might be satisfied in a given situation. I briefly suggested in chapter 3 that these two types of belief can be combined in a single perception. Gibson's notion of an affordance provides an excellent illustration of this. To say that affordances are directly perceived is precisely to say that instrumental relations can feature in the content of perception, or alternatively, that a single protobelief can be both perceptual and instrumental. Nonetheless, this unity is not necessary. Instrumental and perceptual protobeliefs can be separated at the nonconceptual level.

Perceptual protobeliefs are canonically present-tense (which is, of course, equivalent to saying that they are not tensed at all). They have to do with here-and-now features of the occurrent environment. The most basic form of instrumental protobeliefs are either to be understood on the model of Gibsonian affordances or to be modeled as expectations about possible outcomes.[11] These may be hard-wired, or they may be acquired through some form of exposure to the phenomena in question (and thus may be the result of conditioning). One important feature distinguishing both perceptual and instrumental protobeliefs from their conceptual analogues is that there is no distinction at the nonconceptual level between entertaining a protobelief content and holding it to be true. The ability to entertain a representational state without assenting to it is a high-level cognitive ability. It is associated with, inter alia, the capacity for deliberation and what is often termed practical reasoning. These are not, I take it, operative at the nonconceptual level. Of course, a creature may have more than one instrumental protobelief in a situation in which he can only act on one of them. But to say that he can only act on one of them is not to say that he can decide which of them he is going to act on. It is natural to assume that the weighting of instrumental protobeliefs is determined by, among other things, the comparative strengths of the relevant motivational states.

There is a delicate balance to be struck in positing protobeliefs as explanatory tools at the nonconceptual level. If the differences between protobeliefs and conceptual beliefs are stressed, then one can raise the question of how two such dissimilar states can play comparable roles in the explanation of behavior. On the other hand, assimilating protobeliefs and conceptual beliefs leaves one open to the objection that crucial differences are being overlooked. On the plus side, protobeliefs and conceptual beliefs are thus far comparable in that they both satisfy the four criteria for genuinely representational states offered in chapter 3. On the debit side, some crucial differences have just been mentioned. There is one important issue that has not yet been touched upon, however.

It is as unanimously agreed among philosophers as anything is that intentional mental states are nonextensional, where this means that in specifying the contents of an intentional mental state, coreferential terms cannot always be substituted *salva veritate* (without changing the truth value of the content ascription). The nonextensionality of mental states is connected to the fact that they involve thinking about objects under particular modes of presentation. Thought about an object is not about that object *tout court,* but rather about that object as grasped or conceived in a certain way. The question, then, is whether the states that I am describing as protobeliefs can exhibit anything analogous to this property of nonextensionality.

It has seemed obvious to some philosophers, even those most sympathetic to the idea that a form of cognition can exist in the absence of language, that thinking about objects under particular modes of presentation is only available to language-using creatures. Consider the following passage from Charles Taylor:

> Now it is a feature of our language that, in applying a description to something, in picking something out under a concept, we are picking out something to which other descriptions also apply, which falls under other concepts as well. . . . Thus for language users the expression 'thinking of something *as* an *X*' has a specific force, for of these it is true that they could also think of (what they recognize as) the same thing under some other description. . . . But for an animal, thinking of or fearing something "as a so-and-so" cannot be given this sense. For of an animal we could never say that he was conscious of this same thing (that is, what to him is the same thing) under two different descriptions, either at one time or on different occasions. . . . This means that the only type of consciousness of the objects around them that we can attribute to animals is a consciousness of their immediate relevance to their behaviour. The red object is something to fly from, the meat something to be eaten, and so on, but the animal is not aware of the object *as* something he must fly from, or of the meat as something to be eaten. (Taylor 1964, 67–68)

Taylor's reasoning here seems clear. Thinking of an object under a nonextensional mode of presentation is, he claims, equivalent to thinking of it under a particular description. And thinking of an object under a particular description is only available to language users, because descriptions are linguistic phenomena. This leaves Taylor with only a restricted sense in which the cognition of animals and infants is cognition at all. According to Taylor, an animal "is not aware of the object as something he must fly from." What happens, presumably, is that the animal perceptually registers the object in a way that triggers a certain reaction. On Taylor's view, it is the type of action or reaction triggered that determines whether we are dealing with behavior that requires intentional explanation or not. It is the directedness of actions that renders them appropriate for intentional rather than mechanical explanation. He explains his position:

> In short, we have at least *prima facie* grounds for classing them as agents. . . . That is to say, we want to class them as beings who direct their behaviour, such that attributing a given direction to a given segment of an animal's behaviour is

not simply saying that this segment has a certain end-product, or that it is to be explained by certain laws, but rather that, whatever the explanation, and whether it achieves its end or not, it is given this direction by the animal. (Taylor 1964, 67)

So if an animal perceptually registers an object and acts in a manner that it is appropriate to describe as fleeing from the object, then it is engaging in behaviour that needs to be explained intentionally. Thus does Taylor explain the possibility of intentional behavior even in creatures incapable of thinking about objects under particular modes of presentation.

This compromise position has its difficulties, however. If behavior of this type really is to be significantly analogous to the intentional behavior of language-using human beings, then it must render the creature's behavior comprehensible as a response to its perceptually registering the object that triggered the appropriate response. The explanation will be of the form 'The animal fled because it perceptually registered that object'. But for this explanation to be informative, it must also explain why perceptually registering *that* object should make fleeing an appropriate response. It must explain why the perception generates the response of fleeing. This cannot be done, however, if what the animal perceives (the content of the animal's perception of the object) does not include the object as something potentially dangerous. Without this, there will be no (intentional) explanation of why the animal flees from the object, rather than approaching or ignoring it. But the problem, of course, is that this is impossible if, as Taylor maintains, the animal "is not aware of the object as something he must fly from," simply because to be aware of an object as something dangerous is to be aware of it under a nonextensional mode of presentation.

So if Taylor is right and the cognitive repertoire of non-language-users does not include something analogous to the capacity to think of objects under nonextensional modes of presentation, then the possibility of giving satisfactory intentional explanations of their actions seems to be severely compromised. This would be a very unwelcome conclusion. Fortunately, though, taking seriously the ecological account of perception provides a way of making sense of the idea that non-language-using creatures are capable of thinking about objects under nonextensional modes of presentation. The concept of an affordance is, of course, the key. The central idea at work in analyzing perception in terms of affordances is that the environment is not perceived in neutral terms. What are perceived are the possibilities that the environment affords for action and reaction. These include, of course, the potential of various locations for providing shelter, concealment, or nourishment. And, of course, the fact that a particular place is perceived as affording shelter explains why an animal will seek shelter there. The animal does not perceive a place neutrally and then seek shelter there. What the animal perceives is a possibility of shelter, and it acts accordingly. The visual cliff offers a dramatic example, as do the more day-to-day examples of affordances that emerge from visual kinesthetics, such as looming.

The perception of affordances, therefore, provides a way in which we can understand how perceptual protobeliefs can have an analogue of the property of nonextensionality. Perceptual protobeliefs are not neutral. They involve perceiving objects under modes of presentation, where these modes of presentation are given by the possibilities for action and reaction that those objects afford. This analogue of nonextensionality can be pressed even further. We can, for example, make perfectly good sense of two or more perceptual protobeliefs being about the same object under different modes of presentation. An object can present different affordances, depending on the angle from which it is approached and perceived. As an animal moves around the object, its perceptual protobeliefs will change accordingly. The same object can also be perceived on different occasions under different modes of presentation. Suppose that an animal catches sight of a predator. The predator is perceived, of course, as affording danger, and the animal responds appropriately by fleeing. Suppose that some time later the animal encounters the same predator, only this time the predator is lying dead. Now the predator is perceived as affording nourishment, and the animal feeds accordingly. Here we have two different affordances, which yield two different modes of presentation, and the difference between the modes of presentation is what explains the difference in behavior.

To draw the strands of this section together, what we learn from Gibson's ecological approach to perception is that perceptual experience is itself a source of nonconceptual first-person contents. These nonconceptual first-person contents are crucial to the intentional explanation of the behavior of non-language-using creatures. Such intentional explanation proceeds in terms of protodesires and protobeliefs, and the protobeliefs have nonconceptual first-person contents derived from perception that render them immediately salient to the perceiver's behavior. These proto-beliefs with nonconceptual first-person contents have properties importantly analogous to the nonextensionality of the mental states of language-using creatures, particularly the property of involving objects under particular modes of presentation.

5.3   The Ecological Self in Infancy

It will be remembered from chapter 1 that part of the paradox of self-consciousness is how to explain how young children can bootstrap themselves into self-conscious thought. If self-consciousness is understood in terms of the capacity for first-person thoughts involving reflexive self-reference and yet the capacity for reflexive self-reference presupposes the capacity to think first-person thoughts, then we are confronted with a circle of interlocking concepts. This seems to breach certain plausible constraints on the acquisition of cognitive abilities. If the interdependence of reflexive self-reference and first-person thought is complete, it follows that there are no more-basic cognitive abilities in terms of which self-consciousness can be explained, and hence that there are no more-basic cognitive abilities from which self-consciousness can emerge in the normal course of cognitive development. The acquisition of self-consciousness then becomes a complete mystery. Self-consciousness depends upon the capacity to take a first-person perspective (to think first-person thoughts), but we have no understanding of how entry into that first-person perspective is possible.

The discussion of ecological optics in this chapter presents us with the possibility of a radically new perspective on the problem. When perception is understood in ecological terms, and subject to the constraints already discussed, perception itself is a source of first-person contents. These first-person contents are autonomous nonconceptual contents, in the sense discussed in chapter 3, and as such are available to young infants as well as to animals. This opens up the following possibility. If it can be shown that these nonconceptual first-person contents are available more or less from the start of life, then the whole problem of how entry into the first-person perspective is possible fails to arise. If very young infants are capable of entertaining perceptual states with nonconceptual first-person contents, then they are already in the first-person perspective, and the apparent paradoxicality of trying to explain how a creature can acquire the capacity for first-person thought without already possessing that capacity disappears (although, of course, there will remain questions regarding the transition to the conceptual level).

Of course, this is a stage in the argument at which empirical work must come to the fore, because the question now arises of whether there is evidence to support the proposal that nonconceptual first-person contents are available from more or less the beginning of life. Fortunately, a considerable amount of work has been done by developmental psychologists inspired by Gibson's theories of perception. Some workers in the field have found the evidence so convincing that they have introduced the term 'ecological self' to capture how self-specifying information is picked up from the beginning of life. Consider the following passage from an important paper by Ulric Neisser:

The information that specifies the ecological self is omnipresent, and babies are not slow to pick it up. They respond to looming and optical flow from a very early age, discriminate among objects, and easily distinguish the immediate consequences of their own actions from events of other kinds. The old hypothesis that a young infant cannot tell the difference between itself and its environment, or between itself and its mother, can be decisively rejected. The ecological self is present from the first. (1988, 40)[12]

What Neisser and others mean by 'ecological self' is not quite the same as what I have been discussing as nonconceptual first-person contents, but it is sufficiently close that the evidence adduced to support theories of the ecological self also supports the thesis that nonconceptual first-person contents can be present from the beginning of life. In this section I briefly review some of the important developmental evidence for this conclusion.[13]

Neonatal distress crying

There is strong experimental evidence suggesting that infants have an innate tendency to cry in response to the crying of other infants at more or less the same age (Simner 1971). When Martin and Clark (1982) replicated some of these experiments using infants with a mean age of 18.3 hours, they noticed by chance that five crying male infants stopped crying when they heard a recording of themselves crying. To investigate this more systematically, they tested 47 infants within a day after birth. Both calm and already crying babies were played tape recordings either of themselves crying or of another newborn baby crying, and then the total amount of crying over a 4-minute period was measured. The experimenters found that infants who were calm when the test began cried significantly more when they heard another infant crying than when they heard themselves crying, while infants who were already crying cried less after hearing themselves cry than after hearing another infant crying.

Here we seem to have a clear case of self-perception in newborn infants. The infants can discriminate their own crying from the crying of other infants of the same age. What is particularly interesting is that the sense of hearing is the relevant modality. Although most of the discussion of self-specifying invariants in perception has focused on vision, these experiments suggest that auditory information is equally self-specifying.

Neonatal imitation

On the traditional view of cognitive development, associated with Jean Piaget, the capacity for facial imitation is a high-level cognitive ability, occurring only towards the end of the second year. What makes facial imitation so important is the fact that awareness of the behavior to be imitated and the awareness of the imitating behavior occur in different sensory modalities. Facial imitation involves matching a seen gesture with an unseen gesture, since in normal circumstances one is aware of one's own face only haptically or proprioceptively. If successful facial imitation is to take place, a visual awareness of someone else's face must be apprehended so that it can be reproduced on one's own face.[14]

Meltzoff and Moore (1977) found that infants between 12 and 21 days old could successfully imitate three distinct facial acts (lip protrusion, mouth opening, and tongue protrusion) and one manual act (sequential finger movement). The infants were prevented by a dummy placed in their mouths from responding before the model gesture was complete. The dummy was then removed and the infants were videoed close up. Independent judges then decided what gestures the infants were trying to make. The judges did this without knowing what model gestures the infants were responding to. The results of the experiment seemed clearly to show that imitation behavior was going on here. Meltzoff and Moore (1983) then looked for evidence of imitation capabilities in infants just after birth. Here too they were successful. The average age of the infants was 32 hours, with the youngest infant only 42 minutes old. Two gestures were employed (mouth opening and tongue protrusion) and once again the scorer was looking at videotapes of the infants without any information about the gesture the experimenter had made. Here too the evidence was clearly in support of imitation. These results have been interestingly replicated and extended by T. M. Field and his coworkers (1982), who found that newborn infants, 2 days old, could consistently imitate the facial expressions of an adult model when that model either smiled, frowned, or displayed an expression of surprise.

There are very good reasons to think neonatal imitation behavior needs to be explained in intentional terms. In the first place, the behavior involves memory and representations. As mentioned earlier, the infants had a dummy placed in their mouths to prevent them from responding before the experimenter had completed the model gesture. By the time the infants are in a position to imitate the gesture, the experimenter has reverted to his normal facial expression. Clearly, then, there must be some sort of stored representation of the model gesture, and this stored representation triggers the imitation response in a way that seems incompatible with many accounts of the functioning of innate reflexes and innate releasing mechanisms. Furthermore, the infants correct their response over time until their own gesture has homed in on the model gesture. Such a trial-and-error approach is not characteristic of reflex behavior.

What is most striking about neonatal imitation behavior, though, is the richness of self-specifying information that it implicates in the perceptual experience of infants just after birth. The infants are perceiving the experimenter as a being just like themselves, not only as structurally similar but also as capable of behaving in similar ways. It is not simply a case of grasping the intermodal equivalence of, say, a perceived tongue protrusion and their own act of protruding their tongue, because they also have to grasp that the perceived tongue protrusion is *the sort of thing that they can imitate,* as opposed, for example, to the movement of a nipple, to which they respond by sucking rather than by trying to imitate it. The point can be put in more straightforwardly Gibsonian terms by saying that when these infants perceive the face of the experimenter, they perceive their own possibilities for acting as the experimenter is acting. They perceive a set of affordances, but these are no ordinary affordances, because they reveal to the infants information not only about how they can behave but also about their physical makeup.

Infants' reaching behavior
It is not only the complicated affordances revealed in the perceptions driving neonatal imitation behavior that involve self-specifying information. Perceptions of even the most basic affordances involve self-specifying information. Reaching behavior is a case in point. Reaching behavior is driven by the perception that an object is within reach (by the perception that the object affords reaching), and this is, of course, a form of self-specifying information. It is interesting, therefore, that the capacity for fairly accurate perception of whether or not objects are within reach appears early on in infancy, particularly since infants' reaching distance is in a constant state of flux, because of not only their rapid growth but also rapid changes in their motor capacities. An interesting illustration comes from experiments performed by Jeffrey Field (1976). He found that the reaching behavior of 15-week-old infants is adjusted to the physical distance separating them from the object, as measured by the reduction in the probability of their making relevant movements as their distance from the object increased. Earlier work by T. G. R. Bower (1972) suggested that this adjustment is in place as early as two weeks. He found that when an object is placed out of all possible reach, there is a marked reduction in the frequency with which infants extend their arms toward it.

Reaching behavior is a good index of how infants perceive affordances. Also relevant in this context are the catching skills of very young infants. Even newborn infants try to intercept objects that are moving past them and within reach, and the experimental evidence shows that babies are capable of adapting the speed of their reach to the speed of the moving object (Von Hofsten 1982). Here we are dealing with behavior that involves reaching toward objects in motion, rather than at rest, but it is appropriate to describe what is going on in similar terms. Infants are perceiving the affordance of reachability in a way that has immediate implications for their behavior.

Visual kinesthesis in prelocomotive infants

Visual kinesthesis is an important instance of the pick-up of self-specifying information, and there is a range of experimental evidence suggesting that the capacity to pick up this type of information is present very early on in infancy. Looming is a case in point, and much work has been done on how young infants react in moving-room situations, where information from the optic flow specifies the imminence of a nonexistent collision. The original work was done in babies who were already able to walk, and as I mentioned in the previous section, the babies fell over when they tried to compensate for what they registered as a loss of balance (Lee and Aronson 1974). When these experiments were extended to infants who could crawl but were unable to walk or stand, compensatory movements were also observed (Butterworth and Hicks 1977). The same was found in completely prelocomotive infants from the age of 8 weeks (Pope 1984). In prelocomotive infants the compensatory movements were head movements—the infants were seated in a baby seat and their head movements were measured in relation to the movements of their surroundings.[15]

5.4   Moving beyond Perception

The conclusion to be drawn from the experimental evidence briefly discussed in the previous section is that nonconceptual first-person contents are available from the beginning of life. This has extremely interesting implications for one of the strands in the paradox of self-consciousness. If perception itself can be a source of nonconceptual first-person contents by supplying self-specifying information, and if the pick-up of self-specifying information starts at the very beginning of life, then there ceases to be so much of a problem about how entry into the first-person perspective is achieved. In a very important sense, infants are born into the first-person perspective. It is not something that they have to acquire ab initio. Of course, the first-person perspective that infants have at birth is extremely limited. The range of self-specifying information that they are capable of picking up is tiny in comparison with that of older children and adults. But it is there all the same and provides a foundation on which a greater sensitivity to different types of self-specifying information can be built as the perception of simple affordances grows into the perception of more complex ones and awareness of visual kinesthesis becomes more subtle and differentiated.

Of course, this is still only the very beginnings of a solution. I have identified a class of primitive first-person contents. These contents are primitive both conceptually and ontogenetically. There are no more-primitive types of first-person content in terms of which the first-person contents of perceptual experience can be understood.[16] Nor are there any contents that are ontogenetically more primitive. But this still leaves us with the theoretical task of explaining how this fits into a fully articulated theory of self-consciousness. What is required is an account of how these primitive forms of first-person content are built up into full-fledged self-consciousness. In giving such an account, I will need to be sensitive to the factual dimension—to the actual developmental progression by which children acquire the capacity for different forms of first-person thought. Clearly, though, it is no use thinking that a properly articulated theory of self-consciousness can be gained by simply describing the developmental progression from first-person perceptual contents to full-fledged first-person thought. A properly articulated theory of self-consciousness is required to give the conceptual framework for any such description. Nonetheless, developmental considerations do circumscribe the form that such an account will take, in virtue of the Acquisition Constraint, as formulated in chapter 1. A theory of self-consciousness that starts with the primitive first-person contents that can exist in perceptual states must conform to the Acquisition Constraint. It must show how full-fledged self-consciousness can be constructed from such primitive first-person contents in a way that makes it comprehensible how each increasingly developed form of self-consciousness can emerge ontogenetically from its predecessors. Before embarking on that project, however, I need to draw attention to a further class of primitive first-person contents, and I will discuss such contents in the next chapter.

6

Somatic Proprioception and the Bodily Self

The picture that emerged from the previous chapter is of a form of primitive self-consciousness operative in the very structure of perception. Gibson's analysis of the pick-up of information about the self through the interplay of self-specifying and other-specifying invariants provides evidence for a primitive form of self-consciousness implicated in the basic mechanisms of perception and action from the earliest days in infancy onward. The self that is thus perceived (what some psychologists have called the *ecological self*) is an embodied self. Most of the self-specifying information implicated in ecological perception is information about the body: the disposition of bodily parts and their movement. But it is not only through ecological perception that information is acquired about the embodied self. Gibson's great insight was that vision (and the other exteroceptive sense modalities) are only "windows onto the world" to the extent that they provide relational information about the perceiver's position, movement, and other bodily properties. But there are other sources of such information. The highly complex *somatic proprioceptive system* provides even more fine-grained and detailed information about the perceiver's position, movement, limb disposition, and other bodily properties.

No less than visual perception, somatic proprioception is a form of experience with nonconceptual first-person contents. Like the self-specifying information in ecological perception, somatic proprioception is a form of primitive self-consciousness. Also like the self-specifying information in ecological perception, somatic proprioception of the embodied self is available from birth (and indeed before). These two forms of primitive self-consciousness are the foundations for the higher levels of self-consciousness that will be discussed later on in this book. They are the building-blocks for the bootstrapping process that will eventually result in mastery of the first-person concept and the capacity for full-fledged self-consciousness.

The significance of somatic proprioception for the analysis of self-consciousness has not been properly recognized by philosophers. There are several reasons for this. The first is that philosophers have tended to operate with a narrow and restrictive conception of somatic proprioception (but see the essays in Bermúdez, Marcel, and Eilan 1995). This restrictive conception of somatic proprioception is partly responsible for an unwillingness among philosophers to consider somatic proprioception as a perceptual modality. But an important role has also been played by philosophical arguments purporting to show that somatic proprioception cannot be a form of perception. In this chapter I will attempt to lay these conceptions to rest. I will develop an account of somatic proprioception on which it qualifies as a form of perception whose object is the embodied self. Section 6.3 explains why somatic proprioception is a form of perception with the embodied self as its object, and section 6.4 outlines the criteria on which this qualifies as a form of self-consciousness. In section 6.5, I offer an account of the content of somatic proprioception that explains in more detail the form of consciousness of the self that is implicated in somatic proprioception. The first step, though, is to get clear on the phenomena under discussion.

6.1   The Modes of Somatic Proprioception

Somatic proprioception is not a simple or unitary phenomenon.[1] The best place to begin is by considering some of the internal information systems involved. The general introduction to Bermúdez, Marcel, and Eilan 1995 offers the following as some of the principal types of information deployed in somatic proprioception and an indication of their physiological sources:

• Information about pressure, temperature, and friction from receptors on the skin and beneath its surface
• Information about the relation of body segments from receptors in the joints, some sensitive to static position, some to movement

• Information about balance and posture from the vestibular system in the inner ear and the head/trunk dispositional system and information from pressure on any parts of the body that might be in contact with a gravity-resisting surface

• Information about bodily disposition and volume obtained from skin stretch

• Information about nutrition and other homeostatic states from receptors in the internal organs

• Information about muscular fatigue from receptors in the muscles

• Information about general fatigue from cerebral systems sensitive to blood composition

• Information about bodily disturbances derived from nociceptors

These *somatic information systems* vary along several dimensions. First, they vary according to whether the information they provide is information *solely* about the body (e.g., the systems providing information about general fatigue and nutrition), as opposed to information about the relation between the body and the environment (e.g., the vestibular system, which is concerned with bodily balance). Other systems can be deployed to yield information either about the body or about the environment. Receptors in the hand sensitive to skin stretch, for example, can provide information about the hand's shape and disposition at a given time or about the shape of small objects. Similarly, receptors in joints and muscles can yield information about how the relevant limbs are distributed in space or, through haptic exploration, about the contours and shape of large objects.

Second, not every system yields information that is consciously registered. Most information about balance and limb position, for example, feeds directly into the control of posture. There are also significant differences in how different types of information come to consciousness. It is important to distinguish two different types of conscious somatic proprioception (*mediate* somatic proprioception and *immediate* somatic proprioception), distinguished according to the role played by bodily sensation. The experience of pain is a paradigm example of mediate somatic proprioception, because the sensation of pain is a constitutive part of the experience. Pain is something we *feel*, as are itches, tickles, and so forth. But this cannot be the model for conscious somatic proprioception in general. There are ways of finding out about our bodily posture and movements that count as instances of somatic proprioception (because they are derived from somatic information systems) and yet that are not based on sensations. The systems involved tend to be discussed by psychologists as joint-position sense and kinesthetic awareness respectively. Joint-position sense is the awareness that we have of how our body parts are distributed in space and relative to each other. Kinesthetic awareness is the awareness of limb movement.

There are at least two compelling reasons for denying that kinesthetic awareness and joint-position sense provide a mediate sensation-based awareness of limb position and movement.[2] That sensations are not necessary is shown by the many occasions when we are capable of reporting on limb position and movement without being able to identify any sensations yielding the awareness on which such reports are based. That sensations are not sufficient emerges when one reflects that bodily sensations are rarely of sufficiently fine a grain to yield the relatively precise awareness we have of posture and movement, let alone the extremely precise awareness required to maintain balance and control action. Bodily sensations— pain is again a paradigm example—are rough indicators of large-scale events in the body, too rough to provide a detailed awareness of posture and movement.

The classification that emerges from these distinctions is as follows. Somatic proprioception must be understood in terms of the operations of internal somatic-information systems. Some of these information systems operate completely below the threshold of conscious awareness. Other information systems do yield information that is consciously registered. Of this second category, some information systems operate through the medium of bodily sensations, such as pain, hunger, and fatigue. These are instances of mediate somatic proprioception. They contrast with immediate somatic proprioception, where bodily sensations are at best concomitant (if present at all). The paradigm examples of immediate somatic proprioception are kinaesthetic awareness and joint-position sense.

6.2   Somatic Proprioception and the Simple Argument

Despite the range of different phenomena that come under the heading of somatic proprioception, there is a relatively simple argument showing the direct relevance of an important class of the different modes of somatic proprioception to philosophical accounts of self-consciousness. The class in question is, of course, the class of conscious modes of somatic proprioception and the argument is as follows:

1. The self is embodied. [Premise]
2. Somatic proprioception provides perceptions of bodily properties.[3] [Premise]
3. Somatic proprioception is a form of self-perception.
4. Therefore, somatic proprioception is a form of self-consciousness.

I shall call this the *simple argument*. I am simply assuming premise (1) of the simple argument. It is something that only a dualist would deny. The parts of the simple argument that require more discussion are premise (2) and the conclusion (4). Clearly, if somatic proprioception is a form of perception, then it will provide perceptions of bodily properties. What might not appear so obvious, however, is that somatic proprioception counts as a form of perception at all. In the next section I explain how somatic proprioception satisfies a plausible and stringent set of constraints for anything to count as an instance of perception, thereby establishing the truth of (2). It will be apparent that (3) follows from (2) in at least the following sense: proprioception counts as self-perception because it involves the perception of properties that are in fact properties of one's self. The real question, of course, is whether proprioception qualifies as an instance of self-perception in any sense sufficiently rich to count as a form of self-consciousness and hence to underwrite the conclusion (4). In section 6.4, I offer an affirmative answer to this question.

6.3   Somatic Proprioception as a Form of Perception

First I need to substantiate the claim that somatic proprioception is a form of perception. This will obviously depend upon one's chosen account of perception. The most developed arguments in this area have been formulated by Sydney Shoemaker (particularly 1994, but see also 1986), and I will take his discussion as the framework for this section.

Shoemaker is explicitly concerned with the question of whether introspective self-knowledge is a form of inner perception. He proceeds by identifying the defining features of two distinct models or stereotypes of perception and then asking whether introspective self-knowledge possesses those features. These two models of perception are the *object-perception model* and the *broad perceptual model,* with the defining features of the second being a subset of the defining features of the first. The first applies paradigmatically to vision and rests on the idea that perception is a relation in which one stands to objects. On the second model, perception is a relation not to objects but to facts. Clearly, to motivate lemma (3) in the simple argument, it needs to be shown that somatic proprioception falls under the object-perception model.[4]

Here are the features that Shoemaker finds distinctive of the object model of perception (1994, 252–254). (I have taken the liberty of naming the features.)

The object constraint   While sense perception provides one with awareness of facts, this awareness of facts is a function of awareness of the objects involved in these facts in a sense-experience distinct from the object of perception.

Shoemaker characterizes the second feature in these terms:

The identification constraint   Sense perception involves "identification information" which allows one to pick out the object of perception through its relational and nonrelational properties. Such information enables the "tracking" of the object over time, and its reidentification from one time to another.

Within this constraint I think it is helpful to distinguish the identification constraint proper (that sense perception involves identification information) from the following precondition of its being satisfied:

The multiple-objects constraint   Ordinary modes of perception admit of our perceiving, successively or simultaneously, a multiplicity of different objects, all of which are on a par as nonfactual objects of perception. (Shoemaker 1986, 107)

Shoemaker's argument that the self cannot be the object of any form of inner perception corresponding to the object-perception model concentrates on these three constraints.

Shoemaker takes it as uncontroversial that there is no form of self-perception satisfying the object constraint:

No one thinks that in being aware of a sensation or sensory experience one has yet another sensation or experience that is "of" the first one, and constitutes its appearing to one in a certain way. . . . And no one thinks that there is such a thing as an introspective sense-experience of oneself, an introspective appearance of oneself that relates to one's beliefs about oneself as the visual experience of things one sees relate to one's beliefs about those things. (Shoemaker 1994, 254–255)

The first denial is indeed uncontroversially true, but the second is more problematic. Shoemaker clearly thinks that if the object constraint were satisfied, there would be two separate things going on: ordinary sensory experiences and a putative introspective sense-experience of oneself. But this is precisely what the defender of the simple argument denies, because the claim of that argument is just that instances of somatic proprioception are both ordinary sensory experiences *and* introspective sense-experiences. Somatic proprioception can provide sensory experience of the body. There is a clear impasse here. Both sides have a way of interpreting the object constraint that supports their own position, and it seems best to make the interpretation of the object constraint depend on the outcome of the other constraints.[5]

The identification and multiple-object constraints are the most problematic for somatic proprioception, because it is tempting to argue that somatic proprioception necessarily yields information *solely* about the body. This would entail that the multiple-objects constraint cannot be met by somatic proprioception. But if there is necessarily only one object of somatic proprioception, then there are good reasons for thinking that the identification constraint cannot be satisfied either, since it is not clear what it would mean to have identifying information about an object that is necessarily the only object of the type of awareness in question.

An initial counter to this would be that the sense of touch is a source of somatic proprioception (as stressed in the first section). It is obviously not the case that the body is the sole object of the sense of touch, because touch can be put to work to yield proprioceptive or exteroceptive information (information about the body or information about nonbodily objects in space). And when the sense of touch is being used to yield exteroceptive information, it obviously involves the possibility of perceiving a range of different objects both simultaneously and successively. Nonetheless, it might still be possible for us to draw a clear distinction between exteroceptive and proprioceptive instances of tactile perception, partitioning instances of touch into two mutually exclusive groups, and then to argue that the multiple-objects constraint is only satisfied for exteroceptive touch and that this has no implications for those occasions when the information systems that subserve the sense of touch are being put to a proprioceptive use.

However, the phenomenology of tactile awareness does not generally support this sort of partition (Gordon 1978, O'Shaughnessy 1989, Martin 1992). Consider an instance of exploratory haptic perception, as when one discerns the shape of an object in the dark by running one's fingers over it.[6] The following two things are both true of such a perception. First, through one's awareness of the changing spatial properties of one's fingers, one gains an awareness of the spatial properties of the object. That is to say, there is an important sense in which exploratory touch is *representational.* This is a very basic point, following from the fact that the vehicle of exploratory touch is experienced stimulation at or near the surface of the skin.[7] Second, tactile awareness of the spatial properties of the explored object is not gained by conscious inference from a prior and independent awareness of the contours and movement of our fingers. In paradigm cases of haptic exploration, the perceiver attends directly to the shape and other spatial properties of the explored object. Understanding the phenomenology of touch is understanding how these can both be true.

Although in haptic exploration the perceiver's attention is paradigmatically directed toward properties of the nonbodily objects being explored, this need not be the case. An attention shift is all that is required for the properties of the limb doing the exploring to become the focus of attention, and this does not involve a complete change in the structure and content of awareness. Relevant here is some form of the distinction between focal awareness and peripheral awareness, in particular, the possibility of awareness of something even though one is not attending to it. This idea is most familiar from vision, where it seems clear that items at the boundaries of the visual field are consciously registered, even though they are not being attended to. Peripheral awareness seems to require at least the following. First, items in peripheral awareness can generally be brought into focal awareness, either by moving the body into an appropriate perceptual relation to an object (by turning one's head, for example) or by focusing on one element in a complicated perceptual experience (as when one tries just to listen to the violins in a symphony). Second, instances of peripheral awareness can have implications for action and reaction without bringing focal awareness to bear, as when one flinches from something seen out of the corner of the eye.

The best description of the phenomenology of touch is that tactile experience is always both exteroceptive and proprioceptive. Attention can be directed either proprioceptively or exteroceptively, and it can be shifted from one to the other, but this should be viewed as an alteration of the balance between focal and peripheral awareness. When attention is directed exteroceptively toward the spatial properties of an object, the perceiver remains peripherally aware of the spatial properties of the relevant limb, and vice versa. And this shows how the tactile elements of somatic proprioception can meet the multiple-objects constraint. Even when the attention is fixed firmly on the proprioceptive dimension of tactile awareness, the exteroceptive dimension remains phenomenologically salient in background awareness (Martin 1995). And since it is uncontroversial that deploying the sense of touch exteroceptively permits both the simultaneous and successive perception of a range of distinct objects, it follows that the multiple-objects constraint is satisfied in all instances of tactile somatic proprioception, although, of course, in different ways.

Nonetheless, tactile somatic proprioception is only a part of somatic proprioception as a whole, and even if the multiple-objects constraint is satisfied in this limited sphere, it is illegitimate to extrapolate from this to somatic proprioception as a whole. Fortunately, though, there is another independent line of argument that can be adduced to show that the multiple-objects constraint is satisfied by somatic proprioception. This is also an argument from the phenomenology of somatic proprioception, but it emerges from reflection on the phenomenology of sense experience in general.

It is wrong to think that the senses form five distinct modes of experiencing the world (or six, if proprioception is included), each with its own proper objects. One reason for discomfort with this suggestion is that it creates epistemological problems with the cross-modal integration of what, ever since Aristotle, have been known as the common sensibles. Objects have spatial properties that can be detected by more than one sense, corresponding more or less to what philosophers have classified as primary qualities. These common sensibles are obviously the key to any experience of an objective spatial world, since they define the spatial properties of such a world, but the possibility of such experience seems to be cast in doubt if, for example, the senses of touch and vision have modality-specific objects (Evans 1985).

These problems, moreover, are not simply epistemological. The very possibility of acting on the world demands an integration of visual and tactile information. To reach out for an object successfully, for example, one has to integrate visual perceptions of the object (and of one's own hand) with the proprioceptive feedback, tactile and otherwise, about limb position and movement and with the experienced shape of the object. Even movements as simple as this would pose enormous computational demands if the thesis of modality specificity were correct.

There is, however, powerful empirical evidence that the perceptual information systems subserving perceptual experience are not, in fact, modality-specific. One important set of evidence comes from the experimental work on neonatal imitation discussed in earlier chapters. The ability of neonates to imitate facial movements like mouth opening and tongue protrusion can be interpreted in a way that clearly implies that tactile proprioception and visual perception do not have different proper objects.[8] Facial imitation requires a complex cross-modal integration of tactile proprioception and vision. And the particular significance of neonatal imitation is that because the imitation behavior can take place almost immediately after birth, this integration cannot have been the product of association or empirical correlation.

Another important set of empirical evidence comes from choice reaction-time tasks, tasks involving two or more stimuli to which the subject has to make a selective response that is timed. Some such tasks are *matching* tasks, where the spatial properties of the stimulus are isomorphic (to at least a limited degree) with the spatial properties of the response. In *mapping* tasks, however, there is no such isomorphism. The relation between spatial properties is arbitrary. The experimental evidence shows fairly conclusively that matching tasks are performed with much greater fluency and speed than mapping tasks. This has been taken to show that there is a common coding structure between visual input and motor output (Prinz 1990, Brewer 1993). Since motor output depends on kinesthetic feedback from tactile proprioception, this in turn clearly implicates a common coding structure between vision and tactile proprioception.

A third set of empirical evidence comes from recent work in the neurophysiology of space perception. It is well known that lesions to the posterior parietal cortex produce spatial deficits in humans and nonhuman primates, and the inference frequently drawn is that the posterior parietal cortex is the brain area where the representation of space is computed. Recent neurophysiological work based on recordings from single neurons has suggested that the distinctive contribution of the posterior parietal cortex is combining information from various modalities to generate head-centered, body-centered, and world-centered coordinate systems (Andersen 1995). Information about visual stimuli is initially transmitted in retinal coordinates. Calibrating this with information about eye position yields head-centered coordinates, and further calibration with information about body position (perhaps derived from the vestibular system) yields a body-centered frame of reference.[9] The distal targets of reaching movements are encoded on this modality-free frame of reference, as are motor commands and proprioceptive information about limb position.[10]

We need to move a step further, though, from considering the structure and coding of information systems to the phenomenology of the perceptual awareness that those systems subserve. The crucial point here is that our perceptual awareness of the world is cross-modal. Our perceptions of the world form what Michael Ayers has described as an *integrated sensory field*. He captures the phenomenology of the situation as follows:

A judgement which links the objects of different senses may itself be, and very often is, an immediate *perceptual* judgement, directly grounded on the deliverance of sense. Thus it is not normally as a result of inference, habitual association or the like (although in a few peculiar cases of disorientation some form of inference may be to the point) that I *judge* the object I feel with my hand to be the object I see. Quite simply, I *perceive* it as the same: the identity enters into the intentional content of sensation, and of my total sensory 'field'. (Ayers 1991, 2: 187)

It seems to me that Ayers's description is absolutely right. What we experience in sense perception is a presentation of the world that integrates information from all modalities. It is in fact very rare that we have modality-specific perceptions. This is clearly the case when we are dealing with the perception of common sensibles. The shape that I see is seen as the very same shape that I could close my hand around. But it also applies to the special sensibles. As Ayers points out, when I taste something in my mouth, my gustatory awareness of its taste is integrated with my tactile awareness of its taste and my proprioceptive awareness of its heat. These are different, although often attentively distinguishable, components of a single perceptual experience. The same applies to auditory experience of sounds as coming from a particular direction. Such experiences are inherently relational, and only one of the relata is itself heard. Somatic proprioception needs to be brought to bear to provide the directionality.

A striking result of this cross-modal integration is that all experience emerges as inherently spatial. One way of capturing this idea of an integrated sensory field would be through the concept of an egocentric space.[11] Sense perception generally involves localizing what is perceived within an egocentric frame of reference centered on the perceiver's body. Within this space the body, of course, occupies a privileged position, because objects are located relative to axes whose origin lies in the body, and this is part of the overall significance of somatic proprioception. Somatic proprioception provides the sort of information that makes possible orientation and action within egocentric space. An example of the significance of somatic proprioception is provided by familiar experiments with lenses that invert the visual field. As is well known, the brain adjusts to the inverting lenses after a relatively short period of time, and the perceiver starts to see the world the right way up again. The information about correct orientation that results in the visual field being successfully reinverted clearly does not come from vision, because all visual information is inverted. It must be information derived from the known orientation of the body, and hence with its source in somatic proprioception. The same holds for the integration of vision and action. The locus of action is egocentric, or body-relative, space, and the possibility of action depends both on correct information about the location of objects relative to body-centered axes and on correct information about the location and movement of body-parts. Somatic proprioception is crucial for both of these tasks.

The picture that is emerging is of perceptual experience involving a sensory field that is integrated across modalities and in which somatic proprioception plays a crucial role. Now, according to the multiple-objects constraint, genuine instances of sense perception permit the perception of a range of objects, either simultaneously or successively. It was initially suggested that somatic proprioception could not possibly satisfy this constraint, because somatic proprioception has the body as its sole object of awareness. We have already explored how this seems false in the case of tactile somatic proprioception. But it now seems that we can extend this point to somatic proprioception as a whole. What has been confusing the issue here is the thought that somatic proprioception should be considered in isolation, as a distinctive set of information systems subserving several different forms of awareness. When proprioception is so considered, it does seem natural to think that its sole object of awareness is the body. But, although somatic proprioception does give us information about our bodies, it does so as one of a range of ways we have of finding out about the properties of our bodies in the context of an overall perceptual field, which most emphatically does satisfy the multiple-objects constraint. Quite possibly, if we were so constituted as to experience the world in the fragmented and disjointed way assumed by many of the early empiricists, then it would be proper to deny that somatic proprioception can meet the multiple-objects constraint. But because of how we are constituted and how somatic proprioception is integrated into the general sensory field, the multiple-objects constraint is satisfied.

I turn now to the identification constraint. One reason for denying that it can be satisfied by somatic proprioception would be that genuine instances of identification involve the possibility of misidentification and hence cannot be *immune to error through misidentification relative to the first-person pronoun* (in the sense identified in section 1.2). Since somatic proprioception *is* immune to this sort of error, it might be thought that somatic proprioception cannot satisfy the identification constraint. A fundamental problem, however, with interpreting the identification constraint in terms of being subject to error through misidentification is that it seems to exclude paradigm cases of perceptual awareness. Perceptual demonstrative judgements are themselves immune to error through misidentification (relative to the demonstrative pronoun). When I perceive an object and judge 'That is green', I cannot misidentify the reference of the pronoun 'that', although I may, of course, fail to refer (Shoemaker 1986, Cassam 1995). It follows from this, of course, that being subject to error through misidentification cannot be a necessary feature of perceptual awareness, and hence that a broader reading must be given of what is to count as perceptual identification for the purpose of the identification constraint.

A plausible proposal here would be to view perceptual identification in terms of the capacity to keep track of an object over time. The relevant type of error then becomes losing track of an object, as opposed to misidentification. But it is far from clear that somatic proprioception does exclude losing track of an object, *pace* Cassam 1995. It does seem that one can lose track of one's body over time, or at least of various parts of one's body. This happens, for example, when one absent-mindedly walks home on automatic pilot instead of to the shops or taps one's foot in time to a piece of music without noticing. The best reason for describing these as cases of losing track of what one's body is doing is the feeling of surprise that comes when one notices what has been going on. What can confuse matters here is a failure to make the distinction stressed earlier between proprioceptive awareness and the operation of the proprioceptive information systems. In the two examples just given, the proprioceptive information systems are functioning as they must if actions like walking are even to be possible. But just because they are functioning, this doesn't mean that the subject is keeping track of his body, any more than does the fact that the proprioceptive information systems continue to function while one is asleep. What counts is the lack of the appropriate sort of proprioceptive awareness.

This is not to imply that somatic proprioception is subject to error through misidentification relative to the first-person pronoun.[12] Quite the contrary. Although it is true that if, *per impossibile*, one were proprioceptively to misidentify another's body for one's own one would have lost track of one's own body, it does not follow (nor is it true) that losing track of one's body means misidentifying another's body for one's own, or that when I am in touch with my body I can be mistaken about whether it is mine or not.[13] This is very important because of the close connection between judgements that are immune to error through misidentification relative to the first-person pronoun and genuinely first-person judgements— a connection stressed by Shoemaker himself (1968), as well as by other philosophers (Evans 1982, chap. 7).[14] As I shall argue in the next section, the fact that somatic proprioception is itself immune to error through misidentification relative to the first-person pronoun provides vital support for the claim that somatic proprioception counts as a genuine form of self-consciousness. For present purposes, the important point to note is that, although somatic proprioception can count as a form of perception only in virtue of meeting the multiple-object and identification constraints, this does not mean that it is subject to error through misidentification.

Moreover, this conception of how the identification constraint is satisfied through keeping track of one's body fits well with the general picture of the phenomenology of sense perception sketched earlier in terms of an integrated sensory field. If the phenomenology of sense perception is indeed integrated rather than fragmented, then the body will appear as one object among the range of objects that appear in the integrated sensory field. Of course, even though this might be enough to ensure that the body appears perceptually in a way that satisfies the multiple-objects constraint, it is undeniable that (at least in normal subjects) the body appears as a highly distinctive object. This is due partly to certain aspects of the phenomenology of visual proprioception but principally to the normal functioning of the proprioceptive awareness that keeps track of the body as the center and focal point of body-relative egocentric space. Proprioceptive awareness is critically responsible for the body appearing as a distinctive object in the integrated sensory field.

That leaves just the object constraint, and since neither of the other constraints are effective against the simple argument, it seems justifiable to interpret the object constraint in a manner favorable to the thesis that somatic proprioception is a form of self-perception. As far as the simple argument is concerned, lines (2) and (3) have been vindicated. In the following section I turn to line (4) and the claim that the self-perception yielded by somatic proprioception is a form of self-consciousness.

6.4   Somatic Proprioception as a Form of Self-Consciousness

The move from (3) to (4) in the simple argument might be attacked as resting on the fallacy of equivocation. What makes somatic proprioception a form of self-perception, it might be argued, is that it involves perceiving certain bodily properties that are properties of one's self. But this is not enough to make it a form of self-consciousness. Genuine self-consciousness requires the further feature that those bodily properties should be perceived *as* properties of one's self. And then one might

suggest both that there are no reasons to think that somatic proprioception involves anything along those lines and that genuine self-
consciousness of this sort is only available to creatures who have mastered
the first-person pronoun.

There are two considerations, however, that militate against this sort
of objection. The first is that if the distinction between self-perception
and genuine self-consciousness is to apply to somatic proprioception of
one's own bodily properties, then it should also apply to introspection of
one's own psychological properties. This would mean that introspection
of one's own psychological properties could also fail to count as a form
of self-consciousness, and that seems to be a rather bizarre conclusion.
Of course, it is open to the objector to bite the bullet here, but there is a
prima facie implausibility in any view that denies that my awareness of
my own psychological properties is a form of self-consciousness. It is
equally implausible, I feel, to deny that there is a parallel between somatic
proprioception and introspection. What the objector is claiming is that
an individual can perceive certain bodily properties through somatic proprioception without perceiving that those properties are his own properties. Such a perception might be specified as follows:

(1) x thinks 'That leg is flexing'.

The objector maintains that (1), as contrasted, for example, with (2), is
not a genuine form of self-consciousness.

(2) x thinks 'My leg is flexing'.

Note, however that an exactly parallel distinction can be made for the
introspection of psychological properties. Compare (3) and (4):

(3) x thinks 'That's a feeling of jealousy'.

(4) x thinks 'I'm jealous'.

Both (3) and (4) are introspectively based judgements. If the distinction
between (1) and (2) is telling against the view that somatic proprioception
is a form of self-consciousness, the parallel distinction between (3) and
(4) should be telling against the view that introspection is a form of self-
consciousness.[15]

But, of course, neither the distinction between (1) and (2) nor that between (3) and (4) is relevant here. Neither somatic proprioception nor

introspection can support as sharp a distinction between "mere" self-perception and "genuine" self-consciousness as the objection requires. To see why, consider the following example, where there really is precisely such a sharp distinction. Suppose, for example, that I catch sight of somebody in a mirror without realizing that the person is myself and I think 'That person has got clenched fists'. This would be a situation that might perhaps be described as an instance of self-perception, but it is clearly not an instance of self-consciousness, and this, of course, is precisely the distinction that the objection is trying to capture. What is not clear, however, is that this distinction carries over in any straightforward way to the case of somatic proprioception. What is distinctive about the mirror case (and what makes it so obviously not an example of genuine self-consciousness) is the fact that I misidentify myself. I correctly identify certain bodily properties but fail to recognize that they are properties of my own body and misattribute them to somebody else. But nothing like this goes on in somatic proprioception. In fact, nothing like this *can* go on in somatic proprioception. One of the distinctive features of somatic proprioception is that it is subserved by information channels that do not yield information about anybody's bodily properties except my own (just as introspection does not yield information about anybody's psychological properties except my own). It follows from the simple fact that I somatically proprioceive particular bodily properties and introspect particular psychological properties that those bodily and psychological properties are my own. This feature of somatic proprioception (that, as mentioned earlier, it is derived from information that is immune to error through misidentification relative to the first-person pronoun) militates strongly against the idea that the proposed contrast between (putatively accidental) self-perception and genuine self-consciousness is sharply defined in either somatic proprioception or introspection.[16]

Still, granting that somatic proprioception can be a source of thoughts that are about oneself in a way that provides no purchase for the distinction between accidental and genuine self-reference does not explain why somatic proprioception is properly described as a form of self-consciousness. There is a substantive issue here, which is whether somatic proprioception falls within the same cognitive kind as those forms of "full-fledged self-consciousness" that center around the competent employment of the first-person pronoun. But how can we reach a nonstipulative solution to this question? The strategy I propose is to identify what might be termed the core requirements of genuinely self-conscious thought. If those core features can be specified without presupposing mastery of the first-person pronoun and if those features are also shared by somatic proprioception, then we will have a principled reason for holding that somatic proprioception is properly described as a form of self-consciousness.

So what are the core requirements for genuinely self-conscious thought? It seems to me that there are two such requirements. The first has already been discussed in this section. This is the requirement that genuinely self-conscious thought should be about oneself in a way that is nonaccidental. It cannot be the case that genuinely self-conscious thought ascribes properties to an individual who is in fact oneself without one's being aware that the individual in question actually is oneself. The second requirement is closely related to this requirement of nonaccidental self-reference. Suppose that we ask why accidental self-reference fails to count as genuine self-consciousness. The obvious answer is that thoughts that accidentally self-refer fail to have the immediate implications for action found in genuinely self-conscious thoughts, as has been made familiar by Castañeda (1966) and Perry (1979). This second identifying feature of genuinely self-conscious thoughts—that they feed directly and immediately into action—is an essential part of the functional characterization of first-person thoughts (as emerged in chapter 5).

I have already suggested that somatic proprioception cannot give rise to thoughts that are accidentally about oneself in this manner. This flows out of the discussion of immunity to error through misidentification relative to the first-person pronoun. And it is equally clear that somatic proprioception does have immediate and direct implications for action. This holds true both of self-directed action (like scratching itches) and of action whose target is not the body. And the role of the various somatic information systems in providing feedback about limb movement and balance provides sufficient testimony to these implications for action. I will return to the connections between somatic proprioception and action in the final section.

That somatic proprioception satisfies these two requirements does not, however, exhaust the sense in which somatic proprioception counts as a form of self-consciousness. To make further progress here, we need to distinguish between two distinct modes of self-consciousness yielded by somatic proprioception: the narrow and the broad. What I have been discussing so far is properly described as narrow self-consciousness. It might be described as a form of self-knowledge, knowledge of one's bodily properties. In addition to this, however, somatic proprioception yields a form of broad self-consciousness. At the core of the notion of broad self-consciousness is the recognition of what developmental psychologists call *self-world dualism.* Any subject properly described as self-conscious must be able to register the distinction between himself and the world. Of course, this is a distinction that can be registered in a variety of different ways. The capacity for self-ascription of thoughts and experiences, in combination with the capacity to conceptualize the world as a spatial and causally structured system of mind-independent objects, is a high-level way of registering this distinction. But there are more primitive ways of registering the distinction, provided by somatic proprioception. Somatic proprioception provides a way, perhaps the most primitive way, of registering the distinction between self and nonself. This is a weaker distinction than the distinction between self and world, of course, but it is certainly a necessary component of it. There are two key elements to the self/nonself distinction yielded by somatic proprioception. The self here is, of course, the material self, and it is useful to characterize these two elements in terms of the different ways of grasping the bodily self that these elements involve and provide.

The first element of broad self-consciousness that somatic proprioception provides is an awareness of the limits of the body. The sense of touch is primarily responsible for this. The felt boundaries of the body define the limits between self and nonself. This is directly a function of the points about the joint proprioceptive and exteroceptive structure of tactile awareness mentioned earlier in the context of the multiple-objects constraint. Both the proprioceptive and the exteroceptive dimension of touch are phenomenologically salient (and possible objects of attention) in tactile experience. Because of this, there is an important sense in which the distinction between self and nonself is itself phenomenologically salient.

This offers a way of grasping the body as a spatially extended and bounded object.

A second element of broad self-consciousness emerges when one reflects that somatic proprioception is one of the key ways by which one becomes aware that the body is responsive to one's will. The feedback gained through kinesthesia, joint-position sense, and the vestibular system makes one aware that the body is responding to motor commands. In combination with the previous mode of broad self-consciousness, this yields a way of grasping the body as an object that is responsive to the will. True, much of the body is not at all responsive to the will—the internal organs are obvious examples. But strikingly, the scope of the will does seem clearly to encompass all bodily surfaces and extremities (whether directly or indirectly). Although not every portion of the bodily surface can be moved at will, every portion of the bodily surface can nonetheless be experienced as moving in response to an act of the will. Take an arbitrary area on the top of the head, for example. Although I cannot move that area at will (in isolation), I can nonetheless experience it as moving when I move my head as a whole. It seems fair to say that the limits of the will mark the distinction between the self and the nonself just as much as does the skin, although in a different way.

Philosophers dealing with bodily awareness have to balance two facets that pull in opposite directions. There is, first, the obvious fact that the body is a physical object in the world, which leads to the plausible thought that awareness of the body must be somehow awareness of the body as an object in the world. Second and equally obvious is the fact that the body is (at least from a first-person perspective) quite unlike any other physical object, which leads to the equally plausible thought that awareness of the body is somehow fundamentally different from awareness of the body as an object in the world. The two different facets just isolated offer a way of reconciling the apparent conflict. What somatic proprioception offers is an awareness of the body as a spatially extended and bounded physical object that is distinctive in being responsive to the will.

It is important to stress, however, that narrow self-consciousness and broad self-consciousness are not distinct existences. On the contrary, broad self-consciousness features ineliminably in the content of narrow somatic self-consciousness. This is the final step in the argument that so-matic proprioception counts as a genuine form of self-consciousness. To see why, reflect that the critic of the simple argument who finds a fallacy of equivocation is effectively drawing precisely the distinction between broad and narrow self-consciousness. He is pointing out that narrow self-consciousness is all that follows from the conjunction of (1) and (2), whereas something more like broad self-consciousness is required for (4). To appreciate why this suggestion is fundamentally mistaken, however, a closer look at the content of somatic proprioception is required.

6.5   The Content of Somatic Proprioception

It has been noted by several authors that the content of proprioception is a form of spatial content (O'Shaughnessy 1980, Brewer 1993). The bodily states that form the objects of proprioception are proprioperceived in a way that locates them within a space that is usually (although not always) bounded by the limits of the body. The qualification is needed because of two well-documented phenomena from clinical medicine. Pa-tients with amputated limbs often report feeling "phantom limbs," as do some patients with congenital absence of limbs. In cases of phantom limbs the limits of the proprioperceived body extend beyond the limits of the physical body, with sensations located elsewhere in the body being referred to and experienced in the phantom (Melzack 1992, Ramachan-dran 1994).[17] Phantoms are often highly incorporated into the body scheme. There are widespread reports of patients being able to move their phantoms voluntarily, and the patient F. A. studied by Ramachandran regularly attempted to employ his phantom right arm to ward off blows, grasp objects, or break a fall. The example of phantom limbs clearly shows that the space of the proprioceived body sometimes extends be-yond the bounds of the physical body. A converse set of disorders, the so-called somatoparaphrenic delusions, shows that the space of the pro-prioceived body can be narrower than the bounds of the physical body. Patients who have suffered from right-hemisphere stroke damage (usually in conjunction with damage to the right parietal lobe) are often *anosag-nosic* about their deficit (that is, they deny its existence). A small subset of such patients are led by their anosagnosia to deny that the paralyzed limb belongs to them.[18] Nonetheless, in both these pathological cases, proprioceptive states are still experienced within the frame of a *body-relative space*. The first question that arises in thinking about proprioceptive content, therefore, is how we should think about the frame of reference that determines how proprioceptive states are located within body-relative space.

Proprioception is not, of course, the only source of body-relative spatial contents. It is highly plausible to view perception and basic bodily actions as respectively providing or based on body-relative spatial contents, and it is natural to suggest that perception, proprioception, and the intentions controlling basic bodily actions must have spatial contents coded on comparable frames of reference. This would make it relatively easy to answer the question about the frame of reference of proprioceptive content, since the spatial content of perception and basic bodily intentions is relatively well understood. The spatial locations of perceived objects and objects featuring in the contents of intentions are given relative to axes whose origin lies in the body—what is often termed an *egocentric frame of reference*.[19] An initial proposal, therefore, might be that the axes that determine particular proprioceptive frames of reference are centered on particular body parts, just as are the axes determining the frames of reference for perceptual content and basic intentions.[20]

Despite its appealing economy, however, this account is ultimately unacceptable, because of a fundamental disanalogy between the *bodily space* of proprioception and the egocentric space of perception and action. To appreciate the problem, consider what reason there could be for locating the origin of proprioception in one body part rather than another. In the case of vision or exteroceptive touch it is natural to think that there is a perceptual field bounded so as to determine a particular point as its origin. If, for example, the visual field is described as the solid angle of light picked up by the visual system, then the origin of the visual field can be taken to be the apex of that solid angle. Similarly, one might suggest that the origin of the frame of reference for exploratory touch is a point in the center of the palm of the relevant hand. But somatic proprioception is not like this at all. It is not clear what possible reason there could be for offering one part of the body as the origin of the proprioceptive frame of reference.

In contrast with vision, audition, and the other canonically exteroceptive modalities, there are certain spatial notions that do not seem to be applicable to somatic proprioception. For any two objects that are visually perceived, it makes obvious sense to ask both of the following questions: (a) Which of these two objects is farther away? (b) Do these objects lie in the same direction? Moreover, the possibility of asking and answering these questions is very closely bound up with the fact that visual perception takes place relative to a frame of reference that does indeed have an origin. Posing question (a) is more or less equivalent to asking whether a line between the origin and one object would be longer or shorter than a corresponding line between the origin and the other object. Question (b) is just the question of whether, if a line were drawn from the origin to the object farther away, it would pass through the nearer object. This, of course, is an important part of the explanation of why we can normally answer questions like (a) and (b) at a glance.

Neither of these questions makes sense, however, with respect to proprioception. One does not find oneself asking whether this proprioceptively detected hand movement is farther away than this itch, or whether this pain is in the same direction as that pain. Nor, of course, is this merely a peculiarity of our language. What I am really asking when I ask which of two objects is farther away is which of the two objects is farther away from me, and a similar tacit self-reference is included when I ask whether two objects are in the same direction. The reason one cannot ask these questions with regard to somatic proprioception is that the events about which one learns through somatic proprioception take place within the confines of the body, and there is no privileged part of the body that counts as me for the purpose of discussing the spatial relations they bear to each other (in the way that, for example, the origin of the visual frame of reference can count as me when those questions arise for visually presented objects).

The conclusion to draw from this is that the spatial content of somatic proprioception cannot be specified within a frame of reference that takes the form of axes centered on an origin. So if somatic proprioception is to have a content at all, it must be understood in a fundamentally different way. In the remainder of this chapter I will develop an account that captures these distinctive features of proprioceptive content.

Let me begin by distinguishing two distinct aspects of proprioceptive content: the *descriptive* and the *spatial*. Roughly speaking (and to anticipate somewhat) the content of somatic proprioception is that certain events are taking place at particular bodily locations. The nature of such an event is specified by the descriptive aspect of proprioceptive content, while the spatial aspect specifies the bodily location at which such an event takes place. I will begin by discussing the spatial aspect of proprioceptive content.

A satisfactory account of any form of spatial content needs to explain how places are individuated by providing criteria for sameness of place. In the case of somatic proprioception, of course, we need criteria for sameness of bodily location. What complicates matters here is that on the face of it there seem to be several different forms of criteria for sameness of bodily location that individuate places in different ways. Consider the following two situations:

1. I have a pain at a point on the sole of my right foot when I am standing up, and my right foot is resting on the ground in front of me.
2. I have a pain at the same point on the sole of my right foot when I am sitting down, and my right ankle is resting on my left knee.

According to one set of criteria, the pain is in the same bodily location in (1) and (2), that is to say, it is at a given point on the sole of my foot.[21] According to another set of criteria, however, the pain is in different bodily locations in (1) and (2) because the sole of my foot has moved relative to my other body parts. Let me term these the A *location* and B *location* respectively. Note that the B location is independent of the actual location of the pain in objective space. The B location of the pain in (2) would be the same if I happened to be sitting in the same posture five feet to the left.

With bodily sensations still as paradigms of somatic proprioception, both A location and B location are ineliminable components of the phenomenology of bodily sensations. I take it that the phenomenology of (1) is fundamentally different from the phenomenology of (2), which shows that specifications of proprioceptive content must be sensitive to B locations. But it is also true that it would be hopelessly incomplete to report the phenomenology of (2) by saying merely that I feel a pain just above and to the left of my left knee down and slightly left of my left shoulder, although (some version of) that would be sufficient to pick out the *B* location. This shows that specifications of proprioceptive content must also be sensitive to *A* locations.

Now both the *A* location and *B* location need to be specified relative to a frame of reference, which requires taking a fixed point or set of fixed points relative to which spatial location is to be fixed. Since it emerged earlier that it would not be right to take a single fixed point as an origin, it follows that we must look for a set of fixed, or at least relatively fixed, points in terms of which we can fix the *A* location and *B* location of a given bodily event.

In thinking about the possibility of such a frame of reference we need to bear in mind that the human body has both moveable and (relatively) immoveable body parts. On a large scale, the human body can be viewed as an immoveable torso to which are appended moveable limbs: the head, arms, and legs. Within the moveable limbs there are small-scale body parts that can be moved directly in response to the will (like the fingers, the toes, and the lower jaw) and others that cannot (like the base of the skull), but all the small-scale body parts within the moveable limbs are moveable in the limited sense that their position can be altered relative to any given point in the (relatively) immoveable torso.[22] Let me now introduce the technical concept of a *hinge*. The intuitive idea that I want to capture with this term is the idea of a body part that allows one to move a further body part. Examples of hinges are the neck, the jaw socket, the shoulders, the elbows, the wrists, the knuckles, the finger joints, the leg sockets, the knees, and the ankles. The distinction between moveable and immoveable body parts, together with the concept of a hinge, creates the following picture of how the human body is segmented. A relatively immoveable torso is linked by hinges to five moveable limbs (the head, two legs, and two arms), each of which is further segmented by means of further hinges.

It is, I think, to the hinges that we need to turn to find the fixed points in terms of which we can give the particular *A* location and *B* location of individual body parts at a time. One good reason for this is that an awareness of the location of the hinges, as well as of the possibilities for movement that they afford, can plausibly be viewed as an inevitable concomitant of learning to act with one's body in early childhood. Another good reason is that individual body parts are paradigmatically identified in terms of hinges. The forearm, for example, is the volume between the elbow and the wrist. The palm of the hand is the volume bounded by the wrist and the knuckles. The calf is the volume of leg that falls between the knee and the ankle. Using hinges provides a nonarbitrary way of segmenting the body that accords pretty closely with how we classify body parts in everyday thought and speech.

Let me start by explaining how the hinges can be deployed to determine any given A location. A particular bodily A location is specified relative to the hinges that bound the body part within which it is located. A particular point in the forearm is specified relative to the elbow and the wrist. It is the point that lies on the surface of the skin at such and such a distance and direction from the wrist and such and such a distance and direction from the elbow.[23] This mode of determining A locations secures the defining feature of an A location, which is that a given point in a given body part will have the same A location irrespective of how the body as a whole moves or of how the relevant body part moves relative to other body parts. The A location of a given point in a given body part will remain constant in both those movements, because neither of those movements brings about any changes in its distance and direction from the relevant hinges. Note, however, that this holds true only if the fixed points are restricted to those hinges that bound the relevant body part. If the number of fixed points were expanded to include nonbounding hinges, this would have the undesirable consequence that the A location would vary.

I turn now to the more complicated issue of B location. The first point to observe is that it is individual A locations that have particular B locations. This is clear from situations (1) and (2) described above, in which a pain retains a constant A location in two different B locations. In each situation what has the relevant B location is the pain that is A-located at a particular point in the sole of my foot. It is not the pain simpliciter that in (2) is B-located just above and to the left of my left knee and down and slightly left of my left shoulder, but the pain in the sole of my foot. This provides an important clue as to how the account of B location ought to proceed. If what has a given B location is an A location and A locations are identified within given body parts (relative to the hinges that bound those body parts), then it seems we can map an A location onto a B location if we can plot the location of the given body part. How might this be done?

Body parts have been defined as body segments bounded by hinges. These hinges afford a range of movements in three dimensions (with some hinges, like the shoulder, affording a greater range of movements than others, like the elbow). A hinge such as the wrist allows the hand to be positioned in one of a range of orientations relative to the lower arm. The basic idea in mapping *A* locations onto *B* locations is to specify what orientation the body part is in relative to the hinge. Take a point in the center of the palm of the hand. That point has its *A* location relative to the hinges that bound the palm of the hand, while its *B* location is given by the orientation of the palm of the hand relative to the wrist. Of course, this is not enough to fix a unique *B* location, for it fails to register the changing *B* location of a point in the center of the palm of my hand as I keep my hand in the same orientation relative to my wrist but raise it above my head. Accommodating such changes in *B* locations is possible only if the orientation of the relevant body part is relativized more widely. In the example of the point in the palm of the hand, the orientation of the wrist needs to be fixed relative to the elbow, and the orientation of the elbow relative to the shoulder. That would provide a unique *B* location within the arm and would also specify the location of the arm relative to the torso.

The general model, then, for the identification of *B* locations is as follows. A particular constant *A* location is determined relative to the hinges that bound the body part in which it falls. That *A* location will either fall within the (relatively) immoveable torso, or it will fall within a moveable limb. If it falls within the (relatively) immoveable torso, then its *B* location will also be fixed relative to the hinges that bound the torso (neck, shoulders, and leg sockets). If, however, that *A* location falls within a moveable limb, then its *B* location will be fixed recursively relative to the hinges that lie between it and the immoveable torso. This enables any given *B* location to be calibrated with any other. Suppose that I want to scratch an itch in my left arm with the tip of the middle finger of my right hand. Both *A* locations have *B* locations recursively specified as above. Each of those recursive specifications will relativize the *B* location to the respective shoulder. Thus, all that is needed for those *B* locations to be fixed relative to each other (and hence for me to locate the itch in my arm with the middle finger of my right hand) is a specification of the position of each shoulder relative to the other.

This account remains faithful to the phenomenology of bodily experience. An important part of the phenomenology of bodily experience is, as several writers have stressed, that bodily sensations such as pain are presented not only as being at a particular point relative to other parts of the body but also as located within a particular body part (Martin 1993, Brewer 1993). This is captured very clearly by the distinction between and interdependence of A locations and B locations.[24] A bodily sensation has a particular B location (relative to the body as a whole) only insofar as it has a particular A location (within a particular body part), because B locations are fixed on the basis of A locations. Moreover, the interrelation between A locations and B locations captures the further phenomenological point that body parts are perceived as belonging to the body as a whole (Martin 1995). But explaining properly why this is so brings us to what I have termed the descriptive dimension of proprioceptive content.

Earlier I contrasted characterizing the nature of a proprioperceived event within the body (the descriptive dimension) with specifying where that event is in the body (the spatial dimension). The first question to be asked of the descriptive dimension of proprioceptive content concerns the nature of the proprioperceived event. What is the direct object of proprioception? The answer to this question can be read off from the understanding that we now have of the spatial dimension of proprioceptive content. The direct object of proprioception is the state of the body at a particular location. In terms of A location and B location, this means that the direct object of proprioception will be the state of the body at a particular location in a given body part, which is itself located relative to the rest of the body. Note one consequence of this, to which I will return at the end of this section. The body as a whole features in the descriptive dimension of proprioceptive content, just as it does in the spatial dimension.

The descriptive aspect of proprioceptive content is that the body at a particular location is in a particular state. But what sort of state? It may be helpful to consider the range of bodily states that feature in proprioceptive content under the familiar headings of 'quality' and 'quantity'. The qualitative states are those familiar from the phenomenology of bodily sensation. Obvious examples are the states of being bruised, being damaged, being tickled, being itchy, being tender, being hot. Most of the qualitative states featuring in proprioceptive content share the feature of departing from what one might term bodily equilibrium. One prominent reason for the body to obtrude on consciousness is that it is in an abnormal condition of one form or another. This is a respect in which the qualitative states generally differ from the quantitative ones. The sensation that a limb is moving in a particular direction or the feeling that one's legs are crossed are paradigm quantitative states. Generally, these are not, of course, departures from bodily equilibrium but rather ways in which one keeps track of one's body in its normal operations and activities. Of course, the states that are the objects of particular proprioceptive contents can have both qualitative and quantitative features, as when one feels that one's bruised ankle is swollen. They can also have several qualitative and/or quantitative features at once, as when one clasps one's hands together and moves them (perhaps to hit a volleyball).

Now any acceptable account of content must explain the correctness conditions of the relevant content-bearing states. Of course, any given proprioceptive content will be correct if and only if there is an event taking place at the appropriate bodily location with the relevant qualitative and/or quantitative features. This is true but uninformative, however. What we really need is some indication of the criteria by which one might recognize whether these correctness conditions are satisfied or not. This is, of course, an epistemic rather than a constitutive issue. Let me make some brief comments in this direction.

The key to understanding how the correctness conditions of proprioceptive content can be applied is the functional role of content-bearing proprioceptive states with regard to the events that cause them and the actions to which they give rise. Some of these actions are explicitly directed towards the body (e.g., scratching an itch). Others are implicitly directed towards the body (e.g., snatching one's hand away from a flame). Others are not body-directed at all (e.g., the role of what I termed quantitative features in controlling action). In each of these cases, however, it is possible to employ the concept of an appropriate action to illuminate the correctness conditions. The correctness conditions for explicitly body-directed actions, like scratching itches, are that the action should be appropriate to the disturbance that causes the proprioceptive state. This requires, of course, that there actually be a disturbance at the bodily location at which the action is directed (which would satisfy the correctness condition for the spatial aspect) and that the action be appropriate to the disturbance there (which would satisfy the correctness condition for the descriptive aspect). For proprioceptive states that cause implicitly body-directed actions, the correctness conditions are similar. One might view an appropriate action in both of these cases as an action that would tend to restore bodily equilibrium, for example, by relieving the pain.

The correctness conditions of proprioceptive states that cause non-body-directed actions are slightly more complicated in that (unlike bodily sensations) they are not necessarily linked to isolated and easily identifiable events taking place in the body. Typically, these are proprioceptive states reporting what I termed quantitative features, like general limb disposition and movement. Here, though, we can see how the correctness conditions might be brought to bear by considering the model sketched earlier, in which two different types of proprioceptive information (about initial limb disposition and then feedback about limb movement) are implicated in paradigm cases of intentional action where a motivational state and a perceptual state jointly produce an intentional command. The obvious fact that correctness of the proprioceptive information is a necessary condition of the success of the intentional action illustrates how one might recognize whether the correctness conditions are satisfied: the correctness conditions are satisfied if the relevant perception is true and the relevant motivational state is satisfied.[25]

This brief sketch leaves many questions unanswered, but I take it that the account so far is secure enough for me to bring this discussion of proprioceptive content to bear on the argument that somatic proprioception is a genuine form of self-consciousness. In the previous section I distinguished between broad self-consciousness (awareness of the material self as a spatially extended and bounded physical object distinctive in its responsiveness to the will) and narrow self-consciousness (the material self's knowledge of its bodily properties as given in proprioceptive contents of the type I have been discussing). Instances of narrow self-consciousness will have contents with both spatial and descriptive dimensions. The body as a whole features in both of these dimensions of content. This is particularly clear in the case of the spatial dimension, which involves an awareness of the body as an articulated structure of body parts separated by what I have termed hinges. This implicates an awareness of the self as spatially extended and bounded. But it also implicates the second component of broad self-consciousness (awareness of the bodily self as responsive to the will). This is because awareness of the hinges is closely bound up with awareness of the body's possibilities for action. The body presents itself phenomenologically as segmented into body parts separated by hinges because those are the natural units for movement. In the descriptive aspect of proprioceptive content, moreover, it is once again the body as a whole that features. The content of somatic proprioception is that the body, at a particular A location and a particular B location, is in a particular state with certain qualitative and/or quantitative features. Each such content exemplifies both broad and narrow self-consciousness.

6.6   Summary

In section 6.2, I offered the simple argument to show that somatic proprioception is a form of primitive self-consciousness. The crucial claims in the simple argument were, first, that somatic proprioception is a form of perception and, second, that as self-perception it is a form of self-consciousness. These claims were defended in sections 6.3 and 6.4 respectively. The soundness of the simple argument shows that somatic proprioception is a source of what in earlier chapters I described as first-person contents. Like the first-person perceptual contents discussed in the previous chapter, these contents are primitive and available more or less from birth.[26] In at least one respect, the contents of somatic proprioception are richer than the first-person contents of perceptual protobeliefs. As has emerged from the discussion of the content of somatic proprioception, they encompass a genuine awareness of the limits and responsiveness to the will of the embodied self. Somatic proprioception is a source of information not just about particular properties of the embodied self but also about the nature of the embodied self itself.

The pick-up of self-specifying information in ecological perception and the nonconceptual first-person contents of somatic proprioception are the most primitive forms of self-consciousness. One implication of this is that it widens the scope of what might be termed the first-person perspective far beyond the domain of humans, and even the higher mammals. This is particularly significant for any philosopher who shares the plausible view that self-consciousness, even in its primitive forms, carries with it a degree of moral significance. A further implication more relevant to present concerns is that the first-person nonconceptual contents of ecological perception and somatic proprioception are the basic building blocks from which the full-fledged self-consciousness associated with mastery of the first-person pronoun will eventually emerge, and hence are the raw material from which to construct both an account of how the acquisition constraint can be met for full-fledged self-conscious thought and a noncircular explanation of the conditions of mastery of the first-person pronoun.

7

Points of View

The previous two chapters have shown how somatic proprioception and the structure of exteroceptive perceptual experience can be a source of nonconceptual first-person contents from the very beginning of life. This is an important start in dissolving the paradox of self-consciousness, because it disproves the central assumption generating the paradox, namely, that it is incoherent to ascribe thoughts with first-person content to an individual who is not capable of employing the first-person pronoun to achieve reflexive self-reference. But it is just a start, and what is required now is an understanding of how we get from the primitive first-person contents implicated in perceptual experience at the ecological level and in somatic proprioception to the various high-level forms of first-person thought that involve reflexive self-reference. How do we build up from the pick-up of self-specifying information to full-fledged self-consciousness? One promising strategy here is to identify certain fundamental dimensions of self-consciousness that neither the perceptual pick-up of self-specifying information nor the degree of self-awareness yielded by somatic proprioception can do justice to, and then to consider how such basic-level information pick-up needs to be augmented if those dimensions of self-consciousness are to come into play.

7.1 Conceptual Points of View and Nonconceptual Points of View

The previous chapter showed how somatic proprioception offers an awareness of the body as a spatially extended and bounded object that is responsive to the will. A major part of the significance of this is that it offers the subject a way of registering the distinction between self and nonself. It does this by marking the boundaries of the self. The boundaries of the self emerge in somatic proprioception both as the limits of the will and as the limits of felt feedback about the disposition and movement of body parts. Crucial to this emergence is the sense of touch, which, because it is simultaneously proprioceptive and exteroceptive, provides an interface between the self and the nonself. As was also pointed out in the previous chapter, registering the distinction between self and nonself is a very primitive form of self-awareness. This is because self-awareness has a very significant contrastive dimension. A central way of considering a creature's degree of self-awareness is in terms of its capacity to distinguish itself from its environment, and no creature would be able to distinguish itself from its environment if it did not have a minimal degree of self-awareness to begin with. But once that minimal degree of self-awareness is in place, the richness of the self-awareness that accompanies the capacity to distinguish the self from the environment is directly proportionate to the richness of the awareness of the environment from which the self is being distinguished. There is, of course, very little such richness in somatic proprioception, which, although it has an exteroceptive dimension, provides relatively little information about the organization and structure of the world. The world that manifests itself in somatic proprioception is a world of surfaces, textures, and resistances—primitive indeed in comparison with the causally structured world of physical objects. And the form of self-awareness that emerges from somatic proprioception is correspondingly primitive.

Thus, to make progress beyond the minimal registering of the distinction between self and nonself that comes with somatic proprioception, we need to consider the subject's awareness of its environment. Philosophers discussing self-awareness often place a lot of weight upon metaphors of 'perspective' and 'point of view'. The point of these metaphors is to capture certain characteristic aspects of how the environment is disclosed to self-conscious subjects, as opposed to how it is disclosed to impartial scientific investigation. There is more at stake here than a simple metaphorical restatement of traditional and rather vague distinctions between subjectivity and objectivity. The metaphors themselves put a distinctive spin on the notion of subjectivity involved. In particular, they bring out the centrality of spatiality in understanding self-conscious thought, because the most obvious way of understanding how the environment can be apprehended from a particular perspective or point of view is in spatial terms. Having a distinctive perspective or point of view on the environment is something that a self-conscious subject does at least partly in virtue of occupying a particular spatial position. Of course, though, as I stressed in my discussion of Gibson's ecological optics, it is a mistake to view this in an atomistic way. It is only in the experimental laboratory that cognition takes place from a fixed spatial point. Perspectives and points of view move through the world, retaining continuity through change. The real challenge is understanding what this sort of perspectival movement involves.

Kant is the philosopher who has had the clearest grip on the relation between self-awareness and awareness of the environment, and the whole of the Transcendental Analytic in the *Critique of Pure Reason* can be viewed as a sustained working out of the interdependence between them. To go into the details of Kant's treatment, although fascinating, would take us into murky waters far from the matter at hand. I propose to use P. F. Strawson's (1966) discussion of Kant's transcendental deduction of the categories as the philosophical point of departure. Strawson felicitously uses the notion of a point of view and places it at the very heart of Kant's treatment of the interdependence between self-awareness and awareness of the environment.

To appreciate what is going on here, we need to step back a little. Strawson's Kant is concerned with the structure of self-conscious experience. What, he asks, are the necessary conditions that must be fulfilled for self-conscious experience to be a genuine possibility? What must hold for a series of thoughts and experiences to belong to a single, unitary self-conscious subject? He begins thus:

It is a shining fact about such a series of experiences, whether self-ascribed or not, that its members collectively build up or yield, though not all of them contribute to, a picture of an unified objective world through which the experiences themselves constitute a single, subjective, experiential route, one among other possible subjective routes through the same objective world. (Strawson 1966, 104)

According to Strawson this "shining fact" is the key to understanding the conditions that Kant places upon the possibility of genuinely self-conscious experience. The central condition is that a subject's experiences must "determine a distinction between the subjective route of his experiences and the objective world through which it is a route" (Strawson 1966, 104). And it is this, of course, that Strawson terms the subject's point of view on the world. He explains:

A series of experiences satisfying the Kantian provision has a certain double aspect. On the one hand it cumulatively builds up a picture of the world in which objects and happenings (with their particular characteristics) are presented as possessing an objective order, an order which is logically independent of any particular experiential route through the world. On the other hand it possesses its own order as a series of experiences of objects. If we thought of such a series of experiences as continuously articulated in a series of detailed judgements, then, taking their order and content together, those judgements would be such as to yield, on the one hand, a (potential) description of an objective world and on the other the chart of the course of a single subjective experience of that world (Strawson 1966, 105).

Strawson's fleshes out the notion of a point of view in a way that draws together two distinct (sets of) conceptual capacities: the capacity for self-ascription of experiences and the capacity to grasp the objectivity of the world.

Let us take a further step back and ask why Strawson's Kant thinks that these two sets of conceptual abilities need to be brought together. The first point is that the question of the possibility of self-conscious experience is inextricably bound up with the question of the possibility of any form of experience. Strawson brings this out by considering the hypothesis that there might be an experience whose objects were sense data: "red, round patches, brown oblongs, flashes, whistles, tickling sensations, smells" (Strawson 1966, 99). This would not count as anything recognizable as experience, he maintains, because it would not permit any distinction to be drawn between a subject's experiences and the objects of which they are experiences. In such a case, the *esse* (being) of the putative "objects of experience" would be their *percipi* (being perceived). There would be no distinction between the order of experiences and the order of the "objects of experience," and this, according to Strawson, effectively means that we cannot talk either about objects of experience or about a subject of experience, and hence we cannot talk about experience at all.

Strawson's central claim is that no creature can count as a subject of experience unless it is capable of drawing certain very basic distinctions between its experiences and the objects of which they are experiences.

Experience that reflects a temporally extended point of view on the world will ipso facto permit these basic distinctions to be drawn in virtue of possessing the "double aspect" outlined in the passage quoted earlier. The matter can be further clarified through the concept of a *nonsolipsistic* consciousness, which Strawson introduces in *Individuals*. There he refers to "the consciousness of a being who has a use for the distinction between himself and his states on the one hand, and something not himself or a state of himself, of which he has experience, on the other" (Strawson 1959, 69). The notion of a point of view elucidates what any creature's experience must be like for it to count as nonsolipsistic in this sense.

Nonetheless, Strawson's conception of a point of view needs some modification before it can be fitted into the current framework. As Strawson understands the matter (unsurprisingly, given his Kantian inspiration), experience reflecting the double aspect required for the development of a point of view is available only to creatures who have mastered both the sophisticated conceptual skills involved in being able to ascribe experiences to themselves and the basic concepts required for understanding the objectivity of the world. Although he does not offer an explicit argument for why the notion of a point of view must be defined in that way, I think the following captures his position:

1. Genuine nonsolipsistic consciousness requires the capacity to distinguish one's experiences from the objects experienced.
2. That requires the capacity to identify one's experiences as one's experiences.
3. Identifying one's experiences as one's experiences is a form of self-ascription.
4. The self-ascription of experiences requires reflexive self-reference.

The discussion of nonconceptual first-person contents in the preceding two chapters, however, should have generated a certain suspicion of this line of argument. The previous chapter in particular showed that nonsolipsistic experience both can and does exist in the absence of the sort of conceptual skills that Strawson takes (without argument) to be necessary for it. A creature who, in virtue of somatic proprioception, can register the distinction between self and nonself has clearly arrived at a form of nonsolipsistic consciousness.

We can keep the essential thrust of Strawson's position by reformulating it as follows. Taking the central distinction to be between subjective experience and what that subjective experience is experience of allows us to capture the crucial feature missing in the hypothesized purely sense-datum experience without immediately demanding any relevant conceptual capacities on the part of the subject. Using this as the central notion, we can reformulate the original characterization: having a temporally extended point of view on the world involves taking a particular route through space-time in such a way that one's perception of the world is informed by an awareness that one is taking such a route, where such an awareness requires being able to distinguish over time between subjective experience and what it is experience of. For obvious reasons I term this a *nonconceptual point of view.*

7.2   Self-Specifying Information and the Notion of a Nonconceptual Point of View

Once the notion of a point of view has been formulated so that no relevant conceptual requirements are built into it, one might naturally think that the analysis of perceptual experience and somatic proprioception in chapters 5 and 6 already shows us how to make sense of the notion of a nonconceptual point of view. No special argument is needed to show that it is possible to have a nonconceptual point of view, it might be suggested, because such a nonconceptual point of view is built into our experience of the world from the very beginning. Much of the self-specifying information picked up in perceptual experience is information about the spatiotemporal route that one is taking through the world. This is, of course, particularly apparent in kinesthetic experience, both visual and proprioceptive. It might thus seem that one does in fact have a continuous awareness of oneself taking a particular route through the world that does not require the exercise of any conceptual abilities, in virtue of having a constant flow of information about oneself as a physical object moving through the world. The suggestion is that the ecological coperception of self and environment, together with the proprioceptively derived distinction between self and nonself, is all that is needed for experience from a nonconceptual point of view. This suggestion is a very natural one. But it is misplaced, and seeing why it is misplaced is an important first step in the project of moving from basic-level information pick-up to full self-consciousness.

We need to begin by exploring in more detail why a point of view has been described as temporally extended. Is it the nonconceptual point of view itself that is temporally extended, or simply the lifespan of the creature that has the point of view? The issue can be focused with a thought experiment. Suppose that we imagine a creature whose experience takes place completely within a continuous present and lacks any sense of past or future. The hypothesis is that every experience that this creature has is completely novel. Could such a creature have experience reflecting a nonconceptual point of view? If the answer is affirmative, then it follows that a nonconceptual point of view has to be temporally extended only in the limited sense that it is enjoyed by creatures who move through the world over time. If negative, we will have to look for a new sense of temporal extension.

Reflection on this thought experiment leads, I think, to the conclusion that the capacity to make the basic distinctions at the heart of the notion of a nonconceptual point of view would be absent in the case under discussion. A creature whose experience takes place completely within a continuous present cannot draw the fundamental nonsolipsistic distinction between its experience and what it is experience of. A minimal requirement on being able to make such a distinction is that what is being experienced should be grasped as existing independently of any particular experience of it. What we are trying to avoid, it will be remembered, is a situation in which the *esse* of the putative "objects of experience" is their *percipi,* and this requires "a component of recognition or judgement which is not simply identical with, or wholly absorbed by, the particular item which is recognised, which forms the topic of the judgement" (Strawson 1966, 100). There must be recognition that the object of experience has an existence transcending the particular occasion on which it is apprehended. At the most basic level, such a grasp of independent existence itself involves an understanding that what is being experienced at the moment either has existed in the past or will exist in the future, that it has an existence transcending the present moment. By definition, however, a creature that experiences only a continuous present cannot have any such understanding.

There is a possible confusion here that it is important to clear up. The distinction between self and nonself that has been seen to be present in somatic proprioception is emphatically not equivalent to the distinction between experience and what it is experience of that is currently at issue. What could potentially confuse matters is that both distinctions appear to qualify as instances of what Strawson terms nonsolipsistic consciousness. A nonsolipsistic consciousness is "the consciousness of a being who has a use for the distinction between himself and his states on the one hand, and something not himself or a state of himself, of which he has experience, on the other" (Strawson 1959, 69). A creature who, in virtue of somatic proprioception, has a grasp of the boundaries and limits of the self, and hence of the distinction between self and other, can be described as "having a use for the distinction between himself and his states, on the one hand, and something not himself or a state of himself on the other." The same holds for a creature who has grasped the distinction between experience and what it is experience of. But it would be a mistake to think that a grasp of the first distinction would automatically bring with it a grasp of the second. The distinction between self and nonself has nothing to do with the concept of experience. Moreover, there is an important difference in the respective temporal dimensions of the two distinctions. The distinction between self and nonself is available purely *synchronically*. It does not require taking into account times other than the present, unlike the distinction between experience and what it is experience of. That second distinction is *diachronic*, as will emerge shortly.

The important question as far as this second distinction is concerned, therefore, seems to be this: What form must experience take if it is to incorporate an awareness that what is being experienced does not exist only when it is being experienced? And in particular, what must the temporal form of any such experience be? Clearly, such an awareness would be incorporated in the experience of any creature that had a grasp of the basic temporal concepts of past, present, and future, but we are looking for something at a more primitive nonconceptual level. What I would suggest is that certain basic recognitional capacities offer the right sort of escape from the continuous present without demanding conceptual mastery. Consider the act of recognizing a particular object. Because such an act involves drawing a connection between current experience of an object and a previous experience of it, it brings with it an awareness that what is being experienced has an existence transcending the present moment. Of course, not all such acts of recognition will involve an awareness that what is being experienced exists independently of being experienced. Reference to a previous experience can occur in the absence of any awareness that the object of experience exists unperceived, as is the case, for example, when a particular sensation or subjective feeling is recognized. It is certainly possible to recognize an experience as one previously experienced without any grasp of the distinction between experience and what it is experience of. Clearly, the recognitional capacities must be exercised on something extraneous to the experiences themselves. But what?

Physical objects are obvious candidates, and any creature that could recognize physical objects would have experience that involves drawing the right sort of distinctions. However, one might wonder whether the distinctions could be drawn at a level of experience that does not involve objects, and in fact it is hard to see how there could be such a thing as a nonconceptual point of view if the distinctions could not be drawn at a more primitive level. Strawson (following Kant) is surely right to assume that a full understanding of the nature of objects comes only with a core set of conceptual abilities. It is important, then, that there should be "things" that can be recognized but that are not physical objects, but what are they? One natural suggestion to make here would be that such "things" are places. The thought here is that the fundamentally spatial nature of the experienced world provides the most basic material for the exercise of basic recognitional capacities. The experience of creatures who cannot manipulate concepts in the manner required to think about an objective spatial world of mind-independent objects can nonetheless reflect the spatiality of their lived environment in terms of the primitive capacity to think about places.

There is an obvious problem, though, that this proposal has to deal with. The identification of places and the identification of objects seem so inextricably bound together that it is not clear how there can be reidentification of places without thought about objects. The connection between objects and places has been thought to hold in both directions. It is certainly clear that the criteria of identity for any given material object involve spatiotemporal continuity, and that if I want to establish whether an object at one time is identical with another object at another time, then one of the criteria that has to be satisfied is that they should either be at the same place or that there should be a plausible spatial route between the two places that they occupy. But many have also argued that the interdependence holds also in the opposite direction, that the criteria of identity for places necessarily depend on the criteria of identity for objects (Strawson 1959, Quinton 1973). It is important, however, to be clear on what the terms of the debate are here. One question that might be asked here is whether we, as concept-exercising and language-using creatures, could have anything like the understanding of space and spatial relations that we actually do have without having the capacity to think about objects and to employ those thoughts about objects in identifying places and their relations. But what is relevant here is the more general question of whether any capacity for place reidentification could be available to creatures who lack the capacity to think in terms of enduring material objects occupying spatial positions (Campbell 1993).

The problem arises, of course, because places themselves cannot be recognised simpliciter. They must be recognised in terms of what occupies them. So, to rebut the objection that there cannot be place reidentification without object reidentification, it will be necessary to offer an alternative account of the possible occupants that could make place reidentification possible. It seems to me that, far from material objects being the only such occupants, there are (at least) two distinct alternatives.

One alternative has already been discussed at some length in chapter 3, where I noted that recent work in developmental psychology strongly supports the view that young infants parse their visual perceptions into bounded segments, about whose behavior they have certain expectations, which expectations nonetheless do not qualify as the perception of objects (still less as involving mastery of the concept of an object). I suggested in the final section of chapter 4 that by defining the concept of an object* we could capture at a nonconceptual level how the perceived array can be parsed into spatially extended segments that are more primitive than objects. Drawing on this, I find it natural to propose that objects* could have an important role to play in place reidentification.

We can make a start on the second alternative by noting the view that there are levels of language use that do not involve identifying reference to particular objects (Strawson 1959, Campbell 1993). What is often termed "feature-placing" discourse characterizes the world in terms of features in a manner notably different from the more familiar subject-predicate discourse. Whereas subject-predicate discourse depends upon identifying reference to material particulars, and these are then ascribed qualities or properties (which are sortal universals, appropriate for identifying and classifying material particulars), feature-placing discourse deploys universal terms that are not sortal universals and that are not predicated of material particulars. 'It is raining' is a case in point, as is 'There is food'. In neither of these cases is there a particular thing of which certain properties are predicated, nor are the universal terms involved the sort of terms that can be used to classify particulars. Quine's distinction between mass terms and count terms is very much to the point here (1960, sections 19–20). *Mass terms* are terms that refer cumulatively to general types of stuff, like water, wood, or rain. Any bit of wood is wood, as is any collection of bits of woods, and the question of how many is not an appropriate one to ask once the presence of wood has been identified. In contrast, *count terms* must be provided in order for things to be counted and numbered. They pick out particular things.[1] We can understand feature-placing discourse as a form of language use that operates at the level of mass terms and has no count terms, with the important proviso that the range of available mass terms in such feature-placing discourse is not restricted to those terms that function as mass terms in our own far more complex language.[2]

This notion of primitive feature-placing discourse can be modified to help us understand how place reidentification might take place without thought about objects. Let us assume a fairly primitive creature that nonetheless possesses the capacity to recognize features, such as warmth or food. Let us assume, moreover, that such a creature can navigate its way around the environment in a manner that is not entirely stimulus-driven (according to the criteria discussed in chapter 4). In navigating its way around the environment, it returns to particular places, and this can be made comprehensible in terms of certain features (warmth, food, water, etc.) that exist at those places and that it is appropriate to describe the creature as detecting. Such a situation it is compelling to describe as one in which spatial behaviour is driven by information about features holding at places. This in turn opens the way to the thought that we can understand some forms of place reidentification in terms of feature reidentification.

So we can make sense of place reidentification in terms either of the notion of an object* or that of feature reidentification, or of course in terms of both. This answers the worry that place reidentification depends on object reidentification by showing that at least a primitive form of place recognition can be prior to object identification.[3] But there is an important dimension not yet discussed. We can draw a broad distinction between two types of memory. There are, on the one hand, instances of memory in which past experiences influence present experience but without any sense on the part of the subject of having had the relevant past experiences and, on the other, instances in which past experiences not only influence present experience but also the subject is in some sense aware of having had those past experiences. In the former case what licenses talk of memory is the fact that a subject (or an animal or even a plant) can respond differentially to a stimulus as a function of prior exposure to that stimulus or to similar stimuli. This is not to deny that such a memory can be extremely complex. Quite the contrary, it seems to be central to the acquisition of any skill, even the most developed. The "differential response" does not have to be simple or repetitive. Nonetheless, we can draw a contrast between memory at this level and the various forms of memory that do involve an awareness of having had the relevant past experiences, as, for example, when a memory image comes into one's mind or one successfully recalls what one did the previous day. Clearly, there are many levels of such memory (which I shall term 'conscious memory'), of which autobiographical memory is probably the most sophisticated. One thing that these forms of *conscious* or *explicit* memory all have in common, however, is that previous experience is consciously registered, rather than unconsciously influencing present experience.[4]

This distinction of forms of memories is a crude one, not least because such terms as 'conscious' and 'explicit' are so hazy, but it can be illustrated through some striking experimental work carried out with amnesic patients (Schacter, McAndrews, and Moscovitch 1988). As is well known, amnesia is an inability to remember recent experiences (even from the very recent past) and to learn various types of information, and it results from selective brain damage that leaves perceptual, linguistic, and intellectual skills untouched. Memory deficits in amnesic patients have traditionally been studied using techniques designed to elicit explicit memories. So, for example, amnesic patients might be instructed to think back to a learning episode and either recall information from that episode or say whether a presented item had previously been encountered in the learning episode. On tests like these, amnesic patients perform very badly. What is interesting, though, is that the very same patients who perform badly on these tests of recall and recognition can perform successfully (sometimes as successfully as normal subjects) on tests that do not require thinking back to specific episodes or consciously bringing to mind earlier experiences. The acquisition of skills is a case in point, and there is considerable experimental evidence showing that amnesic patients can acquire both motor and intellectual skills over a series of learning episodes even though they cannot explicitly remember any of the learning episodes. A striking example is the densely amnesic patient who learned how to use a personal computer over numerous sessions, despite declaring at the beginning of each session that he had never used a computer before (Glisky, Schacter, and Tulving 1986). In addition to this sort of capacity to learn over a succession of episodes, amnesics have performed well on single-episode learning tasks (such as completing previously shown words when given 3-letter cues). Experiments like these in amnesic patients clearly reveal the difference between conscious and nonconscious memory, but similar dissociations can be observed in normal subjects, as when performance on indirect tasks reveals the effects of prior events that are not remembered.

Nonetheless, the distinction of forms of memories is not yet as clear as it needs to be, since the distinguishing feature of conscious memories, as so far defined, is that they issue in verbal reports, which is of limited use at the nonconceptual level. To sharpen the distinction further it is helpful to recall that memory is a causal notion (Martin and Deutscher 1966). This holds both of conscious and unconscious memory, although, of course, in different ways. At a very general level, the notion of memory has the following core role to play in the explanation of behavior: we need to appeal to the operations of memory to explain a creature's current behavior where we cannot fully explain that behavior without assuming that it is being being causally affected by previous experiences and/or thoughts (henceforth, 'experiences/thoughts'). But the satisfaction of this core condition counts as an instance of conscious memory if and only if the previous experiences/thoughts are causally efficacious through the medium of occurrent experiences/thoughts that refer back to those previous experiences/thoughts. In the case of unconscious memory, in contrast, this further requirement is not satisfied.

Note that there are two ways in which the further requirement for conscious memory could fail to be satisfied. First, it could be the case that there are no distinctive occurrent experiences/thoughts. Of course, this would not mean that there are no occurrent experiences/thoughts at all. Rather, this case arises when a creature's occurrent experiences/thoughts are precisely those that it would have had if the previous experiences/thoughts had not been causally efficacious. As an example, consider Glisky's amnesic patient encountering his computer at the beginning of his tenth lesson (which, of course, he thinks is his first). Despite the effects of the previous nine lessons, the patient has more or less the same experiences/thoughts that he had when he first encountered the computer. No distinctive experiences/thoughts are caused by his previous encounters with the computer. Nonetheless, those previous encounters could be causally efficacious if, for example, the patient's first action was to switch on the computer and take hold of the mouse. A second way of failing the further requirement would occur if, although the subject in question did have distinctive occurrent experiences/thoughts caused in the appropriate way, those experiences/thoughts do not refer back to the previous experiences and/or thoughts that caused them. One common way in which this occurs is when perceptual discriminative capacities have been sharpened through long experience. Here a creature's occurrent perceptions could be significantly altered by previous experiences/thoughts without there being any reference back to the experiences/thoughts that are causally responsible for the increased discrimination manifest in its occurrent perceptions.

It is important to recognize that neither form of potential failure can be present if we are plausibly to maintain the presence of conscious memory. Conscious memory requires more than that past experience/thoughts causally affect present experiences/thoughts. It requires that they do so in a way that makes them recognized as past experience/thoughts. The grasp of a primitive notion of the past is built into the ascription conditions of conscious memory: to attribute conscious memory is ipso facto to attribute a grasp of times other than and prior to the present.

So, the distinction is between, on the one hand, the processing of retained information derived from past experience and, on the other, the registration of past experience as past experience in conscious awareness. When we apply this distinction to the matter in hand, our working notion of a point of view demands that conscious memory be involved in the recognitional abilities at the heart of having a point of view upon the world. Reflect on the case of a creature, perhaps a swallow, that is perfectly capable of performing complicated feats of navigation (like finding its way back to its nest or to the warmer climes where it spends the winter) but that nonetheless has no conscious memories of repeatedly encountered features or objects* at particular places. Such a creature is clearly sensitive to certain facts about the places, features, or objects* in question, because those facts determine behavior. Moreover, it is quite possible that its occurrent experiences should be causally affected by its previous encounters with those places, features, or objects*. Nonetheless, it is important to recognize that we are applying the concept of reidentification here in a restricted sense. In the case of a creature capable only of nonconscious memory, that creature's capacity to reidentify a place is exhausted by its capacity to find its way back to that place.

But when we consider place reidentification that involves the operations of conscious memory, the situation becomes fundamentally different. When a creature finds its way back to a particular place that it then consciously remembers (or when it consciously remembers an object* or feature at a place to which it has found its way back), it is emerging from a continuous present and moving toward possession of a temporally extended point of view. This is so for two reasons. First, consciously to remember a particular place, object*, or feature is to be aware of having been at that place or encountered that object* or feature before. A creature who can remember having been somewhere before has the beginning of an awareness of movement through space over time. And that in turn is the beginning (and certainly a necessary, although not sufficient, condition) of being able to draw what Strawson terms the distinction between the subjective route of one's experiences and the world through which it is a route. Second, recall that part of the significance of the notion of a point of view is that it provides a sense of self-world dualism richer than the minimal registering of the distinction between self and nonself that emerges from somatic proprioception. As I mentioned earlier, the richness of the self-awareness that accompanies the capacity to distinguish the self from the environment is directly proportionate to the richness of the awareness of the environment from which the self is being distinguished. And what is significant about place reidentification that involves conscious memory is that it makes possible a richer form of awareness of the environment. Without conscious memory, no creature would be able to conceive of their environment as composed of items that have an existence transcending the present moment. What conscious memory offers is the possibility of conceiving of objects as having existed in the past.

These two reasons for why place reidentification involving conscious memory is so central here depend on how conscious memory implicates a form of temporal orientation toward the past. There are, of course, different types and degrees of temporal orientation toward the past, and one question that arises is, what type of understanding of the past does conscious memory contribute to the acquisition of a nonconceptual point of view upon the world? An important distinction in this area has been made by John Campbell (1994, section 2.1). Campbell distinguishes between what he terms *temporal orientation with respect to phase* (henceforth *phasal orientation*) and *temporal orientation with respect to particular time* (henceforth *particular orientation*). He illustrates the distinction as follows:

Consider an animal that hibernates. Through the part of the year for which it is awake, it regulates its activity depending on the season. Such an animal certainly has a use for temporal orientation. It can recognize that it is late spring, perhaps by keeping track of how long it has been since winter, and realize that soon it will be summer. But it may not have the conception of the seasons as particular times; it may be incapable of differentiating between the autumn of one year and the autumn of another. It simply has no use for the conception of a particular autumn, as opposed to the general idea of the season. So while the animal is capable of orientation with respect to phases, it is not capable of orientation with respect to particular times. (Campbell 1994, 38)

At issue here is the capacity to think about event tokens, as opposed to the capacity to think about event types. Phasal orientation does not involve distinguishing between event types and event tokens. Phasal orientation is concerned simply with where one is on a given temporal cycle and does not provide the resources for thinking about the relations, temporal or otherwise, between that temporal cycle and another. In a particular orientation, in contrast, event tokens are discriminated by means of a temporal frame of reference that places all event tokens within a single linear series ordered by the relations of temporal priority and temporal simultaneity.

Does the work to which I am putting the concept of conscious memory require a phasal orientation or a particular orientation toward the past? Conscious memory offers the beginning of both an awareness of movement through space over time and an awareness that the environment is composed of items that have an existence transcending the present moment. Temporal orientation toward the past is at the heart of both of these forms of awareness. There seems no good reason to think that phasal orientation will not be sufficient here. The creature described by Campbell in the passage just quoted has both an awareness of movement through space over time and an awareness that the environment is composed of items whose existence transcends the present moment, despite its inability to orient itself toward particular times. Although place reidentification involves reidentifying a *particular* place, it does not follow that if reidentification is to involve conscious memory, then the memory in question must be a memory of having previously encountered that place at a particular time. A memory of having previously encountered the place at a particular stage in a temporal cycle would be quite sufficient.

Certainly, a conscious memory of having previously encountered a particular place is a memory of a particular happening or event that occurred at a particular time. But it does not follow that the memory must refer to a particular time within a temporal frame of reference, as associated with the particular orientation toward the past. This is tied up with the fact that memory is a causal notion. The causal dimension of memory is captured particularly clearly in the influential and widely accepted account of memory offered by Martin and Deutscher (1966), which I will use to illustrate the point. The core of the account is given by the following three conditions:

A remembers a particular event or thing ϕ if and only if

i. within certain limits of accuracy he represents ϕ as having been encountered in the past;

ii. if ϕ was public, he observed ϕ; if ϕ was private, then it was "his";

iii. his past experience of ϕ was (causally) operative in producing a state or succession of states that ultimately produced his representation of ϕ. (Martin and Deutscher 1966, 166)

I take this to be a relatively uncontroversial theory of memory. Conditions (i) to (iii) can be satisfied whether or not ϕ is located by *A* within a temporal frame of reference associated with the particular orientation toward the past. If *A* is capable only of phasal orientation toward the past, then it follows, of course, that he is not capable of representing the temporal difference between ϕ in temporal phase *P* and ϕ' in temporal phase *P'*, and hence the particular times at which they occur. But if *A* currently represents ϕ and his current representation is causally derived from his experience of ϕ, then, given that ϕ is a particular event occurring at a particular time, it follows from conditions (i) to (iii) that *A* is enjoying a memory of a particular event that occurred at a particular time.

It might be objected, though, that *A* is not properly described as representing ϕ in the situation described. Let us assume that two particular events ϕ and ϕ' within temporal cycles *P* and *P'* are phenomenologically indistinguishable for *A*. If this were the case, then a subject would only be able to distinguish them by referring them to different points in a single temporal series that includes both *P* and *P'*, and this, ex hypothesi, is something that *A* cannot do. In such a case, the objection runs, *A* cannot be properly described as representing ϕ rather than ϕ', and hence would not satisfy condition (i). The point of the causal theory, however, is that whether *A* is representing ϕ or ϕ' is determined by the causal history of *A*'s current representation. It is, of course, perfectly possible that there is no single determinate causal history, and that *A* is really representing a generic ϕ-type event or object in a manner causally traceable to the conjunction of its experiences of ϕ, ϕ', ϕ'', ... But it would be a mistake to think that this is all that *A* can properly be described as doing. Memory is best analyzed as a form of perception, and it cannot generally be a requirement upon perceiving a particular ϕ that one be able to distinguish that ϕ from any other ϕ-type event or object that might have been causally responsible for one's current perception.

This is a good moment to comment on some potential ambiguities in the concept of episodic memory. Campbell defines 'episodic memory' so that it counts as an instance of the particular orientation: "I will be interpreting 'episodic memory' to mean memory of a past happening conceived as having a particular past time at which it took place" (Campbell 1994, 40). I have no objection to this stipulation. But it is important to bear in mind that many psychologists operate with a simple binary distinction between memory of things happening and memory for facts and skills (semantic and procedural memory). If memory is classified in this binary way, then accepting Campbell's definition will have the consequence that all memories of things happening will count as instances of particular orientation toward the past. This is an unwelcome conclusion, because it makes analytically true a claim that is controversial and in any case (as I have just argued) false. It would be helpful to enrich the vocabulary here by distinguishing the class of *autobiographical memories* within the more inclusive class of episodic memories.[5] Autobiographical memories are those memories of particular events that are temporally indexed so that they fit within a linear, autobiographical frame of reference.

Let me take stock. I have used the notion of a temporally extended point of view to characterize the structure of experience in a creature capable of making a rudimentary distinction between its experiences and what those experiences are experiences of. When we looked more deeply at this idea, it emerged that the capacity to make such a distinction is available only to creatures who are capable of exercising certain basic recognitional abilities: the interlocking abilities to recognize places and features. Moreover, these recognitional abilities must involve the exercise of explicit or conscious memory. Putting the matter like this, however, brings out into the open two important problems that need to be confronted. The first is a practical problem. It is relatively straightforward to establish the presence of explicit or conscious memory in language-using subjects, since their subjective reports are usually a reliable source. But when we are dealing with nonlinguistic animals, all we have to go on are observable facts about differential responses to stimuli as a function of previous exposure. How can we decide whether to explain these responses in terms of implicit or explicit memory? The second problem is theoretical, and more radical. It emerges because we are looking for cognitive abilities that it makes sense to ascribe to non-concept-using creatures, like young infants and many animals. But many philosophers are skeptical about the very possibility of nonconceptual recognitional abilities. At the very least, then, this skepticism must be set to rest.

To begin with the skeptical worry, one reason for thinking that the notion of nonconceptual recognition does not make sense is the thought that recognition is essentially an activity of classification that involves relating objects of experience under concepts. There is, I think, a simple reply to this. If there were no nonconceptual recognition, then it would be impossible to see how any concepts could ever be acquired. Whatever detailed theory of concept acquisition we adopt, it is obviously true that the acquisition of observational and perceptual concepts takes place on the basis of perceived resemblances between items.[6] But there can be no perceived resemblances without basic recognitional abilities. Recognition is the most fundamental step in categorization and classification, and it is correspondingly absurd to make it depend on more sophisticated cognitive abilities.[7] But in contrast to the very clear sense we have of what it is to classify things under concepts, we have very little understanding of what nonconceptual recognition might consist in at the level of conscious or explicit phenomenal experience (i.e., when we are dealing with recognitional abilities that cannot be understood solely in terms of nonconscious information processing). There are three points that it is worth making in this context.

First, it is a mistake to hold that there can be no organized experience without the experience of conceptually classifiable particulars. On the contrary, we have already looked at two ways in which experience can be organized without the application of concepts. The first emerged in my first discussion of nonconceptual content in chapter 3, where I noted that infants seem to be capable of parsing their experience into bounded segments that support certain basic expectations. This is a clear example of experience being organized without the application of concepts. Comparable types of organization emerged earlier in this section with feature-placing modes of thought. Of course, neither of these types of experience can count as experience of particular items, if 'particular items' is read to mean 'enduring material objects', but that would be a question-begging reading.

A second point is that there seems room for an unanalyzable feeling of familiarity as a basic building block for cognition. The notion of familiarity is at the heart of the theory of memory that Russell offered in *The Analysis of Mind,* and it has by and large not received good press among philosophers (Russell 1921, Pears 1975). According to Russell, the feeling of familiarity integral to the content of memory images gives rise to the belief that the image refers to the past. One significant, perhaps conclusive, difficulty for this theory is describing the feeling of familiarity in a way that clearly distinguishes it from the belief to which it is supposed to give rise, and the result has been a general distrust of appealing to feelings of familiarity in the context of memory. But this general distrust must be mistaken. An enormous part of learning, and hence of cognition as a whole, depends upon grasping that one event is similar to another, that something is the same as something else, and at the most basic level, it is hard to see how this could ever be apprehended without some sort of feeling of familiarity. Learning depends on the appreciation of similarity, as Quine has noted on many occasions, and familiarity is just an appreciated similarity. This is certainly not compromised by granting the anti-Russellian point that, in the case of belief-forming and language-using creatures, this feeling of familiarity is not clearly distinguishable from beliefs about the pastness of the remembered event to which it gives rise, since we are interested in familiarity as experienced by creatures incapable of entertaining beliefs about the pastness of past events.

Third, there is a close relation among recognitional abilities, features, and basic inductive generalizations. When an animal recognizes a particular place through recognizing a particular feature, that feature will, of course, be something in which it has a direct interest and that is directly relevant to its behavior. Recognizing a given feature is closely bound up with recognizing possibilities for action relative to that feature, and when this is performed over a period of time, it is appropriate to speak of the formation of a basic inductive generalization about what to expect at a particular place. The induction is generated by the experience of repeated conjunctions (which is itself presumably underwritten by feelings of familiarity). This gives us a further important element in nonconceptual recognition, because the expectancies to which such inductive generalizations give rise are presumably part of what it is like to recognize a place in terms of a feature.

These basic inductive generalizations are to be distinguished from the instrumental protobeliefs discussed in chapter 5. Those instrumental protobeliefs, involved in explaining the simplest and most basic forms of intentional activity, were elucidated in terms of present-tense expectancies about the behavior of objects in the environment. They do not count as instances of conscious memory. In fact, they fail to satisfy the criteria for conscious memory in the second of the two ways identified earlier. Although instrumental protobeliefs have, of course, been produced by past experiences, they contain no reference back to the past experiences causally responsible for those effects.

There is room for a strong claim about the connection between recognitional abilities and basic inductive generalizations at the nonconceptual level. There is a very important question about how memories can have have implications for current behavior. Jonathan Bennett has posed the question and solved it (note, though, that his terminology is rather different from mine):

> Non-linguistic behaviour is essentially a manipulation of a present environment, and the immediately relevant beliefs must be ones about the present. If an item of behaviour of this kind is also to show that the agent has a certain belief about the past, this must presumably be because the attribution of the past belief helps to explain the present one. But that requires that the two be somehow linked by the agent, and I do not see how they can be linked except through a general belief. (Bennett 1976, 104)

It is through the medium of basic inductive generalizations that a creature can bring its conscious memories to bear upon current behavior. Here is Bennett's illustration:

> Suppose that *a* chases a victim *v* up a tree, guards the foot of the tree for a while, and then climbs up after *v*. We could discover that *a* climbs the tree because he believes that *v* is in the tree. Can that belief be explained as arising from the belief that *v* was earlier in the tree? Only, I suggest, if *a* is also credited with the linking belief that *v*-like animals leave trees only by climbing down them (or that *v*-like animals never fly, or some such). (Bennett 1976, 105)

In his earlier book *Rationality* Bennett argued that the interdependence of basic inductive generalizations and conscious memories (in my terms) meant that neither could be ascribed to nonlinguistic creatures. Only linguistic creatures, he claimed, could manifest these two cognitive abilities separately. Only in language can one manifest a conscious memory without a related inductive generalization, and vice versa. This yields his restriction of these abilities to language users when coupled with the assumption that a creature that cannot manifest two different types of cognitive ability separately cannot properly be credited with either of them.[8]

As Bennett subsequently realized, however, the fact that basic inductive generalizations and conscious memories always coexist in the explanation of behavior if they feature in it at all does not mean that they cannot be separated out on behavioral grounds. Suppose that we are faced with a particular piece of behavior that appears to demand explanation in terms of a conscious memory of a particular place and a concomitant inductive generalization. Different inductive generalizations dictate different forms of behavior in different circumstances. By examining what a creature does in different circumstances, we can work out which inductive generalizations are governing its behavior and apply this back to the original behavior. Similarly, a given conscious memory of a place may, in conjunction with different inductive generalizations, dictate identifiable forms of behavior relative to that place. By comparing different candidate conscious memories with different candidate inductive generalizations, it should be possible in principle to narrow the field down to a single memory-generalization pair.

This interdependence of conscious memories and basic inductive generalizations is very significant in dealing with the practical problem identified earlier: how are we to establish the presence of explicit or conscious memory in nonlinguistic creatures, given the importance of verbal reports in deciding what memories to ascribe to linguistic creatures? Let me set the scene by describing two sets of experiments in the animal learning literature. The first is a set of experiments on monkeys (rhesus and pig-tailed macaques) carried out by Gaffan (1977). Monkeys were trained to watch a screen on which 25 colored slides were presented twice at random during a testing session. The monkeys were tested for their capacity to detect whether a given slide was being presented for the first or second time during a training session. Pressing a lever during the second presentation of a slide was rewarded with a sugar pellet, but pressing the lever during the first presentation was not. The two rhesus monkeys tested were able (after training) to discriminate with 90 percent accuracy between first and second presentation, although an average of 9 slides intervened between the two presentations.

Contrast Gaffan's experiments with the superficially more complicated memory experiments performed by Davis and Fitts (1976) on rhesus monkeys and pig-tailed macaques. In these experiments, pictures pasted onto boards were used to cover wells in which food rewards could be placed. The monkeys were presented with a sample picture, which they pushed off the well to discover whether the sample was rewarded or not. After a short delay, two pictures were presented simultaneously: one the sample and the other completely novel. If the sample had originally been rewarded it was rewarded again, while if the well under the sample had originally been empty, then the novel picture was rewarded. The monkeys mastered this principle.

In some ways this second set of experiments seems to involve more complicated memory operations than the previously described experiments. The animals are being asked to remember not just whether a picture has been presented before but also whether it was rewarded or not. This is a two-way classification. On the other hand, however, there is correspondingly less reason to hypothesize that conscious recognition and familiarity are driving the behavior in the experimental situation. Mastering the principle can be explained in terms of the direct reinforcement of associations. The first such association is the straightforward association between the sample and the reward. The second is the association between an unrewarded sample and the novel picture. To revert back to the original characterization of conscious memory, it does not seem necessary in explaining what is going on to appeal to more than the causal efficacy of previous experience on present behavior. But there does not seem to be a similar explanation of what is going on in Gaffan's recognition experiments. That is because the relevant association there involves familiarity and recognition. It is an association between rewards and the familiarity of a presented image. Successful performance in the Gaffan experiments rests upon successful mastery of a basic inductive generalization along the lines of 'Pressing a lever when something seen before is seen again leads to a reward' in conjunction with specific individual conscious memories of the form 'This has been seen before'. Specific individual conscious memories are required to learn this basic inductive generalization. I offer Gaffan's experiments as a clear example of behavior that demonstrably requires explanation in terms of conscious memories.

Let me relate this back to the concept of a nonconceptual point of view. The conclusion so far is that any creature who has a temporally extended point of view on the world must possess conscious recognitional abilities. This enables us to return to the issue with which this chapter began. We set out to identify certain fundamental dimensions of self-consciousness to which the perceptual pick-up of self-specifying information cannot do justice, and then to consider how basic-level information pick-up needs to be augmented if those dimensions of self-consciousness are to come into play. I put forward the notion of a nonconceptual point of view as just such a fundamental dimension of self-consciousness, and I suggested at the beginning of this section that the perceptual pick-up of self-specifying information might be sufficient for experience to reflect a point of view on the world. We are now in a position, though, to see why it cannot be sufficient.

On the ecological view, perception is fundamentally a process of extracting and abstracting invariants from the flowing optical array. Organisms perceive an environment that has both persisting surfaces and changing surfaces, and the interplay between them allows the organism to pick up the sort of information that specifies, for example, visual kinesthesis. The key to how that information is picked up is the idea of direct perception. The mistake made by existing theories of perception, according to Gibson, is construing the process of perception in terms of a hierarchical processing of sensory inputs, with various cognitive processes employed to organize and categorize sensations. A crucial element of this serial processing is bringing memories to bear upon present experience. As emphasised in chapter 5, Gibson rejects this whole picture of perception. Accepting that present experience is partly a function of past experience, he firmly denies that this sensitivity to past experience is generated by processing memories and sensations together. His alternative account rests on the idea that the senses as perceptual systems become more sensitive over time to particular forms of information as a function of prior exposure.[9] Although Gibson was rather polemical about what he termed "the muddle of memory," it would seem that his account seems to involve no more than a differential response to stimuli as a function of past experience. Gibson's position seems to be that conscious recognition is not implicated in ecological perception, although it might or might not develop out of such ecological perception. It is perfectly possible for a creature to have experience at the ecological level without any conscious recognitional capacities at all. If, then, a capacity for conscious place recognition is a necessary condition of having experience that involves a temporally extended point of view, then it seems that the dual structure of experience involved in the ecological coperception of self and environment must be significantly enriched before yielding a point of view.

The point, of course, is not that this creates any problem for the basic idea of ecological perception; rather, it is that the materials offered by Gibson's own account need to be supplemented if they are to be employed in the theoretical project under discussion, and it is perfectly possible that Gibson's concepts of information pick-up and direct "resonance" to information in the ambient environment could have a crucial role to play in such an extension of the basic way in which ecological perception is sensitive to past experience (as they are, for example, in the account of perception and memory developed in Neisser 1976). Gibson's account alone cannot do all the work it was earlier suggested it might be able to do, because the capacity for conscious place recognition needs to be added onto the ecological coperception of self and environment.

7.3   Three Intersecting Distinctions and the Acquisition Constraint

In chapter 5, I argued that the pick-up of self-specifying information in perceptual experience was a source of nonconceptual first-person contents. In chapter 6, I argued the same for somatic proprioception. I also suggested that these are the most primitive types of first-person contents—the building blocks from which we can construct a principled account of both the nature and the acquisition of self-consciousness. One obvious question that this raises is, are we committed to the view that any creature whose perceptual experience is a source of nonconceptual first-person contents ipso facto counts as self-conscious? This would, in the eyes of most theorists, be a reductio ad absurdum of the position under discussion. My discussion of the notion of a nonconceptual point of view in this chapter has offered a way to avoid this conclusion. We now have the conceptual machinery to impose a division within the class of creatures whose perceptual experience supports nonconceptual first-person contents. This division divides those creatures that have a nonconceptual point of view on the world from those creatures that do not. This distinction can be employed to mark a significant substantive sense of self-consciousness.

Still, several important issues remain to be discussed. First, more needs to be said about the notion of a nonconceptual point of view. The discussion in this chapter has been devoted principally to establishing conscious place recognition as a necessary condition for possession of a nonconceptual point of view, and it should be obvious that it is far from a sufficient condition. In the next chapter I will discuss in more detail how the capacity for conscious place recognition is put to work to provide a nonconceptual point of view on the world. A second set of issues emerges when we ask how the distinction stressed in this chapter maps onto certain other distinctions, one of which has already been discussed. In particular, something needs to be said about how the distinction between conscious place recognition and nonconscious place recognition relates, first, to the distinction between conscious and nonconscious creatures and, second, to the distinction discussed in chapter 4 between behavior that supports an intentional interpretation and behavior that does not. A third point that needs to be discussed is how the conclusions of this chapter mesh with the Acquisition Constraint, which governs the overall project of showing how full-fledged self-consciousness can be built up from the pick-up of self-specifying information in perceptual experience.

Describing the type of memory implicated in experience reflecting a nonconceptual point of view as conscious memory can make it tempting to think that all and only creatures capable of conscious place recognition are conscious. This is certainly suggested by the contrast drawn between conscious place recognition and unconsciously generated differential responses due to prior exposure to stimuli. Nonetheless, there is nothing incoherent about the idea that a creature inhabiting what I termed the continuous present could have conscious experiences. Of course, it could not have conscious experiences if we stipulate, as Strawson does, that conscious experiences are available only to creatures with a point of view on the world. But there are no good grounds for making this stipulation. Perceptual experiences with first-person nonconceptual contents derived from the pick-up of self-specifying information can be entertained by creatures who lack a point of view on the world in virtue of lacking conscious recognitional abilities. I can think of no non-question-begging reason to deny that these are experiences. And in any case, even someone determined to deny that such states could count as experiences in some rich and as yet unspecified sense of the word would nonetheless have to accept that such a creature could still be conscious in virtue of having sensations.[10]

We should not assume that only creatures possessed of the appropriate conscious recognitional capacities can behave in ways that demand intentional explanation. The operational criteria for the appropriateness of intentional explanation discussed in chapter 4 neither make any reference to, nor imply the existence of, conscious recognitional abilities. These criteria derive from the basic thought that representational perceptual states are intermediaries between sensory input and behavioral output to which appeal needs to be made when there is no invariant connection between input and output. There is no reason to think that a creature moving around the world and acting on the basis of self-specifying information in the various ways described by Gibson could not be capable of behavior that is plastic and flexible enough to require intentional explanation. And if the behavior is suitably plastic and flexible, then, as discussed in chapter 5, the first-person nonconceptual contents derivable from the pick-up of self-specifying information are particularly well suited to capture the contents of perceptual protobeliefs in way that explains their direct relevance to action. Intentional explanation can enter into the picture prior to the emergence of the conscious recognitional abilities necessary for possession of a point of view on the world.

This point can be brought home by reflecting on the strong pressures to concede that at least some instrumentally conditioned behavior is intentional (Russell 1980, Dickinson 1988). Instrumental conditioning certainly does not require conscious recognitional capacities, being perfectly explicable on Gibsonian lines in terms of increasing perceptual sensitivity to a particular affordance. All that instrumental conditioning requires is consciousness in the very weak sense of sentience, since reinforcement depends on the capacity to feel sensations. It is reasonable, I think, to hold that the capacity for intentional behavior is restricted to creatures that are conscious in the weak sense of being able to feel sensations. But the converse does not hold. Creatures whose behavior is not intentional can be perfectly capable of feeling sensations. This is presumably what makes possible the various types of instrumental conditioning that do not result in intentional behavior.

The conclusion to draw, then, is that that we are dealing here with three intersecting distinctions, rather than three different ways of describing the same distinction. None of the three distinctions map cleanly on to any of the others. Nonetheless, it does seem that these three distinctions give us a hierarchy of cognitive abilities, ordered according to the relations of dependence among these abilities. Basic consciousness is clearly the most primitive of the three abilities. It is presupposed by both the others, while itself presupposing neither of them. In fact, it is very plausible to think that it is innate (Gazzaniga 1995). Next comes the capacity for intentional behavior, which requires consciousness in the weak sense of sentience but is independent of the conscious recognitional abilities that we have seen to be necessary conditions for possession of a nonconceptual point of view. It is perfectly possible, as I have stressed, for the first-person nonconceptual contents yielded by the pick-up of self-specifying information to occur at this level. Subject to the conditions discussed in this chapter, such contents can interact with the highest of the three cognitive abilities, which is the capacity to entertain conscious recognitional abilities of the sort discussed in this chapter.

It seems reasonable to think that the categorization of these three factors in terms of their degrees of primitiveness provides useful clues to answering the more general developmental question of how the capacity for conscious recognition can arise, both ontogenetically and phylogenetically. It will be remembered that the following constraint was suggested as a means of ensuring that an articulated theory of self-consciousness is suitably sensitive to the developmental progression from first-person perceptual contents to first-person thought:

The Acquisition Constraint   If a given psychological capacity is psychologically real, then there must be an explanation of how it is possible for an individual in the normal course of development to acquire that capacity.

The application of the acquisition constraint to the present case is straightforward. We have a modest hierarchy of three stages, intended to capture relations of logical dependence. But how plausible is this hierarchy in developmental terms? Do the abilities associated with each level provide sufficient resources for the acquisition of the abilities associated with higher levels? The first level is basic sentience. This really presents no ontogenetic difficulties, since the capacity to feel sensations is innate and certainly present long before birth. There is no need to explain how the capacity to feel sensations arises in the developing individual.[11] I have also discussed how positing a primitive feeling of familiarity can help with understanding the transition from intentional behavior without conscious recognitional abilities to intentional behavior that does incorporate conscious recognitional abilities. The real problems come with the transition from basic sentience to intentional behaviour. How can this transition take place?

The first point to make is that the key to the whole procedure will be provided by associations between stimuli and sensations. A vital part of the evolutionary purpose of the capacity to feel sensations must presumably be to make it possible for organisms to learn from their environment. In its most basic form, this will take the form of correlations between painful stimuli and harmful sensations and corresponding correlations between pleasurable stimuli and beneficial sensations. The mechanisms that allow such correlations to emerge support the basic form of learning: learning that enables the organism to avoid things that are harmful to it while actively pursuing things that are beneficial to it. At this level we are, of course, dealing with stimulus-response behavior and the question is, how and why does stimulus-response behavior develop into behavior showing the flexibility and plasticity characteristic of intentional behavior? The answer I tentatively offer is that intentional behavior emerges when the number of stimulus-response correlations potentially relevant to any given action becomes so great that the need arises to choose between a range of possible responses to a given situation. The real point about intentional behavior is that a creature behaving intentionally behaves in a way that it need not have (which is why one important criterion for intentional behavior is whether or not there is a lawlike correlation between environmental stimulus and behavioral response). It is plausible to see this sort of situation arising because there are so many ways in which the creature could have behaved. The most primitive form of intentional action surely arises when a decision procedure emerges for deciding between competing possible courses of action, each of which may itself have a nonintentional ancestry. Intentional behavior should be understood at least in part as a response to a computational problem.

8

Navigation and Spatial Reasoning

Previous chapters have uncovered some of the basic elements of primitive self-consciousness. In chapter 5, I used ecological theories of perception to show how nonconceptual first-person contents can feature in the structure of perception, particularly visual perception. Chapter 6 explored conscious somatic proprioception as a comparable source of self-specifying contents. Both of these are ground-level forms of self-consciousness in the sense that, although they are not on their own sufficient to warrant the ascription of self-consciousness in anything but a derivative sense, they will be crucial building blocks in states that are properly described as self-conscious. In chapter 7, I began to show how one works up to self-conscious states by developing the notion of experience that reflects a nonconceptual point of view on the world, understanding this to involve taking a particular route through space-time in such a way that one's perception of the world is informed by an awareness that one is taking such a route. I have so far examined only one aspect of what it is to have a nonconceptual point of view on the world, namely, that it must involve conscious or explicit memory as a condition of conscious place recognition. This chapter will complete the account.

8.1 From Place Recognition to a Nonconceptual Point of View: Navigation and Spatial Awareness

At the heart of the notion of a nonconceptual point of view is registration of the nonsolipsistic distinction between experience and what is experienced. A minimal requirement of being able to make such a distinction is that what is being experienced should be grasped as having an existence independent of any particular apprehension of it. This in turn requires recognition that what is experienced exists at times other than the particular occasion on which it is apprehended. This is where conscious memory deployed in recognition enters the picture, as a basic way of recognizing this independent existence, because recognizing something involves correlating past and present experience of that object. I then suggested that recognizing places in terms of features present at those places is the most basic way in which this can be carried out. This already takes us beyond the account given of somatic proprioception and beyond Gibson's account of first-person contents gained through the pick-up of self-specifying information, but it still leaves us short of the notion of a nonconceptual point of view on the world for reasons that will emerge in this section.

Although conscious place recognition has been offered as a way of registering the distinction between subjective experience and what it is experience of, it is not yet clear that we have an account of place recognition rich enough for the job. In the previous chapter, place recognition was explained through the recognition of features or objects* at particular places. This indirect way of thinking about places needs to be distinguished from the more direct way of thinking about places that registers that they are places. Only the second of these ways manifests what can properly be described as an understanding of space, because understanding the nature of space involves understanding that a network of spatial relations holds between *places* independently of the spatial relations that hold at any given time between the various objects* or features found at those places. It is potentially misleading to say, as many philosophers have said, that space is a single system of spatial relations. Certainly, there is only a single system of spatial relations in the sense that all places are interconnected, that is, in the sense that there cannot be two or more spaces that are spatially insulated from each other. Nonetheless, for practical purposes, there are two importantly different types of spatial relations. There is the static and relatively unchanging system of spatial relations holding between places, and there is the highly changeable system of spatial relations holding between things always located at a particular place but not always at the same place.

The essence of navigation, and spatial thought in general, is bringing these two types of spatial relations into harmony—being able to calculate, for example, that if a creature C has moved a certain distance at a certain speed relative to creature D and if creature D is now at place P, then creature C will be found at place P^*. Spatial thought depends on a grasp of the fact that spatial relations between places will stay constant even though the spatial relations between objects vary, because a significant component of it uses those constant spatial relations as a means of mapping and keeping track of the changing spatial relations. Consequently, any understanding of the nature of space must respect the distinction between these two different systems of spatial relations. Moreover, this distinction also seems to be integral to the notion of a nonconceptual point of view. Possessing a nonconceptual point of view on the world involves being aware that one is taking a particular route through space-time as one navigates that route, and an adequate awareness that one is taking a particular route through space-time clearly presupposes a degree of understanding of the nature of space.

Obviously, though, the account of place recognition in the previous chapter does not respect this distinction, or more cautiously, the demands placed upon place recognition could be satisfied by a creature with no inkling of the distinction. It is perfectly possible for a creature to be capable of recognizing features as features that it has seen before and to put these recognitional abilities to work in navigating from one feature to another, without apprehending that there are spatial relations holding between the places at which those features are instantiated and that those spatial relations hold independently of the spatial relations between the features. Place recognition in the minimal sense discussed in the previous chapter can exist without an understanding of space. Such minimal place recognition involves the recognition of things that are places but does not demand that they be recognised as places. This indicates one dimension along which my minimal account of place recognition needs to be developed if it is to be built up into the notion of a nonconceptual point of view.

There is a second, related limitation in the minimal account of place recognition. The exercise of conscious memory in the recognition of places reflects a sense of the nonsolipsistic distinction between experience and what is experienced, but I have said nothing about the functions that this serves within the life of any creature capable of it. We are trying to capture the basic degree of self-consciousness implicated in a creature's having a point of view or perspective on the world, and it is reasonable to expect that this degree of self-consciousness will be implicated across a broad spectrum of cognitive and practical abilities. There seem to be three important questions at issue here, none of which has yet been discussed. First, what part does this nonsolipsistic distinction play within cognitive and practical life more widely construed? Second, what further cognitive and practical abilities are made available by the possibility of conscious place recognition? Third, what is the relevance of any of these cognitive and practical abilities to the possession of a nonconceptual point of view on the world and to primitive self-consciousness in general?

There are, then, two dimensions along which I am obligated to develop the minimal account of place recognition, and there are good reasons to think that the concept of navigation will be centrally implicated in both of them. Different types of navigation involve different levels of spatial awareness, with correspondingly different modes of understanding places. It is highly plausible that the move from the minimal grasp of place already in play to the fuller spatial understanding implicated in the notion of a nonconceptual point of view can be profitably analysed as a move from one form of navigational competence to another. Thus the concept of navigation seems very helpful in fulfilling the first obligation. Moreover, the ability to navigate through a spatial environment is itself at the intersection of a range of other cognitive and practical abilities, and hence seems equally promising with respect to my second obligation.

In the following sections of this chapter I will be primarily concerned with substantiating this general idea that careful attention to different types of navigational ability will help to bridge the theoretical gap between minimal place recognition and full-fledged possession of a nonconceptual point of view. Before moving on to this, however, it is important clearly to articulate the different elements that have emerged in my discussion of the notion of a nonconceptual point of view so that we can be clear about the end point to which we are moving.

The most general characterization of the notion of a nonconceptual point of view is this: having a nonconceptual point of view on the world involves being aware that one is taking a particular route through space-time as one navigates that route. But what exactly does this entail? A minimal requirement upon any creature to whom a nonconceptual point of view can correctly be ascribed is that it be capable of registering the distinction between experience and the experienced. This is the nonsolipsistic requirement that, as I argued in the previous chapter, can be satisfied only by forms of experience that do not take place wholly within a continuous present. The temporal implications of the nonsolipsistic requirement arise because grasping that an object of experience has an existence transcending the particular occasion on which it is experienced implies grasping that what is being experienced at a particular time has either existed in the past or will exist in the future. The possession of recognitional abilities involving conscious memory provides the most basic way in which the nonsolipsistic requirement can be satisfied, and I suggested that the recognition of places in terms of features is the most basic such recognitional ability.

In addition to this nonsolipsistic dimension of the notion of a nonconceptual point of view, there is a second dimension. A nonconceptual point of view requires awareness that one is taking a particular route through space-time, and this brings with it the need for a degree of spatial awareness. Recognizing places places cannot take place in isolation or purely passively; it goes hand in hand with navigating from one place to another. The navigational capacities that this involves will be a crucial element in possessing a nonconceptual point of view on the world. When the particular route through space-time that a creature takes is determined by its navigational abilities, its awareness of that route (demanded by its possession of a nonconceptual point of view) will have to reflect the fact that it is navigating through the world. This in turn demands a degree of understanding of the nature of space. In particular, it demands an understanding of the distinction between the spatial relations that hold between things and the spatial relations that hold between places.

Let me then provisionally break down the notion of a nonconceptual point of view into the following constituent elements:

The nonsolipsistic component (the distinction between experience and what that experience is experience of) requires

a. grasping that an object of experience exists independently of a particular apprehension of it, which requires

b. grasping that what is experienced exists at times other than those at which it is experienced, which requires

c. the exercise of recognitional abilities involving conscious memory, which is most primitively manifested in

d. feature-based recognition of places.

The spatial awareness component (putting place recognition to work for navigational purposes) requires

a. awareness that one is navigating through the environment, which requires

b. an understanding of the nature of space, which requires

c. a grasp of the distinction between the spatial relations that hold between places and the spatial relations that hold between things.

8.2   Spatial Awareness and Self-Consciousness

The issues raised by the close relationship between spatial awareness, self-consciousness, and an understanding of the mind-independence of the objects of experience has been discussed in the philosophical literature relatively frequently since Kant opened the debate in the *Critique of Pure Reason.* Two recent and influential treatments of the issues will be found in Christopher Peacocke's *A Study of Concepts* (1992) and John Campbell's *Past, Space, and Self* (1994). The juxtaposition of their respective positions poses an important challenge, which it will be the aim of the rest of this chapter to answer.

Christopher Peacocke has argued that any well-founded attribution to a creature of a capacity for the reidentification of places presupposes that the creature in question has mastery of the first-person concept.[1] If sound, this argument will have disastrous implications for the argument of this book, for it directly entails the incoherence of the notion of a nonconceptual point of view. Let me schematize his argument:

1. The attribution of genuine spatial representational content to a creature is justified only if that creature is capable of reidentifying places over time.

2. Reidentifying places requires the capacity to identify one's current location with a location previously encountered.

3. Reidentifying places in this way involves building up an integrated representation of the environment over time.

4. Neither (3) nor (4) would be possible unless the subject possessed at least a primitive form of the first-person concept.

To appreciate the significance of (4), it is important to remember the Priority Thesis, discussed and endorsed in chapter 2:

The Priority Principle   Conceptual abilities are constitutively linked with linguistic abilities in such a way that conceptual abilities cannot be possessed by nonlinguistic creatures.

According to the Priority Principle, concept possession goes hand in hand with linguistic mastery. Thus if Peacocke's argument is sound, it entails that what he is calling place reidentification cannot be available either to nonlinguistic creatures or to linguistic creatures that lack mastery of the first-person pronoun. Hence, on the assumption that Peacocke's place reidentification is an element in what I term possession of a nonconceptual point of view on the world, his argument is a direct threat to the position that I am developing.

Let us look more carefully at how Peacocke understands place reidentification. Place reidentification is the ability to identify a current place with a previously encountered place. This seems comparable to what I have been describing as place recognition involving conscious memory. In (3), however, the notion of place reidentification is made rather richer with the suggestion that place reidentification is available only to those creatures capable of building up an integrated representation of the environment over time:

To identify places over time requires the subject to be able to integrate the representational contents of his successive perceptions into an integrated representation of the world around him, both near and far, past and present. I label this the ability to engage in spatial reasoning. . . . Spatial reasoning involves the subject's building up a consistent representation of the world around him and of his location in it. (Peacocke 1992, 91)

Although Peacocke does not go into details about what is to count as "a consistent representation of the world around the subject," it is plausible to assume that it is rather comparable to elements (b) and (c) of what I term the spatial awareness component, namely, that a representation of the spatial layout of the environment registers an understanding of the nature of space, and in particular, of the distinction between the spatial relations that hold between places and those that hold between things.

So it is only with (4) that the position I am developing differs from Pea-cocke's position. It is clear, therefore, that Peacocke's argument presents a challenge that has to be met: the challenge of showing how the ability to engage in spatial reasoning is available to creatures who do not possess the capacity for reflexive self-reference.

One way of trying to meet this challenge would be to deny the strong conditions that Peacocke places on the capacity for place reidentification. In particular, one might query his suggestion that place reidentification is available only to creatures who have the capacity to construct suitably integrated representations of their environment and to engage in spatial reasoning in a way that necessarily involves grasp of the first-person pro-noun. This could be done, for example, by appealing to the notion of causally indexical comprehension developed by John Campbell (1994).[2] Grasping a causally indexical notion just is grasping its implications for one's own actions. Examples of such causally indexical notions are that something is too heavy for one to lift, or that something else is within reach. As Campbell points out, grasp of causally indexical notions may be linked with a reflective understanding of one's own capacities and of the relevant properties of the object. On the other hand, it need not be so linked: he maintains that it makes sense to ascribe to creatures a grasp of such causally indexical notions without ascribing to them any grasp of notions that are not causally indexical (even though those causally non-indexical notions might be essential to characterize the causally indexical notions), because the significance of such notions is exhausted by their implications for perception and action. And as such, causally indexical mental states qualify as states with nonconceptual content.

In the present context, then, one might suggest that there is no need to place the theoretical weight that Peacocke does on disengaged reflective and reasoning abilities. Rather, we should be looking at how a given crea-ture interacts with its surroundings, because that will be how it manifests its grasp of the spatial properties of its environment (of the connectedness of places, for example). On such a view, a creature could be capable of spatial reasoning in the absence of any capacity to reflect on its interac-tions with its environment. If this line is pursued, then it seems to provide a way in which we can hang on to the idea of place reidentification with-out accepting Peacocke's claim that it implicates possession of a primitive form of the first-person concept, precisely because it denies Peacocke's claim that any creature capable of place reidentification must be capable of explicitly representing itself and its location in its surroundings.

The trouble with this suggestion, however, is that Campbell's understanding of causally indexical spatial reasoning is rather orthogonal to the account I have been developing of the essential features of experience reflecting a nonconceptual point of view. Campbell calls upon the distinction between causal indexicality and causal nonindexicality to perform a variety of tasks and to give concrete sense to a range of other distinctions. One of these distinctions is that between absolute and egocentric ways of representing space, where an absolute representation of space is one that is not explicable in terms of an organism's interactions with space. Campbell wants to argue against the pragmatist's denial that there are any such absolute representations of space and to defend the view that there are ways of thinking about space that are completely independent of one's engagement with it, where such engagement is construed in navigational terms. This is all very well but, as usually happens with these "either"/ "or" distinctions, far too many discrete and rather different phenomena get lumped together on one side of the divide. In particular, Campbell's notion of causal indexicality has little or nothing to say about how the environment must be represented to make different types of navigation possible (Campbell 1993, 25). Different types of navigation are classified together because they all presuppose that places are physically significant in terms of their implications for perception and action. But this glosses over crucial distinctions, one of which is the distinction between those forms of navigation that do presuppose an integrated representation of the environment over time and those forms of navigation that do not. Of course, one might think that possession of an integrated representation of the environment over time is available only to creatures who are capable of representing space absolutely, which for Campbell means that it is available only to language-using adult humans (Campbell 1993, 25). But this is surely an empirical claim open to empirical refutation. It is not something that can be assumed at the beginning of enquiry.

The positions staked out by Peacocke and Campbell provide the framework for an account of spatial reasoning. Such an account will show, I hope, how the ability to engage in spatial reasoning can be available to creatures who do not possess the capacity for linguistic self-reference, without weakening the notion of spatial reasoning so far that it loses touch with the core of the notion of a nonconceptual point of view. How can this double challenge be met? Let me return briefly to Peacocke's characterization of spatial reasoning. Recall that the crux of spatial reasoning, as Peacocke defines it, is that it involves building up an integrated representation of the environment over time. And it is precisely this integrated representation of the environment that is lacking in Campbell's conception of causally indexical spatial comprehension. The contrast that Campbell draws between causally indexical and causally nonindexical thought is a contrast between practical engagement with the environment and detached and reflective contemplation of the environment, and his discussion of the contrast makes clear that (in his view, at least) the sort of integrated spatial reasoning under consideration falls on the "detached and reflective" side of the divide. What is needed is an account of spatial reasoning invoking a mode of representing the environment that is richer than what Campbell offers but yet does not involve the sophisticated skills that Peacocke builds into his notion of spatial reasoning.

If it can be shown that it does indeed make sense to attribute to prelinguistic creatures an integrated representation of their environment, then the double challenge will have been met. But how might this be done? Everything depends, of course, on how the notion of an integrated representation of the environment is understood, and it is unfortunate that Peacocke does not go into much detail on this. The first step, therefore, is to offer a more detailed account of the notion of an integrated representation of the environment over time. I shall argue in the following section that this more detailed account is best achieved through considering what is distinctive of behavior governed by spatial reasoning involving such a representation—and in particular, through considering what navigational capacities are available only through such spatial reasoning. The next section offers an account that emphasizes four such navigational abilities, citing experimental evidence that shows that those navigational abilities are available to nonlinguistic creatures. In the final section I make explicit the implications of this for primitive self-consciousness and illustrate how such an integrated representation of the environment might emerge from the perception of affordances (as discussed in chapter 5).

8.3   Cognitive Maps and Integrated Representations of the Environment

Readers familiar with recent work in the philosophy and psychology of spatial representation will notice the connection between the notion of an integrated representation of the environment over time and what psychologists often call a cognitive map. Indeed, it might seem natural to think that there is no difference between them and that the notion of possessing an integrated representation of the environment over time is best elucidated through the notion of a cognitive map. This seems to me to be a serious mistake, however, for reasons that I try to bring out in this section.

Here is a definition of what is meant by a cognitive map from one of the most significant recent works on animal-learning theory: "A cognitive map is a record in the central nervous system of macroscopic geometric relations among surfaces in the environment used to plan movements through the environment" (Gallistel 1990, 103). This conception of a cognitive map as a record in the nervous system of geometric relations between surfaces in the environment is not at all what this chapter is trying to capture. What I am interested in is the spatial-awareness component of primitive self-consciousness, and that spatial-awareness component is a personal-level state. Records in the nervous system, however, are subpersonal states. Of course, as I have argued elsewhere (Bermúdez 1995b, 1995d, 1995e), it is a mistake to make a rigid distinction between personal and subpersonal levels of explanation. It is compelling to think that for any creature to have the sort of conscious spatial awareness implicated in primitive self-consciousness, it must have a suitable record in the nervous system of the geometrical relations between environmental surfaces. It is equally compelling (at least to my mind) to think that any *adequate explanation* of conscious spatial awareness must appeal to subpersonal facts about the recording of geometric relations in the nervous system. But the fact remains that these are two very different things.

One of the factors that makes it tempting to equate conscious spatial awareness with possession of a cognitive map is that many psychologists and philosophers who place theoretical weight on cognitive maps do so within the context of a distinction between different levels of spatial awareness. The most sophisticated level of spatial awareness is usually described in terms of possession of a cognitive map. One way in which this point is often put is that possession of a cognitive map goes hand in hand with the possibility of identifying places on an environment-centered (allocentric), rather than body-centered (egocentric), frame of reference. Many have thought that the representation of space through a cognitive map is a crucial element in the detachment from practical concerns that allows us to anchor the coordinates of our spatial thought on something other than our own bodies. One philosopher who has placed much stress on this thought is Gareth Evans, who sees possession of a cognitive map as one of the crucial differentia between engagement in a spatial world and representation of a spatial world: "The network of input-output connections which underlie the idea of an egocentric space could never be regarded as supporting a way of representing space (even egocentric space) if it could not be brought by the subject into coincidence with some such larger spatial representation of the world as is constituted by a cognitive map" (Evans 1982, 163). But what does the expression 'cognitive map' mean in claims like these?

One thing that seems clear is that Evans's use of the expression 'cognitive map' must be very different from what Gallistel takes it to mean, namely the storage of geometric information in the nervous system. Gallistel makes a very plausible case that possession of a cognitive map in his sense is not at all restricted to creatures capable of what Evans would recognize as representation of a spatial world. Chapters 5 and 6 of *The Organization of Learning* (Gallistel 1990) defend the thesis that all animals from insects upward deploy cognitive maps with the same formal characteristics in navigating around in the environment. Gallistel argues that the cognitive maps that control movement in animals all preserve the same set of geometric relations within a system of earth-centered (*geocentric*) coordinates. These relations are metric relations, the relations studied by metric geometry, of which Euclidean geometry is the best-known example. The distinctive feature of a metric geometry is that it preserves all the geometric relations between the points in the coordinate system. Gallistel's thesis is thus in direct opposition to the widely held view that the spatial representations of lower animals are weaker than those of higher animals because they can record only a limited set of geometric relations. He maintains that, although the cognitive maps of lower animals have far fewer places on them, they record the same geometrical relations between those points as humans and other higher animals. Moreover, he offers a uniform account of how such metric cognitive maps are constructed in the animal kingdom:

I suggest that the surveying procedures by which animals construct their cognitive map of their environment may be broken down into two inter-related sets of processes, which together permit the construction of geocentric metric maps. One set of processes constructs a metric representation in egocentric coordinates of the relative positions of currently perceptible points, lines and surfaces—a representation of what is perceived from one's current vantage point. The other process, dead reckoning, provides a representation in geocentric coordinates of the vantage points and the angles of view (headings). Combining geocentric representations of vantage points and angles of view with egocentric representations of the segment of the world perceived from each vantage point yields a representation of the shape of the behaviourally relevant environment in a system of coordinates anchored to the earth, a geocentric cognitive map. (Gallistel 1990, 106)

Dead reckoning (the process of keeping track of changes in velocity over time) yields an earth-centered representation of vantage points and angles of view that combines with current perceptual experience of the environment to yield an earth-centered cognitive map.

The clear implication of Gallistel's account of animal representation is that his sense of 'cognitive map' is of no use in distinguishing different forms of spatial awareness, since it is presupposed by just about every form of spatial awareness. How about the other senses of the expression? Another commonly encountered way of understanding 'cognitive map' is in imagistic terms, as a mental picture that the mind consults to solve navigational problems, but this is even more clearly a nonstarter. When we put to one side the imagistic and subpersonal understandings of the notion of a cognitive map, we seem to be left with a notion that is rather amorphous. Gareth Evans offers the following definition: "a representation in which the spatial relations of several distinct things are simultaneously represented" (1982, 151). This is not very helpful. Despite Evans's insistence on seeing possession of a cognitive map as the key to objective thought about space, this definition does not distinguish between egocentric and allocentric frames of reference. And it is no more helpful to be told by E. C. Tolman, who coined the phrase, that a cognitive map is the mental analogue of a topographic map, for this is only as clear as the notion of a mental analogue.

As this brief examination of the concept of a cognitive map shows, it is a concept rather unsuited to the task of helping explain what it is to have an integrated representation of one's environment over time. The clearest sense of a cognitive map is Gallistel's construal in terms of the storage of metric information in the nervous system, but this is not going to explain how possession of an integrated representation of the environment over time differs from other forms of spatial representation. None of the other senses of 'cognitive map' is really clear enough to explain anything. The conclusion to draw from this, I think, is that to make any progress on the notion of an integrated representation of the environment over time, we need to proceed in broadly functional or operational terms. That is, we need to consider what forms and types of navigational behavior should be taken as appropriate criteria for the ascription to a creature of an integrated representation of the environment. I shall go on to discuss four such types of navigational ability in the next section. Before moving on, however, there is an important loose end to tie up.

In the previous section I argued for the importance of developing a position midway between the cognitivist account of spatial reasoning favored by Christopher Peacocke and the theory of causally indexical spatial awareness favored by John Campbell. But it might be asked at this point if the proposal to consider what it is to possess an integrated representation of the environment over time in broadly functional and operational terms is compatible with that stated aim. I argued that Campbell's notion of an awareness that is exhausted in its implications for action and perception is not rich enough to capture the spatial-awareness component of a nonconceptual point of view. But it is open to a defender of Campbell's position to argue that construing spatial representation in functional or operational terms is simply offering up a causally indexical account under another name. Surely, it might be argued, a functional or operational construal of spatial representation suffers from precisely the same defects attributed to the view that spatial representation is exhausted in its implications for action and perception, simply because it is construing spatial representation purely in terms of its behavioral outputs.

Let me begin evaluating this objection by recalling a familiar distinction between criterial and constitutive accounts of a particular phenomenon. A constitutive account is intended to explain what the phenomenon in question is, whereas a criterial account is intended to identify the conditions whose satisfaction will be the basis (on causal explanatory grounds) for a warranted claim that the phenomenon is indeed present. The first point to make is that the operational and functional construal would have to be construed as a constitutive account of spatial representation for the objection to stick. But, of course, it is not being offered as a constitutive account. It is a criterial account. The two different forms of explanation should not be confused. The central tenet of functional/operational explanation is that the best way of studying a psychological phenomenon is in terms of the causal relations that it bears to certain inputs and certain outputs, and it would be a caricature of this position to say that it identifies the psychological phenomenon with these inputs and outputs. That, after all, is the crux of the distinction between functionalism and crude behaviorism. The sort of functional/operational analysis that I shall propose in the next section identifies certain forms of navigational abilities that seem to be explicable only on the assumption that the behavior in question is governed by an integrated representation of the environment over time. The procedure here is, of course, inference to the best explanation. As I shall try to bring out, the empirical evidence overwhelmingly supports the view that there is a principled class of navigational abilities for which inference to the best explanation demands the attribution of an integrated representation of the environment over time.

8.4 Navigation Deploying an Integrated Representation of the Environment over Time

A good deal of the most interesting work on the representation of space has been carried out by animal-learning theorists. There is a very good reason for this. Animal-learning theorists study nonlinguistic creatures, and so have no access to verbal reports as a source of evidence for the presence of mental representations. Of necessity, therefore, they have been forced to consider the representational abilities of animals indirectly and to develop very sophisticated ways of evaluating the evidence for the presence of those cognitive abilities and testing to make sure that there are no more-parsimonious explanations available that do not involve mental representations. Similar points hold of those developmental psychologists primarily concerned with prelinguistic infants. Here too we find a highly sophisticated battery of experimental techniques designed to isolate precisely those behavioral responses that can be explained only intentionally. It will be no surprise, therefore, to find that animal-learning theory and developmental psychology will feature heavily in this section.

Let me begin by stating two basic conditions that must be satisfied before there is any possibility of ascribing to a creature integrated representations of the environment. These are necessary but not sufficient conditions. They correspond to the four conditions that, in chapter 4, I placed on any behavior whose explanation requires appeal to content-bearing psychological states. Just as these four conditions mark out those forms of behavior that can properly be described as representation-driven, there are two conditions that must be satisfied by any form of navigation properly describable as driven by the representation of spatial features of the environment (which is not the same as what I am terming an integrated representation of the environment over time).

The first of these conditions has long been recognized to be important by animal-learning theorists. This is the condition that genuine spatial-navigation behavior should be place-driven rather than response-driven (or, in terms of what is by now a familiar distinction, that it be the result of place learning rather than response learning). The first question that must be asked of any putatively spatial behavior is whether the apparently spatial movement is reducible to a particular sequence of motor movements, as opposed to being targeted at a particular place. The point of this condition is that it maps very neatly onto the general requirement that no genuinely representational behavior can be explicable in stimulus-response terms, because particular sequences of movements are paradigms of what can be learned as responses to stimuli. The standard stimulus-response explanation of maze learning in rats is that the animal learns a series of responses that are reinforced by the rewards that follow correct responses. At each point in the maze where there is more than one possible path (the "choice points") the rat learns to go right or go straight ahead, where these responses can be coded in terms of the sequences of movements that they involve, and it is these sequences of movements that are rewarded.

The direct reinforcement of particular sequences of movements is a paradigm of the mechanistic explanations of behavior that stimulus-response theory attempts to provide. This means that it will be a necessary condition on any behavior genuinely driven by an integrated representation of the environment over time that it not be reducible to particular sequences of movements. But what is the difference between behavior reducible to particular sequences of movements and behavior not so reducible? A classic and elegant experiment by Tolman, Ritchie, and Kalish (1946) is a paradigm illustration of the difference between place learning and response learning. Tolman used a cross maze with four endpoints (north, south, east, west—although these are labels rather than compass directions). Rats were started at north and south on alternate trials. One group of rats were rewarded by food located at the same endpoint, say east— the point being that the same turning response would not invariably return them to the reward. For the other group, the location of the food reward was shifted between east and west so that, whether they started at north or south, the same turning response would be required to obtain the reward. This simple experiment shows very clearly the distinction between place learning and response learning. To learn to run the maze and obtain the reward, the first group of rats (those for which the food was always in the same place, although their starting-points differed) must represent the reward as being at a particular place and control their movements accordingly. If they merely repeated the same response, they would only succeed in reaching the food reward on half of the trials. For the second group, though, repeating the same turning response would invariably bring them to the reward, irrespective of the starting point.

Tolman found that the first group of rats learned to run the maze much more quickly than the second group. From this he drew conclusions about the nature of animal learning in general, namely that it is easier for animals to code spatial information in terms of places rather than in terms of particular sequences of movements. This general thesis—one that many subsequent researchers have been unwilling to accept—is not (at least for my purposes) the most interesting aspect of Tolman's experiment. What is more interesting, I think, is that the distinction that his experimental paradigm brings out offers an excellent operational illustration of a minimal condition that has to be fulfilled before one can even start to enquire whether or not a creature's behavior is governed by an integrated representation of its environment. The minimal condition is simply that the behavior cannot be understood in terms of learned responses that can be coded in terms of bodily movements rather than their distal targets.

This initial baseline condition cannot stand alone, however. There is a second condition on the class of navigation-behaviors driven by spatial representation of the environment. Although the contrast between response learning and place learning is clear enough to illustrate how behavior driven by information coded in terms of chained movement sequences cannot count as driven by spatial representation of the environment, it is not clear that we are in a position to affirm the converse proposition, namely, that all behavior that resists explanation in terms of learned responses is ipso facto driven by spatial representation of the environment. In other words, the distinction on which the first minimal condition rests is not exhaustive. This can be appreciated by considering the possibility that a creature's navigational behavior might be driven neither by coded movement responses nor by the representation of places but instead by sensitivity to features of the environment that covary with spatial features. Let me give an example.

Animal behaviorists puzzled by the extraordinary homing abilities of birds, particularly of homing pigeons, have put forward several different explanations of how a bird released into completely unfamiliar territory hundreds of miles from its home can almost immediately set a fairly direct course for home. On the widely accepted assumption that homing behavior cannot be explained in terms of any form of dead reckoning, the birds must be reacting to stimuli that convey spatial information, and the challenge is to identify those stimuli and how they are registered. The explanations put forward fall into two broad categories (Gallistel 1990, 144–148). One set of explanations propose that the birds are registering the angle of arrival of nonvisual stimuli propagated from their home position, such as odors or low frequency sounds. A second class of explanations appeals to the possibility of bicoordinate navigation. Bicoordinate navigation is navigation in terms of stimuli that can be perceived from any point on the earth's surface and that covary with latitude and longitude, such as the position of the sun and stars and/or the earth's magnetic field. Bicoordinate navigation on the basis of magnetic information can illustrate the difference between sensitivity to spatial features of the environment and sensitivity to features of the environment that covary with spatial features. Although we are obviously dealing with navigation that is representationally far richer than learned movement responses, in neither case do we yet have behavior driven by direct sensitivity to spatial features of the environment. The fact that the magnetic field increases in strength toward the poles, for example, might perhaps offer a way of obtaining compass orientation, but it is not itself a spatial feature of the environment. Nor are odors or low frequency sounds emanating from the home position spatial features of that home position. If navigation behavior is driven by the computation of magnetic information, then there is no need to appeal to the distal target in explaining what is going on. And if the behavior is explained through quite extraordinary sensitivity to nonspatial stimuli then, even though the distal target will play a crucial role in the explanation, those features of it involved in the explanation will not be spatial features.

This gives us two minimal necessary (negative) conditions that must be satisfied before there is any possibility of describing a creature's behavior as driven by representations of the spatial features of its environment. It must be the case both that the behavior in question is *not* reducible to coded sequences of bodily movements and that it is *not* driven by sensitivity to features of the environment that merely covary with spatial features. While noting that it does not seem to be true that the conjunction of these conditions provides a sufficient condition for the existence of behavior driven by representation of spatial features of the environment, let me pass over the question of how exactly to specify such a sufficient condition and turn to the further question of how one might build up from behavior that satisfies these two minimal necessary conditions to behavior that reflects possession of an integrated representation of the world. Here it seems that there are three further and more sophisticated conditions that capture the core of this more advanced form of spatial representation.

Possessing an integrated representation of the world involves appreciating a system of simultaneous spatial relations. This entails that, for any given route between two places, a subject who possesses an integrated representation of the world will appreciate that the route is not the only possible route. In fact, it seems to be a central aspect of appreciating that something is a route between two points that one appreciate that there are other possible routes between those same two points. This is, of course, a vital element in appreciating the connectivity of space. One key way of giving practical significance to the idea that all places are connected with each other is by appreciating that there are multiple routes between any two places. But how are we to understand this in operational terms? What navigational abilities would count as practical manifestations of the grasp that any given route between two points is merely one of a set of possible routes?

In general terms, the relevant navigational ability is the capacity to think about different routes to the same place. This navigational ability can, of course, take many specific practical forms. One very obvious such practical form is the capacity to navigate around obstacles. A good index of a creature's possession of an integrated representation of a given spatial environment is that, should it find its customary route to a particular place (say a source of water) blocked for some reason, it will try to navigate around that obstacle. An interesting illustration of how the capacity to think about different routes to the same place and the capacity to navigate around obstacles can come together can be found in a set of experiments carried out by Tolman and Honzik (1930a). Tolman and Honzik ran rats through a maze in which three different routes of varying length led from the starting point to a food reward. Unsurprisingly, the rats quickly learned to follow the shortest route to the reward, and when the shortest route was blocked, they quickly learned to use the middle-length route. The interesting result occurred when the shortest route was blocked at a point after the middle-length route had rejoined it. According to Tolman and Honzik, in such a situation their rats did not attempt to take the middle-length route but instead moved straight from the shortest

Figure 8.1
A creature that displays perspectival sensitivity will take the shortest path to obtain food at point *C*. This entails that if the creature sees food at *C* while at *A* and later moves to *B*, to go to *C*, it will follow the path *BC*.

route to the longest. Here the rats are representing the maze as comprising different intersecting routes to a single point and are actively comparing those routes to each other. They have an integrated representation over time of at least the local environment of the maze.

As I mentioned earlier in the chapter, there are two importantly different systems of spatial relations. There is a static and unchanging system of spatial relations holding between places and a highly changing system of spatial relations holding between things that are always located at a particular place but not always at the same place. Possessing an integrated representation of space involves grasping how these two systems of spatial relations map onto each other and being able to bring them into harmony for navigational purposes. Part of what makes this integrated representation so central is that all creatures capable of representing space are themselves moving through space. This gives a second condition upon possession of an integrated representation of the environment, namely that any creature who can plausibly be ascribed such a representation must be capable of reacting to the spatial properties of the objects and stimuli it encounters in a way that is sensitive to its own changing position.

The importance of this latter condition has been stressed by Christopher Peacocke in the notion of perspectival sensitivity that he develops in *Sense and Content*. Let me begin by explaining how Peacocke understands the notion. Peacocke illustrates what he means with the following example. In figure 8.1 we are to suppose that a creature at place *A* can perceive an object at place *B* and is accustomed to obtain food at place *C*. According to Peacocke, a subject who satisfies the requirement of perspectival sensitivity, after he has moved from *A* to *B* by a path that he recognizes as taking him from *A* to *B*, will move directly along the line

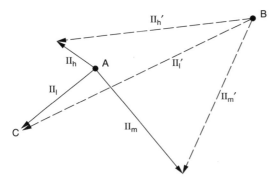

Figure 8.2
An intentional web initially centered on place *A* and then recentered on place *B*.
A subject who wants to move from *A* to *C* but finds himself having to move from
A to *B* before implementing his intention will follow the route given by Π_l' *if he
displays perspectival sensitivity*. (From Peacocke 1983, 68. Redrawn by permission of Oxford University Press.)

BC, rather than by moving from *B* along a path parallel to *AC*, when he
desires the food that he ordinarily obtains at *C*. Note, moreover, that this
requirement of perspectival sensitivity is richer than the requirement mentioned earlier that spatial responses not be reducible to particular sequences of movements. Although it is true that any subject for whom the
route from *A* to *C* is coded in terms of the movements required to get from *A*
to *C* will fail to display perspectival sensitivity, the converse does not hold.

Accepting Peacocke's illustration of perspectival sensitivity does not
mean, however, that we should accept without qualification his positive
account of what is going on when perspectival sensitivity is displayed.
The account he gives seems, in one important respect, to be too impoverished. Let me explain. Peacocke's account of perspectival sensitivity is
based upon the notion of an *intentional web*. Consider figure 8.2. In the
figure Π_h, Π_l, and Π_m represent experience types in which given objects
are perceptually presented, and the arrows represent the distances and
directions in which a subject would have to move were he to decide to
move toward those objects. This diagram is what Peacocke terms an intentional web. It is important to realize that the experience types Π_h, Π_l,
and Π_m are individuated in terms of what Peacocke terms sensational
properties, that is, the nonrepresentational properties that an experience

has in virtue of what it is like to have that experience (Peacocke 1983, 5). This provides the material for understanding his notion of perspectival sensitivity, as follows:

A simplified general statement of the requirement of perspectival sensitivity would be this: if the subject moves from one place to another, his intentional web must be recentered on the place determined in normal circumstances by the change in the sensational properties of his experience. . . . Perspectival sensitivity is literally a matter, in actual and counterfactual circumstances, of the sensitivity of the subject's intentional actions to variations in his perspective on the world. (Peacocke 1983, 69)

The sense in which this account of perspectival sensitivity is too impoverished seems to me to lie in its restriction of the notion of an intentional web to occurrently perceived objects and routes to those objects. This neglects the importance of spatial memory. A subject's intentional web must also include remembered locations and the routes to those locations. This is so for the following reason. A perspectively sensitive subject will be sensitive to how the spatial properties of objects are altered as a function of his changing position. Among these spatial properties will be the spatial relations in which occurrently perceived objects stand to objects that have been encountered in the past and will be encountered in the future. If these spatial relations are left out of the equation, then the practical significance of perspectival sensitivity will be severely diminished. I propose, therefore, to take over Peacocke's notion of perspectival sensitivity, subject to this expansion of the core notion of an intentional web.

Three examples will show how this notion of perspectival sensitivity can be practically deployed in operational terms. Consider the following experiment carried out by Chapuis and Varlet (1987). The experiment was performed outdoors with Alsatian dogs. The dogs were taken on a leash along the path *ADB* shown in the diagram and shown, but not allowed to eat, pieces of meat at *A* and *B* (see figure 8.3). The three points were all far enough apart to be invisible from each other.[3] On the assumption that the dogs, when released, would want to obtain food from both *A* and *B* it is clear what perspectival sensitivity would demand in this situation, namely, that if the dogs go first to *A*, they then proceed directly to *B* along the dotted line *AB*, and vice versa. And this is in fact what occurred in 96 percent of the trials. It is important to realize that what is going on here is different from what is going on in the Tolman and

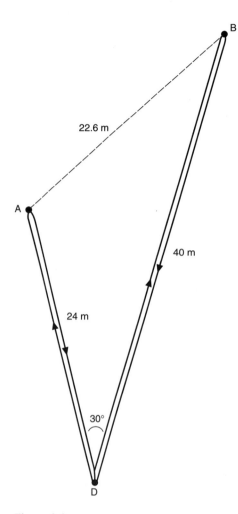

Figure 8.3
Perspectival sensitivity in dogs. *D* is the starting point, and *A* and *B* the food points. The solid lines represent exploratory runs with the dogs on leashes, and the dotted line the shortcut taken by the dogs when released. (From Chapuis and Varlet 1987.)

Honzik experiments discussed above. The rats in those experiments (as interpreted by the experimenters) are comparing three paths to a given goal with which they are already familiar. The rats register that there are different, though interconnected, paths to a single goal and make calculations about their relative efficiency, but this falls short of perspectival sensitivity in Peacocke's sense. What distinguishes the behavior of the dogs is that they are using information about routes with which they are familiar to devise a shortcut between two points in a way that depends on sensitivity to their changing spatial position.

Another good example of behavior for which the demands of inference to the best explanation seem to require the attribution of perspectival sensitivity (behavior displaying perhaps an even greater spatial mastery) is the performance of a young chimpanzee in the so-called traveling-salesman combinatorial problem (Menzel 1973). The chimpanzee was carried by an experimenter who hid food at 18 different locations, so the chimpanzee was able to see every location and the routes between them. When left to its own devices, the chimpanzee recovered almost all of the food, employing an optimal path considerably more economical in terms both of distance and of preference (when the foods were of different values). The chimp is able to construct an optimal recovery route only because it can track spatial relations in a way that is sensitive to its changing position.

Perspectival sensitivity can clearly be demonstrated in young infants, as is shown by a experimental paradigm employed by Acredolo, Adams, and Goodwyn (1984). The paradigm comprises two containers surrounded on three sides by transparent screens (figure 8.4). From the position marked *A* in the diagram the experimental infants were shown an object hidden in one of the two containers. Because of the glass walls, however, they could reach it only by crawling around to the gap in the wall on the opposite side of the apparatus (point *B*). The location of the object relative to the infant is, of course, inverted as he moves around from point *A* to point *B* (the container that was formerly on the infant's right is now on his left, and vice versa). The infants' successes reported by Acredolo, Adams, and Goodwyn clearly indicates sensitivity on the part of the experimental infants to the spatial implications of their changing position.

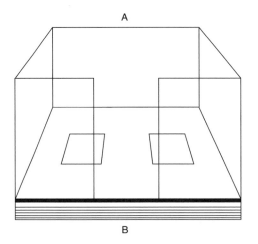

Figure 8.4
Perspectival sensitivity in infancy. The infant sees an object hidden in one of the containers but is prevented from reaching the object by transparent glass screens. To obtain the object, the infant must crawl around the array to *B*. (From Acredolo, Adams, and Goodwyn 1984.)

Let me turn now to the third component in possessing an integrated representation of one's environment. As I have already mentioned several times, the representation of space involves the capacity to represent two different classes of spatial relations: the relatively unchanging spatial relations that hold between places and the far more dynamic relations that hold between things, which change positions. The constraint of perspectival sensitivity provides one condition on a proper grasp of how these two different types of spatial relations interact, a condition that follows from the fact that the perceiving subject is himself a moving thing. But this is a further condition that needs to be extracted here. If a creature is to be able to harmonize these two types of spatial relations, it must be able to grasp at some level that there are two different types of spatial relations, and this in turn seems to demand a grasp that places are distinct from the things found at those places. This holds even when 'thing' is understood weakly, so that features count as "things." A creature that can think about a particular spatial location only in terms of an object* or feature existing at that location has not grasped the nature of space in the way required to possess an integrated representation of its environment over time (any more than a creature who can think about a particular object only in terms of a single spatial location). There is a crucial requirement here, namely that a creature should be able to recognize that places persist through changes in the objects* or features located at those places. This in turn seems to require the capacity to recognize and reidentify places independently of objects or features located at those places.

Another set of experiments carried out on rats in mazes by Tolman provide a good illustration of how this capacity might be practically manifested. These experiments are the so-called "latent learning" experiments (Tolman and Honzik 1930b). Two different groups of rats were run through a maze for several days. One group were provided with rewards at the end of the maze, while the second group went unrewarded. As one might expect, the rats that found food at the end of the maze quickly learned to run the maze, while the unrewarded rats just seemed to wander aimlessly about, turning into as many blind alleys at the end of the test period as they had at the beginning. Much more striking, though, was what happened when a food reward was put into the maze of a rat that had hitherto been unrewarded. The rats who previously appeared not to have learned the correct sequence choices required to run the maze were almost immediately able to run the maze more or less perfectly once they encountered the food reward. Placed back at the beginning of the maze the day after finding the reward, they took the most direct path to the end of the maze, rather than repeat the (apparently random) movements that had originally taken them there.

The most obvious way of interpreting these results (and certainly the way they were interpreted by Tolman and Honzik) is to hold that the rats were already familiar with the quickest way through the maze by the time the food reward was introduced but simply had no reason to put their "latent learning" into practice before encountering the food reward. What is interesting for present purposes is how latent learning illustrates the representation of space. Latent learning depends upon the rats registering that the place where they encounter the food is the same as the place that they had previously visited without encountering any food. If the rats could only think about a particular place in terms of a particular object or feature that they find there, then latent learning would be impossible. The behavior revealed in the latent-learning experiments is a good example of the exercise of the capacity to think about places as persisting through changes of features or objects located at those places.

8.5   The Notion of a Nonconceptual Point of View and Primitive Self-Consciousness

Earlier in this chapter I broke the notion of a nonconceptual point of view down into two main components, which I termed the *nonsolipsistic component* and the *spatial-awareness component*. This chapter has been primarily concerned with the second of these two components. Let me begin this section by adding the final details to this structural account of the notion of a nonconceptual point of view.

The nonsolipsistic component (the distinction between experience and what that experience is experience of) requires

a. grasping that an object of experience exists independently of a particular experience of it, which requires

b. grasping that a thing exists at times other than those at which it is experienced, which requires

c. the exercise of recognitional abilities involving conscious memory, which is most primitively manifested in

d. feature-based recognition of places.

The spatial-awareness component (putting place recognition to work for navigational purposes) requires

a. awareness that one is navigating through the environment, which requires

b. a degree of understanding of the nature of space, which requires

c. a grasp of the distinction between the spatial relations that hold between places and the spatial relations that hold between things, which is manifested in navigational behavior that

d. satisfies the following two minimal conditions:

   i. not being reducible to particular sequences of bodily movements,

   ii. not being driven by sensitivity to features of the environment that merely covary with spatial features of the environment;

e. and implicates the following three cognitive capacities:

   i. the capacity to think about different routes to the same place,

   ii. the capacity to keep track of changes in spatial relations between things caused by one's own movements relative to those things,

iii. the capacity to think about places independently of the objects*
or features located at those places.

A very natural question to raise when confronted with an apparently bi-
partite notion like that just put forward is, In what sense, if any, do the
two components mesh together to form a cognitive 'natural kind'? An
unsympathetic reader might be inclined to say that the notion of a nonconceptual point of view has been gerrymandered out of two distinct sets
of cognitive abilities that happen both to involve some notion of place
recognition and place reidentification. But this would be a serious mistake. To put the point briefly, the significance of the structured notion of
a nonconceptual point of view is that it allows us to understand how the
forms of first-person perceptual content discussed in chapters 5 and 6 can
be put to work to yield a genuine form of primitive self-consciousness.
This is what unites the two central components.

The notion of a nonconceptual point of view brings together the capacity to register one's distinctness from the physical environment and various navigational capacities that manifest a degree of understanding of
the spatial nature of the physical environment. One very basic reason for
thinking that these two elements must be considered together emerges
from a point made at the beginning of the previous chapter: the richness
of the self-awareness that accompanies the capacity to distinguish the self
from the environment is directly proportionate to the richness of the
awareness of the environment from which the self is being distinguished.
So no creature can understand its own distinctness from the physical environment without having an independent understanding of the nature of
the physical environment, and since the physical environment is essentially
spatial, this requires an understanding of the spatial nature of the physical
environment. But this cannot be the whole story. It leaves unexplained
why an understanding should be required of *this* particular essential feature of the physical environment. After all, it is also an essential feature
of the physical environment that it be composed of objects that have both
primary and secondary qualities, but there is no reflection of this in the
notion of a nonconceptual point of view. More is needed to understand
the significance of spatiality.

Let me step back briefly from primitive self-consciousness to consider
the account of self-identifying first-person thoughts given in Gareth

Evans's *Varieties of Reference* (1982). Evans places considerable stress on the connection between the sophisticated form of self-consciousness that he is considering and a grasp of the spatial nature of the world. As far as Evans is concerned, the capacity to think genuine first-person thoughts implicates a capacity for self-location, which he construes in terms of a thinker's ability to conceive of himself as identical with an element of the objective order. Though I don't endorse the particular gloss that Evans puts on this, the general idea is very powerful. The relevance of spatiality to self-consciousness comes about not merely because the world is spatial but also because the self-conscious subject is himself a spatial element of the world. One cannot be self-conscious without being aware that one is a spatial element of the world, and one cannot be aware that one is a spatial element of the world without a grasp of the spatial nature of the world. Evans tends to stress a dependence in the opposite direction between these notions:

The very idea of a perceivable, objective spatial world brings with it the idea of the subject as being *in* the world, with the course of his perceptions due to his changing position in the world and to the more or less stable way the world is. The idea that there is an objective world and the idea that the subject is *somewhere* cannot be separated, and where he is is given by what he can perceive. (Evans 1982, 222)

But the thrust of his work is very much that the dependence holds equally in the opposite direction.

It seems to me that this general idea can be extrapolated and brought to bear on the notion of a nonconceptual point of view. What binds together the two apparently discrete components of a nonconceptual point of view is precisely the fact that a creature's self-awareness must be awareness of itself as a spatial being that acts upon and is acted upon by the spatial world. Evans's own gloss on how a subject's self-awareness is awareness of himself as a spatial being involves the subject's mastery of a simple theory explaining how the world makes his perceptions as they are, with principles like 'I perceive that such and such; such and such holds at P; so (probably) I am at P' and 'I am at P; such and such does not hold at P, so I can't really be perceiving such and such, even though it appears that I am' (Evans 1982, 223). This is not very satisfactory, though. If the claim is that the subject must explicitly hold these principles, then it is clearly false. If, on the other hand, the claim is that these are the principles of a theory that a self-conscious subject must tacitly know, then the claim seems very uninformative in the absence of a specification of the precise forms of behavior that can only be explained by the ascription of such a body of tacit knowledge. We need an account of what it is for a subject to be correctly described as possessing such a simple theory of perception. My own view is that some of the navigational abilities discussed in this chapter will have a central role to play in this account. But there is no need for present purposes to make a claim that strong. The point I wish to stress is simply that the notion of a nonconceptual point of view as I have presented it can be viewed as capturing, at a more primitive level, precisely the same phenomenon that Evans is trying to capture with his notion of a simple theory of perception.

There is an important respect, though, in which Evans's emphasis on a simple theory of perception can be misleading. Although usefully highlighting the spatiality of the self-conscious subject, it focuses attention on the passive "input" side of that spatiality, rather than the active "output" side. A vital element in a self-conscious subject's grasp of how he himself is a part of the physical world is indeed derived from an understanding of how his perceptions are a function of his location in precisely the way that Evans brings out. But it must not be forgotten that a vital role in this is played by the subject's own actions and movement. Appreciating the spatiality of the environment and one's place in it is largely a function of grasping one's possibilities for action within that environment: realizing that if one wants to return to a particular place from *here* one must pass through these intermediate places, or that if there is something *there* that one wants, one should take *this* route to obtain it. That this is something that Evans's account could potentially overlook emerges when one reflects that a simple theory of perception of the form that he describes could be possessed and deployed by a subject that only moves passively. I take it to be an advantage of the notion sketched in this chapter that it incorporates the dimension of action by emphasizing the practicalities of navigation.

Moreover, stressing the importance of action and movement indicates how the notion of a nonconceptual point of view might be grounded in the self-specifying information to be found in visual perception. I am thinking here particularly of the concept of an affordance so central to

Gibsonian theories of perception. One important type of self-specifying information in the visual field is information about the possibilities for action and reaction that the environment affords the perceiver, and I suggested earlier (in chapter 5) that affordances are nonconceptual first-person contents that serve as building blocks in the development of self-consciousness (though there are certain qualifications that emerged in chapter 7 that have to do with the importance of conscious memory). We are now in a position to give this idea a little more focus (albeit programmatically). The development of a nonconceptual point of view clearly involves certain forms of reasoning, which I earlier followed Peacocke in calling spatial reasoning. Clearly, we will not have a full understanding of the notion of a nonconceptual point of view until we have an explanation of how this reasoning can take place. What I would suggest, though, is that Gibsonian affordances form one important class of representations over which this reasoning takes place. The spatial reasoning involved in developing a nonconceptual point of view upon the world is largely a matter of calibrating different affordances into an integrated representation of the world. This idea obviously needs to be worked out in detail, but let me make some brief comments about what might be involved in such a process of calibration and how it relates to discussion earlier in this chapter.

Calibrating different affordances into an integrated representation of the world will be a function of a creature's understanding how those affordances are spatially related to each other, and the basic materials for such a calibration will, of course, be the navigational abilities involved in getting from one affordance to another. Let me give some examples of what might be involved here. I will assume that when a creature is able to navigate from one affordance to another in a way that satisfies the two minimal conditions discussed earlier, it is appropriate to describe it as having an understanding of the spatial relation between those affordances. The question is how an understanding of individual spatial relations of that sort becomes an integrated representation of the environment.

One very basic point here is that the spatial relations holding between affordances have the properties of symmetry and transitivity. Correspondingly, calibrating affordances involves recognizing such symmetry and transitivity. Let me term this a grasp of *affordance symmetry* and *af-*

fordance transitivity. If a particular route R leads from affordance A to affordance A', then a creature who has grasped affordance symmetry will recognize that reversing the route will take him from affordance A' to affordance A. By the same token, a creature who has grasped affordance transitivity will recognize that if route R leads from affordance A to affordance A' and route R' leads from affordance A' to affordance A'', then R followed by R' will take him from A to A'', and so on for any combination of connected routes.

At a more sophisticated level, consider the following. Calibrating affordances into an integrated representation of the world will involve the capacity to distinguish affordances from the places at which those affordances hold, and vice versa. A grasp of what I would term *affordance identities* is one fundamental component of this capacity. Grasping affordance identities is grasping that a given place can have different affordances over time and, correlatively, that a different affordance does not necessarily mean a different place. Understanding affordance identities will involve, for example, understanding that the spatial relations holding between a given affordance A at a particular place P and other affordances A', A'', . . . at other places P', P'', . . . will continue to hold even if A intermittently ceases to hold at P and is replaced by A^*. More concretely, suppose that an animal lives near a watering hole, from which it is safe to drink at all times of day except early morning and dusk when it is visited by predators. Here we have a place P (the watering hole) with two different affordances: A (water) and A^* (serious danger). A creature who has grasped the identity of A and A^* will understand that the spatial relations that hold between A and other affordances A', A'', . . . at P', P'', . . . hold equally between A^* and those other affordances. For example, suppose the creature is familiar with the route from a particular tree to the watering hole and usually visits the watering hole after visiting the tree. If the creature has grasped the affordance identity of A and A^*, it will know not to take that route at dawn or dusk.

Suppose that a creature moves towards an integrated representation of its environment by applying its understanding of affordance symmetry, affordance transitivity, and affordance identity to its understanding of the spatial relations holding between individual affordances. When does the process end? When would it be right to say that the creature has an integrated representation of its environment? Let me define the number of affordances with which a creature is familiar as its *affordance space,* and let a section of an affordance space be *connected* if and only if the creature in question recognizes that there is a route from any given affordance to any other given affordance. It seems clear that no creature can possess an integrated representation of its environment unless its affordance space is connected, or at least close to being connected. Moreover, repeated application of affordance symmetry, affordance transitivity, and affordance identity could yield just such a connected affordance space. This is not to say, of course, that a connected affordance space is sufficient for an integrated representation of the environment. As discussed in the previous section, there are conditions on navigational behavior that any creature possessing an integrated representation of its environment must satisfy, and it is possible that a creature might fail to satisfy those conditions despite possessing a connected affordance space. After all, a connected affordance space does not automatically generate the capacity to keep track of those changes in spatial relations between objects caused by one's own movements relative to those objects, for example. Nor will every connected affordance space be able to serve as a basis for further types of spatial reasoning. The London Underground map is an example of a connected affordance space, but not one that would enable a navigator to devise shortcuts not marked on the map. At the very least, a connected affordance space must be sensitive to the distance and direction between affordances.

Nonetheless, once a creature has a connected affordance space, or something close to it, it is relatively straightforward to see how it might progress toward an integrated representation of its environment by acquiring the further capacities discussed in the previous section. It is plausible that the capacity for thinking about different routes to the same place could emerge naturally out of a fully connected affordance space, particularly one in which there is a range of affordance identities. Likewise for the capacity to think about places independently of the objects or features located at those places.

The concept of an affordance, therefore, is the key to seeing how my discussion of spatial reasoning and of integrated representations of the environment meets the Acquisition Constraint in the manner outlined in chapter 1. The constraint demands, in effect, that any learned cognitive ability be constructible out of more primitive abilities already in existence. As emerged in chapter 5, there are good reasons to think that the perception of affordances is innate. And so if, as I have suggested, the perception of affordances is the key to the acquisition of an integrated spatial representation of the environment via the recognition of affordance symmetries, affordance transitivities, and affordance identities, then it is perfectly conceivable that the capacities implicated in an integrated representation of the world could emerge nonmysteriously from innate abilities.

9

Psychological Self-Awareness: Self and Others

Let me take stock. Chapter 5 showed how the very structure of perceptual experience can be a source of nonconceptual first-person contents through the pick-up of self-specifying information. In chapter 6, I argued that somatic proprioception can also be a source of first-person contents, and that those first-person contents incorporate an awareness of the body as a spatially extended and bounded object that is distinctive in virtue of its responsiveness to the will. The next two chapters explored how these basic building blocks could be developed into a more sophisticated form of self-awareness that I termed a *nonconceptual point of view*. The key elements of a nonconceptual point of view are, first, a more sophisticated registering of the distinction between self and environment than is available in either perceptual experience or somatic proprioception and, second, a capacity for spatial reasoning that brings with it an awareness of oneself as moving within, acting upon, and being acted upon by, the spatial environment.

These forms of self-awareness so far discussed are predominantly physical and bodily. What we have been dealing with is largely awareness of the embodied self as a bearer of physical properties. There has so far been little discussion of the explicitly psychological dimension of self-awareness. But awareness of the embodied self as a bearer of psychological properties is an equally significant strand in self-awareness and, moreover, of central importance in solving the paradox of self-consciousness. It will be the subject of this chapter.

9.1   The Symmetry Thesis: An Unsuccessful Defence

An initial question that arises in thinking about psychological self-awareness is the relation between psychological self-awareness and awareness of other minds. As a way of broaching the issue, let me start with the relation between psychological self-awareness and awareness of other minds in subjects who are capable of fully conceptual thought and linguistic mastery. As I have already mentioned, psychological predicates have a constant sense, whether they are applied to oneself or to others. It is not the case that psychological predicates have a first-person sense, on the one hand, and a second- and third-person sense, on the other. This is prima facie evidence for a commonality between psychological self-awareness and awareness of other minds, at least at the conceptual level. Let me offer the following as a way of capturing this prima facie commonality more generally:

The Symmetry Thesis   A subject's psychological self-awareness is constitutively linked to his awareness of other minds.

The Symmetry Thesis will be the subject of this section and the next. I will consider two arguments in support of the Symmetry Thesis, only one of which will turn out ultimately to be sound. First, though, let me discuss the Symmetry Thesis a little further.

The Symmetry Thesis has both a weak reading and a strong reading, which it is useful to distinguish. The weak reading is that there can be no psychological self-awareness without awareness of other minds. I am taking awareness of other minds to involve the capacity to discriminate at least some psychological-state types in other subjects of experience. This means that the Symmetry Thesis is directly antithetical to any view on which psychological self-awareness is conceptually distinct from awareness of other minds. Let me put the point another way. On the weak reading, the Symmetry Thesis implies that to the extent that psychological awareness in general is a matter of applying psychological predicates, it is impossible for a subject's repertoire of psychological predicates to be composed solely of predicates that have only a first-person application.[1] The same point can be put in a way that does not make it a point about language mastery. If we define a psychological representation as a mental representation that enables a subject to discriminate psychological-state types, the weak reading of the Symmetry Thesis maintains that not all of a subject's psychological representations can be applicable only to the first person.

Thus, the Symmetry Thesis, as weakly construed, is incompatible with the notion that psychological self-awareness is independent of awareness of other minds, in, for example, the way that seems to be implied by those versions of the argument from analogy that hold that our capacity to ascribe psychological properties to others is derived by analogy and extension from our logically independent capacity to ascribe psychological properties to ourselves. On most versions of the argument from analogy, there is no constitutive connection between first-person and third-person ascriptions of psychological properties. The analogy approach to awareness of other minds generally appears within the context of a debate predicated on the assumption that it makes perfectly good sense for a psychologically self-aware subject not to be aware that there are any other minds at all. Consider the following well-known passage from John Stuart Mill:

> By what evidence do I know, or by what considerations am I led to believe, that there exist other sentient creatures; that the walking and speaking figures which I see and hear, have sensations and thoughts, or in other words, possess Minds? . . . I conclude it from certain things, which my experience of my own states of feeling proves to me to be marks of it. . . . I am conscious in myself of a series of facts connected by a uniform sequence, of which the beginning is modifications of my body, the middle is feelings, and the end is outward demeanour. In the case of other human beings I have the evidence of my senses for the first and last links of the series, but not for the intermediate link. . . . Experience, therefore, obliges me to conclude that there must be an intermediate link. (1889, 243)

The implication here is clearly that apprehending the connections between the three links in the sequence is independent of the identifying the presence of two of those links in other subjects and could take place in its absence. Even on its weak construal, the Symmetry Thesis rules this possibility out.

A second and stronger reading of the Symmetry Thesis would be that no subject can discriminate in himself psychological-state types that he cannot discriminate in other subjects. This is stronger than the first implication, which leaves open the possibility that, despite the impossibility of a psychologically self-aware subject being completely unaware of the existence of other minds, that subject's understanding of other minds might be impoverished relative to his psychological self-understanding. This point can be put in a way that matches the previous point: to the extent that psychological awareness is a matter of ascribing psychological predicates, whether to oneself or to others, there can be no psychological predicates which have only a first-person application. Alternatively, and more broadly, whatever psychological representations a subject has, none of those psychological representations can have only a first-person application.

It is important to note, however, that the Symmetry Thesis does not have any implications for the obvious fact that our ways of finding out about our own psychological properties can differ fundamentally from our ways of finding out about the psychological properties of other people. Typically, we find out about many of our psychological properties without any need to observe our behavior, whereas observation of behavior is often required to find out about other people's psychological properties. No theory that denied this obvious fact could be true. The Symmetry Thesis, though, says no more than that the set of capacities that we put to work in finding out whether or not we instantiate any of a given set of psychological properties cannot exist in the absence of a comparable set of capacities to determine whether other people instantiate any of that same set of psychological properties. It does not require that it be the same capacities performing both tasks, or that those capacities be structurally similar in any way.

Let me turn now to the question of why one might think that the Symmetry Thesis is true. I have already suggested one prima facie piece of evidence, which is the constancy of sense of psychological predicates across first-person, second-person and third-person applications. But this is no more than prima facie evidence. The fact that where a psychological predicate can be applied in first-, second-, and third-person ways, it means the same in each application does not entail either that if a subject has some psychological predicates, he must have at least some with a third-person application (the weak reading) or that none of those psychological predicates can have only a first-person application (the strong reading).

To move beyond prima facie evidence, the first argument in support of the Symmetry Thesis that I want to consider draws on a widely accepted claim about the nature of concept mastery. Although the argument's most articulate development has come from Gareth Evans, its origins seem to lie in some terse remarks of Strawson's. Here is how Strawson puts the conclusion of the argument: "It is a necessary condition of one's ascribing states of consciousness, experiences, to oneself in the way one does, that one should also ascribe them, or be prepared to ascribe them, to others who are not oneself" (Strawson 1959, 99). This seems close to what I have termed the strong reading of the Symmetry Thesis, namely that no subject can discriminate in himself psychological-state types that he cannot discriminate in others. Note, however, that this argument, if sound (which I shall argue that it is not), would prove the Symmetry Thesis in a manner that might well turn out to be too restricted. Because it rests crucially upon a particular view of the requirements for concept mastery, it is restricted to the discrimination of psychological-state types at the conceptual level, unless it can be shown that the requirements in question are not exclusive to conceptual representation.

This following sentence from Strawson conveys the essentials of Strawson's and Evans's position: "The main point here is a purely logical one: the idea of a predicate is correlative with that of a range of distinguishable individuals of which the predicate can be significantly, though not necessarily truly affirmed" (Strawson 1959, 99, n. 1). From this requirement on predicates in general it follows that psychological predicates must have a range of distinguishable individuals to which they can be applied. And this seems to lead to the conclusion that no psychological predicate can have only a first-person application. Evans has developed the same point into what he terms the Generality Constraint:

What we have from Strawson's observation is that any thought which we can interpret as having the content that a is F involves the exercise of an ability—knowledge of what it is for something to be F—which can be exercised in indefinitely many distinct thoughts, and would be exercised in, for instance, the thought that b is F. And this of course implies the existence of a corresponding kind of ability, the ability to think of a particular object. (Evans 1982, 103)

We thus see the thought that a is F lying at the intersection of two series of thoughts: on the one hand, the series of thoughts that a is F, that b is F, that c is F, . . . and, on the other hand, the series of thoughts that a is F, that a is G, that a is H. (Evans 1982, 104, n. 1)

Evans's Generality Constraint imposes a stronger requirement than the comments from Strawson that gave rise to it. Evans imposes a requirement of general recombinability, suggesting that mastery of the concept *F* requires being able to think that *x* is *F* for arbitrary *x*, whereas Strawson is requiring simply the ability to think that *x* is *F* for a range of objects. This difference is not relevant to the following, and for the sake of simplicity, I shall refer to both Evans and Strawson as defending forms of the Generality Constraint.

Evans's Generality Constraint has the advantage of precision, and it is clear how it might be put to work in support of the Symmetry Thesis. Let me offer a schematic argument:

1. Self-ascription of psychological states in subject-predicate form is the paradigm form of psychological self-awareness.
2. Self-ascription of psychological states requires conceptual mastery of both subject and predicate.
3. The Generality Constraint applied to (2) requires the ability to generalize both the subject and the predicate.
4. Generalizing the predicate involves the ability to apply that predicate to arbitrary distinguishable individuals.
5. Since the predicate is a psychological predicate, these arbitrary distinguishable individuals will include other psychological subjects.

From (5), the Symmetry Thesis follows straightforwardly. Note, moreover, that it is the strong reading of the Symmetry Thesis that is supported. The conclusion (5) implies that no psychological predicate can have only a first-person application.

In evaluating this argument, we need to distinguish clearly between the following two questions:

(A)   *If* an individual is aware of the existence of other psychological subjects, does the Generality Constraint require that any individual properly credited with mastery of a given psychological predicate be able to apply that psychological predicate to those other subjects?

(B)   *If* an individual is not aware of the existence of other psychological subjects, does this mean that he cannot satisfy the Generality Constraint?

These two questions have very different implications for the Symmetry Thesis. An affirmative answer to the first question leaves open the possibility that would be denied by an affirmative answer to the second question, namely that an individual unaware of the existence of other psychological subjects might nonetheless have genuine mastery of a psychological predicate. No defence of the Symmetry Thesis can allow this to be a genuine possibility. Since the weight of the argument falls on the Generality Constraint, the Generality Constraint must yield an affirmative answer not just to (A) but also to (B). Unless this is so, stage (5) in the Strawson and Evans argument will not go through.

But it is not clear that the Generality Constraint does yield an affirmative answer to (B). There are ways in which the Generality Constraint could be satisfied by an individual unaware of the existence of other psychological subjects. Everything here hinges on how we understand the concept of an arbitrary distinguishable individual. Recall that we are dealing here with truth-evaluable subject-predicate sentences. The Generality Constraint does not prescribe (nor is there any reason why it should) that thoughts that would show that the constraint was satisfied by a given subject-predicate thought must have the same truth value as the original thought. From this one might conclude that there is no need for the range of distinguishable individuals to include other psychological subjects. Why is the Generality Constraint not satisfied by a subject's capacity to entertain the thought that a given psychological predicate does not apply to any one of a range of inanimate objects?

It might be objected that this is self-defeating because, simply in virtue of entertaining the thought that an inanimate object does not have a given psychological property, one is (mistakenly) treating it as a psychological subject. This cannot be right, however. A minimal requirement for something to be a psychological subject is surely that at least some psychological predicates must be true of it. It is not clear to me that to entertain the thought that a given psychological predicate does not apply to a given inanimate object is somehow to commit a category mistake. How, after all, can it be a category mistake if it is a true thought?

In any case, however, there are other grounds on which one can object to the Strawson and Evans argument. The basic thought motivating acceptance of the Generality Constraint is that there is a deep incoherence in the idea of a predicate that is applicable only on a single occasion: to a given individual at a given time. Predicates must be multiply instantiable. That, it seems to me, is the force of Strawson's claim that "the idea of a predicate is correlative with that of a range of distinguishable individuals of which the predicate can be significantly, though not necessarily truly affirmed." [2] It is unfortunate, however, that both Evans and Strawson take a very synchronic view of the satisfaction conditions for their respective constraints. Had they taken a more diachronic perspective, they would have recognized that a subject himself can, over time, provide a range of different occasions on which a predicate may be significantly affirmed. To appreciate the significance of this, recall some comments that Strawson makes in the footnote from which I have already quoted: "A necessary condition of one's ascribing predicates of a certain class to one individual, i.e. oneself, is that one should be prepared, or ready, on appropriate occasions, to ascribe them to other individuals, and hence that one should have a conception of what those appropriate occasions for ascribing them would be" (Strawson 1959, 99, n. 1).[3] Strawson's view is that ascribing predicates to other individuals, or being prepared so to ascribe them, implicates a conception of the appropriate ascription conditions for those predicates. Presumably, the argument is completed by noting that possessing such a conception is a necessary condition of being able to apply the predicate at all. I can see no reason, however, why a conception of the appropriate ascription conditions is not equally implicated by ascribing, or being prepared to ascribe, predicates to oneself at different times.

Combining this with the earlier point provides a compelling counterweight to the move from (4) to (5) in the Strawson and Evans argument. Although it is (arguably) the case that mastery of a given psychological predicate requires the capacity to apply it to arbitrary distinguishable individuals, it does not follow that these arbitrary distinguishable individuals must include other psychological subjects. In such a case, therefore, the Generality Constraint cannot be used to argue that psychological predicates must have second- and third-person uses, as well as first-person uses. Without this, though, the Strawson and Evans argument cannot provide a satisfactory defence of the Symmetry Thesis. Evans writes, "No judgment will have the content of a psychological self-ascription, unless the judger can be regarded as ascribing to himself a property which he can conceive as being satisfied by a being not necessarily himself—a state of affairs which he will have to conceive as involving a persisting subject of experience" (Evans 1982, 232). To maintain this, however, we need more than the Generality Constraint. In the next section I offer what I take to be a more powerful defence of the Symmetry Thesis. In one respect this defence will be wider in scope than the Strawson and Evans argument, because it will not be restricted to conceptual thought. In another respect, though, it will be narrower in scope, because it will not support a strong reading of the Symmetry Thesis.

9.2   The Symmetry Thesis: A Neo-Lockean Defence

The argument in support of the Symmetry Thesis that I will offer in this section is much briefer than the unsuccessful argument from the Generality Constraint just examined. It starts not from putative requirements on concept mastery and psychological self-ascription but from a point about self-awareness that has already been discussed. This is the point that self-awareness has a fundamentally contrastive dimension. The contrastive dimension of self-awareness had an important part to play in developing the notion of a nonconceptual point of view. At the core of the notion of a nonconceptual point of view is the capacity to distinguish self from the environment, and the richness of the self-awareness that accompanies this capacity is directly proportionate to the richness of the awareness of the environment from which the self is being distinguished. A similar thought is the key to seeing why the Symmetry Thesis is true.

Let me begin, though, by bringing out in a little more detail what I mean by the contrastive dimension of self-awareness. As I have emphasized, an important element in self-awareness is a subject's capacity to distinguish himself from the environment and its contents. I will use the phrase 'distinguishing self-awareness' as a shorthand for this. The discussion of somatic proprioception in chapter 6 provided a clear example of distinguishing self-awareness. I showed how an awareness of the body as a spatially extended object distinctive in virtue of its responsiveness to the will was part of the content of somatic proprioception. As I noted, however, this awareness is only a limited form of distinguishing self-awareness, yielding little more than a basic distinction between self and nonself. The reason for this awareness being so restricted is simply that somatic proprioception does not implicate (though, of course, it can be accompanied by) a particularly rich conception of what the self is opposed to. The conception of the environment emerging from somatic proprioception need not be anything richer than what is *not* responsive to the will, and this yields little more than a conception of basic numerical distinctness. Clearly, if a richer conception of the environment were in play, then the distinguishing self-awareness in somatic proprioception would be correspondingly richer. For example, if a subject were able to conceive of his environment as containing spatially extended objects, then he would be capable of distinguishing self-awareness as a spatially extended object that is distinctive within the class of spatially extended objects. The significance of possession of a nonconceptual point of view is precisely that it provides a richer awareness of the environment, thus making for a correspondingly richer degree of distinguishing self-awareness. There is, I conjecture, a general principle to be extracted here. Distinguishing self-awareness implies tacit reference to what might be termed a *contrast space*. I have distinguishing self-awareness of myself as ϕ only to the extent that I can distinguish myself from other things that are ϕ. These other things that are ϕ form the contrast space. This principle about contrast spaces can be seen as an extension of a familiar neo-Lockean point about identity (Mackie 1976, chap. 5; Wiggins 1980; Ayers 1991, vol. 2).

The neo-Lockean point about identity is that questions about identity over time can only be posed and answered relative to a given categorization. It does not make sense to ask whether something that exists at a particular time is or is not identical with something that exists at a later time. What we have to ask is whether this thing is the same x as that thing, where 'x' is a sortal representation that picks out a category or kind. A sortal representation, as I propose to use the term, is a mental representation, not necessarily linguistic, that classifies things as members of a given kind. The kind in question may, but need not, be a natural kind. What distinguishes a sortal representation from an ordinary descriptive or functional representation is that it is associated with more or less determinate criteria of application and identity, from which it follows that once we have a given sortal representation in play, we will know what criteria of identity to look for. Of course, distinctness being the opposite of identity, it follows that we cannot ask simply whether this is or is not distinct from that. What we must ask is whether this is a distinct x from that, where 'x' picks out a category or type of object.

Let me term the Lockean thesis the *restricted thesis of relative identity over time.* To hold the restricted thesis of relative identity is to hold that questions of identity over time are always relative to a given sortal representation. This needs to be kept separate from the *unrestricted thesis of relative identity over time,* according to which two individuals x and y may be identical with respect to one sortal representation but distinct with respect to another. Let me illustrate this with the very relevant example of personal identity. Locke's view (which I am not endorsing) is that a single block of flesh and bone can embody two different countable things: a living human being (relative to the sortal representation *man*) and a conscious rational subject capable of memory (relative to the sortal representation *person*). The man and the person are different things that happen most of the time to be physically coextensive. This is a form of restricted relative identity. According to the unrestricted theory of relative identity, on the other hand, the block of flesh and bone is identical with the man and also identical with the person, although the man is not identical with the person. Two good reasons for not endorsing the unrestricted thesis are, first, that it comes into conflict with the principle (Leibniz's Law) that if x and y are identical, then they share all their properties and, second, that it means abandoning the transitivity of identity. Fortunately, the unrestricted thesis is not entailed by the restricted thesis.[4] To reach the unrestricted thesis, one needs to add to the restricted thesis the premise that an individual can be a member of more than one kind, where the kinds in question are not subordinate to one another.

Locke himself believed that questions about identity and distinctness (or diversity, as he put it) were problematic only when considered over time. Recent work on personal identity has not followed him in this. Consideration of split-brain patients in particular has suggested that identity and distinctness at a time can also be very problematic.[5] For example, one (admittedly rather controversial) way of considering split-brain patients would be to hold that at any given time after the severing of the corpus callosum, a block of flesh and bone can embody more than one conscious rational subject, despite embodying only one living human being. Whether or not this is a correct description of split-brain patients, it is a conceivable possibility that theories of personal identity need to take account of by incorporating some of sort of means to answer questions of identity at a time. Presumably, this will require applying criteria of identity in accordance with a version of the restricted thesis of relative identity holding at a time as well as over time. Corresponding to the restricted thesis of relative identity at a time will be a thesis of relative distinctness at a time, according to which questions of distinctness at a time are always relative to a given sortal representation. If this were not so, then because x and y are identical if and only if they are not distinct, it would be possible to answer questions about identity without reference to a given sortal representation, contrary to the thesis of relative identity.

The relevance of this to distinguishing self-awareness is as follows. Distinguishing self-awareness is a general label for the various ways in which a subject can recognize his distinctness from the environment and its contents. According to the restricted thesis of relative distinctness, questions about distinctness are relative to a given sortal representation. But what is involved in answering a question about distinctness relative to a given sortal? The key here, it seems to me, is recognizing that questions of the form 'Are x and y distinct with respect to sortal z?' should really be rephrased in the form 'Can we count more than one instance of sortal z here?'[6] Once this is recognized, the Symmetry Thesis falls out soon enough. Assume that sortal z is a psychological sortal. If a subject is to be capable of recognizing that he is distinct from his environment with respect to sortal z, he must be capable of posing and answering questions of the form 'Can more than one instance of sortal z be counted here?' The capacity to pose such questions presupposes an understanding that sortal z is at least potentially multiply instantiated (that there are, or at least could be, other instances of sortal z), while the capacity to answer them presupposes an ability to distinguish and count instances of sortal z. Putting these together yields the conclusion that, insofar as sortal z is to provide a form of distinguishing self-awareness, it cannot have solely a first-person application. Distinguishing self-awareness requires a contrast space, as a function of what it is to recognize distinctness.

Although the neo-Lockean argument does support the Symmetry Thesis, it supports only the weak reading. The choice, it will be remembered, was between construing the Symmetry Thesis as holding either that if a subject has a range of psychological representations, he must have at least some with a third-person application (the weak reading) or that none of those psychological representations can have only a first-person application (the strong reading). The defence I have offered of the Symmetry

Thesis is based on the requirements of distinguishing self-awareness. It follows, therefore, that a constitutive link between first- and third-person application has been shown to hold only for those psychological representations implicated in distinguishing self-awareness. I have not argued (and do not believe) that the Symmetry Thesis holds in its strong form.

The psychological representations implicated in distinguishing self-awareness are, of course, those psychological representations that define the category (sort or kind) of psychological subjects. So the upshot of the neo-Lockean defence of the Symmetry Thesis is that the psychological representations that define the category of psychological subjects necessarily have first-, second-, and third-person applications. In the next section I will have more to say about what those psychological representations actually are.

Let me turn now to an issue that has been hovering in the background throughout this and the previous section. To what extent are the arguments I have discussed in support of the Symmetry Thesis applicable at the nonconceptual level to non-language-using creatures? The (unsuccessful) argument from the Generality Constraint is closely tied to the putative requirements of concept mastery, and hence is not straightforwardly applicable at nonconceptual levels of representation. But the same is not true of the just-offered neo-Lockean argument from distinguishing self-awareness. The point of the argument is that a subject's distinguishing self-awareness depends on his capacity to discriminate and count individual instances of a given category. I have put this point in terms of a subject's mastery of sortal representations, deliberately leaving open the possibility that the categorization in question might be independent of language mastery.[7] Of course, as in earlier chapters, work is needed to show that the categories in question can be understood and applied at the nonconceptual level, and this task will occupy the final sections of this chapter.

9.3   The Core Notion of a Psychological Subject

The existence of a constitutive link between psychological self-awareness and awareness of other minds implies that the best place to look for primitive forms of psychological self-awareness is in social interactions. A subject's recognition that he is distinct from the environment in virtue of being a psychological subject must take place against the background of a contrast space that includes other psychological subjects. This has a clear implication for the sort of evidence that will settle the question of whether psychological self-awareness can exist in a form that is nonconceptual and independent of language mastery. What we are looking for are social interactions involving prelinguistic or nonlinguistic subjects for which the best explanation involves ascribing the appropriate form of distinguishing self-awareness to a nonlinguistic or prelinguistic subject. Clearly, the first step must be to clarify what exactly the appropriate form of distinguishing self-awareness involves. That will be the subject of this section.

A subject has distinguishing self-awareness to the extent that he is able to distinguish himself from the environment and its contents. He has distinguishing *psychological* self-awareness to the extent that he is able to distinguish himself as a psychological subject within a contrast space of other psychological subjects. What does this require? The discussion in the previous section has shown how this question is to be answered. Distinguishing self-awareness is relative to a given sortal categorization, and psychological self-awareness is relative to the sortal category of psychological subjects. We need to turn our attention to the sortal category of psychological subjects. What are the criteria of identity and application associated with the sortal category of psychological subjects?

The first point to make is that the category of a psychological subject is what one might term a complex sortal category, analyzable in terms of more basic categories. There are several relevant criteria of identity and application for psychological subjects, and each of these criteria of identity pick out a further psychological category. Each of these psychological categories is itself independently analyzable. This is one of the reasons why distinguishing psychological self-awareness is a matter of degree. A subject can master some of the relevant criteria of identity and application without mastering others. A subject in such a position will have a restricted range of psychological categories in terms of which he can distinguish himself from the social environment. The more of these psychological categories a subject acquires, the closer he will move toward distinguishing awareness of himself as a psychological subject.

The category of a psychological subject is vague, in the following standard sense. There are borderline cases of individuals for whom (or which) it is not possible to give a determinate answer to the question of whether or not they qualify as psychological subjects. This is an unsurprising consequence of the point made in the previous paragraph about the category of psychological subjects being a complex sortal category. Given the complexity and diversity of the criteria of identity and application, the different combinations in which they may appear, and the fact that it will not always be straightforward to determine whether a given criterion actually applies, it is unsurprising that there does not appear to be a set of necessary and sufficient conditions that will settle in any given case whether one is dealing with a psychological subject or not. Nor should this be a matter of great concern, since it is not clear that there are any philosophically interesting kinds or sorts that are completely determinate. As far as analyzing distinguishing psychological self-awareness is concerned, the vagueness of the category of a psychological subject means simply that we should concern ourselves with trying to identify the core of the notion of a psychological subject. By the core of the notion of a psychological subject, I mean a set of basic psychological categories whose instantiation by a given individual collectively provides strong prima facie evidence that the individual in question is a psychological subject, where the instantiation of those categories counts as strong prima facie evidence for the presence of ϕ if and only if a judgement based on such evidence would count as warranted. One might define a warranted judgement in this context as a judgement that would often settle a debate as to the presence of ϕ and would at the minimum be taken very seriously in such a debate.[8]

The account of the notion of a self-aware psychological subject I am looking for will take the following form:

(PS$_1$)   Self-aware psychological subjects are aware of themselves as x, y, z, etc.

The schematic letters correspond to the basic psychological categories that collectively count as prima facie evidence for the presence of a psychological subject. Of course, there are indefinitely many psychological categories whose instantiation provides strong prima facie evidence for the presence of a psychological subject. The category of individuals capable of autobiographical memory seems to qualify, for example. This poses an obvious problem. How is one to identify what I am terming the core of the notion of a psychological subject? How is one to distinguish the basic from the nonbasic among all the psychological categories whose instantiation provides strong prima facie evidence for the presence of a psychological subject?

The solution to this puzzle is to distinguish between those psychological categories that one cannot hold to be instantiated without assuming that they are instantiated in a psychological subject and those psychological categories that can be ascribed to an individual without thereby identifying that individual as a psychological subject. To ascribe autobiographical memories to an individual is ipso facto to identify that individual as a psychological subject. So the inference from an individual's possession of autobiographical memories to that individual's being a psychological subject seems somewhat analytic (as would be the inference from an individual's being a milkman to his being a man). On the other hand, one can decide that a creature is sentient (that is to say, capable of feeling pleasure and pain) without ipso facto placing it in the category of psychological subjects. Sentience is not a sufficient condition for psychological-subjecthood. So a creature's sentience can count as one of a range of facts that collectively count as strong prima facie evidence for psychological subjecthood. I thus assume that the psychological categories that feature in a completed version of (PS$_1$) will not individually count as sufficient conditions for psychological subjecthood.

Perhaps the most obvious candidate for inclusion in a completed version of (PS$_1$) that satisfies the requirement just noted will be the psychological category of perceivers of the world. This follows straightforwardly from the fact that perceiving the world in at least one modality is a necessary condition for being ascribed any psychological properties at all, and only creatures to which psychological properties can be ascribed can count as psychological subjects. So, to be aware of oneself as a psychological subject must involve being aware of oneself as a perceiver. It is helpful at this point, I think, to advert back to Gareth Evans' idea of a simple theory of perception, briefly discussed toward the end of the previous chapter. Here is what he says:

Any thinker who has an idea of an objective spatial world—an idea of a world of objects and phenomena which can be perceived but which are not dependent upon being perceived for their existence—must be able to think of his perception of the world as being simultaneously due to his position in the world, and to the condition of the world at that position. The very idea of a perceivable, objective spatial world brings with it the idea of the subject as being *in* the world, with the course of his perceptions due to his changing position in the world and to the more or less stable way the world is. (Evans 1982, 222)

The significance of a subject's mastery of the sort of simple theory of perception that Evans outlines does not lie solely in what it betokens for his command of the objectivity of the spatial environment.[9] It is also highly relevant to his psychological self-awareness. To have mastered a simple theory of perception is quite simply to be aware of oneself as a perceiver of the environment.

Perception, obviously, is necessary but not sufficient for being a psychological subject. The category of psychological subjects is much narrower than the category of perceivers, and the category of psychologically self-aware subjects is correspondingly much narrower than the category of self-aware perceivers. It is a shortcoming in Evans's discussion of simple theories of perception that he gives the impression that mastery of such a theory is somehow the key to self-awareness. The truth of the matter is that a subject's awareness of himself as a perceiver of the environment is just one of the several strands in psychological self-awareness. John Campbell's recent book (1994), which follows Evans in many respects, develops Evans's position at this crucial point. Campbell stresses that we need to think in terms, not just of a theory of perception, but of a joint theory of perception and action. This broaches what I take to be the second strand in the notion of a psychological subject. Psychological subjects are agents who intentionally act upon the world because of their perceptions and desires. Correspondingly, to be aware of oneself as a psychological subject is to be aware of oneself as an agent.[10] The psychological category of agents itself has several strands, one of which emerges in this passage from John Campbell: "This theory explains our perceptions as the joint upshot of the way things are in the world and the way things are with us, and it explains the effects of our actions as the joint consequences of our bodily movements and the way things were around us to begin with" (Campbell 1994, 217). As it stands, however, this is rather incomplete. A subject's actions are not just the joint consequences of bodily movements and the layout of the environment. A subject's bodily movements are what they are because of his intentions, and an action is successful or unsuccessful to the extent that those intentions are satisfied. Lack of success can be due to the particular body movements made not being sufficiently skillful or to their being blocked in some way or to the environment not actually being the way it was perceived and expected to be. A subject will be aware of himself as an agent to the extent that he is capable of recognizing and distinguishing these various factors and possibilities. Again, we are dealing with something that is a matter of degree and that will have an unavoidably vague dimension.

Let me move on to a third strand in the notion of a psychological subject. Psychological subjects do not simply perceive the world and act upon it. There are psychological reactions to the world that are not exhausted by perception and action (although such reactions do, of course, have implications for perception and action). I refer here to moods, emotions, feelings of happiness and unhappiness, which I shall collectively term the reactive psychological states. It is hard to envisage any recognizable psychological life in the absence of such phenomena. Any sentient creature is capable of the subjective valences of pleasure and pain that qualify as the most basic forms of psychological phenomena of this type, and nothing that is not sentient could count as a psychological subject. As an argument for this, consider the following. A necessary condition of being a psychological subject is that a creature should be capable of acting intentionally. Intentional action is constitutively motivated by desires and beliefs (or protodesires and protobeliefs), and no nonsentient creature can have a desire. Desires are not themselves reactive states, but it is hard to see how desires could arise in the absence of reactive psychological states. It follows from this that any individual who is to count as a self-aware psychological subject must be aware of himself as having reactive psychological states, or as bearing reactive psychological attitudes to the world.

In addition to this a priori argument for the thesis that psychological subjects are essentially capable of reactive psychological states, a further set of reasons emerges when one reflects on the functions that emotions and other reactive psychological states serve in maintaining the organism. Some of these functions are physiological. For example, emotional states play a vital role in eliciting autonomic and endocrine responses. The emotion of fear generates changes in heart rate and release of adrenalin. Some byproducts of reactions are psychological, such as the role that emotions play in the storing and triggering of episodic memories. Others are social, the role of emotions in promoting social bonding being an obvious example. It is certainly arguable that no creature lacking these functions would have the behavioral flexibility and cognitive sophistication to count as a psychological subject. As Edmund Rolls (1990, 1995) has stressed, emotional states provide a computationally simple way of integrating sensory input with motor output. The sensory system need transmit only the valence to the appropriate action-generating systems, rather than a full representation of the state of affairs that gave rise to the valence. The emotion of fear is a basic and clear example. There are obvious adaptive advantages in avoidance and flight responses being triggered as quickly as possible. Combining these functional considerations with the a priori suggestions yields a compelling case for seeing the capacity for reactive attitudes as essential to psychological subjects.

So the central psychological categories in terms of which the category of psychological subjects should be understood are the categories of perceivers, agents, and bearers of reactive psychological states. I offer the following as the core of the notion of a self-aware psychological subject:

(PS$_2$)   Psychological subjects with a perspective on the world are aware of themselves as perceivers, as agents, and as having reactive psychological states.

As mentioned earlier it is relatively unimportant whether these turn out to be jointly sufficient or even severally necessary. All of the concepts involved here are complex and vague in ways that make it extremely unlikely that they will each always have determinate criteria of identity. My claim is simply that when we encounter a subject aware of himself as a perceiver, as an agent, and as having psychological states, we have strong prima facie evidence that we are dealing with a self-aware psychological subject.

9.4   The Emergence of Psychological Self-Awareness in Social Interactions

Let me now bring the various strands of this chapter to bear on the issue of psychological self-awareness. According to the weak version of the Symmetry Thesis that has been defended, there is a constitutive link between psychological self-awareness and awareness of other minds. This link holds because a subject's recognition that he is distinct from the environment in virtue of being a psychological subject depends on his ability to identify himself as a psychological subject within a contrast space of other psychological subjects. This self-identification as a psychological subject will take place relative to the set of categories that define the core of the concept of a psychological subject. So a suitably self-aware subject will be capable of distinguishing himself as a perceiver within a contrast space of perceivers, as an agent within a contrast space of agents, and as a bearer of reactive attitudes within a contrast space of other bearers of reactive attitudes. It follows from this that the best place to look for primitive forms of psychological self-awareness is in social interactions. This offers a clear way to proceed that will settle the question of whether psychological self-awareness can exist in a nonconceptual form that is independent of language mastery. In line with the methodology I have been following throughout the book, what would settle the matter would be social interactions involving prelinguistic or nonlinguistic subjects for which inference to the best explanation requires ascribing the appropriate form of distinguishing self-awareness to a nonlinguistic or prelinguistic subject.[11]

Here, as at various points in earlier chapters, we will need to look at empirical work if we are properly to identify and to understand the potential explananda. No doubt there are various areas of ethology and psychology that might be highly relevant here. What I want to concentrate on, however, is an impressive body of developmental results concerning the interactions between infants and their parents during the first year of the infants' lives. There is a concensus of opinion among researchers from a range of different traditions that at about the age of 9 months human infants undergo a social-cognitive revolution. This is a revolution that takes place in several dimensions. One significant point that has been stressed, particularly by Piaget and his followers, is that at 9 months infants become capable of new ways of acting upon objects. At about 9 months (the beginning of Piaget's stage IV) infants start to search for hidden objects and are able to solve the problem of reaching an object placed out of reach on a cloth that is itself within reach: by pulling the cloth toward them until they can grasp the object (Piaget 1954). This development in the perception and representation of objects is not, however, directly relevant to psychological self-awareness, although it will turn out to be indirectly relevant. What I want to focus on is the social dimension of the 9-month revolution. Here is how Colwyn Trevarthen, one of the leading workers in the area, describes the social transition that takes place: "The most important feature of the new behaviour at 9 months is its systematically combining interests of the infant in the physical, privately known reality near him, and his acts of communication addressed to persons. A deliberately sought sharing of experiences about events and things is achieved for the first time" (Trevarthen and Hubley 1978, 184). What I will be proposing is that this new behavior emerging in 9-month-old infants manifests distinguishing self-awareness relative to the three categories at the core of the notion of a psychological subject, in other words, that what we see at 9 months is the emergence of psychological self-awareness in infancy. Let me start, though, by sketching the broad contours of the transition in infant development, and in particular the background against which it takes place.

Infants are social beings from their very earliest days (Trevarthen 1993). An important illustration of this is provided by the work on neonatal imitation cited and briefly discussed in chapter 5. Meltzoff and Moore (1983) found that infants with a mean age of 32 hours (including one as young as 42 minutes) were capable of imitating gestures of mouth opening and tongue protrusion performed by an investigator. As I sketched in chapter 5 (see also Bermúdez 1996), neonatal imitation behavior reveals that infants have a sophisticated social awareness of physical commonalities between themselves and human adults. Infant imitation of facial gestures presupposes a recognition on the part of the infants that the gestures they see in front of them are gestures that they themselves can make (although they cannot see themselves making them). This recognition in turn must rest on an awareness of having a common physical structure with the experimenter, and with other human beings in general. Given that the capacity for imitation behavior seems to set in immediately after birth, it is natural to conclude that this offers one respect in which the human infant is born as a social being.

There is, of course, a range of further empirical evidence supporting the thesis that the infant universe is social from the very start of life. One body of evidence comes from the primitive discriminatory abilities that infants display. Discrimination of voices is a good example. Infants as young as 3-days-old seem to prefer their own mother's voice over the voice of another infant's mother (DeCasper and Fifer 1980). There is also evidence that slightly older infants (2-weeks-old) were more likely to stop crying on hearing their mother's voice than when they heard the sound of a female stranger (Bremner 1988, 157). One possible explanation for this sensitivity to the maternal voice is that it is acquired while the infant is still in the womb. No such explanation is available, however, for some of the striking results that have emerged with respect to young infants' abilities for discriminating faces. Particularly interesting are the results obtained by Field, Woodson, Greenburg, and Cohen (1982) showing that infants with a mean age of 45 hours revealed a clear preference for the face of their mother rather than the face of a stranger. The same study also showed that the same infants, after being repeatedly presented with their mother's face, became habituated to it and would eventually look longer at a stranger's face.

This sensitivity on the part of young infants to perceptually discriminable features of other individuals is matched by a sensitivity to the rather more subtle matter of other people's emotional states. Again, this is something that starts more or less from birth, as is indicated by the phenomenon often termed *empathic arousal,* where infants begin to cry when they hear another infant cry (Sagi and Hoffman 1976). It is worth adverting also to a phenomenon (noted in chapter 5) that was discovered while the experiments revealing empathic arousal were being replicated. Neonates are capable of discriminating their own crying from the crying of other infants (as evidenced by the fact that their distress crying significantly decreases when a recording of themselves crying replaces a recording of another infant crying). As they grow older, infants' capacities for discriminating emotional states become more sophisticated. The 3-month-old infants tested by Kuchuk, Vibbert, and Bornstein (1986) showed a preference for a face with a smiling expression over a face with a neutral expression, and this preference increased with the intensity of the smile.

These different forms of infant social sensitivity manifest themselves in surprisingly complex forms of interaction between infants and their caregivers. By the time they are 2-months-old, infants engage in extended and coordinated protodialogues or protoconversations involving reciprocal vocalization, with each partner taking their turn and adapting their behavior to fit in with the other (Bateson 1975, Trevarthen 1993). An excellent description of a typical episode of protoconversation, worth quoting in full, has been provided by Colwyn Trevarthen:

> The start of communication is marked by orienting of the baby. Babies 6 weeks or older focus on the mother's face and express concentrated interest by stilling of movement and a momentary pause in breathing. The infant's interest as a whole conscious being is indicated by the coordination and directedness of this behaviour, which aims all modalities to gain information about the mother's presence and expressions. Hands and feet move and clasp the mother's body or her supporting hand, the head turns to face her, eyes fix on her eyes or mouth, and ears hold and track her voice.
>
> The next, and crucial, phase is signaled by the infant's making a "statement of feeling" in the form of a movement of the body, a change in hand gesture away from clasping the mother, a smile or a pout, a pleasure sound or a fretful cry. The mother, if she is alert and attentive, reacts in a complementary way. A positive, happy expression of smiling and cooing causes her to make a happy imitation, often complementing or praising the baby in a laughing way, and then the two of them join in a synchronised display that leads the infant to perform a more serious utterance that has a remarkably precocious form.
>
> This infant utterance is the behaviour, in that context of interpersonal coordination and sharing of feelings, which justifies the term *protoconversation*. It looks and sounds as though the infant, in replying to the mother, is offering a message or statement about something it knows and wants to tell. Mothers respond and speak to these bursts of expression as if the infant were really saying something intelligible and propositional that merits a spoken acknowledgment. (1993, 130–132)

An experimental paradigm developed by Murray and Trevarthen (1985) makes a persuasive case for why this sort of behavior is properly described as a primitive form of conversation behavior, rather than simply as the mother accommodating herself to the random vocalizations of her child. Murray and Trevarthen used closed-circuit television to set up remote interactions between 6-to-8-week-old infants and their mothers, with each partner seeing a life-size full-face image of the other. Even in this artificial medium there ensued a fairly normal protoconversation of the sort described above (barring the bodily contact, of course). The experimenters then broke the closed-circuit link and, after a short while, began replaying to the infants videotapes of their mother filmed a few minutes earlier during the real-time interaction. The infants showed real distress at this, despite the fact that the videotapes showed precisely the same images of the mother that had recently given them so much pleasure. The explanation of the infants' distress is, of course, that they miss the contingency of their mothers' utterances and expressions on their own utterances and expressions. They see what is clearly half a dialogue that appears to be directed at them without any sense of participation in that dialogue—without the mutual accommodation, adjustment, and responses that define normal protoconversations.

There is a distinction to be made between thin and thick interpretations of these mother-infant protoconversations and the discriminative abilities that they presuppose and implicate. On the thick reading (which is strongly suggested by Trevarthen's own interpretation of his results), these mother-infant interactions reveal genuine intentional communication involving attempts on the part of both partners to translate their own feelings to the other participant. On this interpretation, the infants' behavior is not only purposeful but also displays recognition that the mothers' responses are equally purposeful. The infants are aware of what they are trying to do and aware of what their mothers are trying to do. Their regulation of the protoconversation is directed toward bringing what they are trying to do in accord with what their mothers are trying to do. Consider Trevarthen's summary of infant development during the first year of life:

We have shown that from birth infants have no trouble in detecting and interacting discriminately and optionally with the mental states of other persons. Very soon after birth, they can enter into a dynamic exchange of mental states that has a conversational potentially intention-and-knowledge-sharing organisation and motivation. The emotional and purposeful quality of these interchanges of motives undergoes rapid differentiation in the games of ensuing months. It becomes more elaborate, more quickly reactive, and more directive in relation to the responses of the other and is protracted into longer narratives of feeling. We say the infant is developing a more assertive, more conscious self, but we mean that the infant's experience of being a performer in the eyes of the other is gaining in power, presence and pleasure. (1993, 161)

This passage makes very clear that if the thick reading is right, explaining what is going on in mother-infant interactions will require ascribing to the young infant a form of distinguishing self-awareness. As defined in the previous section, distinguishing self-awareness involves a recognition of oneself as a perceiver, an agent, and a bearer of reactive attitudes against a contrast space of other perceivers, agents, and bearers of reactive attitudes. It can only make sense to speak of the infant's experience of being a performer in the eyes of the other if the infant is aware of himself as an agent and of his mother as a perceiver. Similarly, talk of intentional interchanges and narratives of feeling presuppose that the infant is aware of himself and his mother as bearers of reactive attitudes.

It seems to me, however, that the view that the components of distinguishing psychological self-awareness are all present in the protoconversations that start in the second month of life glosses over the very important distinction between thinking about something in a particular way and responding differentially to something that has a particular feature. The fact that the infant regulates his behavior in conformity with his mother's responses does not license the conclusion that he is thinking about either himself or his mother in any particular way. It does not license ascribing such thoughts to him because those thoughts are not necessary to explain how he behaves. As has been emphasised in earlier chapters, it is the principle of inference to the best and most parsimonious explanation that we must use to regulate content ascriptions to nonlinguistic and prelinguistic creatures, and this principle does not require us to credit protoconversational infants with distinguishing psychological self-awareness. Simpler explanations are available.[12]

One such possible explanation might employ a version of Piaget's notion of secondary circular reactions (although Piaget sees these as characteristic of his stage IV, which covers the fifth to ninth months of the first year and hence start rather later than protoconversational behavior). Piaget's secondary circular reactions involve a primitive distinction between means and ends, and the stage of development that he characterizes in terms of them is one in which infants manipulate objects with a view to bringing about sights that they find interesting and pleasurable.[13] There are all sorts of reasons why an infant might derive pleasure from protoconversational interactions. The infant might derive pleasure from noting the *physical* contingency between his own bodily movements and the movements of his mother.[14] Or he might derive pleasure from noting (visually, proprioceptively, or both) the match between his own bodily movements and his mother's movements. Or, of course, he might simply find the whole process intrinsically interesting. Note, moreover, that this line of explanation is not necessarily incompatible with an intentional explanation of the infant's behavior (in the sense discussed in chapter 4). It is incompatible only with explanations that describe protoconversational infants as engaged in intentional communication.

Another, and perhaps in this context more plausible, explanation of what is going on in mother-infant protoconversations would take more seriously the idea that protoconversations involve the evocation and regulation of feelings, while denying that this involves the sort of communicative acts postulated by the thick reading. The key to this second possible explanation is the distinction between, on the one hand, having evoked in one a particular feeling and evoking that feeling in another individual and, on the other, communicating to another individual the fact that one has a particular feeling. Only the second of these implicates the thick interpretation of protoconversations. Evoking a feeling in another person does not require thinking about a person in a way that identifies them as a person who has feelings (or, by extension, as a bearer of reactive attitudes). And this is compatible with the behavior that evokes the feeling in the other person being intentional—a point easily missed. Suppose, for example, that I evoke a feeling in you because I have learned that this will result in the same feeling being evoked in me in a heightened form. This evocation could be intentional simply under the description of my intending to bring it about that I experience the same feeling in a heightened form. It can be the case that feelings are transferred and shared intentionally in a way that affects the feelings of each participant without it being the case that the infant is intentionally communicating the fact that he has a certain feeling to an individual whom he identifies as someone capable of having feelings herself. Of course, there is little reason to think that anything like this goes on in normally developed adult subjects (although it is possible that this offers one way of understanding what seem to be social interactions in autistic and psychopathic subjects). Nonetheless, it offers a plausible way of fleshing out the thin reading of what is going on in mother-infant protoconversations.

The plausibility of the thin interpretation of social interactions in early infancy emerges even more clearly when we consider the developments that take place at about 9 months of age, because at this stage infants start to behave in ways that compel one to explain them using the categories deployed by the thick interpretation. In most general terms, what happens at 9 months is a fundamental change in the nature of the infant's interactions with people and objects. I have noted that in the first 9 months of life infants engage in surprisingly complicated social interactions with their caregivers. The same period is also one of keen exploration and manipulation of physical objects. The consensus of opinion among workers in the area is that what is distinctive of infant behavior and cognition in the first 9 months of life is an inability to integrate these two different types of interaction. These young infants can interact with other people in the protoconversational manner described, and they can explore and manipulate objects, but they can only do one task at a time. What happens at 9 months is that infants suddenly become capable, not just of undertaking both types of interaction at the same time, but also of coordinating them in a way that creates a fundamentally new type of interaction. This new type of interaction is *triadic* rather than *dyadic*. Infants become capable of employing their interactions with people in their interactions with objects, and vice versa. Figure 9.1, drawn from Tomasello 1993, illustrates the general structure of the transition. In the remainder of this chapter I will examine three of the new social interactions made possible by this transition from dyadic to triadic interactions. What I will argue to be the best explanation of these interactions involves ascribing to the infants involved the distinguishing psychological self-awareness discussed above. To each of the three types of interaction there corresponds one strand of the core notion of a psychological subject identified in the previous section.

The first type of social interaction has been well studied by developmental psychologists as the phenomenon of *joint selective visual attention*. Joint visual attention is the simplest form of triadic interaction, and the basis of the other two that I shall consider. Joint visual attention occurs when infants attend to objects as a function of where they perceive another individual's gaze to be directed and, conversely, when infants direct another individual's gaze to an object in which they are interested. Let me briefly review the respective evidence for these two aspects of joint visual attention.

I begin with the evidence for the infant's ability to look to where they perceive another individual's gaze to be directed. Scaife and Bruner (1975)

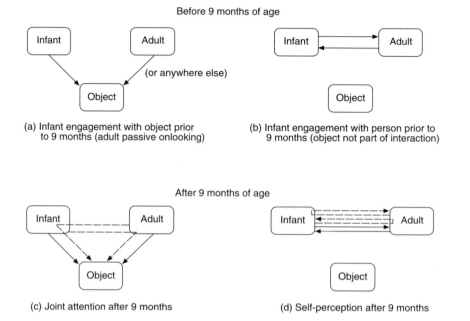

Figure 9.1
Infants' engagements with objects and persons before and after 9 months of age. Solid arrows indicate perception and dashed arrows a comprehension of another's perspective. (From Tomasello 1993, 177.)

set up an experiment in which infants of varying ages were confronted with an experimenter (not a caregiver) who established eye contact with them and then looked away. The aim was to find the age at which infants followed the movement of the experimenter's gaze at a level above chance. The group of infants aged 8 months and over performed considerably better than chance—a particularly significant result in view of the infant's lack of familiarity with the experimenter and the artificiality of the paradigm. Murphy and Messner (1977) showed that 9-month-old infants are capable of recognizing maternal pointing as a cue for directing their attention. Although their ability at that age to follow the invisible line from the pointing hand to the target object is subject to certain limitations (particularly when there is a large angle of separation between the pointing limb and the target object and when there are distracting features), the infants were clearly able to register that their attention is being directed toward the target object. There is evidence also that infants, after follow-ing the direction of the point, look back at the person pointing for feed-back as to whether they have indeed targeted the right object. The implications of these and other findings (Bruner 1975) are summed up by Jerome Bruner in these terms:

What has been mastered at this first stage is a *procedure* for homing in on the attentional locus of another. It is a disclosure and discovery routine and not a naming procedure. It is highly generative within the limited world inhabited by the infant in the sense that it is not limited to specific kinds of objects. It has, moreover, equipped the child with a technique for transcending egocentrism, for insofar as he can appreciate another's line of regard and decipher their marking intentions, he has plainly achieved a basis for what Piaget has called decentration, using a coordinate system for the world other than the one of which he is the centre. (Bruner 1977, 276)

The converse aspect of joint visual attention, the crucial embedding of object-focused attention in social contexts, begins at about the age of 6 months when infants begin to switch their gaze back and forth between object and caregiver (Newson and Newson 1975). These gestures develop during the last third of the first year into attempts on the part of the infant to establish an object as the focus of joint attention (Leung and Rheinhold 1981). Daniel Stern provides an eloquent summary of how infants can take the initiative in generating states of joint visual attention:

Infants begin to point at about nine months of age, though they do so less fre-quently than mothers do. When they do, their gaze alternates between the target and the mother's face, as when she is pointing to see if she has joined in to share the attentional focus. It seems reasonable to assume that, even prior to pointing, the infant's beginning capacity to move about, to crawl or cruise, is crucial in discovering alternative perspectives as is necessary for joint attention. In moving about, the infant continually alters the perspective held on some unknown sta-tionary sight. Perhaps this initial acceptance of serially different perspectives is a necessary precursor to the more generic "realization" that others can be using a different coordinate system from the infant's own. (Stern 1985, 129–130)

It is interesting to consider the conclusions that Stern draws from the development of these two aspects of joint visual attention:

These observations lead one to infer that by nine months infants have some sense that they can have a particular attentional focus, that their mother can also have a particular attentional focus, that these two mental states can be similar or not, and that if they are not they can be brought into alignment and shared. *Inter-attentionality* becomes a reality. (Stern 1985, 130)

Stern's conclusion, in essence, is that joint visual attention illustrates that the infant possesses what I have termed distinguishing psychological self-awareness relative to the category of perceivers of the environment. Let me reconstruct the reasoning that might lead to this conclusion. Recall that we are operating under the constraints of inference to the best explanation, with parsimony taken as a necessary condition upon the best explanation. The explananda in one form of joint visual attention are, first, the fact that the infant's attention tracks the mother's attention and, second, the fact that the infant seeks feedback from the person pointing. Both of these explananda seem to demand ascribing to the infant a recognition that the mother (or the experimenter) perceives the world from a perspective that is different from the infant's own but that the infant can learn about by adjusting the focus of his own attention. Unless the infants do have this recognition, there will be no reason for them to extend their gaze from the pointing finger to the object to which the finger is pointing and certainly no reason for them to look back to the mother for feedback. Built into this recognition on the part of the infant is an awareness of himself as a perceiver, in particular, as a perceiver who is trying to perceive what his mother perceives.

The explanatory requirement to assume that the infant is aware of himself as a perceiver is even clearer in the second form of joint visual attention, where the explanandum is the infant's trying to direct another individual's gaze to an object in which they are interested. This is a means-end activity. The infant is trying to bring about the desired end that his mother look at the object or event in which he is interested. This, of course, implicates a grasp that his mother is a perceiver. That the infant also has a concomitant grasp that he himself is a perceiver emerges more clearly in the means he chooses to bring this end about. In essence what the infant tries to do is to make the mother recognize that he, as a perceiver, is looking at a particular object, with the eventual aim that her recognition that this is what he is trying to do will cause the mother to look in the same direction.

It is interesting now, and will be helpful in the next chapter, to outline some representative first-person contents that seem to be implicated in the best description and explanation of what is going on in joint visual attention. The first type of joint visual attention (where the infant attends to an object as a function of where he sees the other's gaze directed) seems to require attributing to the infant contents like the following:

(1)   The infant recognizes, "Mother wants me to look where she is looking."

Or perhaps:

(2)   The infant recognizes, "Mother is trying to get me to look where she is looking."

In the second type of joint visual attention the direction of fit is reversed: infants are trying to direct the mother's attention to an object they are looking at. Here inference to the best explanation seems to push one toward something like the following psychological attributions. First is a desire:

(3)   The infant desires, "Mother will look where I am looking."

But the desire is efficacious in explaining behavior only when combined with an instrumental protobelief along the following lines:

(4)   The infant recognizes, "Mother will look where I am looking if I look back and forth from her to it."

Of course, particular explanations in particular contexts may well depart from these paradigms. But it does seem that central cases of joint visual attention will need to be explained through the attributions of intentions and protobeliefs like these.

Joint visual attention is, of course, a form of collaborative activity, and it is possible to argue that the infant's efforts in bringing about a redirection of the focus of the mother's attention itself presupposes a degree of distinguishing psychological self-awareness as an agent. The argument might run, for example, like the following. The infant's intention is that the mother's recognition that he is *trying to bring it about* that she look where he is looking, cause her to look where he is looking. If, like many philosophers of action (e.g., O'Shaughnessy [1980]), one takes the presence of a trying to betoken the presence of an action, then the content of the infant's intention seems to include a recognition of his own agency. I do not want to put too much weight on this argument, however, as there is excellent evidence for ascribing to infants a more full-blooded sense of agency at about the same age. This is evidence from the games and collaborative activities that infants engage in with their caregivers (what some workers in the area call *coordinated joint engagement*). As before, I'll start by briefly reviewing the data and then move on to explain their implications.

Much of the most interesting work in this area has taken the form of longitudinal studies that trace the development of a single infant over time. The data that I want to focus on comes from Trevarthen and Hubley's (1978) work with an infant called Tracey. They placed Tracey and her mother interacting and playing in a darkened and comfortably furnished room and filmed them unobtrusively from an adjacent room. A total of 32 visits during Tracey's first year provided a detailed perspective on Tracey's development. The room was equipped with toys, and the experimenters were particularly interested in the development of different forms of play. They noted an important transition between 9 and 10 months:

At 40 weeks Tracey's mother became an acknowledged participant in actions. Tracy repeatedly looked up at her mother's face when receiving an object, pausing as if to acknowledge receipt. She also looked up to her mother at breaks in her play, giving the indication of willingness to share experiences as she had never done before. Tracey pulled the cart in by the string, watching it move remote from her hand. She accepted many changes among coloured beads by her mother, pausing in her manipulation to look at what was shown to her. She followed when her mother pointed to a bead while speaking, and calmly accepted removal of an object without loss of interest in the shared play. At one point she gently moved her mother's hand aside so she could get to beads beneath it. When her mother showed her how to make the wheels of the inverted trolley turn and squeak, Tracey watched closely and touched the wheels. When her mother eagerly said "Pull it" Tracey made a move to draw the trolley towards her, but failed because the string was not taut, at the same time, expecting success, she looked up and smiled eagerly at her mother. This was clearly a learned anticipation of the pleasure they usually shared when she did the trick of pulling in the trolley correctly. (Trevarthen and Hubley 1978, 201–204)

This is a clear illustration of what was earlier termed a triadic interaction, in which infants employ their interactions with people in their interactions with objects, and vice versa. In the next few weeks the games Tracey and her mother played became more sophisticated:

At both 45 and 47 weeks a large transformation in the balance of Tracey's communications with her mother was completed, and the effect on her mother was very great. For the first time Tracey gave a play object happily to the mother when asked to do so. They played with one of Tracey's toys, a rattle with a clear plastic globe, and a ball inside it. The globe could be unscrewed from the handle to take out or put in the ball. When the ball was offered to Tracey she promptly put it in the globe, and when her mother assembled the two parts she eagerly shook it. . . . Then Tracey's mother rolled a cloth ball to her saying, "Ready, steady, go!" Tracey caught it in two hands and grinned delightedly banging the table with both hands and the ball, and looking up at her mother's face. As her mother held her hand out palm up to receive the object saying, "Where's the ball?", Tracey hesitated a moment and, distracted by the sound of someone entering the room to the side away from her mother, turned to hold out the ball to the visitor. Her mother continued, "No, here: over this side." Tracey looked at her mother's hand, quickly reached to give her mother the ball, looked to her face and smiled. "Thank you!" said the mother, and Tracey gave a triumphant vocalization and hit the table. (Trevarthen and Hubley 1978, 204–205)

Other longitudinal studies (Bakeman and Adamson 1984) have found similar patterns in infant development.

As Trevarthen and Hubley's descriptions make clear, coordinated joint engagement clearly involves (and indeed presupposes) joint visual attention. Therefore, coordinated joint engagement requires distinguishing psychological self-awareness relative to the category of perceivers. What is distinctive about it, however, is that it also implicates distinguishing psychological self-awareness relative to the category of agents. The pleasure that Tracey takes in the various games is not just pleasure at her own agency (in the way that, for example, many infants show pleasure in the simple ability to bring about changes in the world like moving a mobile) but pleasure at successfully carrying out an intention—a form of pleasure possible only for creatures who are aware of themselves as agents. When the intention that is successfully carried out is a joint intention (as it is in several of the games described), the pleasure shared with the other participant reflects an awareness that they too are agents.

As we did with joint visual attention, let us look at the details of some of the contents that appear to be implicated in the best explanation of coordinated joint engagement. If we are trying to explain why infants take such pleasure when they succeed in various tasks or games, the natural explanation would involve something like the following attribution:

(5)   The infant recognizes, "I have succeeded in what I intended to do."

Similarly, when the task or game is a cooperative one, the content of the intention is first-person plural rather than first-person singular:

(6)   The infant recognizes, "We have succeeded in what we are trying to do."

Of course, in cooperative games (like the game that Trevarthen reports Tracey and her mother playing with the cloth ball) a vital part of what is going on appears to be each party's recognition of the other's intentions. Thus the Tracey manifests intentions with the following content:

(7)   The infant recognizes, "Mother wants me to give her the ball."

It is clear from these specimen contents (again, all first-personal) how coordinated joint engagement implicates distinguishing self-awareness relative to the category of agents. All three contents involve the infant's awareness of herself as an agent, and (6) and (7) combine this with an awareness of the mother's agency.

So the well-documented phenomena of joint visual attention and coordinated joint engagement in infants during the last quarter of the first year provide excellent examples of social interactions for which inference to the best and most parsimonious explanation requires ascribing to the infants in question distinguishing psychological self-awareness relative to the psychological categories of perceiver and agent. Of the three strands of distinguishing self-awareness identified earlier in the chapter, this leaves only the third undiscussed: awareness of oneself as a bearer of reactive attitudes relative to a contrast space of other bearers of reactive attitudes. Once again, the crucial period of infant development that starts at around 9 months of age presents a striking example of social interactions for which the best explanation requires attributing to the infants involved precisely this type of distinguishing self-awareness. The crucial stage is the emergence of what developmental psychologists call *social referencing*.

The essence of social referencing is the regulation of one's own behavior by investigating and being guided by the emotional reactions of others to a particular situation. In its typical manifestation in infancy, the infant will come across a puzzling or perhaps intimidating situation and will look toward his mother for guidance. His subsequent behavior will be influenced by his perception of her emotional reaction to the situation. Like coordinated joint engagement, social referencing presupposes joint visual attention: not only do both mother and infant have to be attending to the same features of the situation for social referencing to take place, but the infant has to be confident that he has successfully captured his mother's attention if he is to trust her reactions. Social referencing, therefore, clearly implicates distinguishing self-awareness as a perceiver. It is richer than joint visual attention and coordinated joint engagement because it opens up the emotional and reactive dimension of self-awareness. Like joint attention and joint engagement, however, the self-awareness emerges in the context of cooperative and interactive behavior into which the infant enters to cope with a world of unfamiliar and often alarming objects and people.

I will cite only one study to illustrate the phenomenon of social referencing: Klinnert et al. 1983. It is particularly interesting because it employs the experimental paradigm of the visual cliff cited in chapter 5 as an important example of how infants are capable of picking up self-specifying visual information almost immediately after birth. Recall that the visual cliff is a table made of clear glass and divided into two halves. On one of the two halves a chequered pattern is placed immediately below the surface of the glass to create an appearance of opacity, while a similar chequered pattern is placed at a variable distance below the surface of the other half to create the appearance of a sudden drop-off. What Klinnert et al. discovered is that 12-month-old infants clearly employ social referencing when they reach the drop-off point as they try to cross the tabletop to their mother. They look down at the deep side and then across to their mother. The mother was in each case instructed to adopt a predetermined facial expression (either fear or happiness). The results clearly showed that the infants registered and responded to the mother's emotional reaction to the situation. Of the 19 infants whose mothers smiled, 14 crossed the deep side, while of the 17 infants whose mothers showed fear, none crossed the deep side to the mother.

What conclusions can be drawn from social referencing? The explananda are that the infants look towards their mothers for guidance when they encounter a surprising or alarming event like the visual cliff and that the mother's facial expression is highly effective in determining their subsequent behavior. Explaining the first of these clearly requires attributing to the infant a comprehension that his mother reacts to things and events in the same way that he does, that she also finds events surprising or alarming. As mentioned earlier, this presupposes, but is not exhausted by, the infant's comprehension that both he and his mother are perceivers of the world. Following the mother's line of sight or the invisible line that leads from her pointing fingertip to an object does nothing more than direct the infant's attention to a particular object or event. It does not tell the infant anything about the object. Social referencing, in contrast, is a way of finding out about things in the world. It is not too fanciful, I think, to draw a linguistic analogy: whereas joint visual attention is a primitive analogue of the linguistic act of reference, social referencing is a primitive analogue of the linguistic act of predication. This means that the effectiveness of social referencing depends upon the infant's recognizing that his mother's emotional reactions are a guide to the nature of the puzzling object or event. This is what explains his willingness to tailor his own emotional reactions to the the emotional reactions that he perceives in his mother, which in turn presupposes an awareness that both he and his mother are bearers of reactive attitudes. This, of course, is just distinguishing self-awareness relative to the category of bearers of reactive attitudes.

Once more, it is worth making explicit specimens of the general type of contents that might feature in descriptions and explanations of social referencing. The infant on the visual cliff looks towards his mother for guidance. Why? The natural explanation is that the infant has an instrumental protobelief to the effect that his mother's reactions will provide an indication of whether the situation really is as bad as it appears:

(8)   The infant recognizes, "Mother is like me and reacts in the same sort of way to events as I do."

Something slightly more complex is required to translate this into action—capturable perhaps by the following pair of contents:

(9)   The infant recognizes, "The expression on her face means that she herself would not go forward."

(10)   The infant intends, "I will do what she would do."

Again, the combination of (8), (9), and (10) clearly implicates the presence of distinguishing psychological self-awareness relative to the category of bearers of reactive attitudes.

9.5   Conclusion

Let me draw the strands of this chapter together. I have been focusing on psychological self-awareness. It emerged early on in the chapter that psychological self-awareness needs to be viewed in the context of what I termed the Symmetry Thesis, namely that a subject's psychological self-awareness is constitutively linked with his awareness of other minds. The neo-Lockean defence of the Symmetry Thesis that I offered led to the thought that the Symmetry Thesis holds for self-awareness relative to the psychological categories that define and form the contrast space for the complex category of psychological subjects. These categories are those of perceivers, agents, and bearers of reactive attitudes.

The central question tackled in this chapter was whether it is legitimate to speak of nonconceptual psychological self-awareness in the way that it has been seen to be legitimate to speak of nonconceptual bodily self-awareness in previous chapters. As in previous chapters, I suggested that an answer to this question needed to be constrained by the requirements of inference to the best and most parsimonious explanation. What is needed to settle the question is clear evidence of forms of behavior for which inference to the best explanation requires attributing to non-linguistic or prelinguistic creatures precisely such psychological self-awareness. In the final section of the chapter I showed how such evidence was to be found in the complex social interactions in which human infants partake during and after the last quarter of the first year. Joint visual attention exemplifies distinguishing psychological self-awareness relative to the category of perceivers. Coordinated joint engagement exemplifies distinguishing psychological self-awareness relative to the category of agents. And social referencing exemplifies distinguishing psychological self-awareness relative to the category of bearers of reactive attitudes. Thus, with respect to these three core elements in the notion of a psychological subject, the notion of nonconceptual psychological self-awareness is indeed legitimate. It remains, however, to see how this can be deployed to solve the paradox of self-conscious. For this I turn to the next and final chapter.

10

Solving the Paradox of Self-Consciousness

The preceding chapters have provided the materials with which to offer a solution to the paradox of self-consciousness identified in chapter 1. In this final chapter I will draw together the various strands of the argument and show how they illuminate the paradox of self-consciousness. The first step, though, must be to recapitulate the paradox and the various moves that have been made towards a satisfactory solution to the paradox.

10.1 A Recapitulation

The paradox of self-consciousness as identified in chapter 1 can be presented as an inconsistency between the following six propositions:

1. The only way to analyze self-consciousness is by analyzing the capacity to think 'I'-thoughts.
2. The only way to analyze the capacity to think a particular range of thoughts is by analyzing the capacity for the canonical linguistic expression of those thoughts (the Thought-Language Principle).
3. 'I'-thoughts are canonically expressed by means of the first-person pronoun.
4. Linguistic mastery of the first-person pronoun requires the capacity to think 'I'-thoughts.
5. A noncircular analysis of self-consciousness is possible.
6. The capacity to think 'I'-thoughts meets the Acquisition Constraint (in the paradigmatic way defined in chapter 1).

It is propositions (5) and (6) that create the paradox. If the Thought-Language Principle is correct, then it does indeed follow that the only way to analyze the capacity to think 'I'-thoughts is through an analysis of the conditions of mastery of the first-person pronoun. But there are two kinds of circularity created by the proposal (as per (1)) that this is the key to providing an analysis of the capacity for self-conscious thought. The first type of circularity, which I termed explanatory circularity, arises because the capacity for self-conscious thought is presupposed in a satisfactory account of mastery of the first-person pronoun. The second type of circularity (capacity circularity) arises because the putative interdependence between self-conscious thought and linguistic mastery of the first-person pronoun rules out the possibility of explaining how the capacity either for self-conscious thought or for linguistic mastery of the first-person pronoun arises in the normal course of human development. Neither capacity is innate, and yet each presupposes the other in a way that seems to imply that neither can be acquired unless the other capacity is already in place.

Clearly, defusing the paradox of self-consciousness requires removing at least one of the propositions (1) to (6) so as to leave the propositions that remain consistent. The proposal that emerged from considering the strengths and shortcomings of the functionalist theory of self-reference in chapter 2 is that it is the Thought-Language Principle that must be rejected. Rejecting the Thought-Language Principle means rejecting the theory of content that underlies it, what I termed the classical conception of content. The classical conception of content has two key components. The first component is the Conceptual-Requirement Principle, that the ascriptions of content to an individual are constrained by the concepts that the individual possesses. The second component is the Priority Principle, to the effect that there is a constitutive connection between conceptual abilities and correlated linguistic abilities such that conceptual abilities cannot be possessed by nonlinguistic creatures. These two components jointly make up the Thought-Language Principle, and rejecting either one of them will be sufficient to reject the Thought-Language Principle. I proposed retaining the Priority Principle and rejecting the principle that ascriptions of content are constrained by concept possession. This makes possible a theory of nonconceptual content, according to which states with representational content can be properly ascribed to individuals without those individuals necessarily possessing the concepts required to specify how those states represent the world.

Of course, rejecting the Thought-Language Principle and the classical conception of content is useless unless it is shown that rejecting the Thought-Language Principle does not affect the truth values of the propositions that remain. The general strategy that I proposed here involves distinguishing between those forms of full-fledged self-consciousness that presuppose mastery of the first-person concept and linguistic mastery of the first-person pronoun and those forms of primitive or nonconceptual self-consciousness that do not presuppose any such linguistic or conceptual mastery. The operative idea was that if the self-consciousness presupposed by linguistic mastery of the first-person pronoun could be construed as nonconceptual rather than full-fledged, then the two forms of circularity that create the paradox of self-consciousness could be neutralized. A noncircular analysis of full-fledged self-consciousness in terms of linguistic mastery of the first-person pronoun would be available if the 'I'-thoughts presupposed by such linguistic mastery turned out to be instances not of full-fledged self-consciousness but instead of nonconceptual self-consciousness. This would also provide the key to showing how linguistic mastery of the first-person pronoun meets the Acquisition Constraint. On the assumption that linguistic mastery of the first-person pronoun can be analyzed satisfactorily in terms of nonconceptual self-consciousness, the Acquisition Constraint will be satisfied if it can be shown that there could be a plausible developmental progression from the cognitive skills and abilities that normal human infants have available to them at birth via the relevant forms of nonconceptual self-consciousness to linguistic mastery of the first-person pronoun.

If a solution to the paradox of self-consciousness along these lines is to be independently plausible, there are several conditions that must be satisfied. First, the rejection of the classical conception of content must be independently motivated. The paradox of self-consciousness cannot be the only reason for rejecting the classical conception of content if the appearance of a purely ad hoc move is to be avoided. A second condition is that the theory of nonconceptual content be subject to general constraints on the ascription of states with representational content. This in turn requires developing a general account of the marks that characterize content-bearing states in general and limiting ascriptions of nonconceptual content to states in which those marks are clearly present. Moreover, some ways of rejecting the classical conception of content to allow the existence of nonconceptual contents are nonetheless incompatible with the proposed solution to the paradox. It might be argued, for example, that states with nonconceptual content can be ascribed only to creatures that have a certain basic conceptual and linguistic mastery. A third condition, therefore, is that the conception of nonconceptual content in play be one that permits representational states with nonconceptual content to be ascribed to creatures that have no linguistic (and hence conceptual) abilities at all, that is, that recognizes the possibility of autonomous nonconceptual contents.

In chapter 3, I undertook to show that these conditions are indeed satisfied. I began by discussing arguments from the theory of perceptual experience in support of the general thesis that not all contents can be conceptual. Those arguments do not, however, support a notion of autonomous nonconceptual content. Accordingly, I then argued that evidence from experiments studying dishabituation in object perception in early infancy shows that the perceptual experience of infants does genuinely represent the world in a content-bearing way. Hence, since these are infants who manifestly lack any linguistic or conceptual abilities, the ways in which they represent the world can only be captured through a notion of autonomous nonconceptual content. In chapter 4, after having thus legitimated the notion of nonconceptual content, I offered an account of the essential marks of content-bearing states that is neutral between conceptual and nonconceptual content and thus provides a principled way of identifying when it is appropriate to ascribe states with nonconceptual content.

Nonetheless, a simple rejection of the classical conception is not sufficient, since there are many philosophers who would be prepared to countenance the possibility of nonconceptual content without accepting that there might be nonconceptual first-person contents, or 'I'-thoughts. Thus, to use the theory of nonconceptual content to solve the paradox of self-consciousness, I must independently motivate the possibility of nonconceptual first-person contents, and hence the possibility of nonconceptual self-consciousness. This is a more substantial task, occupying chapters 5 through 9. The methodology I adopted rested on the first of the marks of content identified in chapter 3, namely that content-bearing states serve to explain behavior in situations where the connections between sensory input and behavioral output cannot be plotted in a lawlike manner. I pointed out in chapter 2 (*pace* the functionalist theory of self-reference) that not every instance of intentional behavior where there are no such lawlike connections between sensory input and behavioral output needs to be explained by attributing to the creature in question representational states with first-person contents. Nonetheless, many such instances of intentional behavior do need to be explained in this way. This offers a way of establishing the legitimacy of nonconceptual first-person contents. What would satisfactorily demonstrate the legitimacy of nonconceptual first-person contents would be the existence of forms of behavior in prelinguistic or nonlinguistic creatures for which inference to the best understanding or explanation (which in this context includes inference to the most parsimonious understanding or explanation) demands the ascription of states with nonconceptual first-person contents.

I applied this methodological principle in four separate domains, each of which yielded a different type of nonconceptual self-consciousness. In chapter 5, drawing on J. J. Gibson's account of perception, I developed the view that the pick-up of self-specifying information in exteroceptive perception is a source of nonconceptual first-person contents from the beginning of life. This was argued partly on the basis of an analysis of the structure of the visual field and of visual experience in general and partly as a form of inference to the best explanation from experimental work on the sensory capacities of human infants. The second domain where I looked for evidence of nonconceptual self-consciousness was somatic proprioception (the various forms of bodily awareness). This occupied chapter 6. I suggested that somatic proprioception was best understood as a form of perception of the body. The best explanation of the phenomenology of bodily self-perception took the form of an account in which somatic proprioception emerged as a distinctive form of awareness of the material self as a spatially extended and bounded physical object that is distinctive in being responsive to the will.

The nonconceptual first-person contents implicated in somatic proprioception and the pick-up of self-specifying information in the structure of exteroceptive perception provide very primitive forms of nonconceptual self-consciousness, albeit forms that can plausibly be viewed as in place from birth or shortly afterward. That such nonconceptual first-person contents exist is a necessary condition of there being a solution to the paradox of self-consciousness, because they are an essential part of the case against the central assumption generating the paradox (namely, that it is incoherent to ascribe thoughts with a first-person content to creatures who lack linguistic mastery of the first-person pronoun). Nonetheless, they are far from sufficient. A solution to the paradox requires showing how we can get from these primitive forms of self-consciousness to the full-fledged self-consciousness that comes with linguistic mastery of the first-person pronoun. This progression will have to be both logical (in a way that will solve the problem of explanatory circularity) and ontogenetic (in a way that will solve the problem of capacity circularity). Clearly, this requires that there be forms of self-consciousness that, while still counting as nonconceptual, are nonetheless more developed than those yielded by somatic proprioception and the structure of exteroceptive perception, and moreover that it be comprehensible how these more developed forms of nonconceptual self-consciousness should have emerged out of basic nonconceptual self-consciousness.

The dimension along which forms of self-consciousness must be compared is the richness of the conception of the self that they provide. Nonetheless, a crucial element in any form of self-consciousness is how it enables the self-conscious subject to distinguish between self and environment—what many developmental psychologists term self-world dualism. In this sense, self-consciousness is essentially a contrastive notion. One implication of this is that a proper understanding of the richness of the conception of the self that a given form of self-consciousness provides requires that we take into account the richness of the conception of the environment with which it is associated. In the case of both somatic proprioception and the pick-up of self-specifying information in exteroceptive perception, there is a relatively impoverished conception of the self associated with a comparably impoverished conception of the environment. One prominent limitation is that both are synchronic rather than diachronic. The distinction between self and environment that they offer is a distinction that is effective at a time but not over time. The contrast between propriospecific and exterospecific invariants in visual perception, for example, provides a way for a creature to distinguish between itself and the world at any given moment, but this is not the same as a conception of oneself as an enduring thing distinguishable over time from an environment that also endures over time.

To capture this diachronic form of self-world dualism, I introduced the notion of a nonconceptual point of view. Having a nonconceptual point of view on the world involves taking a particular route through the environment in such a way that one's perception of the world is informed by an awareness that one is taking such a route. This diachronic awareness that one is taking a particular route through the environment turned out to involve two principal components: a nonsolipsistic component and a spatial awareness component. The nonsolipsistic component is a subject's capacity to draw a distinction between his experiences and what those experiences are experiences of, and hence his ability to grasp that what is experienced exists at times other than those at which it is experienced. This requires the exercise of recognitional abilities involving conscious memory and can be most primitively manifested in the feature-based recognition of places. I glossed the spatial awareness component of a non-conceptual point of view in terms of possession of an integrated representation of the environment over time. That a creature possesses such an integrated representation of the environment is manifested in three central cognitive/navigational capacities: a capacity to think about different routes to the same place, a capacity to keep track of changes in spatial relations between objects caused by one's own movements relative to those objects, and a capacity to think about places independently of the objects or features located at those places. I cited evidence from both ethology and developmental psychology indicating that these central cognitive/navigational capacities are present in both nonlinguistic and prelinguistic creatures. Again, my argumentative strategy was inference to the best explanation.

What is significant about the notion of a nonconceptual point of view is that it manifests an awareness of the self as a spatial element moving within, acting upon, and being acted upon by the spatial environment. This is far richer than anything available through either somatic proprioception or the self-specifying information available in exteroceptive perception. Nonetheless, like these very primitive forms of self-consciousness, a nonconceptual point of view is largely awareness of the material self as a bearer of physical properties. This limitation raises the question of whether there can be a similarly nonconceptual awareness of the material self as a bearer of psychological properties. This question was the subject of chapter 9. In approaching the possibility of nonconceptual psychological self-consciousness, I was guided by the thought that there might be a constitutive link between a subject's psychological self-consciousness and his awareness of other minds (the Symmetry Thesis). In the first part of the chapter I defended a weak version of the Symmetry Thesis, according to which there are some psychological categories that a subject cannot apply to himself without also being able to apply them to other psychological subjects. These psychological categories form the core of the notion of a psychological subject. This is so because a subject's recognition that he is distinct from the environment in virtue of being a psychological subject depends on his ability to identify himself as a psychological subject within a contrast space of other psychological subjects, and this self-identification as a psychological subject takes place relative to a set of categories that collectively define the core of the concept of a psychological subject.

There appear to be three central psychological categories defining the core of the concept of a psychological subject: the category of perceivers, the category of agents, and the category of bearers of reactive attitudes. This, in conjunction with the Symmetry Thesis, offers a clear way of answering the question of whether psychological self-consciousness can exist in a form that is nonconceptual and independent of linguistic mastery. In line with the methodology I adopted previously in this book, what would settle the matter would be social interactions involving prelinguistic or nonlinguistic subjects for which inference to the best explanation requires assuming that those subjects are applying the relevant psychological categories to themselves and to others. In the final section of the chapter I looked at various experimental paradigms of research on the social cognition of infants and showed that there are compelling grounds for attributing to prelinguistic infants in the final quarter of the first year distinguishing psychological self-consciousness relative to the three key categories.

The situation at the moment, therefore, is that four different forms of primitive nonconceptual self-consciousness have been identified and shown to be psychologically real. With this we have the materials for a

solution to the paradox of self-consciousness. The next and final stage is
to show how these materials can be used to circumvent the paradox of
self-consciousness.

10.2   Nonconceptual Self-Consciousness and Explanatory Circularity

What is responsible for explanatory circularity is the fact that an adequate explanation of what linguistic mastery of the first-person pronoun
consists in involves ascribing to the person who has mastered the first-
person pronoun certain first-person thoughts that, by the Thought-
Language Principle, are themselves comprehensible only by ascribing to
the language-user mastery of the first-person pronoun. The first stage in
resolving this aspect of the paradox of self-consciousness is to get clear
on precisely what those first-person thoughts are.

The initial argument in chapter 1 was that a grasp of the token-reflexive
rule governing the reference of the first-person pronoun cannot be sufficient to explain mastery of the first-person pronoun. A minimal requirement upon proper and genuine employment of the first-person pronoun
is that the person who employs a token of the first-person pronoun so as
to secure genuine and proper self-reference should know that he is the
producer of the token in question. This minimal requirement must be
reflected in an account of mastery of the first-person pronoun. A natural
question at this point is whether this minimal requirement is also (in conjunction, of course, with a suitable grasp of the token-reflexive rule) sufficient for linguistic mastery of the first-person pronoun. More precisely,
given that an account of what it is to have mastery of the first-person
pronoun will need to specify the conditions holding on genuine and
proper employment of the first-person pronoun, does such an account
need to specify any conditions other than mastery of the token-reflexive
rule and a knowledge that one is the producer of the relevant token of 'I'?

Brief reflection shows that these conditions cannot be sufficient. There
are straightforward counterexamples in which a language-user produces
a token of 'I' in full understanding of the token-reflexive rule, whereby
every token of 'I' refers to the person who produces it, and in the full
knowledge that he himself is the producer of that token, while nonetheless failing to refer to himself. One such counterexample is provided by

the use of language in fiction. An actor uttering a soliliquy satisfies both conditions but does not refer to himself. Fiction is a difficult case, however, since it is arguable that no genuine and proper reference takes place in fictional discourse. Fortunately, there are two further, straightforward counterexamples that do not depend on any peculiarities of fictional situations. When I dictate a letter to a secretary who writes down at the end of the letter the words 'I look forward to hearing from you', she does so fully comprehending both the token-reflexive rule that the relevant token of 'I' refers to whoever utters or inscribes it and the fact that she is writing down that token. But she is obviously not referring to herself, nor, of course, does she take herself to be referring to herself. The same is true of the simultaneous interpreter who translates my words into French without placing them in *oratio obliqua*. These are all cases where someone knowingly produces a token of 'I' (or 'je') in full comprehension of the token-reflexive rule, and yet it is clear that they neither refer to themselves nor take themselves to be referring to themselves.

Evidently, then, more is required for proper use of the first-person pronoun than knowingly producing a token of 'I' in full comprehension of the token-reflexive rule. A natural suggestion here would be that what is missing in the examples just given is an intention on the part of the language users to use the token of 'I' that they knowingly produce to refer to themselves. Perhaps the reason that neither the secretary nor the interpreter take themselves to be referring to themselves is that they know that they do not intend to refer to themselves. There is an important difference between knowingly producing a token of 'I' that would, in certain circumstances, refer to oneself and producing a token of 'I' knowing that one is intending to refer to oneself. An ostensibly competing explanation would be that the token-reflexive rule does not apply to either the secretary or the translator because neither of them produces the respective token of 'I' in the relevant sense of 'produces'. Indeed, it is highly plausible that there is more to producing a token of 'I' than simply uttering or inscribing it. Yet in spelling out what the production of a token of 'I' involves over and above uttering it or inscribing it, it is natural to advert to the intention to utter or inscribe that token of 'I' with the intention to refer to oneself.

Let me start by trying to get a proper understanding of what is involved in the phenomenon of intentional self-reference by means of the first-

9.2 The Symmetry Thesis: A Neo-Lockean Defence   237

9.3 The Core Notion of a Psychological Subject   241

9.4 The Emergence of Psychological Self-Awareness in Social
Interactions   247

9.5 Conclusion   265

10 **Solving the Paradox of Self-Consciousness   267**

10.1 A Recapitulation   267

10.2 Nonconceptual Self-Consciousness and
Explanatory Circularity   275

10.3 Solving the Problem of Capacity Circularity   291

10.4 The Way Forward   294

Notes   299

References   313

Index   327

person pronoun. What is the content of the relevant intention? The best place to start is with Grice's communication-theoretic account of meaning (1957), on the entirely reasonable assumption that an account of the intention to refer linguistically to oneself can be derived only from an account of communicative intent in general. As is well-known, the general form of Grice's attempt to use the notion of communicative intent to illuminate the notion of meaning is this: that A means something by x is to be understood in terms of A's intention that the utterance of x should produce some effect in an audience by means of the recognition of this intention.[1] Although this general form has been somewhat refined in response to counterexamples (see particularly Grice 1969), we can safely ignore these complexities. What is immediately relevant is a general bifurcation that Grice introduces between two different types of responses that might be communicatively intended—what might be termed the informational and the practical. When an informative message is intended, the response that an utterer intends to produce in his audience is a belief or some other kindred cognitive state. When a practical message is intended, the response that an utterer intends to produce is an action of some form or other. Let me schematize these. Communicatively intending an informational message takes (roughly) the following form:

An utterer u utters x to mean p if and only if u utters x intending

a. that some audience a should come to believe that p,

b. that a should be aware of intention (a),

c. that the awareness mentioned in (b) should be part of a's reason for believing p.

Communicatively intending a practical response takes this form:

An utterer u utters x to mean that an audience a should do ϕ if and only if u utters x intending

a. that a should do ϕ,

b. that a should be aware of intention (a),

c. that the awareness mentioned in (b) should be part of a's reason for doing ϕ.

Other philosophers of language in the communication-theoretic tradition (Armstrong 1971, Bennett 1976) have followed Grice in this bifurcation in the central notion of intending to bring about a response in the audience.

It is not clear from the work of Grice and his successors whether they intend their account of communicative intent to be part of a statement of the necessary and sufficient conditions that must be satisfied on any given occasion of language use, so that whenever a token sentence x is used to mean that p, or to bring about the response ϕ, it must be accompanied by the appropriate communicative intent. Many philosophers would find such a claim psychologically implausible. Let me offer such philosophers a weaker construal of the communicative-intent theory. One way of reading the theory on which it would not have this sort of psychological implausibility would be as an account that operates at the level of sentence types rather than sentence tokens. A weak reading of the claim that the meaning of sentence type X is given by a complex communicative intent of the sort just indicated is that no speaker could be credited with a meaningful use of a token of type X unless he learned how to employ tokens of type X through appreciating the complex communicative intention given by the theory. For the purposes of this chapter I shall stick with the Gricean position as formulated for expository convenience. For what I have to say, however, the weaker reading is perfectly sufficient.

The two-branched analysis of communicative intent in terms of intended informational and practical messages is relatively straightforward at the level of the sentence. There is a simple and easily identifiable distinction between assertoric or declarative sentences, which it is plausible to analyze along the first branch as intended to generate beliefs in the audience, and imperative or injunctive sentences, which it is equally plausible to analyze along the second branch as intended to bring about some act or other on the part of the audience. The particular use to which I wish to put the theoretical notion of communicative intent is in illuminating intentional self-reference, and there are two good reasons why this bifurcated theory of communicative intent cannot be unproblematically applied here.

The first reason is a general one. At a level of analysis below the sentence we are dealing with particular acts like reference and predication, which do not lend themselves to this clean bifurcation. Let me bring this out with respect to the act of reference. If a clear bifurcation between informational and practical communicative intent is to be maintained below the level of the sentence, then reference ought to be construed in terms of informational communicative intent, so that the response that an utterer intends to produce in his audience is a belief. Let us assume, for the sake of simplicity, that we are dealing with the simple subject-predicate sentence 'That is green' uttered in the presence of a green Granny Smith apple to which I am pointing and that I intend to produce in my audience (Jones) the belief that the apple is green. How are we to understand the reference of the demonstrative pronoun 'that'? Straight-forwardly adapting the informational account would yield the thought that my utterance of the demonstrative pronoun (accompanied by a suit-able ostensive gesture) is intended to produce in Jones the belief that the object to which I am pointing is the subject of my sentence through what Bennett helpfully terms the Gricean mechanism (that is, through Jones's recognition of my intention to produce in him that belief). But it is surely not necessary either for Jones to have any such belief or for this to be what I am trying to do, for me successfully to communicate to him the thought that the apple is green. Nor is it necessary for me to intend to produce in him any beliefs about the apple being the subject of my sen-tence. I do, of course, intend to produce in Jones a belief about the apple, namely that it is green. As part of that project I refer demonstratively to the apple. And the apple is indeed the subject of my sentence. But none of this adds up to my intending Jones to form a belief about the apple being what my sentence is about. I shall return to this shortly.

The second reason that the theory of communicative intent is problem-atic at this level is a psychological one highly pertinent to the matter in hand. It is relatively uncontroversial among developmental psychologists that a full-fledged concept of belief emerges relatively late in cognitive development, and certainly long after the emergence of even relatively so-phisticated language use (including, for that matter, competent use of the first-person pronoun). The evidence for the late emergence of the concept of belief is the well-known false-belief task, a beautifully simple paradigm designed to identify whether or not young children can deploy the idea of a mental state representing the world to be a way other than the way it is. In the false-belief task, children are presented with the following situation. A character, Maxi, places some chocolate in a cupboard and then leaves the room. While he is away, the chocolate is moved to another location. The child is asked where Maxi will look for the chocolate when he returns. In order for the child to give the correct answer, he must understand that Maxi still represents the chocolate as being where in fact it is not, namely where Maxi originally left it. And that means that the child must be able to contrast his perception of the situation as it is with Maxi's beliefs about the situation as it is no longer. The experimental evidence is that children consistently fail on this task until well into their fourth year (Wimmer and Perner 1983; see Perner 1991 for further discussion). Now, although there is, of course, much to be said about the false-belief task, the central point for present purposes is that no subject who fails the false-belief task can be ascribed the concept of belief, since possessing the concept of belief requires comprehension of the possibility that another subject represents the world in a way other than it is.[2] This has the straightforward consequence that the concept of belief cannot feature in any communicative intention that is to be ascribed to infant language users younger than three years of age. So, on the assumption that the notion of communicative intent is indeed applicable here, it must at least be possible for there to be an appropriate informational communicative intention that does not take the concept of belief to be central.

To return, then, to the first point, what is the communicative intention governing my demonstrative reference to the apple, since it is not an intention that Jones should come to believe (via the Gricean mechanism) that the apple is the subject of my sentence? The simplest and most straightforward suggestion would be that I intend the demonstrative reference to the apple to draw Jones's attention to the apple. Of course, this is hardly sufficient. I could call Jones's attention to the apple by biting into it or by placing it on my son's head and shooting an arrow at it. These would not be ways of drawing attention to the apple that would count as instances of demonstrative reference, the reason being, of course, that they can be effective without proceeding through Jones's recognition of my intention. Genuine demonstrative reference occurs when I intend Jones's attention to be drawn to the apple by means of the Gricean mechanism, namely that my utterance of the demonstrative pronoun accompanied by a suitable ostensive gesture should identify the apple to Jones in virtue of his recognition that such is my intention.

This proposal brings out what is wrong with the bifurcation between informational and practical communicative intent at the subsentential level. When I intend to draw Jones's attention to the apple, I do not intend simply to produce beliefs in Jones (as the purely informational account of communicative intent at the level of the sentence would maintain). Nor do I intend simply to get Jones to do something. What I intend is that Jones should do something (redirect his attention) in a way that will put him in informational contact with the apple. This is, moreover, fully in line with the second point. When I intend that Jones's attention should be drawn via the Gricean mechanism to the apple, I do not intend Jones to form any beliefs about the subject of my sentence. Nor is it necessary for Jones to form any such beliefs. All that is required is that his attention should in fact be drawn to the apple through the Gricean mechanism in a way that will lead him correctly to realize that the apple is what I am describing as green.

Of course, these observations fall a long way short of a general communication-theoretic account of reference. There are all sorts of other conditions that might arguably be needed. It might be thought necessary, for example, that linguistic reference take place as part of the utterance of a complete sentence. Something also needs to be said (and will be shortly) about the linguistic meaning of the word through which reference is effected. I take it, however, that from what's been said we can derive at least the bare bones of a satisfactory account of the communicative intent that governs linguistic reference. Such an account will proceed along something like the following lines:

An utterer *u* utters *x* to refer to an object *o* if and only if *u* utters *x* intending

a. that some audience *a* should have their attention drawn to *o*,

b. that *a* should be aware of intention (a),

c. that the awareness mentioned in (b) should be part of the explanation for *a*'s attention being drawn to *o*.

This general outline gives us sufficient tools to return to the problem of self-reference.

Recall what led us to communication-theoretic accounts of reference. I originally raised the question of whether it is sufficient for genuine linguistic self-reference that a speaker should knowingly produce a token of 'I' in full knowledge of the token-reflexive rule governing the reference of 'I'. I showed that this is not sufficient and suggested that what would be sufficient would be producing a token of 'I' in full knowledge of the token-reflexive rule and with the intention to refer to oneself. This is what led me to investigate the communicative intent that governs linguistic reference—on the two assumptions, first, that intentional self-reference will be a special case of intentional reference and, second, that the best way to understand intentional reference is in terms of the communicative intent that governs acts of reference. The next step must be to apply this to the first-person pronoun.

A straightforward application of the sketch just given of the communicative intent governing the act of reference yields something like the following:

An utterer u utters 'I' to refer to himself* if and only if u utters 'I' in full comprehension of the token-reflexive rule that tokens of 'I' refer to their producer and with the tripartite intention

a. that some audience a should have their attention drawn to u,

b. that a should be aware of u's intention that a's attention should be drawn to u,

c. that the awareness mentioned in (b) should be part of the explanation for a's attention being drawn to u.

For familiar reasons, this cannot be satisfactory. An utterer's intentional self-reference does not require that he intend to draw attention to himself in the way just mentioned. Utterer u can refer to himself (more accurately, himself*) without intending to draw attention to u. This, after all, is the problem that initially led to the paradox of self-consciousness. It will not be of any use to replace 'u' with 'the utterer of this token' in each of the three parts of the tripartite intention. Although that would undoubtedly secure successful self-reference in cases where, for example, u is unaware that he is u, it is surely only in the most unusual cases that people intend to refer to themselves as producers of tokens of 'I'. This is sufficient to prevent it from featuring in a statement of the communicative intent governing paradigm cases of intentional self-reference. It is, of course, reasoning along precisely these lines that brought us to the paradox of self-consciousness in chapter 1, via the conclusion that any adequate account of linguistic mastery of the first-person pronoun would have to include certain first-person thoughts among its conditions. We can now see the form that such an account will have to take:

An utterer *u* utters 'I' to refer to himself* if and only if *u* utters 'I' in full comprehension of the token-reflexive rule that tokens of 'I' refer to their producer and with the tripartite intention

a. that some audience *a* should have their attention drawn to him*,

b. that *a* should be aware of his* intention that *a*'s attention should be drawn to him*,

c. that the awareness mentioned in (b) should be part of the explanation for *a*'s attention being drawn to him*.

Each of the three clauses of the tripartite intention is a first person thought, in virtue of the presence in each of them of the indirect reflexive pronoun he*.

If this account of linguistic mastery of the first-person pronoun is to escape the explanatory circularity that partly creates the paradox of self-consciousness, then, for reasons that have already been discussed in this chapter, each of the three clauses in the statement of the tripartite communicative intention must be formulable in terms of nonconceptual first-person thoughts. It is at this point that the exploration of nonconceptual first-person thoughts in the main body of this book pays dividends, for we now have the materials to provide such a formulation. That is, the methodology of inference to the best and most parsimonious explanation has shown how we can be warranted in identifying and explaining behavior by means of nonconceptual first-person contents of precisely the sort that would provide a noncircular account of linguistic mastery of the first-person pronoun.

Clause (a) in the tripartite intention is that the utterer should utter a token of 'I' with the intention that some audience should have their attention drawn to himself*. There are two key components here. The first component is that the utterer should intend to draw another's attention to something. That this is possible at the nonconceptual level is clearly shown by my discussion of joint selective visual attention in the previous chapter. The best explanation of joint selective visual attention involving young infants is that they are acting on the intention to direct another individual's attention to an object in which they are interested. Of course, in the cases of joint selective visual attention I examined, the objects in question are not the infants themselves. Accordingly, the second component of clause (a) of the communicative intention is that the utterer should be aware of himself* as a possible object of another's attention. This is largely a matter of physical self-consciousness. The materials here are provided by proprioceptive self-consciousness and the various forms of bodily self-consciousness implicated in possession of a nonconceptual point of view. Proprioceptive self-consciousness in particular provides a conception of the body as a spatially extended and bounded physical object that is unique in its responsiveness to the will. One way, therefore, in which clause (a) of the complex tripartite intention might be satisfied at a nonconceptual level would be through an intention to draw an audience's attention to the material self as revealed in proprioceptive self-consciousness. Another way would be through an intention to draw an audience's attention to the material self as a spatial element moving within, acting upon, and being acted upon by, the spatial environment—the conception of the self that is implicated in possession of a nonconceptual point of view.

In clause (b) the requirement is that the utterer of 'I' should intend that his audience recognize his* intention to draw its attention to him*. This is a reflexive awareness of the intention in the first clause. The real issue that it raises is one about how iterated psychological states can feature in the content of intentions. In the first clause we have what can usefully be described as an *uniterated intention*. An uniterated intention is one in which a psychological state does not feature within the scope of the 'that' clause specifying the content of an intention or any other content-bearing state, or where a psychological state does so feature, that psychological state does not have a further psychological state featuring in the 'that' clause that specifies its content. The first clause in the intention is an uniterated intention in the second of these two senses because the psychological state that features in the content of the intention does not take a further psychological state as its object. A *first-order iteration* occurs when a further psychological state is embedded within the context created by the psychological state featuring within the scope of the 'that' clause specifying the intention. A *second-order iteration* occurs when there is a third psychological state embedded within the context created by that further psychological state. Generally, an *iteration to the order n* occurs when there is an $(n-1)$th order psychological state embedded within the scope of the 'that' clause specifying the content of a given psychological state. Clearly, in clause (b) specifying the communicative intent governing the use of 'I', we have a second-order iteration. There are three psychological states embedded within the scope of the 'that' clause. What complicates the matter further is that one of those psychological states is a first-person state. Moreover, it is a first-person psychological state that has a further psychological state within the scope of the 'that' clause specifying its content. This poses an obvious challenge. Are there resources at the nonconceptual level for thinking an intention of this complexity?

There are two distinguishable questions here. The first question is whether there are resources at the nonconceptual level for thinking a thought whose content contains a second-order iteration. The second question is whether there are resources at the nonconceptual level for embedding a first-person psychological state within a first- or higher-order iteration. Let me take them in reverse order. The discussion of psychological self-consciousness in the previous chapter revealed several examples of first-person psychological states embedded within first- or higher-order iterations. A canonical example comes from joint visual attention, where inference to the best explanation seems to require attributing to infants contents like the following:

(1)   The infant recognizes, "Mother wants me to look where she is looking."

This is a first-person content embedded in a first-order iteration. The structure emerges more clearly when (1) is reformulated less idiomatically as follows:

(2)   The infant recognizes, "Mother wants that I look where she is looking."

Of course, this is not simply a peculiarity of joint visual attention. This sort of embedding of first-person contents in first-order iterations occurs whenever there is recognition of another's intention that one should do something. Recognitional states like these play a crucial role in the cooperative games and projects that are so important in infancy after the last quarter of the first year. An important source of infants' pleasure and enjoyment is their recognition that they have successfully performed what their mothers intended them to. And this implicates an embedding of a first-person content within a first-order iteration.

The fact remains, however, that the descriptions and explanations given of the various examples of joint visual attention, coordinated joint engagement, and social referencing that I have considered do not provide any examples of second or higher-order iterations. They are all forms of cognition and action for which inference to the best explanation can rest satisfied with first-order iterations. Nonetheless, it is possible to describe a consistent and indeed familiar situation for which inference to the best explanation does appear to require attributing a second-order iteration, and indeed, a second-order iteration that embeds a first-person content. This can be done by varying slightly one of the examples of coordinated joint engagement already discussed. Trevarthen and Hubley's longitudinal study of Tracey describes a game with a trolley:

When her mother showed her how to make the wheels of the inverted trolley turn and squeak, Tracey watched closely and touched the wheels. When her mother eagerly said "Pull it" Tracey made a move to draw the trolley towards her, but failed because the string was not taut, at the same time, expecting success, she looked up and smiled eagerly at her mother. (Trevarthen and Hubley 1978, 204)

Explaining Tracey's pleasure in this simple game requires attributing to her the following two true protobeliefs:

(3)   Tracey recognizes, "I have succeeded in what I set out to do."

(4)   Tracey recognizes, "Mother recognizes that I have succeeded in what I set out to do."

I am assuming that Tracey's expectant smile toward her mother anticipates a reciprocating smile. Suppose, however, another situation in which things are similar except that no such reciprocating smile appears on the mother's face. Tracey* (as I shall call her) is consequently distressed. One way of explaining this state of affairs would be in terms of Tracey*'s recognizing her mother's failure to recognize her intention that her mother should recognize her success. This in turn requires attributing to Tracey* the intention to get her mother to take pleasure when she succeeds in carrying out her intention:

(5)   Tracey* intends, "Mother is pleased when she recognizes that I have succeeded in what I set out to do."

This is a second-order iteration, and moreover a second-order iteration that embeds a first-person content.

It should not be thought that describing such a possible scenario is simply stipulating a solution to the problem, because the possibility of the scenario as described presupposes the coherence of ascribing second-order iterations at the nonconceptual level. Certainly, there would be room for considerable disquiet if the only motivation for believing in the possibility of the scenario was to solve the problem at hand. But this is surely not the case. Not only is the sort of interaction between infant and mother described readily conceivable and indeed familiar, but the explanation proposed can be tested. Suppose, for example, that one is wondering whether Tracey*'s distress ought not to be explained more simply in terms of her being unhappy that her mother had failed to smile when a certain effect was attained. This would, of course, require no more than the following uniterated intention:

(6)   Tracey* intends, "Mother is pleased when such and such occurs."

Now it seems to me that what is at issue between these two interpretations can be empirically tested, because they each implicate different counterfactuals. Suppose that the relevant effect is the moving of the trolley. If the explanation implicating the uniterated intention (6) is correct, then one would expect Tracey* to be distressed whenever the trolley moves and her mother does not smile or otherwise show pleasure. If, on the other hand, the explanation implicating the second-order iteration in intention (5) is correct, then one would expect Tracey* to show distress only in those situations where her mother fails to show pleasure and the movement of the trolley is contingent upon Tracey*'s pulling it. There is nothing puzzling about the thought that this counterfactual might be true rather than the previous one, and hence there must be a genuine and psychologically real distinction between (5) and (6).

I take it, therefore, that clause (b) in the tripartite communicative intent governing the deployment of the first-person pronoun is fully specifiable at the nonconceptual level. That leaves us simply with clause (c) in the tripartite intention, the clause specifying the so-called Gricean mechanism that the intention specified in clause (b) should be part of the explanation for the success of the intention specified in clause (a). Here again are the conditions we are working with:

An utterer u utters 'I' to refer to himself* if and only if u utters 'I' in full comprehension of the token-reflexive rule that tokens of 'I' refer to their producer and with the tripartite intention

a. that some audience a should have their attention drawn to him*,

b. that a should be aware of his* intention that a's attention should be drawn to him*,

c. that the awareness mentioned in (b) should be part of the explanation for a's attention being drawn to him*.

The first point to make here is that the iteration involved in clause (c) is not at a higher level than the iteration involved in clause (b). It is not that (a) is embedded in (b). Rather, the content of the intention in (c) is that there be a certain relation between (a) and (b). What is this relation? In Gricean accounts of meaning, the relation is often glossed in terms of the awareness mentioned in (b) being a reason for the success of the intention in (a). This does not seem appropriate, however, since the notion of a reason is not operative at the level of nonconceptual content.[3] What is needed is a nonconceptual analog of the reason-giving interpretation of the Gricean mechanism. Some form of causal interpretation is the obvious alternative. Suppose that we reformulate (c) as follows:

c′. that the awareness in (b) should bring it about that a's attention be drawn to him*

Now since (b) has already been explained and since the intention that a's attention be drawn to him* is the content of (a), which has also already been explained, the only new element to be explained here is the causal relation of bringing-it-about-that and how it can form part of an intention linking (a) and (b). There is a reason for referring to the causal relation of bringing-of-about-that, rather than to the notion of cause. The concept of cause brings with it a degree of theory that does not seem to be required to manipulate the Gricean mechanism. For example, the concept of cause has clear modal elements with respect to the necessary connection between cause and effect and the concomitant impossibility of the cause not being followed by the relevant effect. These modal elements are not required for the Gricean mechanism to be understood and employed. Consequently, the concept of cause need not feature in the content of the communicative intention defining mastery of the first-person pronoun. The notion of bringing-it-about-that is intended to indicate a causal relation that can be understood without a full-fledged understanding of full-fledged causation.[4]

The causal relation of bringing-it-about-that is integral to the notion of a nonconceptual point of view and to the self-consciousness that it implicates. Possession of a nonconceptual point of view involves an awareness of the self as acting upon and being acted upon by the spatial environment, and this, of course, depends crucially on understanding both the general notion of one's bringing it about that a certain effect occurs (without which intentional action would be impossible) and the general notion of things being brought about in virtue of, for example, interactions between objects (without which it would be impossible to make predictions about the future other than those based on the most simple correlations of features). Of course, there is a distinction to be made between physical causation and psychological causation. The causal relation of bringing-it-about-that implicated in a nonconceptual point of view is a physical notion, while the type of bringing-it-about-that involved in understanding the operation of the Gricean mechanism is clearly psychological. So if the intention in (c′) is to be available at the nonconceptual level, there must be warrant for attributing a grasp of the psychological bringing-it-about-that relation to prelinguistic creatures.

Not every form of psychological bringing-it-about-that will be sufficient to underwrite comprehension of the Gricean mechanism. Awareness of oneself as an agent presumably involves a comprehension that one's intentions can be effective in bringing about changes in the world, and this is obviously a form of psychological bringing-it-about-that. Nonetheless, it is important to distinguish between what might be termed mind-to-world bringing-it-about-that and mind-to-mind bringing-it-about-that. It is the second of these that is required. Comprehension of the Gricean mechanism requires understanding that one's manifest intentions can be efficacious in bringing about changes in the mental states of others. Such an understanding is, of course, available at the nonconceptual level, as emerged during my discussion of psychological self-consciousness in the previous chapter. Both coordinated joint engagement and joint visual attention depend on both participants comprehending the possibility of mind-to-mind bringing-it-about-that. Here is one example of a proto-belief that might feature in the explanation of canonical instances of joint visual attention:

(7)   The infant recognises, "Mother will look where I am looking if I look back and forth from her to it."

This instrumental protobelief is a recognition of mind-to-mind bringing-it-about-that. The infant recognizes that his looking back and forth from his mother to the object will bring it about that she looks where he is looking.

Once the comprehension of mind-to-mind bringing-it-about-that at the nonconceptual level is granted, the legitimacy of clause (c′) in the communicative intention governing use of the first-person pronoun swiftly follows. Clause (c′) comprises the following intention:

c′. that the awareness in (b) should bring it about that *a*'s attention be drawn to him*

This can be broken down into three elements—specifically, a relation of mind-to-mind bringing-it-about-that between *a*'s awareness of the utterer's intention that *a*'s attention be drawn to him* and *a*'s awareness actually being drawn to him. All three elements have now been accommodated at the nonconceptual level, so there is no obstacle to the thought that their combination in (c′) can be accommodated at the nonconceptual level.

Is this sufficient to solve the problem of explanatory circularity that is one of the two planks of the paradox of self-consciousness? The problem of explanatory circularity derives from the fact that the capacity for self-conscious thought is presupposed in a satisfactory account of mastery of the first-person pronoun. This appears to render circular the project of elucidating the capacity for self-conscious thought through mastery of the first-person pronoun. We are now in a position, however, to see why the circularity here is apparent rather than real. A communication-theoretic account of the requirements on mastery of the first-person pronoun does indeed involve, in addition to mastery of the token-reflexive rule, three intentions with first-person contents. A real and vicious circularity would arise only if the first-person thoughts implicated in mastery of the first-person pronoun themselves implicate mastery of the first-person pronoun. What has emerged, however, is that these first-person thoughts are of a kind that can be nonconceptual in a way that makes them logically independent of mastery of the first-person pronoun. They can be used to explain the requirements on linguistic mastery of the first-person pronoun without themselves presupposing linguistic mastery of the first person. I take it that this is sufficient to solve the problem of explanatory circularity. It also holds considerable promise for solving the problem of capacity circularity, which I take up in the next section of the book.

10.3   Solving the Problem of Capacity Circularity

The problem of capacity circularity arose in chapter 1 in the context of a constraint on the psychological reality of cognitive abilities that I termed the Acquisition Constraint:

The Acquisition Constraint   If a given cognitive capacity is psychologically real, then there must be an explanation of how it is possible for an individual in the normal course of human development to acquire that cognitive capacity.

The Acquisition Constraint is not a very strong constraint. It does not require that any account be provided of how the cognitive ability in question is actually acquired. Nor in fact does it require that any such account be epistemically available. What it does provide is a negative test. If, for any designated cognitive ability, there are good reasons to think that it cannot be acquired in the normal course of human development, then its psychological reality is cast in doubt.

Of course, the force of the Acquisition Constraint depends upon how the notion of acquisition is to be understood. After all, one way in which the Acquisition Constraint could be satisfied for a given cognitive capacity would be if it turned out that the emergence of that cognitive capacity was due to the maturation of an innate module. One might be forgiven for feeling that this makes the Acquisition Constraint too weak a tool. With this apparently catch-all way of potentially satisfying the Acquisition Constraint, how could anything fail to meet it? But what makes matters slightly simpler here is that it is often part of our understanding of a given psychological capacity that it should have been acquired in a certain way. So when we ask whether a given cognitive capacity is psychologically real, the specification of that cognitive ability will often include an outline conception of how it is acquired. This is certainly the case with the multiple cognitive capacities implicated in language mastery. We understand these cognitive capacities to have been acquired through a process of learning, a process that typically starts in the second year of life and continues for several years afterwards. This conception of how language is acquired is so deeply embedded in our understanding of language that the question of how the various cognitive capacities implicated in language use meet the Acquisition Constraint is the question of how they are learned. And should it turn out that one or more of these capacities cannot be learned then, although it might of course meet the Acquisition Constraint in some other way, it seems fair to say that the capacity as we understand it is not psychologically real.

In chapter 1, I gave the following more-detailed account of how, for the purposes of this book, the Acquisition Constraint was canonically to be understood. Every individual has an innate set of cognitive capacities that he possesses at birth. Let me call that set S_0. At any given time t after birth, an individual will have a particular set of cognitive capacities. Let me call this set S_t. Now consider a given cognitive capacity c putatively in S_t. Suppose that for any time $t - n$ the following two conditions are satisfied. First, it is conceivable how c could have emerged from capacities present in S_{t-n}. Second, it is conceivable how the capacities present in S_{t-n} could have emerged from the capacities present in S_0. By it being conceivable that one capacity could emerge from a given set of capacities, I mean that it is intelligible that the individual in question could deploy the cognitive capacities it already has to acquire the new capacity. If these conditions are satisfied, then we have a paradigm case of learning.

If mastery of the first-person pronoun is to meet the Acquisition Constraint (at least on this canonical construal), then clearly there must be some time t when S_t includes the capacity for linguistic mastery of the first-person pronoun, and a corresponding time $t - n$ when S_{t-n} does not include that capacity but includes other capacities on the basis of which it is intelligible that an individual could acquire the capacity for linguistic mastery of the first-person pronoun. This creates an apparent circularity, because any such S_{t-n} will have to contain the capacity to think thoughts with first-person contents, and it is natural to think that the capacity to think thoughts with first-person contents cannot exist in the absence of the capacity for linguistic mastery of the first-person pronoun.

Can the problem of capacity circularity be dealt with in a way that shows how the Acquisition Constraint can be canonically met by linguistic mastery of the first-person pronoun? The solution to this problem is similar in general form to the solution to the problem of explanatory circularity discussed in the previous section. The apparent vicious circularity is removed by showing that the first-person contents implicated in the complex communicative intention governing mastery of the first-person pronoun can be understood at the nonconceptual level, and hence independently of linguistic mastery of the first-person pronoun. In the terms used above, although it is true that the capacities present in S_{t-n} do indeed include the capacity to think certain thoughts with first-person contents, this does not mean that the capacities in S_{t-n} must also include linguistic mastery of the first-person pronoun, because the crucial thoughts involved in learning how to use the first-person pronoun can be nonconceptual and hence independent of language mastery. This emerges particularly clearly if the neo-Gricean specification of the communicative intent governing the correct use of the first-person pronoun is read, as I suggested in section 10.2, as offering conditions on learning the proper use of the token-reflexive rule. If that suggestion is accepted, then we have, first, a clear specification of a set of first-person thoughts that must be grasped by anybody who successfully learns the first-person pronoun and, second, an illustration of how those first-person thoughts can be nonconceptual. This is sufficient, I think, to remove the threat posed by capacity circularity, because it dispels the idea that the first-person thoughts required for the acquisition of mastery of the first-person pronoun could not exist unless mastery of the first-person pronoun was already in play.

I have made various suggestions about how the sophisticated but nonetheless nonconceptual first-person contents required to explain mastery of the first-person pronoun emerge from the primitive first-person contents in an individual's innate endowment. Some of these suggestions are best viewed as selective rational reconstructions of how this process might take place. One example would be the discussion at the end of chapter 8 of how an integrated representation of the spatial environment might emerge from the propriospecific information present in the structure of visual perception. I suggested there that the calibration of what Gibson calls affordances through recognition of affordance symmetries, affordance transitivities, and affordance identities could bridge the gap between the perception of individual spatial relations and the construction of an integrated representation of the environment. I certainly do not claim that the rational reconstructions I have offered are complete or anything near it. Nor do I claim that the various suggestions I have made about how certain cognitive abilities might conceivably emerge from others must feature in a true account of this emergence. What I do claim to have done, however, is to have dispelled worries that there are principled reasons for thinking that no such account will be forthcoming.

10.4   The Way Forward

The principal aim of this book has been to offer a solution to the paradox of self-consciousness by illuminating the various different forms of non-conceptual self-consciousness that are both logically and ontogenetically more primitive than the higher forms of self-consciousness that are more usually the focus of philosophical debate. What philosophers tend to think of as the unitary phenomenon of self-consciousness has a complex and multilayered structure, which is all too often neglected not least because so much of it lies concealed beneath the surface of language. I have tried to compensate by exposing the nonconceptual foundations on which the structure rests. A full account of the structure of self-consciousness, however, will need to illuminate those higher, conceptual forms of self-consciousness to which I have devoted little attention in this book. Let me end this book with a few programmatic comments about the form that I believe such an account will take and about how it might emerge from some of the points that I have made in this book.

   In chapter 1, I considered what I termed the *deflationary theory of self-consciousness*. The starting point of the deflationary theory is the thought that an explanation of everything that is distinctive about self-consciousness will emerge out of an account of what it is for a subject to be capable of thinking about himself. The conceptual forms of self-consciousness—specimens of which are the abilities to entertain autobiographical memories, to make plans for the future, and to formulate second-order desires (desires about desires that one should have)—can all be understood as involving propositional attitudes to first-person conceptual contents. Deflationary theorists are rightly impressed by the thought that all of the conceptual abilities deployed in such first-person contents are, with a single exception, also deployable with the same sense in contents that are not first-personal. Since illumination of the distinctive features of self-consciousness will not emerge from considering those conceptual abilities that can feature indifferently in contents that are first-personal and contents that are not, the deflationary theorist is driven to the thought that an explanation of mastery of the first-person concept is all that is required for a theoretical elucidation of the conceptual forms of self-conscious thought.

If the deflationary theory is correct, then it might be natural to think that an account of mastery of the first-person pronoun (and hence of what it is to possess the first-person concept) based upon the discussion in this book could come close to providing a complete philosophical elucidation of self-consciousness. Sadly, however, this would be premature. The deflationary theory rests on insights that have an important role to play in the development of a complete account of the higher, conceptual forms of self-consciousness, but it would be a grave error to think that such an account will be so easily forthcoming.

Let me grant the first part of the deflationary position, namely that an account of the higher forms of self-consciousness will be an account of the varieties of self-conscious thought at the conceptual level. It is natural to agree with the deflationary theory that such an account will have two components. The first component will elucidate the contents of first-person thoughts at the conceptual level, while the second component will elucidate the nature of the complex propositional attitudes (such as memory and desire) that a thinker can bear to those first-person thoughts. The deflationary theory takes its stand on a clear demarcation between these two components, viewing the second component as the business not of the theory of self-consciousness but of a general theory of propositional attitudes and the first component as exhausted by an account of what it is to possess the first-person concept in conjunction with a general account of concepts.

It is certainly true that there are no propositional attitudes that can be taken only to first-person contents. Autobiographical memory, for example, is best understood not as a distinctively first-person propositional attitude but rather in terms of a distinctive set of first-person contents to which the attitude of remembering can be taken. By the same token, second-order desires are best understood in terms of a distinctive set of first-person contents to which the attitude of desire can be taken. Nonetheless, in both of these cases there are crucial facts, indeed defining facts, about the distinctive set of first-person contents to which the relevant attitude can be taken that cannot be captured by the deflationary theory.

Part of what makes something an autobiographical memory is that it stands in certain inferential relations to other autobiographical memories and to other first-person contents. Similarly, second-order desires have a distinctive role to play in practical reasoning that is also capturable in terms of the inferential relations in which they stand and the dispositions (both cognitive and behavioral) to which they give rise. More generally, each of the higher, conceptual forms of self-consciousness is partially individuated by a different set of inferential patterns and dispositions to behavior that govern any first-person content to which that attitude is taken. Now, as suggested earlier, these inferential patterns and behavioral dispositions must be described at the level of content rather than the level of attitude. What makes memories autobiographical memories, or desires second-order desires, is simply that they are memories or desires with distinctive first-person contents. Of course, for the very reasons at the heart of the deflationary theory, it is at the level of the first-person concept that we will need to explain what this distinctiveness amounts to and how it emerges. This is quite compatible with the deflationary theorist's central tenet that an account of the first-person concept is the key to explaining the conceptual forms of self-consciousness. On the other hand, it seems to be clearly incompatible with the deflationary theorist's proposal for implementing that central tenet, namely that an account of the first-person concept will be derivable from an account of linguistic mastery of the first-person pronoun. There are no facts about linguistic mastery of the first-person pronoun that will determine or explain what might, following David Kaplan, be termed the *cognitive dynamics* of the first-person concept.

The way forward for a theory of self-consciousness, it seems to me, is, first, to chart the characteristic features individuating the various distinct conceptual forms of self-consciousness in a way that will provide a taxonomy of self-consciousness and then, second, to show how these characteristic features can be determined at the level of content. What I hope is now clear is that these higher forms of self-consciousness emerge from a rich foundation of nonconceptual first-person thought, which I have tried to expose and clarify in this book. It is my firm conviction that these different forms of nonconceptual first-person thought hold the key, not just to an eventual account of how mastery of the first-person pronoun meets the Acquisition Constraint, but to a proper understanding of the complex phenomenon of self-consciousness.

Notes

Chapter 1

1. Pears 1988, vol. 2, chapter 10, is an illuminating discussion of the background to Wittgenstein's thinking about the self in *The Blue and Brown Books*.

2. This is still not quite right. A further technical problem is noted in Evans 1982, pp. 189–191, but need not detain us here.

3. A more involved argument for a similar conclusion can be found in Noonan 1979.

4. Compare Shoemaker 1968, 9–10. He amends his view in 1970, nn. 3 and 5. His claim in the latter work is that one can make self-reference immune to error through misidentification with names and definite descriptions, provided that in using them the speaker intends to refer to himself. This is a valid point, but a circumscribed one, since it seems that intending to refer to oneself via a name or definite description can only be done if certain further thoughts are presupposed, and those further thoughts will be first-personal and involve identifying oneself as the referent of that name or definite description.

5. What I am calling the deflationary account of self-consciousness has not been adopted as such in the literature. It is, however, suggested in Shoemaker 1968, subject to the qualifications in n. 4 above.

6. It will be clear from what follows that these problems are not peculiar to the deflationary theory. On the contrary, as I will bring out at the end of the chapter, they fall naturally out of a set of assumptions that are intuitively highly plausible. I am focusing on the deflationary theory here because the paradox of self-consciousness is best appreciated within the confines of a theory of self-consciousness and the deflationary theory is relatively straightforward to expound, as well as having a certain intuitive plausibility. Although this book will offer a solution to the paradox of self-consciousness, this solution is not intended to rehabilitate the deflationary theory. I shall return to the deflationary theory in section 10.4.

7. It is natural to relativize specifications of the token-reflexive rule to the present tense. This clearly holds for linguistic utterances of 'I'. It does not hold for written

inscriptions, however. Adequately specifying the temporal dimension of self-reference will doubtless require some ingenuity. For present purposes, however, the various rough-and-ready formulations I offer will suffice.

8. For a stimulating discussion of how such an explanation might be derived, see Altham 1979. The thought that the token-reflexive rule cannot give the meaning of 'I' as a result of the interdependence between the indirect reflexive pronoun and the first-person pronoun has been emphasised by Anscombe (1975, 47–48). Anscombe puts this to work in support of her eccentric claim that the first-person pronoun is not a referring expression. As far as this claim is concerned, I am fully in agreement with the careful and perceptive criticisms to be found in Taschek 1985. It should be noted that Taschek has no quarrel with Anscombe's point about the circularity of the token-reflexive rule as an explanation of the semantical role of 'I' (1985, 640). I do quarrel with it, however. See pp. 16–17.

9. This is the formulation favoured by Campbell (1994, 102). I have discussed Campbell's use of this rule in Bermúdez 1995a.

10. Compare Nozick 1981, 79–84.

11. All that my argument requires at this point is that such knowledge should be a necessary condition for mastery of the semantics of the first-person pronoun. In chapter 10, where I give a full account of how such mastery is to be understood, it will emerge that it is not a sufficient condition.

12. See Peacocke 1979 for a discussion of several such local holisms. Grice and Strawson (1956) defend what they see as a local holism in the theory of meaning against what is effectively a charge of explanatory circularity in Quine 1951. Hurley, forthcoming, is a sustained examination of the local holism formed by perception and action.

13. I discuss the question of how philosophy and psychology might profitably interact in Bermúdez 1995d and criticize some of the grounds for which philosophers try to keep them apart in Bermúdez 1995b.

14. The sense of 'module' here is importantly different from that pioneered in Fodor 1983. Among their other defining characteristics, Fodor's modules operate at the input-output level, are informationally encapsulated, and are domain-specific. None of these features hold of the modules proposed to explain how language mastery and understanding of other minds meet the acquisition constraint. See Karmiloff-Smith 1992 and Segal 1996 for further discussion.

15. The linguistic arguments in favor of the nativist theory are reviewed in Pinker 1979. For a recent and philosophically driven presentation of Chomsky's view, see Chomsky 1995. For further philosophical discussion, see the essays in George 1989.

16. The debate was opened in the context of chimpanzees in Premack and Woodruff 1978. The idea that the psychological abilities that emerge between the ages of 3 and 4 years should be explained in terms of a theory-of-mind module (ToMM) was suggested in Leslie 1987 and has recently been vigourously argued in Baron-Cohen 1993. Baron-Cohen also suggests a possible ontogenesis for

ToMM in terms of more primitive modules, such as the eye-direction-detector module (EDDM) and the shared-attention module (SAM). Karmiloff-Smith 1992 provides a sustained critique of such extreme nativist theories, both in the area of children's theory of mind and in the area of language acquisition.

Chapter 2

1. The account I favor does not actually speak of the contents of belief as composed of concepts. Rather, it maintains that belief contents (and the contents of propositional attitudes in general) are conceptual, where a conceptual content is one that cannot be ascribed to a creature unless that creature possesses the concepts involved in specifying that content. See chapter 3.

2. Perry 1979 provides the classic discussion of the relation between first-person thoughts and action.

3. And indeed, the account that I shall give below is a broadly functional account.

4. As I shall stress in chapter 4, there are different degrees of structure associated with different types of representations. I shall defend there the view that all genuine representation of the world involves a minimal degree of structure. This needs to be kept firmly distinguished, however, from the view that all genuine representations involve the sort of structure to be found in natural languages. It is certainly not true that all genuine representations permit the sort of universal and generalized recombinability characteristic of natural language. That view would be hard to maintain in conjunction with a rejection of the thought-language principle.

Chapter 3

1. The original impetus came from Evans 1982. It is important to note, though, that Evans's understanding of nonconceptual content is distinctive. He holds that it applies to perceptual-information states, which do not become conscious perceptual experiences until they are engaged with a concept-applying and reasoning system (1982, 226–227).

2. This view doesn't follow from the preceding, since I have said nothing to rule out the possibility that perceptual beliefs might have nonconceptual contents.

3. I take it that there are comparable normative dimensions for the propositional attitudes other than belief.

4. This is what I tried to capture by including the Conceptual-Requirement Principle as part of the classical view of content.

5. There seem, however, to be possible versions of developmental explanation that are compatible with denying the Autonomy Principle. For example, it could be argued that, although in general nonconceptual and conceptual contents form a holism, there are certain conceptual contents that develop out of nonconceptual contents.

6. This is Peacocke's own position. I have criticised it in Bermúdez 1994, and he replies in Peacocke 1994.

7. I shall return to this in the final section of this chapter.

8. This is stressed in Peacocke 1992.

9. This is certainly Spelke's own view: "The earliest developing conceptions of physical objects are the most central conceptions guiding mature object perception and physical reasoning. For adults, such conceptions are overlaid by a wealth of knowledge about the appearances and the behavior of particular kinds of objects. Even this more specific and limited knowledge, however, reflects the core knowledge from which it grew" (Spelke and Van de Walle 1993, 157).

10. It is worth mentioning in this context that, although developmental psychologists seem to find unproblematic the conclusion that infants show surprise in the drawbridge experiments because it is *impossible* for the screen to pass through the object, this is at best questionable. On the inferential interpretation, the surprise would be due to the infant's identifying an object and inferring from their knowledge of how objects behave that what they see is impossible. But why say this rather than that the infants show surprise simply because there are no precedents for what they see? Certainly, more argument is needed than simply pointing out that what the infants see is really impossible.

11. I am grateful to Jim Russell for pressing me here.

12. Some qualifications are required here. It is known from studies of adult subjects, for example, that perceptual predictions of object transformations and interactions tend to be based on kinematic, rather than dynamic, principles and information (Cooper and Munger 1993). This has obvious computational advantages and clearly shows that ordinary object perception need not always involve the perceptual pick-up of the full range of object properties. But that is no objection to the claim that perception of objects depends on perceptual sensitivity to object properties. Perceptual sensitivity to object properties needs to be understood at the level of competence rather than performance.

13. The experiments on infant expectations in collision events reported in Baillargeon 1995 are an excellent example of how detailed work might be carried out on infant sensitivity to object properties.

14. This would be consistent with the general view of the importance of agency in mental development outlined in Russell 1996, and is of course a modern version of a broadly Piagetian position.

15. The inference to an apelike (pongid) neural organization is based on the location of the lunate sulcus, on the assumption that the massively expanded posterior parietal cortex characteristic of the human brain pushed the lunate sulcus backwards and downwards to the position it occupies in the human brain.

16. It has occasionally been suggested in the literature that Neanderthal hominids had a completely modern superlaryngeal vocal tract. Liebermann (1991) compellingly argues that this would have meant that Neanderthal's larynx was in his chest.

17. The crucial claim is, of course, that the emergence of language did not significantly precede the descent of the larynx. This presupposes an equation of language with speech. Some authors have objected to this, suggesting that a gestural language might have preceded spoken language (Corballis 1991), or that *Homo erectus* had a protolanguage comparable to that of a 2-year-old child (Parker and Gibson 1979). Both these suggestions remain at the level of conjecture, however.

18. Farah (1990) distinguishes between two types of simultagnosia, which she terms dorsal and ventral (after the location of the relevant lesion site). Although ventral simultagnosics cannot recognize multiple objects, they can nonetheless *see* multiple objects (unlike dorsal simultagnosics).

19. Farah (1990) questions whether patients with associative object agnosias really do have intact visual perception, noting that they often fail more sophisticated visual tests. Nonetheless, they generally seem to have relatively unimpaired visual perception in comparison with apperceptive agnosics, which seems enough to suggest a significant distinction between the two groups of disorders.

20. See Shallice 1988, section 8.4, for an illuminating discussion of the connections between Marr's theory and relevant neuropsychological findings.

21. This is not to deny that the 3D sketch is itself a content-bearing state. See Bermúdez 1995e for further discussion.

Chapter 4

1. The minimal account is an account of what it is in general for a state to have content. This is a different level of theorizing from specific theories of content. A possible-worlds account of content is an example of such a specific theory, as is Peacocke's own theory of scenario content. The general theory explains what the specific theories have in common.

2. The importance of an exceptionless connection for the theory of information is stressed in Dretske 1981, chap. 3. He gives several arguments for refusing to accept conditional probabilities of less than 1. The most important are the following. First, doing otherwise would admit the possibility that a signal could carry the information that s is G and the information that s is F, but not the information that s is G and F (because the probability of s being F and G might be below the acceptable value of conditional probability). Second, the flow of information is transitive and that this transitivity would be lost if the value of conditional probability were less than one.

3. It is this that led Dretske substantially to modify the theory proposed in Dretske 1981. See Dretske 1990 and chapter 3 of Dretske 1992.

4. This is central to J. J. Gibson's notion of the direct perception of affordances, which will be discussed in the next chapter.

5. Although the number of approaches to the magazines for rats in the omission schedule eventually fell below the level for the control group, for which the

instrumental contingency was maintained, it remained significantly higher than the level for a second control group, for which food and tone were unpaired.

6. This is noted in Peacocke 1983, 61.

7. In fact, this is precisely the form that Bennett adopts for the teleological laws that he thinks explain much animal behavior. The form of a teleological law for Bennett is this:

$(x)(F)(t)((Rx \ \& \ x$ registers that F/Gx at time $t) \rightarrow Fx$ at time $t + d)$

Rx is to be read as the claim that suitable enabling conditions are satisfied (including the animal's having the satisfaction of G as a goal); F/Gx as the claim that x is so structured that the truth of Fx at a later time $(t + d)$ is causally sufficient for Gx at a still later time.

8. The core of Smolensky's proposal is that compositional structure can be captured within a network if the network represents particular "fillers" (e.g., a noun) occupying particular roles (e.g., the role of a grammatical object). But there are other ways in which PDP researchers have suggested that the compositionality requirement might be satisfied without collapsing into CTC. Ramsey (1992), for example, describes a class of connectionist networks in which the different syntactic roles of particular atomic units are encoded via slightly different patterns of activation. These different patterns of activation legitimate different types of molecular combination.

Chapter 5

1. Although Gibson himself displayed little interest in the matter, there are important processing questions about the relation between retinal flow and flow in the optic array. See Harris, Freeman, and Willis 1992 for a framework within which these questions might be addressed.

2. An interesting illustration of the explanatory powers of the theory of invariants comes with the traditional problem of size constancy. Depending on one's distance from an object, the solid visual angle that it subtends will vary. So why does the object not seem smaller or larger, depending on one's distance from it? There is a perceptual invariant that might well explain why objects are perceived as being of a constant size, irrespective of their distance from the perceiver. The relevant invariant is the ratio of an object's height to the distance between its base and the horizon. This ratio remains constant irrespective of the object's distance from the perceiver.

3. This is, of course, one of the ways in which Gibson himself describes it.

4. The efference copy is a perception of the motor command as it leaves the motor apparatus. The efference copy is usually distinguished from what is known as the corollary discharge (Gallistel 1980, chap. 7). 'Efference copy' and 'corollary discharge' both refer to the same signal, but there are two different theories about the role that the signal plays in controlling action, and in particular in allowing

the organism to distinguish between exafferent signals (due to the motion of the environment) from reafferent signals (due to the organism's own motion). According to corollary-discharge theory, the copy of the motor signal directly inhibits the action of any functional unit (such as the *optokinetic unit*) that would compensate for reafference by blocking the relevant action (as would an unchecked optokinetic reaction). In efference-copy theory, on the other hand, a copy of the motor signal is passed on by the relevant functional unit (e.g., the optokinetic unit) as if it were a command from that unit. This allows the efference copy and the reafference to cancel each other out. As Gallistel notes, however, the difference between the two theories emerges only when reafference is abnormal.

5. For interesting and provocative discussion of some of the ontological implications of ecological optics, see Reed 1987.

6. See also Rock 1975, 124–129.

7. See further the experimental evidence reviewed in the next section.

8. It is important to recognize the differences between misperception and perceptual illusions. In addition to the familiar examples of visual illusions, like the waterfall illusion, there are well-documented cases of artificially induced disorders of bodily perception in which subjects report experiencing limbs in anatomically and physically impossible positions (Lackner 1988). These are fundamentally different from the misperception of affordances, because there is no way in which they involve the pick-up of misinformation. In neither the proprioceptive cases nor the visual cases is there a direct pick-up of information from the optical flow. The perceptual systems are confronted with artificially induced sensory input that they are forced to make sense of in any way they can.

9. The source for this is, of course, Perry 1979. For an opposed view, see Millikan 1990.

10. I am referring here to the level of *autonomous* nonconceptual content, in the sense brought out in chapter 3.

11. I will discuss more complicated forms of instrumental protobeliefs in chapter 7. These emerge with the advent of memory.

12. See also Neisser 1991, Butterworth and Hicks 1990, and the papers collected in Neisser 1993.

13. Comprehensive reviews will be found in the essays collected in Neisser 1993 and Rochat 1995.

14. I have discussed the philosophical significance of neonatal imitation from the viewpoint of applied ethics in my 1996 essay.

15. Through the course of their development there are interesting variations in the extent to which infants are susceptible to discrepant visual information. Experience in sitting and crawling decreases susceptibility. See Butterworth and Hicks 1990 for further discussion.

16. This is not to rule out, though, the possibility that the first-person contents of perceptual experience can be understood in terms of the states of visual-

processing subsystems in the brain, and that the states of such subsystems might be representational and have content (Bermúdez 1995e). My suggestion is simply that these subpersonal representational states, despite having contents, will not have first-person contents.

Chapter 6

1. I am following closely the general introduction to Bermúdez, Marcel, and Eilan 1995.

2. Such reasons are discussed by Anscombe (1962), who develops a position ultimately derived from Wittgenstein (see Budd 1989).

3. In this and the following I will drop the explicit restriction to conscious somatic proprioception. Unless there is any indication to the contrary, I will use 'somatic proprioception' to refer only to the conscious modes of somatic proprioception.

4. Although Shoemaker himself does not explicitly consider somatic proprioception, he does explicitly argue for the Humean conclusion that the self cannot be the object of any form of inner perception, as in the object-perception model.

5. When Shoemaker continues his discussion of the object constraint on pp. 256–257, he modulates into what I am calling the multiple-objects constraint by defining a notion of 'object awareness' in such a way that it must be possible for one to bear it to a range of different objects.

6. It is important to distinguish exploratory or active touch from passive touch. It is well known that the tactile discrimination of differently textured surfaces is greatly increased when the finger moves relative to the surface, but it does not seem to matter whether the movement is carried out by the subject or not. For more complicated discrimination tasks, such as the discrimination of three-dimensional shapes and the determination of their structural and material properties, however, active movement is essential (Gordon 1978, Lederman and Klatzky 1987).

7. The physiology of exploratory or active touch has been well researched, at least with respect to the hand (Gordon 1978). Active touch depends on the joint processing of proprioceptive and exteroceptive information. Proprioceptive information about the movement of the hand is required so that predictable information stemming from the subject's own movement can be separated out from the novel information about the contours of the object.

8. Of course, this is subject to the proviso that the behavior really is intentional. For further discussion, see Meltzoff 1993 and Bermúdez 1996.

9. It is not yet known whether the process of coordinate transformation proceeds in a hierarchical fashion, with each representation actually computed in increasing order of complexity, or whether there is a single highly distributed body-centered representation that can integrate signals with different coordinate frames.

10. Moreover, as shown by the movement errors discussed in Ghez et al. 1995, visual information about initial limb position (and not just the position of the target) has an essential role to play in controlling action. Both visual and proprioceptive information are integrated at every stage of visually guided reaching.

11. For further discussion, see the papers in part 1 of Eilan, McCarthy, and Brewer 1993.

12. Of course, it is possible to imagine complicated scenarios in which one's proprioceptive system is hooked up to another's body so that misidentification is possible. This is explored in Armstrong 1984 and Cassam 1995. As Cassam notes, if this really is a coherent possibility, then there is no logical necessity about immunity to error. But it is not clear why one would expect logical necessity for something that is ultimately determined by contingent facts about the human body. The sense of necessity relevant here is nomological necessity (i.e., truth in all possible worlds with the same laws of nature as this world), and so we will have to demonstrate that any proposed counterexample to the modal claim is nomologically possible rather than merely logically possible. But how is one to decide whether being hooked up to somebody else's body so as to feel their sensations really is nomologically possible? How would one convince those who are sure that it is not? In any case, though, and this is the second point, it is far from clear that the modal claim really is so important. If Armstrong-type scenarios are indeed nomologically possible, and were it ever to come about that they are more common than the sort of somatic proprioception under consideration, in which there is de facto only one object of awareness, then clearly we would need to develop both a new theory of somatic proprioception and a new theory of self-awareness. But there seems little reason why that should influence how we decide the question of whether somatic proprioception, in the form that we are familiar with, can be a form of self-awareness, also in the form that we are familiar with. Let me weaken the claim about immunity to accommodate Armstrong-style scenarios as follows: necessarily, in a body with unsupplemented somatic proprioceptive information systems, there is only one object of somatic proprioception, which is the body itself. This is quite enough to be getting on with.

13. Something like this conflation appears in Evans 1982, 237.

14. Let me stress, though, that my way of spelling out this connection is rather different from Shoemaker's or Evans's. See n. 16 below.

15. The only counter to this would be via the claim that psychological properties somehow manifest themselves to introspection in an explicitly first-person way, so that it is impossible to introspect in the manner that (3) attempts to capture. Something like this view is defended in Chisholm 1969.

16. This is a good place to distinguish my use of the notion of immunity to error through misidentification as a criterion of self-awareness from Evans's. Evans treats the first-person pronoun on the model of a perceptual demonstrative. He tries to show that demonstrative self-reference achieved with 'I' depends on epistemological links with one's embodied self that are comparable to the perceptual links that make possible demonstrative reference to perceived objects. The

epistemological links are provided by information channels, one of which is what I have been terming somatic proprioception. Evans identifies the relevant information channels as all and only those channels that give rise to judgments immune to error through misidentification relative to the first-person pronoun. There are certain features of Evans's position that sharply distinguish it from mine, however. The first is that he denies that genuine self-awareness is available in the absence of mastery of the first-person pronoun. Moreover, and this is perhaps part of the explanation for this denial, he thinks that states of the somatic proprioceptive system (and indeed information-carrying states generally) do not qualify as experiences until conceptual and reasoning abilities are brought to bear upon them. Against this I am arguing that somatic proprioception (as opposed to judgments based on proprioceptive information channels) is itself a source of self-awareness. As will be made clear in section 6.5, I find it perfectly intelligible, and indeed necessary, to talk of proprioceptive experiences in the absence of conceptual and reasoning abilities, and it is these experiences (not the first-person judgments that might or might not be based on them) that are the sources of self-awareness.

17. Ramachandran suggests that the referral of sensations should be explained through what he terms the "remapping hypothesis," namely that the area in the somatosensory cortex originally responsible for processing sensory information from the amputated limb becomes reorganized and sensitive to sensory information from parts of the body originally processed by adjacent areas of the somatosensory cortex. It is well known that adjacent areas in the somatosensory cortex do not represent adjacent body parts. This explains why there are well-defined distributions of points on the body surface that yield referred sensations in amputated limbs.

18. See the essays in Prigatano and Schacter 1991 for further discussion.

19. See the papers cited in n. 11 for further discussion.

20. A form of this proposal is to be found in Peacocke 1992, chap. 3.

21. Nothing hangs on the vocabulary of pains, or other bodily sensations, existing at particular places. I am not assuming that there are such things as pains that are the objects of somatic proprioception, as will become clear in my account of the descriptive aspect of proprioceptive content.

22. I shall henceforth use 'moveable' in this limited sense. The sense in which the torso is immoveable is similarly restricted. Of course, I can move my torso by leaning forward or by turning at the waist, but the range of movement is very limited.

23. Strictly speaking, of course, one of these specifications will be sufficient to fix the location. This doesn't mean, however, that only one specification need feature in the frame of reference. Compare the situation of twenty ships moving in convoy flanked by four tugs, which keep the same position relative to each other. The fact that the location of any given ship can be fixed by its distance and direction from any one of the tugs is compatible with all four tugs' constituting the frame of reference.

24. Certain documented phenomena prima facie seem hard to reconcile with the description of the phenomenology of bodily experience just made, and hence with the account of the spatial content of proprioception that I have been offering. Some subjects have reported feeling sensations in space or even in the bodies of others (Shapiro, Fink, and Bender 1952; Békésy 1967). See Martin 1993 for an interesting discussion. Can phenomena like this be accommodated in terms of *A* locations and *B* locations? Clearly, they cannot have *A* locations, in the sense of being experienced as being located in identifiable body parts (unlike, for example, pains that are felt in phantom limbs). But they might plausibly be ascribed *B* locations. As Martin notes, exosomesthetic sensations tend to be felt in extensions of the body, albeit indeterminate ones. This suggests that it might make sense to attribute to them a *B* location based upon their coordinates relative to the nearest hinges. Of course, this would be radically different from the ascriptions of ordinary *B* locations, but this might be seen as reflecting the bizarre phenomenology of the situation.

25. Let me stress that these are not intended to be constitutive accounts. The proposal is not that actions, or even dispositions to act, constitute proprioceptive content in that the correctness conditions are given by the success or failure of the relevant actions. That would have the unacceptable consequence that states with proprioceptive content would in principle be unavailable to a paraplegic. The representational states that cause the relevant actions are what have correctness conditions, and those correctness conditions are bodily events. The actions provide illustrations of how one might recognize when and if the correctness conditions are satisfied.

26. In fact, they may even be available before birth. See the evidence discussed in Gallagher 1996.

Chapter 7

1. Note, moreover, that 'object*' qualifies as a count term rather than a mass term.

2. The point is that certain terms that we employ as count terms to individuate particular objects can have a more primitive deployment as mass terms. As Campbell puts the point, "There may be a use of 'tiger' as a mass term which is prior to its use as a count noun. This use of 'Tiger!' would be merely a response to the presence of tigerhood, by someone who might be quite incapable of making the distinction between one tiger and two being present, or having the idea of its being the same tiger again as was here previously" (1993, 65).

3. This primitive form of place recognition falls significantly short of the capacity to identify places in a way that would reflect a more general understanding of space. In the next chapter I discuss how primitive place recognition might be built up into this more sophisticated way of thinking about space.

4. This is just one aspect of a more general distinction between conscious and nonconscious information processing that can be observed in various neuro-

psychological disorders, such as blindsight and prosopagnosia, as well as in associative-priming experiments on normal patients. A general survey of the neuropsychological issues will be found in Schacter, McAndrews, and Moscovitch 1988. For associative priming, see Marcel 1983.

5. Campbell himself makes such a distinction (1994, 236).

6. For some recent discussions of psychological theories of concept acquisition, and in particular the turn away from prototype theories, see the essays collected in Neisser 1987.

7. Compare Price 1953, chap. 2. It is also, I think, Kant's view that primitive recognition is at the root of all cognition. This seems to me to be the upshot of the discussion of the threefold synthesis in the transcendental deduction of the categories (see Kant 1781/1964, A98–A110).

8. Bennett does not offer an argument in support of this assumption, but it could be defended along the following lines. Only if the two cognitive abilities could be separately manifested would it be possible to come up with a determinate answer to the question of which particular ability is implicated in a given situation.

9. There are some difficulties in disentangling Gibson's defensible points from his untenable diatribes against information-processing accounts of perception (Fodor and Pylyshyn 1981). It is clear that what Gibson notes about "direct perception" does not mean that there is no processing at all going on, although that appeared to be his own view. Some explanation needs to be given at the neurophysiological and other subpersonal levels of how the organism can be sensitive to perceptual invariants. Useful suggestions for how Gibson's insights can be accommodated within a more traditional information-processing theory will be found in McCarthy 1993.

10. This would be a weak sense of what has come to be known in the literature as phenomenal consciousness, as opposed to access consciousness. See the Introduction to Davies and Humphreys 1993 for an explanation of the distinction.

11. This is one of the points at which ontogeny and phylogeny come apart, since there *is* a pressing need to give an explanation of why and, more importantly, how the capacity to feel sensations should have emerged during evolution.

Chapter 8

1. See Peacocke 1992, 90–92. This argument is offered in opposition to the Autonomy Principle, discussed in chapter 3 above. My 1994 essay argues that this argument cannot be satisfactorily deployed against the Autonomy Principle. Peacocke replies to this argument in 1994.

2. There is further discussion of Campbell's book in my 1995a and 1997 essays.

3. Note that this means that Peacocke's original notion of perspectival sensitivity would not be applicable here.

Chapter 9

1. I am describing predicates as having a first-person application when the subject using them is capable of understanding that they can apply to himself. Similarly with second- and third-person predicates. By extension, therefore, a predicate will have only a first-person application when the subject using it is capable only of understanding that it applies to himself.

2. This is very relevant to some of the points made against Evans's development of the Generality Constraint in an acute paper by Charles Travis (1994). Travis objects that satisfying Evans's Generality Constraint for a and F is not a necessary condition of being able to think the thought that a is F, because thinking the thought that a is F requires a degree of context sensitivity that a subject may not have for the thought that b is F. This point is well taken. Nonetheless, it doesn't affect the more general point about the unacceptability of uniquely instantiable predicates that inspires Evans and Strawson.

3. A source of confusion is that although Strawson makes these points in discussing an objection to his own position, they are claims that he endorses. The passage continues "but not necessarily that one should do so on any occasion"—it is this continuation that Strawson has qualms about.

4. See Wiggins 1980 for an extended discussion and Mackie 1976, 160–161, for a more concise one.

5. Nagel 1971 has been very influential in this respect.

6. I am assuming, for simplicity's sake, that x and y are both perceptually present to the subject.

7. Of course, if (as I shall argue) the relevant categories can be apprehended and applied by nonlinguistic and prelinguistic creatures, then the weak and strong readings of the Symmetry Thesis will need to be reformulated.

8. Note that I am not claiming that the instantiation of any one of these psychological categories on its own provides strong prima facie evidence for the presence of a psychological subject. Nor am I ruling out the possibility that a subset of these psychological categories might provide strong prima facie evidence.

9. See pp. 221–223.

10. It is purely for convenience of exposition that I am treating perception and action as separate strands. It seems clear that at every level of analysis, from the neuronal upward, perception and action are inextricably linked. See the essays in Hurley, 1998, for a sustained defense of the noninstrumental interdependence of perception and action. She develops a picture of man and other animals as complex-, dynamic-feedback systems structured by feedback loops that run from action to perception, as well as from perception to action.

11. I am assuming here the soundness of the argument provided in section 3.3 for the Priority Principle, so that evidence of distinguishing psychological self-awareness in nonlinguistic or prelinguistic creatures will ipso facto count as

evidence for the possibility of distinguishing psychological self-awareness at the nonconceptual level.

12. I should note at this point that the current account replaces what I said about infant's awareness of their own agency in Bermúdez 1995c.

13. I now think that an interpretation along these lines is most appropriate for the experimental data discussed in my 1995c paper.

14. In chapter 4 and Bermúdez 1996, I suggested that neonatal imitation behavior involved a pick-up of self-specifying information, and hence representations with first-person contents. Nothing that I said implies that those first-person contents implicated a form of psychological self-awareness. On the contrary, the properties picked up are purely physical.

Chapter 10

1. In the following I will use 'utterance' in a broad sense on which inscriptions on pieces of paper and computer disks count as utterances. By the same token, I shall use 'utterer' in such a way that one can qualify as an utterer with one's vocal cords cut.

2. I take it that failing the false-belief task is not prima facie evidence that the subject cannot comprehend the possibility of *himself* representing the world in a way other than it is.

3. See chapter 3.

4. I will hyphenate 'bringing-it-about-that' as a reminder that it is functioning as a sort of technical term.

References

Aaronson, D., and Rieber, R. W. (eds.). 1975. *Developmental Psycholinguistics and Communication Disorders*. New York: New York Academy of Sciences.

Acredolo, L. P., Adams, A., and Goodwyn, S. W. 1984. "The Role of Self-Produced Movement and Visual Tracking in Infant Spatial Orientation." *Journal of Experimental Child Psychology* 38: 312–327.

Altham, J. E. J. 1979. "Indirect Reflexives and Indirect Speech." In Diamond and Teichmann 1979.

Andersen, R. A. 1995. "Coordinate Transformations and Motor Planning in Posterior Parietal Cortex." In Gazzaniga 1995.

Anscombe, G. E. M. 1962. "On Sensations of Position." *Analysis* 22: 55–58.

Anscombe, G. E. M. 1975. "The First Person." In Guttenplan 1975.

Armstrong, D. M. 1968. *A Materialist Theory of the Mind*. London: Routledge and Kegan Paul.

Armstrong, D. M. 1971. "Meaning and Communication." *Philosophical Review* 80: 427–447.

Armstrong, D. M. 1984. "Consciousness and Causality." In Armstrong and Malcolm 1984.

Armstrong, D. M., and Malcolm, N. 1984. *Consciousness and Causality*. Oxford: Basil Blackwell.

Ayers, M. 1991. *Locke: Epistemology and Ontology*. London: Routledge.

Baillargeon, R. 1987. "Object Permanence in 3.5- and 4.5-Month-Old Infants." *Developmental Psychology* 23: 655–664.

Baillargeon, R. 1995. "Physical Reasoning in Infancy." In Gazzaniga 1995.

Bakeman, R., and Adamson, L. B. 1984. "Coordinating Attention to People and Objects in Mother-Infant and Peer-Infant Interaction." *Child Development* 55: 1278–1289.

Baldwin, T. R. 1995. "Objectivity, Causality, and Agency." In Bermúdez, Marcel, and Eilan 1995.

Baron-Cohen, S. 1993. "From Attention-Goal Psychology to Belief-Desire Psychology: The Development of a Theory of Mind and Its Dysfunction." In Baron-Cohen, Tager-Flusberg, and Cohen 1993.

Baron-Cohen, S., Tager-Flusberg, H., and Cohen, D. J. (eds.). 1993. *Understanding Other Minds: Perspectives from Autism.* Oxford: Oxford University Press.

Barwise, J., and Perry, J. 1981. "Situations and Attitudes." *Journal of Philosophy* 78: 669–691.

Bateson, M. C. 1975. "Mother-Infant Exchanges: The Epigenesis of Conversational Interaction." In Aaronson and Rieber 1975.

Békésy, G. von. 1967. *Sensory Inhibition.* Princeton: Princeton University Press.

Bennett, J. 1964. *Rationality.* London: Routledge and Kegan Paul.

Bennett, J. 1976. *Linguistic Behaviour.* Cambridge: Cambridge University Press.

Bermúdez, J. L. 1994. "Peacocke's Argument against the Autonomy of Nonconceptual Content." *Mind and Language* 9: 402–418.

Bermúdez, J. L. 1995a. "Aspects of the Self." *Inquiry* 38: 489–501.

Bermúdez, J. L. 1995b. "Syntax, Semantics, and Levels of Explanation." *Philosophical Quarterly* 45: 361–367.

Bermúdez, J. L. 1995c. "Ecological Perception and the Notion of a Nonconceptual Point of View." In Bermúdez, Marcel, and Eilan 1995.

Bermúdez, J. L. 1995d. "Transcendental Arguments and Psychology." *Metaphilosophy* 26: 379–401.

Bermúdez, J. L. 1995e. "Nonconceptual Content: From Perceptual Experience to Subpersonal Computational States." *Mind and Language* 10: 333–369.

Bermúdez, J. L. 1996. "The Moral Significance of Birth." *Ethics* 106: 378–403.

Bermúdez, J. L. 1997. "Practical Understanding vs Reflective Understanding." *Philosophy and Phenomenological Research* 57: 635–641.

Bermúdez, J. L., Marcel, A. J., and Eilan, N. (eds.). 1995. *The Body and the Self.* Cambridge: MIT Press.

Boden, M. (ed.). 1990. *The Philosophy of Artificial Intelligence.* Oxford: Oxford University Press.

Bower, T. G. R. 1972. "Object Perception in Infants." *Perception* 1: 15–30.

Bremner, J. G. 1988. *Infancy.* Oxford: Basil Blackwell.

Brewer, B. 1993. "The Integration of Spatial Vision and Action." In Eilan, McCarthy, and Brewer 1993.

Brown, J. W. 1988. *The Life of the Mind.* Hillsdale, N.J.: Laurence Erlbaum.

Bruner, J. S. 1975. "The Ontogenesis of Speech Acts." *Journal of Child Language* 2: 1–19.

Bruner, J. S. 1977. "Early Social Interaction and Language Acquisition." In Schaffer 1977.

Budd, M. 1989. *Wittgenstein's Philosophy of Psychology*. London: Routledge.

Butterworth, G. E., and Hicks, L. 1977. "Visual Proprioception and Postural Stability in Infancy: A Developmental Study." *Perception* 6: 255–262.

Butterworth, G. E., and Hicks, L. 1990. "Self-Perception in Infancy." In Cicchetti and Beeghly 1990.

Campbell, J. 1993. "The Role of Physical Objects in Spatial Thinking." In Eilan, McCarthy, and Brewer 1993.

Campbell, J. 1994. *Past, Space, and Self*. Cambridge: MIT Press.

Carey, S. 1982. "Semantic Development: The State of the Art." In Wanner and Gleitman 1982.

Carey, S., and Gelman, R. (eds.). 1991. *The Epigenesis of Mind: Essays on Biology and Cognition*. Hillsdale, N.J.: Lawrence Erlbaum.

Carruthers, P., and Smith, P. K. (eds.). 1996. *Theories of Theories of Mind*. Cambridge: Cambridge University Press.

Cassam, Q. (ed.). 1994. *Self-Knowledge*. Oxford Readings in Philosophy. Oxford: Oxford University Press.

Cassam, Q. 1995. "Introspection and Bodily Self-Ascription." In Bermúdez, Marcel, and Eilan 1995.

Castañeda, H.-N. 1966. " 'He': A Study in the Logic of Self-Consciousness." *Ratio* 8: 130–157.

Castañeda, H.-N. 1969. "On the Phenomeno-logic of the I." In Cassam 1994.

Chapuis, N., and Varlet, C. 1987. "Shortcut by Dogs in Natural Surroundings." *Quarterly Journal of Experimental Psychology* 39: 49–64.

Chisholm, R. M. 1969. "On the Observability of the Self." *Philosophy and Phenomenological Research* 30: 7–21.

Chomsky, N. 1981. *Lectures on Government and Binding Theory*. Dordrecht: Foris Publications.

Chomsky, N. 1995. "Language and Nature." *Mind* 104: 1–61.

Cicchetti, D., and Beeghly, M. (eds.). 1990. *The Self in Transition: Infancy to Childhood*. Chicago: University of Chicago Press.

Clark, A. 1989. *Microcognition*. Cambridge: MIT Press.

Cockburn, D. (ed.). 1991. *Human Beings*. Cambridge: Cambridge University Press.

Cole, J., and Paillard, J. 1995. "Living without Touch and Peripheral Information about Body Position and Movement: Studies with Deafferented Subjects." In Bermúdez, Marcel, and Eilan 1995.

Cooper, L. A., and Munger, M. P. 1993. "Extrapolating and Remembering Positions along Cognitive Trajectories: Uses and Limitations of Analogies to Physical Motion." In Eilan, McCarthy, and Brewer 1993.

Corballis, M. 1991. *The Lopsided Ape: Evolution of the Generative Mind*. Cambridge: Cambridge University Press.

Costall, A., and Still, A. (eds.). 1987. *Cognitive Psychology in Question*. Brighton: Harvester Press.

Crane, T. 1988. "The Waterfall Illusion." *Analysis* 48: 142–147.

Crane, T. (ed.). 1992. *The Contents of Experience*. Cambridge: Cambridge University Press.

Cussins, A. 1990. "The Connectionist Construction of Concepts." In Boden 1990.

Davidson, D. 1975. "Thought and Talk." In Guttenplan 1975.

Davies, M., and Humphreys, G. (eds.). 1993. *Consciousness*. Oxford: Basil Blackwell.

Davis, R. T., and Fitts, S. S. 1976. "Memory and Coding Processes in Discrimination Learning." In Medin, Roberts, and Davis 1976.

Davis, S. (ed.). 1992. *Connectionism: Theory and Practice*. New York: Oxford University Press.

DeCasper, A. J., and Fifer, W. 1980. "Of Human Bonding: Newborns Prefer Their Mothers' Voices." *Science* 208: 1174–1176.

Dennett, D. 1981. *Brainstorms*. Brighton: Harvester Press.

Diamond, A. 1991. "Neuropsychological Insights into the Meaning of Object Concept Development." In Carey and Gelman 1991.

Diamond, C., and Teichmann, J. (eds.). 1979. *Intention and Intentionality: Essays in Honour of G. E. M. Anscombe*. Brighton: Harvester Press.

Dickinson, A. 1980. *Contemporary Animal Learning Theory*. Cambridge: Cambridge University Press.

Dickinson, A. 1988. "Intentionality in Animal Conditioning." In Weiskrantz 1988.

Donald, M. 1991. *Origins of the Modern Mind: Three Stages in the Evolution of Culture and Cognition*. Cambridge: Harvard University Press.

Dretske, F. 1981. *Knowledge and the Flow of Information*. Cambridge: MIT Press.

Dretske, F. 1990. "Misrepresentation." In Lycan 1990.

Dretske, F. 1992. *Explaining Behavior: Reasons in a World of Causes*. Cambridge: MIT Press.

Dummett, M. 1978. *Truth and Other Enigmas*. London: Duckworth.

Dummett, M. 1993. *The Origins of Analytical Philosophy*. London: Duckworth.

Eilan, N., Marcel, A. J., and Bermúdez, J. L. 1995. "Self-Consciousness and the Body: An Interdisciplinary Introduction." In Bermúdez, Marcel, and Eilan 1995.

Eilan, N., McCarthy, R., and Brewer, M. W. (eds.). 1993. *Spatial Representation: Problems in Philosophy and Psychology*. Oxford: Basil Blackwell.

Evans, G. 1982. *The Varieties of Reference*. Oxford: Clarendon Press.

Evans, G. 1985. "Molyneux's Question." In G. Evans, *Collected Papers*. Oxford: Clarendon Press.

Farah, M. J. 1990. *Visual Agnosia: Disorders of Object Recognition and What They Tell Us about Normal Vision*. Cambridge: MIT Press.

Field, J. 1976. "Relation of Young Infants' Reaching Behaviour to Stimulus Distance and Solidity." *Developmental Psychology* 12: 444–448.

Field, T. M., Woodson, R., Greenburg, R., and Cohen, D. 1982. "Discrimination and Imitation of Facial Expression by Neonates." *Science* 218: 179–181.

Fodor, J. A. 1975. *The Language of Thought*. New York: Crowell.

Fodor, J. A. 1983. *The Modularity of Mind*. Cambridge: MIT Press.

Fodor, J. A. 1986. "Why Paramecia Don't Have Mental Representations." In French, Uehling, and Wettstein 1986.

Fodor, J. A. 1987. *Psychosemantics: The Problem of Meaning in the Philosophy of Mind*. Cambridge: MIT Press.

Fodor, J. A., and Pylyshyn, Z. W. 1981. "How Direct Is Visual Perception? Some Reflections on Gibson's Ecological Approach." *Cognition* 6:136–196.

Fodor, J. A., and Pylyshyn, Z. W. 1988. "Connectionism and Cognitive Architecture: A Critical Analysis." *Cognition* 28: 3–71.

French, P. A., Uehling, T. E., and Wettstein, H. K. (eds.). 1986. *Studies in the Philosophy of Mind*. Midwest Studies in Philosophy, no. 10. Minneapolis: University of Minnesota Press.

Gaffan, D. 1977. "Monkeys' Recognition of Complex Pictures and the Effects of Fornix Transection." *Quarterly Journal of Experimental Psychology* 29: 505–514.

Gallagher, S. 1996. "The Moral Significance of Primitive Self-Consciousness: A Response to Bermúdez." *Ethics* 107: 129–140.

Gallistel, C. R. 1980. *The Organization of Action*. Hillsdale, N.J.: Laurence Erlbaum.

Gallistel, C. R. 1990. *The Organization of Learning*. Cambridge: MIT Press.

Gazzaniga, M. S. 1992. *Nature's Mind*. Harmondsworth: Penguin.

Gazzaniga, M. S. (ed.). 1995. *The Cognitive Neurosciences*. Cambridge: MIT Press.

George, A. (ed.). 1989. *Reflections on Chomsky*. Oxford: Basil Blackwell.

Ghez, C., Gordon, J., Ghilardi, M. F., and Sainburg, R. 1995. "Contributions of Vision and Proprioception to Accuracy in Limb Movements." In Gazzaniga 1995.

Gibson, E. J. 1969. *Principles of Perceptual Learning and Development*. New York: Appleton-Century-Crofts.

Gibson, J. J. 1979. *The Ecological Approach to Visual Perception*. Boston: Houghton Mifflin.

Glisky, E. L., Schacter, D. L., and Tulving, E. 1986. "Computer-Learning by Memory-Impaired Patients: Acquisition and Retention of Complex Knowledge." *Neuropsychologia* 24: 313–328.

Gordon, G. (ed.). 1978. *Active Touch*. Oxford: Pergamon Press.

Grice, H. P. 1957. "Meaning." *Philosophical Review* 66: 377–388. Page references to Grice 1989.

Grice, H. P. 1969. "Utterer's Meaning and Intentions." *Philosophical Review* 78: 147–177. Page references to Grice 1989.

Grice, H. P. 1989. *Studies in the Way of Words*. Cambridge: Harvard University Press.

Grice, H. P., and Strawson, P. F. 1956. "In Defence of a Dogma." *Philosophical Review* 65: 141–158.

Guttenplan, S. (ed.). 1975. *Mind and Language*. Oxford: Clarendon Press.

Haegman, L. 1993. *Introduction to Government and Binding Theory*. Oxford: Basil Blackwell.

Hampshire, S. 1959. *Thought and Action*. London: Chatto and Windus.

Harris, M., Freeman, T., and Williams, G. 1992. "Surface Layout from Retinal Flow." In Humphreys 1992.

Holland, D. C. 1979. "Differential Effects of Omission Contingencies on Various Components of Pavlovian Appetitive Responding in Rats." *Journal of Experimental Psychology: Animal Behavior Processes* 5: 65–78.

Horgan, T., and Tienson, J. 1992. "Structured Representations in Connectionist Systems." In Davis 1992.

Hume, D. 1739–1740/1978. *A Treatise of Human Nature*. Edited by L. A. Selby-Bigge and revised by P. H. Nidditch. Oxford: Clarendon Press.

Humphreys, G. W. (ed.). 1992. *Understanding Vision*. Oxford: Basil Blackwell.

Hurley, S. 1998. *Consciousness and Action*. Cambridge: Harvard University Press.

Kant, I. 1781/1964. *Critique of Pure Reason*. Translated by Norman Kemp Smith. London: Macmillan.

Karmiloff-Smith, A. 1992. *Beyond Modularity: A Developmental Perspective on Developmental Psychology*. Cambridge: MIT Press.

Kellman, P. J., and Spelke, E. S. 1983. "Perception of Partly Occluded Objects in Infancy." *Cognitive Psychology* 15: 483–524.

Kitcher, P. 1990. *Kant's Rational Psychology*. Oxford: Clarendon Press.

Klinnert, M. D., Campos, J. J., Sorce, J. F., Emde, R. N., and Svejda, M. 1983. "Emotions as Behaviour Regulators: Social Referencing in Infancy." In Plutchik and Kellerman 1983.

Kuchuk, A., Vibbert, M., and Bornstein, M. H. 1986. "The Perception of Smiling and Its Correlates in Three-Month-Old Infants." *Child Development* 57: 1054–1061.

Lackner, J. R. 1988. "Some Proprioceptive Influences on the Perceptual Representation of Body Shape and Orientation." *Brain* 111: 281–297.

Lederman, S. J., and Klatzky, R. L. 1987. "Hand Movements: A Window into Haptic Object Recognition." *Cognitive Psychology* 19: 342–368.

Lee, D. N., and Aronson, E. 1974. "Visual Proprioceptive Control of Standing in Human Infants." *Perception and Psychophysics* 15: 529–532.

Lehrer, K. 1974. *Knowledge.* Oxford: Clarendon Press.

Leslie, A. M. 1987. "Pretense and Representation: The Origins of 'Theory of Mind'." *Psychological Review* 94: 412–426.

Leung, E., and Rheinhold, H. 1981. "Development of Pointing as a Social Gesture." *Developmental Psychology* 17: 215–220.

Lieberman, P. 1991. *Uniquely Human: The Evolution of Speech, Thought, and Selfless Behavior.* Cambridge: Harvard University Press.

Lishman, J. R., and Lee, D. N. 1973. "The Autonomy of Visual Kinaesthetics." *Perception* 2: 287–294.

Lock, A. (ed.). 1978. *Action, Gesture, Symbol: The Emergence of Language.* London: Academic Press.

Loewer, B., and Rey, G. (eds.). 1991. *Meaning in Mind: Fodor and His Critics.* Oxford: Basil Blackwell.

Lycan, W. G. (ed.). 1990. *Mind and Cognition: A Reader.* Cambridge, Mass.: Basil Blackwell.

Mackie, J. L. 1976. *Problems from Locke.* Oxford: Clarendon Press.

MacWhinney, B. (ed.). 1987. *Mechanism of Language Acquisition.* Hillsdale, N.J.: Lawrence Erlbaum.

Marcel, A. J. 1983. "Conscious and Unconscious Perception: Experiments on Visual Masking and Word Recognition." *Cognitive Psychology* 15: 197–237.

Marr, D. 1982. *Vision.* San Francisco: W. H. Freeman and Sons.

Marr, D., and Nishihara, H. K. 1978. "Representation and Recognition of the Spatial Organisation of Three-Dimensional Shapes." *Proceedings of the Royal Society of London* B204: 269–294.

Martin, G. B., and Clark, R. D. 1982. "Distress Crying in Neonates: Species and Peer Specificity." *Developmental Psychology* 18: 3–9.

Martin, C. B., and Deutscher, M. 1966. "Remembering." *Philosophical Review* 75: 161–196.

Martin, M. G. F. 1992. "Sight and Touch." In Crane 1992.

Martin, M. G. F. 1993. "Sense Modalities and Spatial Properties." In Eilan, McCarthy, and Brewer 1993.

Martin, M. G. F. 1995. "Bodily Awareness: A Sense of Ownership." In Bermúdez, Marcel, and Eilan 1995.

McCarthy, R. A. 1993. "Assembling Routines and Addressing Representations:

An Alternative Conceptualization of 'What' and 'Where' in the Human Brain." In Eilan, McCarthy, and Brewer 1993.

McDowell, J. 1994. *Mind and World*. Cambridge: Harvard University Press.

McGinn, C. 1989. *Mental Content*. Oxford: Basil Blackwell.

Medin, D. L., Roberts, W. A., and Davis, R. T. (eds.). 1976. *Processes of Animal Memory*. Hillsdale, N.J.: Lawrence Erlbaum.

Mellor, D. H. 1988–1989. "I and Now." *Proceedings of the Aristotelian Society* 89: 79–94. Page references to Mellor 1991.

Mellor, D. H. 1991. *Matters of Metaphysics*. Cambridge: Cambridge University Press.

Meltzoff, A. N. 1993. "Molyneux's Babies: Cross-Modal Perception, Imitation, and the Mind of the Preverbal Infant." In Eilan, McCarthy, and Brewer 1993.

Meltzoff, A. N., and Moore, M. K. 1977. "Imitation of Facial and Manual Gestures by Human Neonates." *Science* 198: 75–78.

Meltzoff, A. N., and Moore, M. K. 1983. "Newborn Infants Imitate Adult Facial Gestures." *Child Development* 54: 702–709.

Melzack, R. 1992. "Phantom Limbs." *Scientific American* 266: 90–96.

Menzel, E. W. 1973. "Chimpanzee Spatial Memory Organization." *Science* 182: 943–945.

Mill, J. S. 1889. *An Examination of Sir William Hamilton's Philosophy*. Sixth edition. London: Longmans.

Millikan, R. G. 1990. "The Myth of the Essential Indexical." *Noûs* 24: 723–734.

Murphy, C. M., and Messner, D. J. 1977. "Mothers, Infants, and Pointing: A Study of a Gesture." In Schaffer 1977.

Murray, L., and Trevarthen, C. 1985. "Emotional Regulation of Interactions between Two-Month-Olds and Their Mothers." In T. M. Field and N. A. Fox (eds.), *Social Perception in Infancy*. Norwood, N.J.: Ablex.

Nagel, T. 1971. "Brain Bisection and the Unity of Consciousness." *Synthese* 20: 396–413.

Neisser, U. 1976. *Cognition and Reality*. New York: W. H. Freeman.

Neisser, U. (ed.). 1987. *Concepts and Conceptual Development*. Cambridge: Cambridge University Press.

Neisser, U. 1988. "Five Kinds of Self-Knowledge." *Philosophical Psychology* 1: 35–59.

Neisser, U. 1991. "Two Perceptually Given Aspects of the Self and Their Development." *Developmental Review* 11: 197–209.

Neisser, U. (ed.). 1993. *The Perceived Self*. Cambridge: Cambridge University Press.

Neumann, O., and Prinz, W. (eds.). 1990. *Relationships between Perception and Action*. Berlin: Springer Verlag.

Newson, J., and Newson, E. 1975. "Intersubjectivity and the Transmission of Culture." *Bulletin of the British Psychological Society* 28: 437–445.

Noonan, H. 1979. "Identity and the First Person." In Diamond and Teichmann 1979.

Nozick, R. 1981. *Philosophical Explanations.* Oxford: Clarendon Press.

O'Brien, L. 1994. "Anscombe and the Self-Reference Rule." *Analysis* 54: 277–281.

O'Shaugnessy, B. 1980. *The Will.* 2 vols. Cambridge: Cambridge University Press.

O'Shaugnessy, B. 1989. "The Sense of Touch." *Australasian Journal of Philosophy* 67: 37–58.

Parker, S. T., and Gibson, K. P. 1979. "A Developmental Model for the Evolution of Language and Intelligence in Early Hominids." *Behavioral and Brain Sciences* 2: 367–408.

Peacocke, C. 1979. *Holistic Explanation: Action, Space, Interpretation.* Oxford: Clarendon Press.

Peacocke, C. 1983. *Sense and Content.* Oxford: Clarendon Press.

Peacocke, C. 1986. "Analogue Content." *Proceedings of the Aristotelian Society,* suppl. vol. 60: 1–17.

Peacocke, C. 1989. *Transcendental Arguments in the Theory of Content.* Inaugural Lecture. Oxford: Oxford University Press.

Peacocke, C. 1992. *A Study of Concepts.* Cambridge: MIT Press.

Peacocke, C. 1994. "Nonconceptual Content: Kinds, Rationales, and Relations." *Mind and Language* 9: 419–430.

Pears, D. 1975. "Russell's Theories of Memory." In D. Pears, *Questions in the Philosophy of Mind.* London: Duckworth.

Pears, D. 1988. *The False Prison.* 2 vols. Oxford: Clarendon Press.

Perner, J. 1991. *Understanding the Representational Mind.* Cambridge: MIT Press.

Perry, J. 1979. "The Problem of the Essential Indexical." *Noûs* 13: 3–21.

Piaget, J. 1954. *The Construction of Reality in the Child.* Translated by M. Cook. New York: Basic Books.

Piaget, J., and Inhelder, B. 1969. *The Psychology of the Child.* New York: Basic Books.

Piatelli-Palmarini, M. 1989. "Evolution, Selection, and Cognition: From 'Learning' to Parameter Setting in Biology and the Study of Language." *Cognition* 31: 1–44.

Pinker, S. 1979. "Formal Models of Language Learning." *Cognition* 1: 217–283.

Pinker, S. 1987. "The Bootstrapping Problem in Language Acquisition." In MacWhinney 1987.

Pinker, S., and Bloom, P. 1990. "Natural Language and Natural Selection." *Behavioral and Brain Science* 13: 707–784.

Pitcher, G. 1970. "Pain Perception." *Philosophical Review* 79: 368–393.

Plutchik, R., and Kellerman, H. (eds.). 1983. *Emotion: Theory, Research, Experience*. Boston: Academic Press.

Pope, M. J. 1984. "Visual Proprioception in Infant Postural Development." Ph.D. thesis, University of Southampton.

Premack, D., and Woodruff, G. 1978. "Does the Chimpanzee Have a Theory of Mind?" *Behavioral and Brain Science* 4: 515–526.

Price, H. H. 1953. *Thinking and Experience*. London: Hutchinson University Library.

Prigatano, G., and Schacter, D. (eds.). 1991. *Awareness of Deficit after Brain Injury*. Oxford: Oxford University Press.

Prinz, W. 1990. "A Common Coding Approach to Perception and Action." In Neumann and Prinz 1990.

Quine, W. V. O. 1951. "Two Dogmas of Empiricism." *Philosophical Review* 60: 20–43. Page references to Quine 1953.

Quine, W. V. O. 1953. *From a Logical Point of View*. Harvard: Harvard University Press.

Quine, W. V. O. 1960. *Word and Object*. Cambridge: MIT Press.

Quinton, A. 1973. *The Nature of Things*. London: Routledge and Kegan Paul.

Ramachandran, V. S. 1994. "Phantom Limbs, Neglect Syndromes, Repressed Memories, and Freudian Psychology." *International Review of Neurobiology* 37: 291–333.

Ramsey, W. 1992. "Connectionism and the Philosophy of Mental Representation." In Davis 1992.

Reed, E. S. 1987. "Why Do Things Look As They Do? The Implications of J. J. Gibson's *The Ecological Approach to Visual Perception*." In Costall and Still 1987.

Rochat, P. 1995. *The Self in Infancy: Theory and Research*. Amsterdam: Elsevier.

Rock, I. 1975. *An Introduction to Perception*. New York: Macmillan.

Rolls, E. T. 1990. "A Theory of Emotion, and Its Application to Understanding the Neural Basis of Emotion." *Cognition and Emotion* 4: 161–190.

Rolls, E. T. 1995. "A Theory of Emotion and Consciousness, and Its Application to Understanding the Neural Basis of Emotion." In Gazzaniga 1995.

Russell, B. 1921. *The Analysis of Mind*. London: Allen and Unwin.

Russell, J. 1980. "Action from Knowledge and Conditioned Behaviour. Part One: The Stratification of Behaviour." *Behaviorism* 8: 87–98.

Russell, J. 1996. *Agency: Its Role in Mental Development*. Hove: Lawrence Erlbaum.

Sagi, A., and Hoffman, M. 1976. "Empathic Distress in the Newborn." *Developmental Psychology* 12: 175–176.

Scaife, M., and Bruner, J. S. 1975. "The Capacity for Joint Visual Attention in the Infant." *Nature* 253: 265–266.

Schacter, D. L., McAndrews, M. P., and Moscovitch, M. 1988. "Access to Consciousness: Dissociations between Implicit and Explicit Knowledge in Neuropsychological Syndromes." In Weiskrantz 1988.

Schaffer, H. R. (ed.). 1977. *Studies in Mother-Infant Interaction*. Proceedings of the Loch Lomond Symposium, Ross Priory, University of Strathclyde, September 1975. New York: Academic Press.

Schopenhauer, A. 1844/1966. *The World as Will and Representation*. Translated by E. J. F. Payne. 2 vols. New York: Dover Publications.

Segal, G. 1996. "The Modularity of Theory of Mind." In Carruthers and Smith 1996.

Shapiro, M. F., Fink, M., and Bender, M. B. 1952. "Exosomesthesia or Displacement of Cutaneous Sensation onto Extrapersonal Space." *AMA Archives of Neurology and Psychiatry* 68: 481–490.

Shoemaker, S. 1963. *Self-Knowledge and Self-Identity*. Ithaca: Cornell University Press.

Shoemaker, S. 1968. "Self-Reference and Self-Awareness." *Journal of Philosophy* 65: 555–567. Page references to Shoemaker 1984.

Shoemaker, S. 1970. "Persons and Their Pasts." *American Philosophical Quarterly* 7: 269–285. Page references to Shoemaker 1984.

Shoemaker, S. 1984. *Identity, Cause, and Mind*. Cambridge: Cambridge University Press.

Shoemaker, S. 1986. "Introspection and the Self." In French, Uehling, and Wettstein 1986.

Shoemaker, S. 1994. "Self-Knowledge and 'Inner Sense'." *Philosophy and Phenomenological Research* 54: 249–314.

Simner, M. L. 1971. "Newborn's Response to the Cry of Another Infant." *Developmental Psychology* 5: 136–150.

Slater, A., Morrison, V., Somers, M., Mattock, A., and Taylor, D. 1990. "Newborn and Older Infants' Perceptions of Partly Occluded Objects." *Infant Behavior and Development* 13: 33–49.

Smolensky, P. 1991. "Connectionism, Constituency, and the Language of Thought." In Loewer and Rey 1991.

Snowdon, P. F. 1991. "Personal Identity and Brain Transplants." In Cockburn 1991.

Snowdon, P. F. 1995. "Persons, Animals, and Bodies." In Bermúdez, Marcel, and Eilan 1995.

Spelke, E. S. 1988. "The Origins of Thought and Language." In Weiskrantz 1988.

Spelke, E. S. 1990. "Principles of Object Perception." *Cognitive Science* 14: 29–56.

Spelke, E. S., and Van de Walle, G. A. 1993. "Perceiving and Reasoning about Objects: Insights from Infants." In Eilan, McCarthy, and Brewer 1993.

Stern, D. 1985. *The Interpersonal World of the Infant.* New York: Basic Books.

Strawson, P. F. 1959. *Individuals: An Essay in Descriptive Metaphysics.* London: Methuen.

Strawson, P. F. 1966. *The Bounds of Sense.* London: Methuen.

Strawson, P. F. 1994. "The First Person—and Others." In Cassam 1994.

Taschek, W. W. 1985. "Referring to Oneself." *Canadian Journal of Philosophy* 15: 629–652.

Taylor, C. 1964. *The Explanation of Behaviour.* London: Routledge and Kegan Paul.

Tinbergen, N. 1951. *The Study of Instinct.* Oxford: Oxford University Press.

Tobias, P. V. 1987. "The Brain of *Homo habilis*: A New Level of Organization in Cerebral Evolution." *Journal of Human Evolution* 16: 741–765.

Tolman, E. C., and Honzik, C. H. 1930a. " 'Insight' in Rats." *University of California Publications in Psychology* 4: 215–232.

Tolman, E. C., and Honzik, C. H. 1930b. "Introduction and Removal of Reward, and Maze Learning in Rats." *University of California Publications in Psychology* 4: 257–275.

Tolman, E. C., Ritchie, B. F., Kalish, D. 1946. "Studies in Spatial Learning. II: Place Learning vs Response Learning." *Journal of Experimental Psychology* 36: 221–229.

Tomasello, M. 1993. "On the Interpersonal Origins of Self-Concept." In Neisser 1993.

Travis, C. 1994. "On Constraints of Generality." *Proceedings of the Aristotelian Society* 94: 165–188.

Trevarthen, C. 1993. "The Self Born in Intersubjectivity." In Neisser 1993.

Trevarthen, C., and Hubley, P. 1978. "Secondary Intersubjectivity: Confidence, Confiding, and Acts of Meaning in the First Year." In Lock 1978.

Ts'o, D. Y., and Roe, A. W. 1995. "Functional Compartments in Visual Cortex: Segregation and Interaction." In Gazzaniga 1995.

Van Gulick, R. 1990. "Functionalism, Information, and Content." In Lycan 1990.

Von Hofsten, C. 1982. "Foundations for Perceptual Development." *Advances in Infancy Research* 2: 241–261.

Walker, Ralph C. S. 1978. *Kant.* London: Routledge and Kegan Paul.

Wanner, E., and Gleitman, L. R. (eds.). 1982. *Language Acquisition: The State of the Art.* Cambridge: Cambridge University Press.

Weiskrantz, L. (ed.). 1988. *Thought without Language*. Oxford: Clarendon Press.

Wiggins, D. 1980. *Sameness and Substance*. Oxford: Basil Blackwell.

Wimmer, H., and Perner, J. 1983. "Beliefs about Beliefs: Representation and Constraining Function of Wrong Beliefs in Young Children's Understanding of Deception." *Cognition* 13: 103–128.

Wittgenstein, L. 1921/1961. *Tractatus Logico-philosophicus*. Translated by D. F. Pears and B. F. McGuinness. London: Routledge and Kegan Paul.

Wittgenstein, L. 1958. *Preliminary Studies for the "Philosophical Investigations," Generally Known as the Blue and Brown Books*. Oxford: Basil Blackwell.

Woodruff, G., and Premack, D. 1979. "Intentional Communication in the Chimpanzee." *Cognition* 7: 333–362.

Index

Acquisition Constraint, 19–21, 23, 24, 44–45, 129, 162, 189, 191, 226, 267, 269, 291–293, 297
and first-person pronoun, 20, 292–294
introduced, 19
Acredolo, L. P., 217, 218
Adams, A., 217, 218
Adamson, L. B., 261
Affordances, 112–114, 117, 118, 127, 223–227, 293–294. *See also* Ecological optics
affordance identities, 225–226, 293
affordance space, 226–227
affordance symmetry, 224–226, 293
affordance transitivity, 225–226, 293
nonextensionality of, 121–122
Alexia, 80
A location vs. *B* location in proprioception, 154–158
Altham, J. E. J., 300 (n. 8)
Amnesia, 174–175, 176
Andersen, R. A., 141
Animal learning theory, 62, 207
Anosagnosia, 151–152
A, not-*B* error or stage 4 error (Piaget), 70, 75
Anscombe, G. E. M., 16–17, 300 (n. 8), 306 (n. 2)
Apperceptive agnosias, 79–81
Argument from analogy, 231

Aristotle, 139
Armstrong, D. M., 54, 277, 307 (n. 12)
Aronson, E., 111, 128
Associative agnosias, 79–81
Australopithecus, 77
Autonomy Principle, 46, 58–82, 85, 97, 270, 301 (n. 5), 310 (n. 1)
and infant cognition, 62–76
and phylogeny of language, 76–79
stated, 61
and visual agnosias, 79–81
Ayers, M., 141, 238

Baillargeon, R., 64–66, 68, 302 (n. 13)
Bakeman, R., 261
Baron-Cohen, S., 300–301 (n. 16)
Barwise, J., 9
Basic inductive generalizations, 183–186
Bateson, M. C., 251
Behavior
emergence of intentional, 192
intentional vs. nonintentional, explanation of, 36–38, 85–91, 115–118, 246
narrowly vs. broadly construed, 86
stimulus-response explanations of, 88–89, 208–210
Békésy, G. von, 309 (n. 24)

Belief. *See also* Content; Representational states; Subjective beliefs
conditions on ascription of, 33–39
emergence of concept of, 279–280
functionalist view of, 29
necessarily conceptual, 34, 52–54, 301 (n. 1)
normativity of, 52–54
utility conditions of, 29, 34, 37–39
Belief-desire psychology, 36–37, 85
Bender, M. B., 309 (n. 24)
Bennett, J., 88–89, 184–185, 277, 279, 304 (n. 7), 310 (n. 8)
Bermúdez, J. L., 132, 249, 300 (nn. 9, 13), 302 (n. 6), 303 (n. 21), 305–306 (n. 16), 306 (nn. 1, 8), 310 (nn. 1, 2), 312 (nn. 12, 13, 14)
Bicoordinate navigation, 211
Blindsight, 79
Bloom, P., 79
Bodily awareness, 131–162. *See also* Proprioception, somatic
of body as responsive to will, 150, 161, 229, 237, 271, 284
of felt boundaries of body, 149–150, 161, 229, 271, 284
structure of, 152–158
Bodily self. *See* Bodily awareness
Body-relative space, 142, 145, 204
frame of reference of, 152–158
Bornstein, M. H., 250
Bower, T. G. R., 127
Bremner, J. G., 250
Brewer, B., 140, 151, 158, 307 (n. 11)
Bringing-it-about-that, 288–290, 312 (n. 4)
Broca's area, 77–78
Brown, J. W., 76, 80
Bruner, J. S., 255, 257
Budd, M., 306 (n. 2)
Butterworth, G. E., 128, 305 (nn. 12, 15)

Campbell, J., 172, 198, 245, 300 (n. 9), 310 (chap. 7, n. 5; chap. 8, n. 2)
on causally indexical comprehension, 200–202, 206–207
on temporal orientation toward the past, 178–180
Capacity circularity, 18–25, 28, 47, 49, 58, 60, 62, 268
and Acquisition Constraint, 19–20
and developmental explanation, 60, 62
distinguished from explanatory circularity, 18
and innatism, 21–24
introduced, 18
and nonconceptual self-consciousness, 291–294
solution to problem of, 291–294
Carey, S., 70
Cassam, Q., 143–144, 307 (n. 12)
Castañeda, H.-N., 4, 14, 148
Causally indexical comprehension (Campbell), 200–202, 206–207
Causation, concept of, 288
Chapuis, N., 215–216
Chisholm, R., 307 (n. 15)
Choice-reaction-time tasks, 140
Chomsky, N., 22, 300 (n. 15)
Clark, A., 93
Clark, R. D., 124
Cognitive dynamics (Kaplan), 296
Cognitive map, 203–207
and levels of self-awareness, 203–204
as record in nervous system, 203–206
Cohen, D., 250
Cohesion, principle of (Spelke), 63–64, 74
Color perception, 55–57, 96
Common sensibles, 139
Communicative intent, 277–291
of first-person pronoun, 282–283, 293
informational vs. practical, 277
and linguistic reference, 280–281
sentential vs. subsentential, 278–281
Computational theory of cognition (CTC), 93–94, 304 (n. 8)

Computational theory of vision (Marr), 81–82
Concepts
  acquisition of, 22, 60–62, 69–71, 74–76
  conditions on ascription of, 34
  evolution of, 60–62
  inferential role of, 67–68, 69–70
  normativity of, 52–54
  relation of, to language mastery, 41–42, 68, 70–71 (*see also* Priority Principle)
Conceptual-Requirement Principle, 41, 42, 43, 44, 45, 268, 301 (n. 4)
  stated, 41
Conditioning, 36–37, 87–89, 119
  classical/Pavlovian, 36, 89
  instrumental/operant, 36, 89, 190
Consciousness, 30, 189–192, 309–310 (n. 4), 310 (n. 10)
Constancy-of-sense thesis, 12, 13, 24–25, 230, 232
Contact, principle of (Spelke), 64, 74
Content. *See also* Representational states; Thought
  classical view of, 28, 39, 41–43, 45, 49, 269–270
  and concept possession, 41–44 (*see also* Nonconceptual content)
  conditions on ascribing, 33–39, 47, 83–94, 269
  constitutive vs. criterial accounts of, 84–85
  demonstrative, 38, 55–57
  indexical, 38
  and information, 84–85
  nonconceptual (*see* Nonconceptual content)
  of perceptual experience (*see* Perceptual content)
  Russellian, 52
Continuity, principle of (Spelke), 64, 66, 74
Contrast space, 238, 242, 248, 265, 274
Cooper, L. A., 302 (n. 12)

Coordinated joint engagement in infants, 260–262, 263, 265, 285–286, 289
Corballis, M., 77, 78, 303 (n. 17)
Corollary discharge, 304–305 (n. 4)
Count terms, 173, 309 (n. 2)
Criterial vs. constitutive accounts of content, 84, 207
Cussins, A., 60

Davies, M., 310 (n. 10)
Davis, R. T., 186
Dead reckoning, 205, 210
DeCasper, A. J., 250
Deflationary account of self-consciousness, 9–13, 14–21, 31, 32, 294–296, 299 (nn. 5, 6)
  and paradox of self-consciousness, 14–21
  stated, 10–11
Deutscher, M., 175, 179–180
Developmental explanation, 60–62, 74
  and Autonomy Principle, 61–62, 301 (n. 5)
Developmental psychology, 62–76, 149, 172, 208, 248
Diamond, A., 75
Dickinson, A., 36, 62, 87, 190
Dishabituation experiments, 47, 64–66, 68, 72, 75
Distinguishing self-awareness, 237–238
  psychological, 240–241, 242, 249, 252, 255, 261
  and relative identity, 240
Distress crying in neonates, 124–125
Donald, M., 77, 78
Drawbridge experiment (Baillargeon), 64–66, 68, 70
Dretske, F., 84, 303 (nn. 2, 3)
Dummett, M., 12, 41, 42

Ecological optics, 103–129, 165. *See also* Affordances; Gibson, J. J.
  content of, 115–123

Ecological optics (*continued*)
and information-processing accounts, 310 (n. 9)
memory in, 187–188
perceptual invariants in, 108–109
and self-perception in infancy, 123–128
self-specifying information in, 103–114, 223–224
Ecological self, 124, 131. *See also* Ecological optics; Nonconceptual first-person contents
Efference copy, 111, 304–305 (n. 4)
Egocentric space. *See* Body-relative space
Eilan, N., 132, 306 (n. 1), 307 (n. 11)
Emotions, 246–247
Empathic arousal in infants, 250
Evans, G., 5, 6, 50, 59, 92, 139, 144, 299 (n. 2), 301 (n. 1), 307 (nn. 13, 14, 16)
on cognitive maps, 204–205
on first-person thoughts, 221–223
on Generality Constraint, 233–237, 311 (n. 2)
on immunity to error through misidentification, 307–308 (n. 16)
on simple theory of perception, 222–223, 244–245
Exosomesthesia, 309 (n. 24)
Explanation, two senses of, 19
Explanatory circularity, 14–16, 47, 49, 58, 60, 268, 283, 290–291
distinguished from capacity circularity, 18
introduced, 14–16
and nonconceptual self-consciousness, 275–291
and possession-conditions explanation, 60
solution to problem of, 275–291

False-belief task, 279–280, 312 (n. 2)
Farah, M., 80, 303 (nn. 18, 19)
Features and feature-placing thought, 38–39, 172–174, 195

Field, J., 127
Field, T. M., 126, 250
Fifer, W., 250
Fink, M., 309 (n. 24)
First-person contents, 5–12, 27–39, 44–47, 49. *See also* First-person pronoun; Nonconceptual first-person contents; Nonconceptual psychological self-awareness; Subjective beliefs
functionalist theory of, 27–39, 42
identification component of, as basic, 7
identification component vs. predication component of, 5–6, 10
without linguistic self-reference, 27–39 (*see also* Nonconceptual first-person contents)
role of, in explanation of action, 34–35, 116–117, 148
First-person-motivation thesis, 35, 37–39
First-person perspective, entry into, 123–124, 128
First-person pronoun, 3, 9–12, 14–18, 21, 22, 24–25, 27–29, 31, 32, 44–46, 49, 132, 146, 198–199, 267–268
and Acquisition Constraint, 20, 292–294
communicative intent governing use of, 282–291, 293
conditions on proper use of, 275–276
functionalist account of mastery of, 31
guaranteed reference of, 9–10
noncircular account of mastery of, 283–291
as perceptual demonstrative (Evans), 307–308 (n. 16)
not a referring expression (Anscombe), 16–17, 300 (n. 8)
role of nonconceptual content in mastery of, 45, 47, 283–291
semantics of, 9–12 (*see also* Token-reflexive rule)

semantics vs. pragmatics of, 17
used as object vs. used as subject, 5–6, 11
Fitts, S. S., 186
Focal vs. peripheral awareness, 138–139
Fodor, J. A., 77, 86, 89, 93, 300 (n. 14), 310 (n. 9)
Freeman, T., 304 (n. 1)
Functionalist account of first-person thought, 27–39, 42, 46
and mastery of first-person pronoun, 31
and self-reference, 27–30, 271

Gaffan, D., 185–186
Gallagher, S., 309 (n. 26)
Gallistel, C. R., 203–206, 210, 304–305 (n. 4)
Gazzaniga, M., 22
Generality Constraint (Evans), 59, 92, 233–237, 241, 311 (n. 1)
George, A., 300 (n. 15)
Ghez, C., 307 (n. 10)
Gibson, E., 113–114
Gibson, J. J., 46, 103–114, 131, 165, 187–188, 190, 224, 271, 303 (n. 4), 304 (nn. 1, 3), 310 (n. 9)
Gibson, K. P., 303 (n. 17)
Glisky, E. L., 175, 176
Goodwyn, S. W., 217, 218
Gordon, G., 137, 306 (nn. 6, 7)
Government-binding (GB) paradigm (Chomsky), 22
Greenburg, R., 250
Grice, H. P., 277–278, 300 (n. 12)
Gricean mechanisms, 279–281, 287–289. *See also* Communicative intent

Haegman, L., 22
Haptic exploration, 133, 137–138, 152, 306 (nn. 6, 7)
Harris, M., 304 (n. 1)
He*, 4, 14–17, 22, 28, 45, 49
introduced, 4
Hicks, L., 128, 305 (nn. 12, 15)

Hinges in proprioceptive content, 155–157, 161
defined, 157
Hoffman, M., 250
Holland, D. C., 87–88
Homo erectus, 78
Homo habilis, 78
Homo sapiens, 77–78
Honzik, C. H., 212, 217, 219
Hubley, P., 249, 260–261, 287
Hume, D., 104
Humphreys, G. W., 310 (n. 10)
Hurley, S. L., 300 (n. 12), 311 (n. 10)

Identification constraint (Shoemaker), 136–137
Identity. *See also* Relative identity
neo-Lockean conception of, 238–240
of persons, 239
Imitation by neonates, 125–127, 140, 249, 312 (n. 14)
Immunity to error through misidentification, 6–12, 143–145
defined, 7
and guaranteed reference of first-person pronoun, 9–10
and identification component of first-person contents, 11–12
and justification, 6–7
not logically necessary, 307 (n. 12)
of perceptual demonstrative judgements, 143
Shoemaker's definition of, 6
of somatic proprioception, 143–145, 147, 148
Indexical beliefs, 117. *See also* Subjective beliefs
Indirect reflexive pronoun ('he*'), 4, 14–17, 22, 28, 45, 49
introduced, 4
Infant cognition, 62–76, 100, 248–262, 271, 274
and protoconversations, 250–254
revolution in, at 9 months, 248–249, 254–255
triadic vs. dyadic, 255, 260

Inference to best explanation, 46, 100, 207, 217, 248, 253, 259, 265, 271, 273
Innate endowment, 19, 22, 292–293
Innate releasing mechanisms, 36
Innatism, 21–24
Integrated representation of the environment, 199–207, 273
  basic conditions on, 208–211
  and cognitive maps, 203–207
  construction of, 224–227, 294
  and navigational abilities, 207–220
  need for operational understanding of, 206
  place-driven vs. response-driven, 208–210
  and sensitivity to genuine spatial features, 210–211
  and two systems of spatial relations, 213–217
Integrated sensory field (Ayers), 141–142, 145
Intentional web (Peacocke), 214–215
Introspection, 135, 146
Inverting lenses, 142
Iterated psychological states, 284–287
'I'-thoughts, 2–12, 24–25. *See also* First-person contents; First-person pronoun; Nonconceptual first-person contents; Nonconceptual psychological self-awareness
  defined, 4
  and genuine self-consciousness, 2–4
  oratio obliqua vs. *oratio recta*, 3–4, 14–15
  and self-reference, 2–4

Joint selective visual attention in infants, 255–259, 263, 265, 283, 285, 289

Kalish, D., 209
Kant, I., 165–167, 198, 310 (n. 7)
Kaplan, D., 296
Karmiloff-Smith, A., 300 (n. 14), 301 (n. 16)
Kinesthesis, 134, 140, 150, 168

visual, 110–112, 114, 115, 116, 117, 122, 128
Klatzky, R. L., 306 (n. 6)
Klinnert, M. D., 263
Kuchuk, A., 250

Lackner, J. R., 305 (n. 8)
Language
  generativity of, 92
  phylogenesis of, 76–79
Language learning
  and capacity circularity, 20
  innatist theory of, 23–24
  of syntax vs. semantics, 23–24
Latent-learning experiments, 219
Lederman, S. J., 306 (n. 6)
Lee, D. N., 111, 128
Leibniz's Law, 239
Leslie, A., 300 (n. 16)
Leung, E., 257
Lieberman, P., 78, 302 (n. 16)
Lishman, J. R., 111
Local holism (Peacocke), 18, 300 (n. 12)
Locke, J., 239
Looming, 109, 122, 128

Mackie, J. L., 238, 311 (n. 4)
Marcel, A. J., 132, 306 (n. 1), 310 (n. 4)
Marr, D., 76, 80, 108, 303 (n. 20)
Martin, C. B., 175, 179–180
Martin, G. B., 124
Martin, M. G. F., 137, 139, 158, 309 (n. 24)
Mass terms, 173, 309 (n. 2)
Maze learning, 208–209, 219
McAndrews, M. P., 174, 310 (n. 4)
McCarthy, R. A., 307 (n. 11)
McDowell, J., 54–58
Mellor, D. H., 29–39, 42
Meltzoff, A. N., 125–126, 249, 306 (n. 8)
Melzack, R., 151
Memory
  autobiographical, 243–244, 294, 295–296

autobiographical vs. episodic, 181
causal theory of, 175–176, 179–180
conscious, 174–180, 185–186, 193, 194, 273
and ecological optics, 187–188
Menzel, E. W., 217
Messner, D. J., 256
Mill, J. S., 23
Millikan, R. G., 305 (n. 9)
Misrepresentation, 84–85, 88, 89–90, 116
misperception vs. perceptual illusions, 305 (n. 8)
Modality specificity, 139–142
Moore, M. K., 125–126, 249
Moscovitch, M., 174, 310 (n. 4)
Moving-room experiments, 111–112, 116
Multiple-objects constraint (Shoemaker), 136–137, 142–143, 144
Munger, M. P., 302 (n. 12)
Murphy, C. M., 256
Murray, L., 251

Nagel, T., 311 (n. 5)
Nativism (innatism), 21–24
Navigation, 196–198, 201–202. *See also* Integrated representation of the environment; Nonconceptual point of view; Space; Spatial awareness
as evidence for integrated representation of environment, 207–220
around obstacles, 212–213
and two systems of spatial relations, 213–217
Neisser, U., 124, 188, 305 (nn. 12, 13), 310 (n. 6)
Neuroanatomy, 77
Newson, E., 257
Newson, J., 257
Nishihara, H. K., 81
Nonconceptual content, 43–47, 50–82, 268–270. *See also* Nonconceptual first-person contents; Nonconceptual point of view; Nonconceptual psychological self-awareness

autonomous, 58–82, 270–274 (*see also* Autonomy Principle)
and computational theory of vision, 81–82
conditions on ascribing, 83–94, 115–123, 253
defined, 52
and developmental explanation, 60–62
different applications of, 58–62
and infant cognition, 62–76 (*see also* Infant cognition)
nonextensionality of, 119–122
and phylogeny of language, 76–79
and possession-conditions explanation, 58–59
of somatic proprioception, 151–162
and visual agnosias, 79–81
of visual perception, 103–114
Nonconceptual first-person contents, 44–47, 49, 97, 103–104, 114, 163, 167, 188, 193, 224, 229, 271–274
conditions on ascribing, 115–123
in coordinated joint engagement, 261–262, 285–286
in ecological optics, 103–114
embedded within iterated psychological states, 285–287
introduced, 49
in joint visual attention, 258–259, 283, 285
in navigational abilities, 46
role of, in explanation of action, 117–123
role of, in intentional self-reference, 283–291
in social contexts, 46
in social referencing, 264
in somatic proprioception, 131–162
Nonconceptual point of view, 168–192, 193–227, 229, 237, 238
construction of, 224–227
defined, 168
diachronic nature of, 169–170, 272–273
and ecological optics, 168–188
and memory, 174–180

Nonconceptual point of view (*continued*)
  nonsolipsistic component of, 197–
    198, 220, 273
  and spatial awareness, 193–198
  spatial-awareness component of,
    198, 199, 220–221, 273
Nonconceptual psychological self-
    awareness, 248–265, 274
  in coordinated joint engagement,
    261–262
  in joint visual attention, 258–259
  in social referencing, 264
Nonconceptual recognition, 182–184
  and basic inductive generalizations,
    183–186
Nonsolipsistic consciousness (Straw-
    son), 167–170, 178, 193–194, 196.
    See also Nonconceptual point of
    view
Noonan, H., 299 (n. 3)
Nozick, R., 300 (n. 10)

Object*, 100–101, 172, 174, 177,
    309 (n. 1)
  defined, 100
Object, concept of, 67–68, 69–71, 99–
    100, 171–172
Object constraint (Shoemaker), 136–
    137, 145
Object permanence, 62–76, 97, 103,
    302 (n. 10)
Object properties, 72–74, 100–101,
    302 (n. 12)
Object-recognition system, 80
O'Brien, L., 17
Omission schedule, 87–88, 303–304
    (n. 5)
Optic flow, 109–112
O'Shaughnessy, B., 137, 151, 259

Paleoneurology, 77
Paradox of self-consciousness, 1, 16,
    27–28, 43–45, 47–48, 49, 58, 123,
    163, 229, 265, 267, 272, 282, 294.
    See also Capacity circularity; Ex-
    planatory circularity

  functionalist solution to, 28, 31–32
  solution to, 272, 275–294
  stated, 24
Parallel distributed processing (PDP),
    93, 304 (n. 8)
Parietal cortex, 77–78, 140
Parker, S. T., 303 (n. 17)
Peacocke, C., 8, 18, 50, 51, 52, 53,
    59–61, 84, 224, 300 (n. 12), 302
    (nn. 6, 8), 304 (n. 6), 308 (n. 20),
    310 (nn. 1, 3)
  on definition of nonconceptual con-
    tent, 52
  and minimal account of concept pos-
    session, 84
  and perspectival sensitivity, 213–215
  on place reidentification, 198–202
  and possession-conditions explana-
    tion, 59
  and scenario/protopropositional con-
    tent, 95–101, 303 (n. 1)
Pears, D. F., 183, 299 (n. 1)
Perception. *See also* Perceptual
    content
  cross-modal nature of, 139–142
  models of (Shoemaker), 135–136
  sensational properties of, 214–215
  simple theory of (Evans), 222–223,
    244–245
Perceptual content, 46, 50–58. *See
    also* Nonconceptual content
  analogue nature of (Peacocke), 51
  epistemic theory of (Armstrong), 54
  fineness of grain of, 50, 54–56, 96
  in infancy, 62–76
  vs. perceptual belief, 51
Perceptual space, 56
Perner, J., 280
Perry, J., 9, 148, 301 (n. 2), 305 (n. 9)
Perspectival sensitivity (Peacocke),
    213–217
Phantom limb, 151, 308 (n. 17)
Piaget, J., 62, 66, 70, 75, 125, 248,
    253
Piatelli-Palmarini, M., 78
Pinker, S., 23, 79, 300 (n. 15)

Place reidentification/recognition, 171–174, 189, 193. *See also* Integrated representation of the environment; Navigation; Nonconceptual point of view; Spatial awareness and conscious memory, 177–179 and first-person concept, 198–200 types of, 194–195

Point of view, 164–168. *See also* Nonconceptual point of view

Pope, M. J., 128

Possession-conditions explanation (Peacocke), 58–59, 61

P* predicates (Shoemaker), 8

Premack, D., 62, 300 (n. 16)

Price, H. H., 310 (n. 7)

Prigatano, G., 308 (n. 18)

Primitively compelling inference (Peacocke), 8

Principle of cohesion (Spelke), 63–64, 74

Principle of contact (Spelke), 64, 74

Principle of continuity (Spelke), 64, 66, 74

Principle of solidity (Spelke), 64–65, 74

Prinz, W., 140

Priority Principle, 42–44, 61, 68, 199, 268, 311–312 (n. 11) stated, 42

Propositional content, 3, 83–85

Proprioception, somatic, 46, 131–162, 163, 167, 188, 193, 194, 229, 237, 271, 284 *A* location vs. *B* location, 154–158 conscious vs. nonconscious, 133–134 content of, 151–161 correctness conditions of, 159–161, 309 (n. 25) descriptive content of, 158–161 as form of perception, 135–145 as form of self-consciousness, 145–151 mediate vs. immediate, 133–134 and neonatal imitation, 125

proprioceived body vs. physical body, 151–152 spatial content of, 154–158 types of information in, 132–134

Prosopagnosia, 80, 81

Protobeliefs, 118–119, 120, 122, 161, 259, 286 and basic inductive generalizations, 184 instrumental vs. perceptual, 118–119

Protoconversations with infants, 250–254 thick vs. thin interpretations of, 252–254

Protodesires, 118

Protopropositional content (Peacocke), 96–101

Psychological self-awareness, 229–265. *See also* Distinguishing self-awareness; Nonconceptual psychological self-awareness and awareness of other minds, 230–241 criteria for, 242 emergence of, in infancy, 247–264 in social interactions, 241–247

Psychological subject as agent, 245–246 as bearer of reactive attitudes, 246–247 core notion of, 241–247, 274 as perceiver, 244–245

Psychologism, 20

Pylyshyn, Z., 93, 310 (n. 9)

Quasi-indicator. *See* Indirect reflexive pronoun ('he*')

Quine, W. V. O., 173, 183, 300 (n. 12)

Quinton, A., 172

Ramachandran, V. S., 151, 308 (n. 17)

Ramsey, W., 304 (n. 8)

Reaching behavior in infants, 127

Reed, E. S., 305 (n. 5)

Registration (Bennett), 88–89
Reinhold, H., 257
Relative identity
  and distinguishing self-awareness,
    240–241
  restricted vs. unrestricted, 238–239
Remapping hypothesis, 308 (n. 17)
Representational states
  cognitive integration of, 90–91, 94
  holism of, 90–91
  as intermediaries between sensory in-
    put and behavioral output, 86–90,
    94, 115–116, 270–271
  structure of, 38–39, 91–94, 301
    (n. 4)
Ritchie, B. F., 209
Rock, I., 305 (n. 6)
Roe, A. W., 80
Rolls, E. T., 247
Russell, B., 183
Russell, J., 36, 75, 190, 302 (nn. 11,
  14)

Sagi, A., 250
Scaife, M., 255
Scenario content (Peacocke), 95–101
Schacter, D. L., 174, 175, 308 (n. 18),
  310 (n. 4)
Schopenhauer, A., 104, 105, 106,
  107, 108, 109
Secondary circular reactions (Piaget),
  253
Segal, G., 300 (n. 14)
Self
  in content of perception, 103–108
  embodied, 131–162 (see also Proprio-
    ception, somatic)
  introspection of, 104, 136
Self-consciousness. See also
  Deflationary account of self-
  consciousness; First-person contents; Nonconceptual first-person
  contents; Nonconceptual psychological self-awareness; Paradox of self-
  consciousness; Proprioception,
  somatic

broad vs. narrow, 160–161
  as a cognitive state, 1
  contrastive nature of, 164, 221, 237–
    238, 272
  core requirements on, 148–151
  gradations in, 163–164, 187, 189,
    193
  narrow vs. broad, 149–151
  ontogenesis of, 18–19, 291–294
  primitive forms of, 76, 103, 128–
    129, 131–132, 161, 269
  and self-ascription of predicates, 12,
    13
  and spatial awareness, 221–223
Self-reference, 2–4, 14–18, 27–30,
  202. See also First-person contents;
  First-person pronoun
  conditions on, 275–276, 281
  functionalist account of, 27–30, 271
  identification-free, 7–8
  and immunity to error, 9–12, 299
    (n. 4)
  intentional, 282–283
  as production of a given token ('I'),
    15–16
  reflexive vs. accidental, 2–4, 32–33,
    34–35, 147–148, 200
  without self-knowledge, 27–30
Self-world dualism, 149–151,
  163–164
Semantic-bootstrapping hypothesis
  (Pinker), 23
Shallice, T., 303 (n. 20)
Shapiro, M. F., 309 (n. 24)
Shoemaker, S., 6, 8, 135–137, 143,
  144, 299 (nn. 4, 5), 306 (nn. 4, 5),
  307 (n. 14)
Simner, M. L., 124
Simple argument about somatic pro-
  prioception, 134–135, 145
Simultagnosia, 79, 303 (n. 18)
Size constancy, 304 (n. 2)
Slater, A., 100
Smolensky, P., 93–94, 304 (n. 8)
Social referencing in infants, 262–264,
  265

Solid angles in vision, 106–107, 152
Solidity, principle of (Spelke), 64–65, 74
Somatic proprioception. *See* Proprioception, somatic
Somatoparaphrenic delusions, 151–152
Space. *See also* Integrated representation of the environment; Navigation; Nonconceptual point of view; Spatial awareness
absolute vs. egocentric representation of, 201
allocentric vs. egocentric representation of, 204, 205
connectivity of, 212
two types of spatial relations, 194–195, 197, 213–217, 220
understanding, 194–195, 196–197
Spatial-attention system, 80
Spatial awareness
and nonconceptual point of view, 193–198
and self-consciousness, 198, 221–223
understanding places as places, 218–220
Spatial reasoning, 200–202. *See also* Integrated representation of the environment
Spelke, E., 63–66, 302 (n. 9)
on concept of objects, 68
Split-brain patients, 239–240
Stage 4 error or *A*, not-*B* error (Piaget), 70, 75
Stern, D., 257–258
Stimulus-response (S-R). *See* Behavior
Strawson, P. F., 9, 165–168, 169, 171, 172, 233–237, 300 (n. 12), 311 (nn. 2, 3)
Subjective beliefs (Mellor), 29–31, 34, 37–39, 117. *See also* First-person contents; Nonconceptual first-person contents
conscious, 29, 30
defined, 29

second-order, 30
self-reference in, 30
utility conditions of, 29, 34, 37–39
Symmetry Thesis, 230–241, 265, 274, 311 (n. 7)
distinction between weak reading and strong reading of, 230–232
and Generality Constraint, 233–237
neo-Lockean defence of, 237–241, 265
and relative identity, 240
strong reading of, 233
weak reading of, 240–241, 247

Taschek, W. W., 300 (n. 8)
Taylor, C., 85, 120–121
Temporal orientation toward the past, 178–180
Tensor-product representations, 94
Thought. *See also* Content; Representational states
analysis of, through linguistic expression (Dummett), 12–13, 40–41, 43
communicability of (Dummett), 12–41
relation of, to language, 12–13, 39–48
structured vs. unstructured, 38–39
Thought-Language Principle, 12–13, 24–25, 39–45, 267–269, 275, 301 (n. 4)
stated, 13
Tobias, P. V., 78
Token-reflexive rule, 14–18, 275–276, 281–282, 290
different versions of, 14–16
and intentional self-reference, 276
temporal dimension of, 299–300 (n. 7)
Tolman, E. C., 206, 209–210, 212, 215, 219
Tomasello, M., 255, 256
Touch, phenomenology of, 137–139. *See also* Haptic exploration
Transducers, 89
Transformational grammar, 22

Traveling-salesman combinatorial
   problem, 217
Travis, C., 311 (n. 1)
Trevarthen, C., 249, 251–252, 260–
   261, 286
Ts'o, D. Y., 80
Tulving, E., 175

Universality-of-belief thesis, 35–37, 46

Valences, 113
Van de Walle, G. A., 63, 302 (n. 9)
Van Gulick, R., 90
Varlet, C., 215–216
Vestibular system, 133, 141, 150
Vibbert, M., 250
Visual agnosias, 79–81, 303 (n. 19)
Visual-cliff experiments, 113–114,
   116, 263, 264
Visual kinesthesis. *See* Kinesthesis
Von Hofsten, C., 127

Wernicke's area, 77
Wiggins, D., 238, 311 (n. 4)
Williams, G., 304 (n. 1)
Wimmer, H., 280
Wittgenstein, L., 5–6, 7, 104, 105, 106,
   107, 108, 109, 299 (n. 1), 306 (n. 2)
Woodruff, G., 62, 300 (n. 16)
Woodson, R., 250